W9-CAZ-918

MAN'S JOURNEY

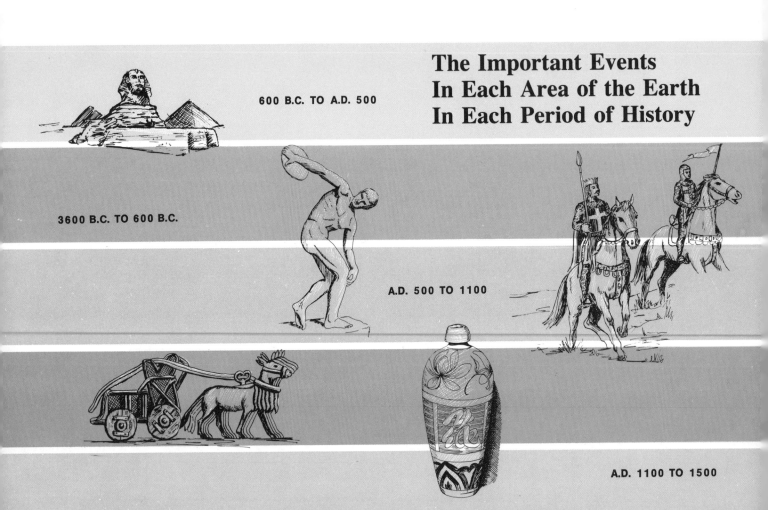

The Important Events
In Each Area of the Earth
In Each Period of History

600 B.C. TO A.D. 500

3600 B.C. TO 600 B.C.

A.D. 500 TO 1100

A.D. 1100 TO 1500

THROUGH TIME

by

MILTON HESSEL

A.D. 1900 TO 1974

Designed and
Illustrated by

JUDY STRICKLAND

A.D. 1500 TO 1900

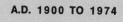

Wanderer Books New York

ACKNOWLEDGMENTS

Among the many people who have aided in the development and preparation of *Man's Journey Through Time,* I am especially grateful to Lee Hessel, my wife, who from the beginning has been my partner and co-worker in every phase of the book's production; to Judy Strickland, whose masterful design and beautiful illustrations more than warrant including her name on the title page with mine; to Marie Smith, who, throughout the manuscript's preparation, acted as consultant, critic and adviser on content and literary style; to my son, Andrew Robert Hessel, who so skillfully researched the histories of the earth's lesser-known areas; to Heinz Gelles, who first pointed out that my thoughts on the simultaneous histories of the different areas of the world could be worked into a book, and to Jerry Byrne for his invaluable technical guidance. Finally, I would like to thank the editors and consultants at Simon and Schuster who gave so much of their time and energy in order to bring *Man's Journey Through Time* to press.

Text copyright © 1974 by Milton Hessel
Illustrations copyright © 1974 by Judy Strickland
All rights reserved including the right of
reproduction in whole or in part in any form.
Published by Wanderer Books, a Simon & Schuster
Division of Gulf & Western Corporation, Simon &
Schuster Building, 1230 Avenue of the Americas,
New York, N.Y. 10020.

Manufactured in the United States of America

Library of Congress Cataloging in Publication Data

Hessel, Milton.
  Man's journey through time.

  Includes index.
  SUMMARY: Traces the key events that occurred in five
main geographical areas on earth from the creation of
the solar system to the 20th century exploration of
space.
  1. World history—Juvenile literature. [1. World
history] I. Strickland, Judy. II. Title.
[D21.H57 1978]   909   78-17031
ISBN 0-671-32972-3

For my family,
Lee, Sue, Andy and Robin

CONTENTS

VIII.
100 THE TWENTIETH CENTURY *1900 AD — 2000 AD.*

IX.
MAN'S JOURNEY THROUGH TIME

INTRODUCTION

You are holding in your hands something that is brand-new and very exciting in the world of literature: a book which tells you the story of man, step by step from the formation of his home, the earth, about five billion years ago, right up to his flights to the other planets tomorrow.

Man's Journey Through Time
will tell you
WHAT was happening in each area of the earth in each period of history,
and
WHEN each period occurred in relationship to the total story.

To facilitate this, the earth is divided in the book into five areas of historical development. Each of these areas is assigned a color. Events occurring in any area are always printed against its color background. These areas are:

THE MEDITERRANEAN WORLD and Europe

ASIA, except for Its Mediterranean Lands

OCEANIA

AFRICA, except for Its Mediterranean Lands

THE AMERICAS

In addition, a Time Bar at the beginning of each chapter locates the time of the events in the chapter in relation to overall history.

If you open this book to a time that particularly interests you, say to the era of the American Civil War (from 1850 to 1875), a glance at the Time Bar will tell you the following things about the time of this Civil War period:

1. that it took place just a bit more than one hundred years ago,

2. almost two thousand years after the birth of Christ,

3. and about five thousand years after man's first civilizations developed in Mesopotamia and Egypt.

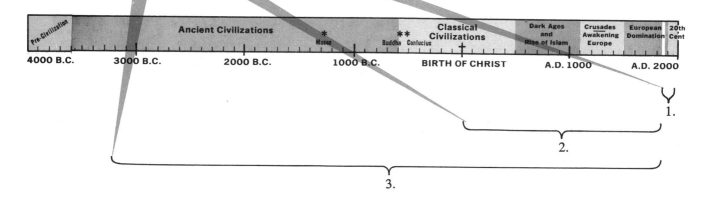

As your eye leaves the Time Bar, you will note among the events occurring elsewhere on the earth during the Civil War period:

that in Europe the German political philosopher Karl Marx was writing *Das Kapital,* the bible of Communism, and the British scientist Charles Darwin was writing *The Origin of Species,* the bible of "evolution," while the French Army was looking down the guns of German troops in the Franco-Prussian War, and in Austria-Hungary, under Emperor Franz Josef, Johann Strauss (1825–1899) was writing delightful music and Gregor Mendel in 1866 was setting down the laws of heredity;

that Japan was being reopened to foreigners as the result of a visit by Commodore Perry of the United States in 1853–1854;

that people were pouring into Australia from all over the earth, hoping to "get rich quick" in the recently discovered gold fields;

that in Africa a rush was on to exploit the continent's newly discovered diamond fields;

and that Mexico was being ruled by the Emperor Maximilian and his beloved wife, Carlota, and that tragedy was in the offing for both of them.

All this and more you will see occurring in this twenty-five year period during which the American Civil War took place.

To summarize, then, *Man's Journey Through Time* will create pictures of events that take place simultaneously across the earth in each successive period of history, and will relate the time of each period to total history. We think it will give you a new and enlightening view of the past, a better understanding of the present, and, we hope, an insight into the future.

I
THE 5 BILLION YEARS
OF OUR EARTH

THE FORMATION OF OUR SOLAR SYSTEM

The Milky Way

On a clear night the stars seem countless. Across one area of the sky they are so thick they look like milk spilled and trailed across the heavens. The billions of stars in this vast cloudlike area of the sky are called, collectively, the Milky Way. Our sun is just one of the stars that compose it.

The sun and the nine planets which circle it (that is, our solar system) make just a tiny speck of light among the billions of other stars composing the Milky Way. In addition to the planet Earth, our solar system's planets are Mercury, Venus, Mars, Jupiter, Saturn, Uranus, Neptune and Pluto. These planets do not give off light or heat, as do our sun and the other stars, but instead receive their light and warmth from the sun around which they orbit.

The Formation of Our Solar System

According to the latest and most widely accepted theory, our solar system of sun and planets was formed about five billion years ago, out of the gases and the dust particles of space which were compressed together by the forces of gravitation. Ever since, the planets have been revolving around the sun, and the entire solar system of sun and planets has been whirling through space as part of the Milky Way.

Astronomers believe that there are literally billions of stars like our sun in the Milky Way, many of them circled by planets which are much like our earth, with similar temperature ranges and comparable atmospheres and supplies of minerals and water.

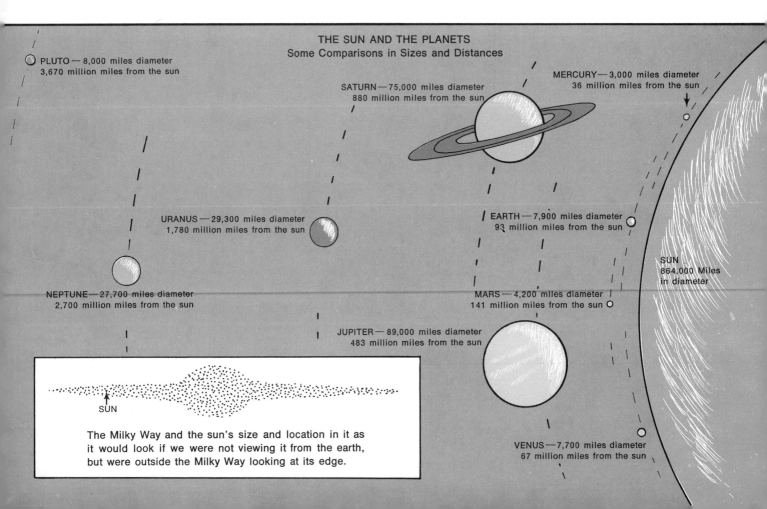

THE SUN AND THE PLANETS
Some Comparisons in Sizes and Distances

PLUTO — 8,000 miles diameter
3,670 million miles from the sun

SATURN — 75,000 miles diameter
880 million miles from the sun

MERCURY — 3,000 miles diameter
36 million miles from the sun

URANUS — 29,300 miles diameter
1,780 million miles from the sun

EARTH — 7,900 miles diameter
93 million miles from the sun

SUN
864,000 Miles
in diameter

NEPTUNE — 27,700 miles diameter
2,700 million miles from the sun

MARS — 4,200 miles diameter
141 million miles from the sun

JUPITER — 89,000 miles diameter
483 million miles from the sun

SUN

The Milky Way and the sun's size and location in it as it would look if we were not viewing it from the earth, but were outside the Milky Way looking at its edge.

VENUS — 7,700 miles diameter
67 million miles from the sun

What Does an Age of Five Billion Years Mean?

We have said that the solar system was formed about five billion years ago. How can we understand a number so large or a span of time so long?

Perhaps we can help by comparing this five-billion-year period of the earth's existence to shorter portions of the earth's history. For example, the latest findings indicate that the first life on earth appeared approximately three billion years ago, when the earth was already two billion years old. This means that our earth was lifeless for about forty percent of its five billion years, and that life began and developed upon it only during the last sixty percent of its existence.

We can also compare the earth's age to man's time upon it. Indications are that our first tool-making ancestors appeared upon the earth about one and three-quarter million years ago. Thus, manlike creatures have wandered over the lands and seas for about 1/3,000th of the earth's history.

Finally, we can compare the time of the earth's existence to the time that has elapsed since the first civilizations appeared in Egypt and Mesopotamia a bit less than six thousand years ago, which tells us that civilization in some form has existed for only about one millionth of the earth's total age.

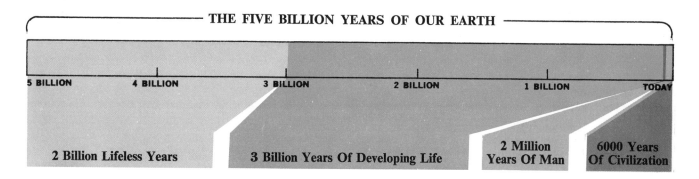

THE FIVE BILLION YEARS OF OUR EARTH

5 BILLION   4 BILLION   3 BILLION   2 BILLION   1 BILLION   TODAY

2 Billion Lifeless Years   3 Billion Years Of Developing Life   2 Million Years Of Man   6000 Years Of Civilization

This, then, is how the earth's five billion years add up: two billion lifeless years and about three billion years of developing life. Out of the three billion years of developing life, manlike creatures have existed for only about one and three-quarter million years; and civilization has existed for, at most, a brief six thousand years.

Is There Life Elsewhere in the Universe?

Most scientists, biologists and astronomers feel that some form of life must exist on millions of planets other than our earth. This conclusion is based on recently acquired evidence that the formation of life (and its development into higher forms) is not an accidental occurrence, but a process that takes place *whenever a planet exists under the right conditions of temperature, atmosphere, moisture and sunshine.* Such life-inducing conditions existed on our earth about three billion years ago when the first earth-life seems to have evolved, and it is assumed that literally millions of other planets throughout our Milky Way, as well as planets in other galaxies, were and are subject to the same conditions that permit the formation of life.

But—and this may be a disappointing exception—it

would seem that such conditions do not exist on any other planet in our own solar system. The other eight planets—Mercury, Venus, Mars, Jupiter, Saturn, Uranus, Neptune and Pluto—have temperatures that are either too hot or too cold to sustain life; or they do not possess the necessary atmosphere; or they have too little or too much moisture; or they receive too little sunshine (or too much) for life to begin and prosper upon them.

Thus, we think that our space explorers are likely to find no life existing on Mercury, Venus, Saturn, Uranus, Neptune and Pluto, and the many "light-years" of distance between us and other solar systems make it seem improbable that at any time in the foreseeable future we will be able to communicate with creatures living upon those planets.

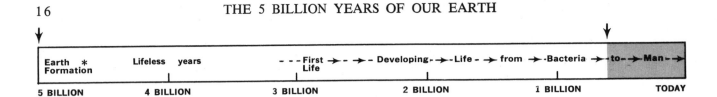

Earth ✱ Formation	Lifeless years	- - -First →- - →- Developing-→-Life -→ from →-Bacteria -→ to-→ Man -→			
5 BILLION	4 BILLION	3 BILLION	2 BILLION	1 BILLION	TODAY

5 BILLION TO 600 MILLION YEARS AGO

The Lifeless Years • The First Life

The Earth's 2 Billion Lifeless Years

Although there were no creatures of any kind on the earth during its two-billion-year period of lifelessness, this doesn't mean that our planet was inactive. For these first years of its existence, the earth was a seething mass of gaseous, liquid and solid materials, widely scattered at first, which were gradually being compressed together and transformed into the bodies of water, land, minerals and air we know now. That is to say that the oceans, continents, islands and mountain ranges, and the concentrations of metals and other minerals, were being formed, reformed, and then formed again.

These same processes are constantly at work upon the earth even up to the present day, but perhaps at a slower pace than during the first 2,000 million lifeless years.

Most important during this lifeless period, the chemical compounds out of which living creatures are created were being produced by the interaction of the sun (and perhaps electricity in the form of lightning) upon the hydrogen, methane, ammonia, water and carbon monoxide which at that time made up the earth's atmosphere. Out of the interactions between the sun's rays, electricity and these chemicals came the compounds called amino acids. It is believed that these amino acids fell into the shallow seas, where they reacted again with each other, sparked by the energy of the sun, to form proteins, the very stuff of life itself.

The Earth's First Life, About 3 Billion Years Ago

The oldest fossils of living creatures yet discovered on our earth are imprints of bacteria found in South Africa in rock formations called black chert. The layer of rock in which they are located is calculated to be three billion years old. The rock was, of course, a soft sediment when the bacteria became imbedded in it. A similar group of fossils of bacteria has been found in Australia in a kind of quartz which is estimated to be only slightly less than three billion years old. It is possible that future discoveries will unearth fossils of similar primitive creatures in rock formations of even greater age than three billion years.

At any rate, we know that life began to exist on the earth at least three billion years ago and that subsequent eons have seen ever more elaborate forms of life develop, leaving behind them the imprints of their bodies in various soft sediments which later hardened into rock.

In addition to such imprints found in very ancient rock, more recent fossils have been found, consisting of the actual hard parts of an animal—teeth, skulls and bones—which have been preserved by being covered by earth or protected in other ways from atmospheric conditions which would ordinarily have caused their deterioration. Fossils of most recent origin are the tools, the pots and other cooking vessels, and the weapons left by primitive men around their campfires, in caves and elsewhere.

In recent years, amazingly accurate methods of determining the age of fossils have been devised. These methods, called the carbon-14 and the argon-40 tests, measure how much radioactive decay has occurred in ancient remains: the greater the decay, the older the fossil. Most gratifying about these new methods of dating fossils is that the information they yield so often confirms the conclusions reached by men who, in the past, had to estimate fossil ages without their aid.

Types of Fossils

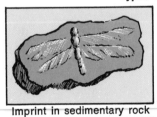

Imprint in sedimentary rock

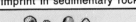

Footprints in sandstone

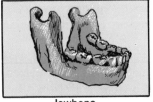

Jawbone

Tools of flint and bone

Earth Formation *	Lifeless years	- - - First Life → - - → - - Developing → Life → from → Bacteria → - to → Man - →
5 BILLION	4 BILLION 3 BILLION	2 BILLION 1 BILLION TODAY

600 MILLION TO 10,000 YEARS AGO

Developing Life on Earth, from the Most Primitive Creatures to Man

For the first two and a half billion years of life on the earth, the fossil record is sketchy and difficult to follow, but during its last 600 million years the record of developing life becomes quite complete and clear. These 600 million years are divided by geologists into three eras:

> The Ancient-Life or Paleozoic Era
> The Middle-Life or Mesozoic Era
> The Recent-Life or Cenozoic Era

Each of these eras is subdivided into lesser expanses of time called "periods."

The evolution of life which took place during those 600 million years, as read in successive layers of rock, is most fascinating. Here is a brief resume of that record:

The Ancient-Life or Paleozoic Era

This era lasted 375 million years. During its earliest segment, called the Cambrian Period, life existed only in the water. All known animals were invertebrates—worms and other forms of soft-bodied creatures which did not have internal skeletons or backbones. Some of these invertebrates had hard external skeletons, or shells, however. Among these were the trilobites, which resembled the horseshoe crabs of today. Other invertebrates were primitive, wingless insects. The only vegetation which left a fossil record is a sea plant called Collenia.

The next 60 million years, or Ordovician Period, began 500 million years ago. During this time the first vertebrates—creatures with internal skeletons and backbones—appeared in the seas. One of these early vertebrates had *both* an internal skeleton and a rigid external covering. It looked like a combination of a fish and a seagoing tank. Floating sea and fresh-water plants called algae are thought also to have evolved during this period. There was still no life on land.

The next 40 million years, the Silurian Period, saw the further evolution of vegetation and animals in lakes and swamps. Giant scorpions up to nine feet in length terrorized other creatures of the seas. There was still no life on land.

The next period, the Devonian, lasted 50 million years, starting 400 million years ago. During this period vigorous plant life began to emerge from the waters and to establish itself on the land. Among these plants were giant ferns with trunks over three feet thick. In the seas, fishes, which included the ancestors of every modern group, developed, including sharks up to twenty feet long. The first animals that lived on the land were amphibians, creatures which lived part of their lives in water and part on land and which crawled out of the

Developing life as seen in fossils found in geologic levels of different ages. The older the level, the closer it would be to the bottom. These geologic levels were formed by different natural forces: here by rivers that laid down layer upon layer of mud which dried into clay, or by deposits of silt or the settling of other solid matter in lakes and oceans; there by a flood of volcanic lava; still elsewhere by mud and debris pushed along by glaciers. There are, of course, no single locations where *all* the levels can be found one on top of another as in the drawing. Instead the fossil record must be read piecemeal from levels of varying age scattered over the earth.

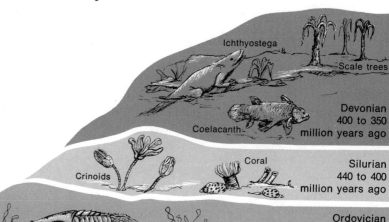

Ichthyostega — Scale trees
Coelacanth — Devonian 400 to 350 million years ago
Crinoids — Coral — Silurian 440 to 400 million years ago
Ostracoderm — Ordovician 500 to 440 million years ago
Sponge — Trilobite — Cambrian 600 to 500 million years ago

waters onto the shores a few tens of millions of years after the first plants had established themselves on land. Spiders and wingless insects were now everywhere.

The next period of time, called the Carboniferous Period, lasted for 80 million years—that is, from 350 million to 270 million years ago. During carboniferous times, fresh-water swamps developed in tropical areas of the earth. Massive ferns grew in these swamps, as did other plants such as conifers up to one hundred feet tall, and still other plants called horsetails. All of these forms of vegetation were eventually buried in sediment which later hardened into rock. Over millions of years, layer upon layer of sediment and vegetation were compressed and carbonized into today's vast fields of coal, which comprises a very important form of fuel and is an open record of the life of the period.

During the Carboniferous Period many amphibians developed, one of them a salamander fifteen feet long. Insects grew wings, and dragonflies attained the size of eagles.

Finally, during a time span called the Permian Period (the Ancient Era's last 45 million years), leaf trees evolved, and the numbers of reptiles and insects increased greatly.

The Middle-Life or Mesozoic Era

The Middle-Life Era lasted a total of 155 million years, from 225 million to 70 million years ago. It is generally known as the Age of Reptiles. During its first 45 million years called the Triassic Period, dinosaurs no more than

six inches long appeared. The first mammals appeared on the earth in the form of small, furry, warm-blooded creatures. Flies and termites evolved, several varieties of pine had developed, and plants called cycads (which looked very much like the palms of today) appeared for the first time.

During the Middle-Life's next period, called the Jurassic, which extended from 180 million to 135 million years ago, reptiles reached fantastic sizes. They swam in the seas (for example, the ichthyosaur, a powerful seagoing carnivore); they flew in the air (the flying pteranodon); they waddled over lands and swamps (the diplodocus, an eighty-foot-long vegetarian). Mammals, however, remained small, about the size of rats.

The Cretaceous Period lasted from 135 million to 70 million years. Fig, magnolia and poplar trees appeared on the earth, and fishes became much as they are today. Giant reptiles still ruled the land, sea, and air; but by the Cretaceous Period's end they had become extinct. It is interesting to note that giant reptiles dominated the earth for nearly 150 million years, whereas manlike creatures have existed on earth less than two million years.

The Recent-Life or Cenozoic Era

The Recent-Life Era, which covers 70 million years, started with the Eocene Period. The warm, moist climate of the period permitted tropical plants to flourish as far north as Greenland. The vacuum left by the extinction of the giant reptiles was beginning to be filled

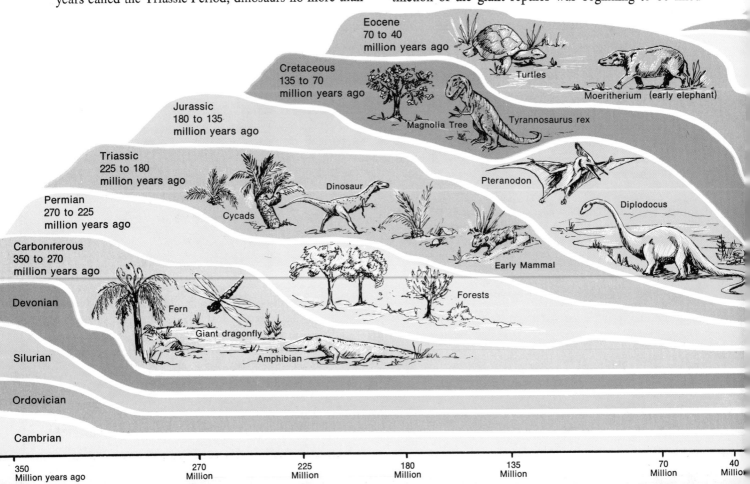

Eocene
70 to 40
million years ago

Turtles

Moeritherium (early elephant)

Cretaceous
135 to 70
million years ago

Magnolia Tree

Tyrannosaurus rex

Jurassic
180 to 135
million years ago

Pteranodon

Diplodocus

Triassic
225 to 180
million years ago

Dinosaur

Permian
270 to 225
million years ago

Cycads

Early Mammal

Carboniferous
350 to 270
million years ago

Devonian

Forests

Fern

Giant dragonfly

Silurian

Amphibian

Ordovician

Cambrian

350 Million years ago	270 Million	225 Million	180 Million	135 Million	70 Million	40 Million

by crocodiles and turtles and all kinds of insects and a great variety of mammals. Pygmy elephants, rhinos, pigs and cattle, and a horse the size of a dog appeared, as did the earliest monkey.

The Recent-Life's next 15 million years are called the Oligocene Period. This lasted from 40 million to 25 million years ago and saw the spread of extensive grasslands which favored the development of grass-eating mammals such as the horse and the cow. In addition, the early dog, the cat and the bear appeared, as did a tailless primitive ape.

The Miocene Period, lasting from 25 million to 11 million years ago, saw the further elaboration of mammals and the development of the anthropoid ape—a creature which often stood on two legs!

During the next two periods, Pliocene, from 11 million to one million, and Pleistocene, from one million to ten thousand years ago, plant and animal life became about as they are today, but their habitats shifted from one portion of the earth to another as the great icecaps advanced and retreated. One and three-quarter million years ago, a manlike tool-using creature lived in Africa,

and somewhat more recently a more advanced manlike creature lived in Asia.

Modern man (*Homo sapiens*) is thought to have appeared in Asia 250,000 years ago, but he probably did not enter Europe until thirty thousand years ago and likely did not appear in the Americas before fourteen thousand years ago.

The Holocene Period covers the present age, beginning ten thousand years ago. It is considered to be a period between glaciers. In the Holocene Period, Stone Age man learned to use fire, to chip and grind stone into tools and weapons, to make bows and arrows and fish hooks, and to farm and domesticate certain animals. Between five and six thousand years ago, men developed the first writing and began to work in metal—first in copper, then in bronze. The development of the earliest civilizations followed shortly thereafter.

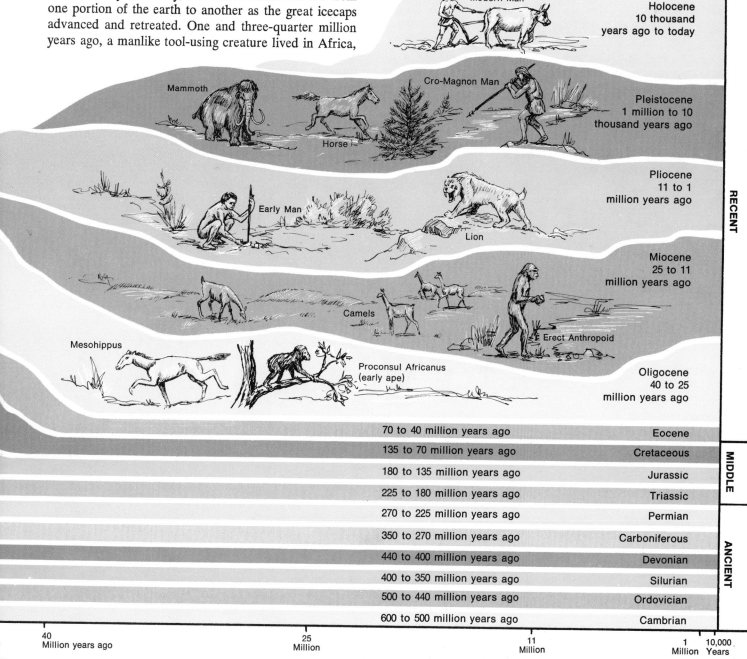

Modern Man	Holocene 10 thousand years ago to today
Mammoth / Horse / Cro-Magnon Man	Pleistocene 1 million to 10 thousand years ago
Early Man / Lion	Pliocene 11 to 1 million years ago
Camels / Erect Anthropoid	Miocene 25 to 11 million years ago
Mesohippus / Proconsul Africanus (early ape)	Oligocene 40 to 25 million years ago
70 to 40 million years ago	Eocene
135 to 70 million years ago	Cretaceous
180 to 135 million years ago	Jurassic
225 to 180 million years ago	Triassic
270 to 225 million years ago	Permian
350 to 270 million years ago	Carboniferous
440 to 400 million years ago	Devonian
400 to 350 million years ago	Silurian
500 to 440 million years ago	Ordovician
600 to 500 million years ago	Cambrian

RECENT / MIDDLE / ANCIENT

40 Million years ago · 25 Million · 11 Million · 1 Million · 10,000 Years

II
THE ALMOST 2 MILLION YEARS
OF MANLIKE CREATURES ON EARTH

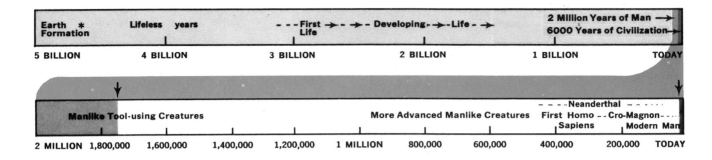

| Earth * Formation | Lifeless years | - - -First → - → - Developing- →-Life - → | | 2 Million Years of Man → 6000 Years of Civilization→ |
| 5 BILLION | 4 BILLION | 3 BILLION | 2 BILLION | 1 BILLION   TODAY |

| Manlike Tool-using Creatures | | More Advanced Manlike Creatures | - - - -Neanderthal - - - - . . . First Homo - -Cro-Magnon- - - Sapiens   Modern Man |
| 2 MILLION 1,800,000   1,600,000   1,400,000   1,200,000 | 1 MILLION   800,000   600,000 | 400,000   200,000   TODAY | |

1,750,000 TO 10,000 YEARS AGO

**Developing Man, the Pre-Civilization Years • Tools • The Brain, the Hand, the Voice •
Geographical Areas of Development**

Tools and the Level of Human Life

Tools, weapons and pottery made and used by succeeding generations of prehistoric man have left us an instructive record of human development. The oldest tools were apparently made of stone, roughly chipped into shapes useful for cutting, hammering or scraping. Wood and bone were no doubt often used in conjunction with the stone (for example as handles), but such materials have long since deteriorated into dust, leaving little record of their existence. This earliest period, when chipped stone was the basic material for tools and weapons, is known as the Old Stone or Paleolithic Age. The makers and users of these rough stone implements lived at first by gathering berries, nuts and grubs. The larger, fiercer animals around them were a constant danger, but gradually they learned to hunt in organized groups, and these more ferocious creatures became less of a threat to their survival. The Paleolithic Age lasted for hundreds of thousands of years and comprised by far the greatest portion of man's total time on earth.

Later, when tools and weapons of stone were finely ground and polished, a new level of human development was attained called the New Stone or Neolithic Age. During Neolithic times, handles for stone spears and hatchets, and shafts for stone arrows, were probably made from wood, as they had been in Paleolithic times. Probably the first crude attempts at agriculture were made during this era, and it appears that the first animals were domesticated—the dog, the pig, the goat,

the sheep and the cow. Also during Neolithic times, men and women first began to live in settled communities; labor became more specialized and the first pottery was fashioned from clay.

With the passing of time, in areas of the earth where copper was obtainable polished stone was replaced by copper in tools and weapons, heralding the advent of what is called the Chalcolithic Age, or Age of Copper. This was followed shortly by the Bronze Age, when men discovered that a blend of copper and tin, called bronze, was much harder than pure copper and provided a better cutting edge. During the Bronze Age, people had already begun, here and there, to cluster together in towns for mutual protection from attack and for ease in trading with one another. Later in the Bronze Age, the first true civilizations developed.

This elevation in the quality of man's tools and man's social organization which we have described did not take place all over the earth at the same time. On the contrary, the first civilizations began appearing about six thousand years ago on lands located at the eastern end of the Mediterranean Sea, but elsewhere most of mankind remained in the most primitive hunting, chipped-stone age of development, while only here and there men had learned to use polished-stone tools and weapons. Even today, some people living in parts of Africa, Australia, New Guinea, Malaysia and South America have not progressed much beyond these primitive stages.

Stone Hand Axe   Awl   Stone Axe with Handle
—— PALEOLITHIC ——

Polished-stone Sickle
—— NEOLITHIC ——

Bronze Spear
BRONZE

The Brain · The Hand · The Voice

More than 100,000 years ago, when men first learned to hunt in groups and to use axes of chipped stone, they started to dominate the other creatures of the earth. In addition, men began to learn to alter their environment to their needs—a process which has continued at an accelerated pace up to the present day.

Quite apparently, these unique abilities of human beings began when man's early ancestors learned to stand upon their hind legs, thus freeing their front paws to develop into marvelous twisting, turning, grasping hands. These hands in partnership with man's superior brain have enabled human beings to do most of the things which make them different from other creatures— everything from fashioning the first crude tools to painting beautiful pictures and (most important) eventually to making a permanent record of *how* to do these things, so that they could be passed along to later generations.

Add to this partnership between brain and hand man's ability to use his voice to communicate in great detail with his fellows, and we have the triumvirate of brain, hand and voice which has enabled men to co-operate with a multitude of other men in a wide variety of activities as diverse as hunting an ancient mammoth and building a modern bridge.

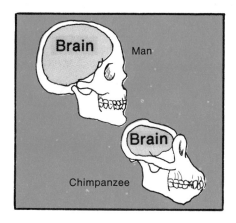
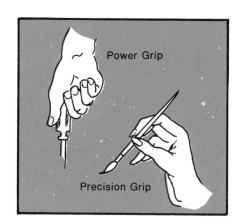

But Why Some Groups of Men More Than Others?

But we must ask ourselves, why only some men? Why have some groups of men developed these skills to so much greater a degree than others? The answer to this question, while generally agreed upon by historians and scientists, is not reassuring to those who would like to proclaim the superiority of one group or race or color of men over another. The answer of history is a simple one. Those men, of whatever race or color, who were in the right place at the right time did well. Those who were not did poorly.

When, about 4000 B.C., the first civilizations developed at the eastern end of the Mediterranean, all colors of skin and many language groups were involved, but dark-skinned peoples predominated. All of these peoples developed means of writing and mathematics, as well as sophisticated systems of government and religion.

It is interesting to note that three thousand years ago the highly civilized dark-skinned peoples of Egypt and Mesopotamia could look upon the contemporary light-skinned Greeks (and later the Romans) as barbarians,

which at that time they certainly were.

About a thousand years later, Cicero, a Roman of distinction, could say, "Do not obtain your slaves from Britain, because they are so stupid and so utterly incapable of being taught that they are not fit to form part of the household of Athens."

And, almost inevitably, when the British in the nineteenth century were taking *their* turn as the most powerful group of men on earth, they tended to dismiss with smug superiority the dark-skinned peoples of their colonies in Asia and North Africa. Yet many of these peoples' ancestors had invented writing and mathematics and built magnificent edifices, when the inhabitants of the British Isles were still painting their bodies blue and dancing naked around their campfires.

Similar attitudes today among citizens of leading nations remind us of the ironies of which history is capable. One wonders what race or color of man will, in its turn, dismiss the descendants of the powerful peoples of the twentieth century as being obviously far inferior to their own uniquely superior selves.

From 10,000 Years Ago to 3600 B.C.: A Survey of Man's Pre-Civilization Years

Throughout the one million years which preceded the first civilizations, huge glaciers several times moved down from the North Pole, enveloping the European, Asian and North American continents, killing vegetation and creating frigid climatic conditions. After long periods of time, each of these ice masses in its turn began to melt, and the edge of the glaciers retreated northward again. In their wake sprang up dense forests filled with game and vast prairies rich with wild grain.

More than ten thousand years ago, when the last of these glaciers was retreating toward the north, the first men to enter the Western Hemisphere are thought to have followed its retreat northward, moving from Asia across the Bering Strait into North America, for it is now known that there was at that time a land bridge between Asia and North America.

About eight thousand years ago, a similar wave of modern men poured into Europe from two directions—from Asia (through Russia and the Balkans) and from Africa (across the Straits of Gibraltar). But the original entry of *Homo sapiens* into Europe had been made about 22,000 years before this new invasion—that is, about thirty thousand years ago—by the Cro-Magnon men who painted the beautiful animal pictures to be seen in the caves of France and Spain.

The retreating icecaps left the Mediterranean lands considerably warmer than either Europe or North America. As a result, the Mediterranean area experienced an intensity of human activity and prosperity (particularly at its eastern end) unknown anywhere else. Here on the rain-watered hillsides, agriculture was practiced as early as 6,500 years before the birth of Christ. Dry areas along the banks of the great rivers (which would one day foster the first civilizations) remained uncultivated, however, because the art of irrigation—threading river waters through the land by canals—would not be developed for another two thousand years—that is, until about 4000 B.C. In the Indian subcontinent and perhaps in the warmer portions of what is now China, similar activity was occurring, but on a lesser scale.

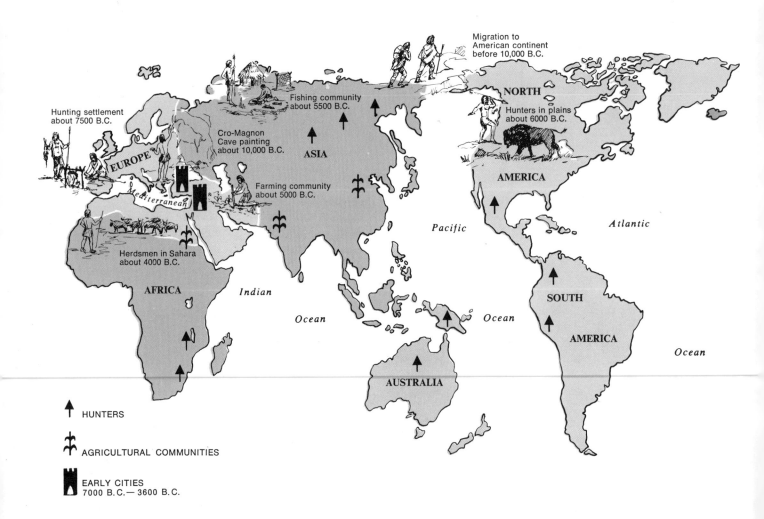

Migration to American continent before 10,000 B.C.

Hunting settlement about 7500 B.C.

Fishing community about 5500 B.C.

Cro-Magnon Cave painting about 10,000 B.C.

EUROPE

ASIA

NORTH

Hunters in plains about 6000 B.C.

Farming community about 5000 B.C.

AMERICA

Mediterranean

Herdsmen in Sahara about 4000 B.C.

AFRICA

Indian

Pacific

Atlantic

Ocean

Ocean

SOUTH

AMERICA

Ocean

AUSTRALIA

↑ HUNTERS

⚹ AGRICULTURAL COMMUNITIES

🏰 EARLY CITIES
7000 B.C.— 3600 B.C.

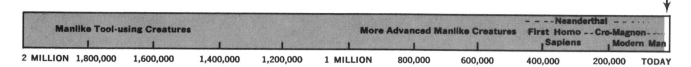

Manlike Tool-using Creatures						More Advanced Manlike Creatures		Neanderthal	
							First Homo	Cro-Magnon	
							Sapiens	Modern Man	
2 MILLION	1,800,000	1,600,000	1,400,000	1,200,000	1 MILLION	800,000	600,000	400,000	200,000	TODAY

8000 B.C. — 3600 B.C.

The Five Geographic Areas of Human Development

We have now reached the point in *Man's Journey Through Time* when individual reports must be made of events occurring simultaneously in different areas of the earth. The peoples of these different areas, separated by natural barriers of mountains, oceans and deserts, developed distinctive cultures and compiled separate historical records, although, of course, no area was ever totally isolated or free from outside influence.

In the five or six thousand years that immediately preceded the first civilizations (and also during a major portion of historical time), the separate areas of human development were about as follows.

THE MEDITERRANEAN WORLD and Europe

those portions of Asia, Africa and Europe lying on the Mediterranean Sea or having easy access to it, plus the rest of the continent of Europe, including European Russia and the British Isles.

ASIA, except for its Mediterranean Lands

four subareas, each so vast as to be almost an area by itself: (1) the Steppes and northern Asia, thousands of miles of prairies, forests and mountains; (2) the Indian subcontinent, now India, Pakistan and Bangladesh; (3) the central land mass, now China, Korea and Japan; (4) Southeast Asia, now the nations of Burma, Thailand, Vietnam, Laos, Cambodia, the Malay Peninsula and Indonesia.

OCEANIA

what is now Australia and New Zealand, as well as the thousands of islands of the vast Pacific Ocean extending to and including Hawaii.

AFRICA, except for its Mediterranean Lands

THE AMERICAS

the two continents of the Western Hemisphere.

MEDITERRANEAN WORLD AND EUROPE

ASIA

OCEANIA

AFRICA

THE AMERICAS

THE MEDITERRANEAN WORLD and Europe

At the Asian end of the Mediterranean, in Palestine and Syria, there were Neolithic cultures dating back to 7000 B.C. As previously noted, agriculture was practiced here as early as 6500 B.C. The town of Jericho, located just north of the Dead Sea, dates from this period. It was protected by stone fortifications, and its houses were made of brick and had polished plaster floors. Jericho's people practiced a religion which made use of human skulls covered over with clay to resemble human features. Handsome painted pottery was widely used throughout the Palestine-Syria area by 5500 B.C.

In Anatolia (also called Asia Minor), there were Neolithic cultures as early as 7000 B.C. Fragmented remains of textiles and sculpture of both clay and stone, have been found here, as have beautiful wall paintings.

In Iran (formerly called Persia), we know of New Stone Age cultures and primitive agriculture dating back to 6000 B.C. Later plant cultivation extending from the western edge of the Zagros Mountains to the Caspian Sea began as early as 5000 B.C.

In Mesopotamia (the area between the Tigris and Euphrates Rivers in present-day Iraq), archaeologists have found evidence of both painted pottery and primitive agriculture dating from about 4500 B.C.

On the African side of the Mediterranean, in the Nile River Valley, primitive agriculture and animal husbandry were practiced as early as 4500 B.C. Shortly after 4000 B.C., vessels with sails were used on the Nile River.

On the European side of the Mediterranean, the island of Crete had a Neolithic culture whose people lived in the island's many caves, perhaps as early as 5000 B.C. About 4000 B.C., emigrants from Asia Minor are thought to have entered Crete and introduced a primitive agriculture to the island. The first products carried in Cretan boats (probably lumber from Crete and obsidian from the island of Melos) were trafficked island to island as early as 4000 B.C.

On the mainland of Greece and on the Greek islands, the people were using polished stone tools as early as 4000 B.C., and seem to have begun a form of primitive agriculture about the same time.

Most of the rest of Europe was populated by Paleolithic hunters and food gatherers using chipped-stone tools, bone fishhooks and wood arrows tipped with flint. In the Balkan Peninsula there are evidences of a Neolithic culture (probably influenced by more advanced people from Asia Minor) that used a handsome painted pottery and practiced primitive agriculture as early as 4000 B.C.

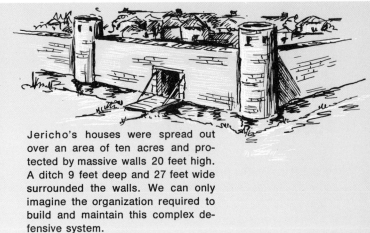

Jericho's houses were spread out over an area of ten acres and protected by massive walls 20 feet high. A ditch 9 feet deep and 27 feet wide surrounded the walls. We can only imagine the organization required to build and maintain this complex defensive system.

Most early farming was done on rain-watered hillsides with permanent villages located closeby. Main crops were grains: barley, wheat, rice and corn.

Egypt was truly a product of the Nile. The river supplied water for man, beasts and crops; its floods regularly fertilized the soil; and (as early as 4000 B.C.) its currents carried sailboats downstream, while the prevailing winds supplied the power to move them back upstream against the current.

The inhabitants of northern-European waterside communities perfected fishhooks, nets, traps, the trident and the feathered arrow—all used in pursuing the fish and game which abounded in their marshes. They even hollowed out canoes to aid in hunting and fishing, and, armed with harpoons, are known to have ventured into the ocean after seals.

ASIA, except for its Mediterranean Lands

The Steppes and the other northern portions of Asia were populated by groups of Paleolithic nomads—wandering groups of Mongolian, Turkic and Indo-European-speaking peoples.

In the Indian subcontinent, sometime before 5000 B.C., Neolithic man lived around the delta and the upper reaches of the Indus River, and in the central plateau of India called the Deccan. In each of these sections there were primitive agriculture, animal husbandry, the weaving of cloth and the production of handmade pottery.

In Asia's central land mass (China, Korea and Japan), prior to 4000 B.C., there is evidence only of Paleolithic inhabitants using chipped-stone tools. Animal hides were used for clothing, and needles and fishhooks were made of bone and wood; but sometime after 4000 B.C., polished-stone tools came into use and pottery was beginning to be produced.

Southeast Asia was inhabited by primitive forest-dwelling men who were hunters and fishermen.

The domestication of sheep and cattle committed early man to a nomadic existence in the ever demanding search for pasture lands for their herds.

OCEANIA

In Oceania, the continent of Australia and the islands of New Zealand, Melanesia and Micronesia were populated by Paleolithic peoples (Negritos and Australoids), who were food gatherers and hunters, using chipped-stone, wood and bone tools. To the best of our knowledge, the outer islands were unpopulated during this period.

AFRICA, except for its Mediterranean Lands

In Africa, modern man was predominantly represented in the period from ten thousand years ago to 3500 B.C. by Negroes who were living under Paleolithic conditions over much of the continent. The ancestors of the modern Bushmen were concentrated in the deserts of the south, and those of the Pygmies in the forests of the

Congo and Guinea. About 5500 B.C., the Sahara Desert began to pass through a "wet stage." What are now barren sands were then relatively cool, fertile lands and pastures. Primitive agriculture was practiced, and there was trade with surrounding areas.

THE AMERICAS

Bands of several hunters (and their families) roamed the countryside in search of game. The fortunate killing of a large animal often meant the difference between weeks of plenty and the barest survival.

In the Americas, well before 10,000 B.C., nomads are believed to have crossed from Siberia to Alaska. By 9000 B.C. they had become food gatherers and small-game hunters in North America's Great Basin. The art of basketmaking was known.

By 8500 B.C. there were big-game hunters in South America's Patagonia, and also in the eastern and central portions of what is now the United States. By 7500 B.C. there were hunters capable of pursuing the larger game throughout most of South America, and between 7000 B.C. and 5000 B.C. primitive cultivation of peppers, gourds, beans and squash had begun in central Mexico.

III
THE ANCIENT CIVILIZATIONS

THE 3,000 YEARS FROM 3600 B.C. TO 600 B.C.

Prologue

About 3,600 years before the birth of Christ, civilized societies began to appear on the lands that lay at the eastern end of the Mediterranean Sea. Somewhat later, other civilizations appeared in India, and, later still, in China. Most of what we know of human accomplishment in these three cradles of civilization on the Mediterranean, in India and in China has been learned from archaeological discoveries made during the last century and a half, and from some made as recently as the last few decades.

Until archaeologists uncovered the remains of societies as ancient as 5,600 years, along with evidence of their amazing attainments in architecture, engineering and writing, mankind had almost forgotten that such ancient groups of people had ever existed. True, there were many references to them in the Bible, in the writings of Herodotus the Greek historian, in the Vedas—the sacred records of the Hindus—and in Chinese tales and legends; but nineteenth- and twentieth-century historians had tended to treat these references as the exaggerations of folklore.

Recent archaeological discoveries, however, have revealed that these Biblical and other sources only hinted at the development achieved by many of these ancient cultures. We now know that some of them lasted more than half of the total of all civilized time, and that from about 3600 B.C. until about 600 B.C. ancient Egypt, Mesopotamia, Crete, India and China, as well as Israel and Phoenicia, made contributions to man's skills and store of knowledge which later peoples have only embellished.

Some Definitions: The Meanings of the Words *Culture* and *Civilization*

From this point on, we shall be using the words *culture* and *civilization* with meanings somewhat different from those they ordinarily have. When we speak of the "culture" of a society, for example, we will be referring to the accumulation of skills by a significant percentage of the society's people, not to the skill of a few of its individuals. If, for example, only some of the society's farmers and craftsmen know how to irrigate and fertilize crops, or how to make tools and jewelry out of bronze, then these activities will properly be regarded as individual skills; but if most of its farmers fertilize and irrigate their crops, and most of its artisans commonly work in such metals as bronze, these activities should be regarded as part of the society's culture.

When we use the word *civilization,* we shall be implying that the society in question has achieved this cultural level in several specific activities, among which are a general knowledge of agriculture and the use of metals, a high society-wide attainment in the arts and sciences, and the development of systems of writing, numbering and measuring. Most important, we will be implying that religion has progressed well beyond the simple nature-worship of primitive peoples. Finally, when we use the word *civilization* we shall be indicating that a government has evolved, capable of providing an environment favorable to the continuance of these varied activities.

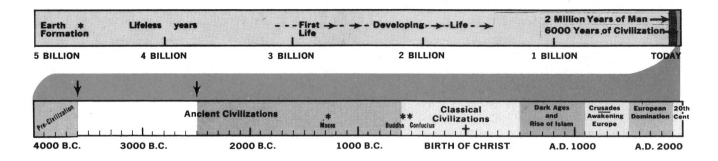

| Earth * Formation | Lifeless years | - - -First → - → Developing - → Life - → Life | 2 Million Years of Man → 6000 Years of Civilization → |

| 5 BILLION | 4 BILLION | 3 BILLION | 2 BILLION | 1 BILLION | TODAY |

| Pre-Civilization | Ancient Civilizations | * Moses | ** Buddha Confucius | Classical Civilizations | Dark Ages and Rise of Islam | Crusades Awakening Europe | European Domination | 20th Cent |

| 4000 B.C. | 3000 B.C. | 2000 B.C. | 1000 B.C. | BIRTH OF CHRIST | A.D. 1000 | A.D. 2000 |

3600 — 2500 B.C.

Breakthrough to Civilization • The First Writing • Bronze Tools and Weapons •
Engineering and Architecture

The first civilizations did not develop in the rain-watered lands of Asia Minor or Syria-Palestine or India, on which the rudiments of farming had been worked out centuries earlier. Such lands, because of agricultural methods then known, could not support the density of population required for a civilized way of life, but the technical skills which had been developed upon them were later transferred to nearby river valleys. Here, in the valleys, irrigation guaranteed a steady supply of water, and annual floods periodically enriched the soil. As a result, farmers were able to produce food beyond their own needs, and the excess of food could then be traded for the products of artisans—for jewelry, wagons, tools and weapons. In fact, such artisans could come into

being only as a *result* of an overabundance of food. Eventually, the continuing surplus of food produced in the river valleys would give rise to still other specialists, to managers, scholars, priests and kings, and out of this diversity would develop the first civilizations.

Another kind of civilization also came into being during these ancient times, based not on superior agricultural lands such as the river valleys, but on superior location for trade. The Minoan civilization on the island of Crete is thought to be the first of these, but in later ancient times trade-oriented civilizations would be developed by the Mycenaeans on what is now the Greek mainland and, later still, by the Phoenicians on islands off the Asian and African shores of the Mediterranean.

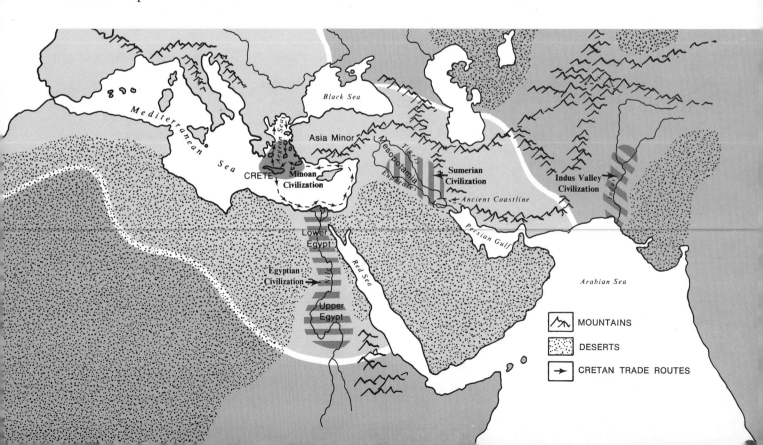

THE MEDITERRANEAN WORLD and Europe

On the Asian side of the Mediterranean, in the twin valleys of the Tigris and Euphrates Rivers, an area called Mesopotamia, a society had been approaching civilization status over a period of one thousand years, under the stewardship of a succession of conquering peoples. We do not know exactly when the dark-skinned Sumerians, in their turn, took over the delta areas of the two rivers, and we are not even sure where they originated, but we do know that they were a remarkable people. Under them the land was called Sumer and it was divided into several independent and often rival city-states. From earliest times the Sumerians lived in relative peace with white-skinned Semitic peoples (Assyrians, Phoenicians, Babylonians, etc., who shared a common language) who also inhabited the area, while farther to the north, in that portion of the twin valleys known as Akkad, the population was predominantly Semitic.

The Sumerians first used pictures to represent whole words, then developed 350 symbols to represent syllables. These symbols were impressed into soft clay tablets with a tool having a triangular tip which produced the characteristic wedge-shaped cuneiform writing.

Either Sumerians or their immediate predecessors in the valleys invented cuneiform writing, the first of mankind's ways of setting down the spoken work. The invention of this first system of writing made possible the recording of history about 3,500 years before the birth of Christ. Cuneiform was to become the means of writing the languages of many other Mediterranean peoples over the next two thousand years. Modern archaeologists are able to read and translate cuneiform writing. The Sumerians developed a number system based on multiples of sixty (as contrasted to such present-day systems as the commonly used decimal system, based on the multiples of ten). They built hydraulic devices to control floods and to regulate the supply of water. They perfected the arts of irrigating and fertilizing the earth, and they designed the first wheeled vehicles.

The influence and skills of the Sumerians spread to lands as far as Egypt in Mediterranean Africa and the Indus River in the Indian subcontinent. The Sumerians used silver ingots of specific weights which were possibly the first money. They invented many of the devices of modern business, such as negotiable notes, letters of credit and contracts; they designed delicate jewelry set with precious stones; and, having little access to stone for construction, they used brick in their handsome and well-designed buildings. Barges loaded with fruit and grain moved along the Tigris and Euphrates Rivers from town to town and along the man-made canals. Sumer was rich.

The rulers of the separate city-states of Sumer (who eventually became priest-kings) were thought to be direct agents of the gods, who lived in and offered protection against a world populated by evil spirits. Obedience to the priest-kings, and through them to the gods, made for the good and safe life. *The Epic of Gilgamesh,* the story of the Great Flood (set down in writing in a later periods), reveals much about this ancient people's search for immortality and their sense of impending doom, for Sumerian religion lacked any consoling belief in an afterlife or in personal salvation.

About 3000 B.C., a few centuries after Sumer reached its pinnacle of development, the Egyptian civilization evolved on the Nile River on the African side of the Mediterranean Sea. The Nile civilization did not experience the thousand years of gradual evolution that can be read in the layers of rubble left in the Tigris-Euphrates Valleys. On the contrary, Egypt seems to have developed from barbarism or primitive culture to civilization in a relatively short time. No doubt Egyptian development was quickened by contact with Sumerian sailors and traders, but, once started, the Nile people built a culture that was wholly their own, one which differed markedly from the Sumerian civilization in many ways.

Egypt, like Sumer, produced a method of writing very early in its history, one which used hieroglyphics, or picture symbols, instead of the wedge-shaped cuneiform. Egyptian engineers built hydraulic devices to control the Nile in flood and to hold back some of its waters for arid periods; artisans wove cloth and built ships and mined copper, and leaders sent out expeditions to other countries to trade for lumber and spices and tin. Like the people of Sumer, the Egyptians made basic discoveries in geometry and the natural sciences; their art was colorful and appealing, their literature alive and very human.

The earliest known use of wheels on a vehicle is seen on a Sumerian sketch dating from about 3500 B.C. The vehicle was a four-wheeled wagon built like a land sledge. The wheels were made of slabs of wood rounded and rigidly fixed to the axles. We must assume that the axle turned at the point of attachment to the wagon.

Partly because the Egyptians had easy access to stone, their massive architecture was more advanced than that of Sumer and even surpassed that of later societies. The Step Pyramid, built in the Third Dynasty, the Pyramids of Cheops, built during the Fourth Dynasty, and the Great Sphinx at Giza, from the same period, are remarkable engineering feats.

The Pyramids are also enduring evidence of the faith that the Egyptian ruler had in life-after-death, a principal concern of Egyptian religion. They are mausoleums and storehouses of all the things the pharaohs would need to carry on their lives in the next world.

There were other, more fundamental differences between Egypt and Sumer, resulting largely from differences in the lands each occupied. Mesopotamia had little natural protection from invasion, and as a result the Tigris-Euphrates Valleys were constantly raided by warring peoples. The twin valleys, in fact, were often occupied at the same time by rival city-states and by a variety of peoples speaking different languages. Economic competition very naturally arose among these various peoples, and a free-market economy developed among those classes not tied to the land.

Egypt's Nile Valley, on the other hand, was protected from invasion by surrounding deserts and sea. The upper and lower portions of the Nile Valley developed separately, but were united about 3100 B.C. by King Menes, who established his capital on the river at the city of Memphis. Egypt then became one land occupied by one people and speaking one language.

In Egypt all land and property belonged to the king, who was believed to be a god. Complete obedience to this god-king and to his appointed agents was enforced. The entire Nile Valley was organized into one great economic unit, with its management (the government) planning and overseeing every detail of farming, craftsmanship and trade. To find comparably regimented societies in history, one must consider the Indus civilization in the Indian subcontinent (about 2500 B.C.), the Inca Indian civilization in South America (about A.D. 1400) and the modern states in Russia and perhaps China.

We know very little about the First and Second Dynasties (family successions) that ruled Egypt, but during the Third to Fifth Dynasties (from 2778 B.C. to 2263 B.C.), a period known as the Old Kingdom, Egypt reached artistic and scientific heights it would never again achieve. The accomplishments of the first several centuries of ancient Egypt were never equaled in the succeeding twelve centuries.

The island of Crete in the Mediterranean Sea greatly expanded its trade during the latter half of this period (3000 B.C. to 2500 B.C.): its boats carried lumber and oil and obsidian from the lands surrounding the Aegean area to Egypt, to Mesopotamia and to the early cities which were developing in Asia Minor, and they returned to Crete with the products of these lands. Bronze was

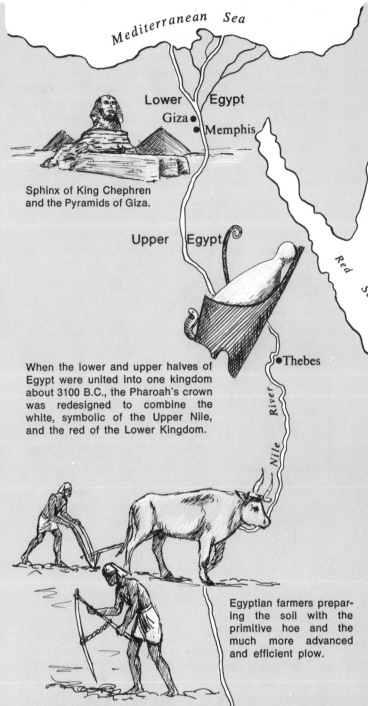

Sphinx of King Chephren and the Pyramids of Giza.

When the lower and upper halves of Egypt were united into one kingdom about 3100 B.C., the Pharoah's crown was redesigned to combine the white, symbolic of the Upper Nile, and the red of the Lower Kingdom.

Egyptian farmers preparing the soil with the primitive hoe and the much more advanced and efficient plow.

introduced into Crete shortly after 3000 B.C., but its early use there was limited. The potter's wheel was unknown, and pottery was still made by hand. The population of Crete throughout this period moved gradually into towns more centrally located, away from the coast.

At this time, between the third and second millennia B.C., the interior of the continent of Europe was still inhabited by Paleolithic hunters who used chipped-stone and wood tools and weapons. However, in areas close to the Mediterranean centers (such as the Balkan Peninsula) polished-stone and, more rarely, copper tools and weapons seem to have been used during this period.

ASIA, except for its Mediterranean Lands

In the Indian subcontinent, around 3000–2800 B.C., permanent agricultural villages began to appear in the Indus River Valley and in the lands close to its delta along the Arabian Sea. A pleasantly painted (but still handmade) pottery was in use. Houses were constructed of mud-brick and stone. Early Indian religion seems to have been a combination of fertility rites and worship of the Mother Goddess.

In central China, about 3500 B.C., scattered peoples along the Yellow River were living in a Neolithic manner, using polished-stone tools and weapons. The bow and arrow were in use, and houses were constructed of mud and wattle, with thatched roofs.

Certain aspects of Chinese history prior to 1500 B.C. are based upon legends which have not been confirmed by archaeological findings. These legends refer to the time from 2852 B.C. to 2205 B.C. as the Age of the Legendary Five Rulers. One of these rulers, the Emperor Huang-ti (about 2697 B.C.), is said to have invented the calendar and a form of writing similar to Egyptian hieroglyphics (although the later-developed character system of Chinese writing is unrelated to this). Legend also would have it that the Emperor's wife taught the people to raise silkworms and to weave cloth. China at this time was not the large country of today. It consisted of an area smaller than the present Honan Province.

Korea, about 3000 B.C., had a Neolithic culture built by tribes which had migrated into the coastal areas from north China and Manchuria.

In Japan, around 3000 B.C., a mixture of Mongolian and Southeast Asian peoples were making pottery by hand, using crudely fashioned stone and bone weapons, and apparently had not begun to practice agriculture.

The earliest Neolithic cultures were developing throughout what is now Vietnam, Laos and Cambodia.

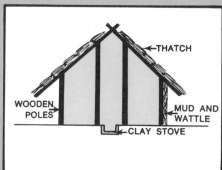

Yellow River huts were of "mud and wattle"—clay reinforced with twigs or straw. A stove (also molded of clay) was located in the center of the conical-shaped buildings.

OCEANIA

The outer islands of Oceania remained largely unoccupied, but Australia, New Zealand and New Guinea were occupied by very primitive peoples.

AFRICA, except for its Mediterranean Lands

Around 3000 B.C., the Sahara Desert was at the height of its "wet stage" and the area was a Neolithic center of farming and trade. About 2500 B.C., however, the Sahara began to lose rainfall, and its people were forced to migrate to African lands to the north, south and east.

THE AMERICAS

In what is now Peru, about 3000 B.C., a culture developed in which fishing and primitive agriculture, including the cultivation of cotton, were practiced. Pottery was in use in what is now Colombia and Ecuador.

In central Mexico, Neolithic people were learning to cultivate many crops, one of which was maize. Permanent pit-houses were being built about 3000 B.C. These were subterranean excavations lined with boulders or sun-dried bricks called adobe, and probably covered with tree limbs and other vegetation where necessary.

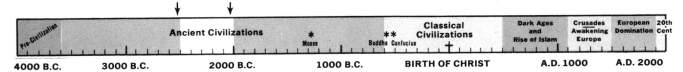

Pre-Civilization	Ancient Civilizations	*Moses	**Buddha Confucius	Classical Civilizations	Dark Ages and Rise of Islam	Crusades Awakening Europe	European Domination	20th Cent

4000 B.C.   3000 B.C.   2000 B.C.   1000 B.C.   BIRTH OF CHRIST   A.D. 1000   A.D. 2000

2500 — 2000 B.C.

Civilization on the Indus River • Expanding Cultural Activity in Crete • The Legendary Hsia Dynasty in China

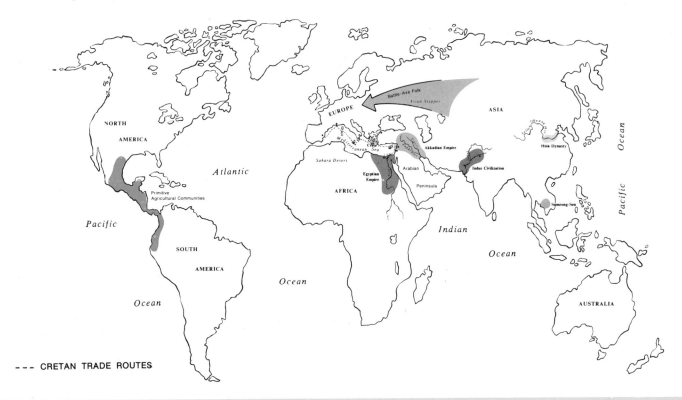

--- CRETAN TRADE ROUTES

THE MEDITERRANEAN WORLD and Europe

The city-states of Sumer were overwhelmed in 2350 B.C. by Semitic conquerors from northern Mesopotamia, led by Sargon of Akkad. Under Sargon, the valleys of the Tigris and the Euphrates were united for the first time into one empire, whose frontiers were then extended east into Elam and west into Syria. Sargon's grandson Naram-Sin expanded the frontiers even farther, east to the mountains of Persia and possibly as far west as the Mediterranean Sea. The Akkadians were overthrown in 2230 B.C. by the Guti, a people who came from the mountains to the east. The Guti ruled a disunited Mesopotamia for the next 150 years, until 2050 B.C., when the Sumerians once again established control over the Tigris-Euphrates Valleys.

Since 2778 B.C., Egypt had flourished under the dynasties of the pharaohs of the Old Kingdom. However, by 2263 B.C., after more than five hundred years of artistic, scientific and commercial achievement, the power of the Old Kingdom's central government had

The Great Ziggurat at the city of Ur was an outstanding example of the tall towers topped with shrines built by the Sumerians to simulate their ancestral mountaintop places of worship. The Biblical "Tower of Babel" may have been such a ziggurat.

so deteriorated that the rule of the Nile Valley was divided among several petty princelings. The next 163 years under this divided and weak government (which ended in 2000 B.C.) are known as the Feudal Period, a time of general regression from the standards and achievements that had made Egypt great.

Crete, by 2500 B.C., had practically monopolized the sources of tin in the Mediterranean area, picking it up in ports of Greece and Spain, and was trading this metal (vital to the making of bronze), along with lumber, oil, pearls and spices, to Egypt, Mesopotamia and the developing cities of Asia Minor. Metalworking in Crete had reached great heights, as had the other arts and sciences. Cretan religion was based in good part on worship of the Mother Goddess and apparently had its origins in Asia Minor; Crete's colorful painting of the time seems to have been greatly influenced by the Egyptians. Yet the mainstream of her culture, as it unfolded, was distinctly Cretan. By the end of this millennium (2000 B.C.) a full-fledged civilization had emerged on the island, but our knowledge of its history and internal structure is limited by the fact that we have been able to translate only one of the several Cretan scripts.

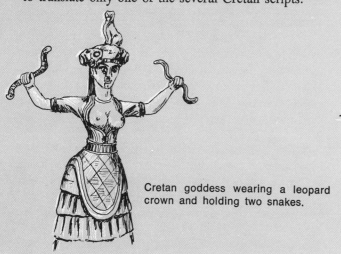

Cretan goddess wearing a leopard crown and holding two snakes.

On Malta, an island in the central Mediterranean, the inhabitants pursued a religion of which impressive evidence remains. They erected huge megaliths—stone monuments—to attest, in some way we do not understand, to their belief in life-after-death. The people of Malta are thought to have spread their religion peacefully and to have erected megaliths throughout the western Mediterranean and, later, along the European Atlantic coasts. Megaliths are to be found in France and Britain, and up to the Baltic shores as far as Sweden. Stonehenge in Britain is believed to be such a megalithic construction, even though it was built after these people had been conquered by Indo-European nomads from Asia. Stonehenge was probably erected under the direction and to the specifications of the conquering Indo-Europeans. In even more recent times, the megalith builders or their disciples apparently erected monuments along the coasts of India. Later still, megaliths were erected along the Southeast Asian shores of the Malay Peninsula and Indonesia.

The basic construction of the temples of the megalith builders on the island of Malta consisted of two upright stones topped by a slab. The islanders apparently had no metal tools with which to cut the stone, and evidence indicates that they used round stone balls as rollers to move the huge slabs.

Beginning about 2100 B.C., people from the Asian Steppes who spoke Indo-European tongues were beginning to penetrate Central Europe. These nomads are known to historians as the Battle-Axe Folk because of the weapons of polished stone with which they armed themselves, weapons which quite evidently had been modeled after Sumerian axes of bronze.

ASIA, except for its Mediterranean Lands

In the Indian subcontinent, a civilization located on the Indus River and its tributaries had come into being by 2500 B.C. or earlier. The remnants of its cities and their contents indicate that this civilization may have been the equal, technologically, of Sumer in Mesopotamia and Egypt in the Nile Valley. We know nothing of its prehistory, and underground water has made it nearly impossible for archaeologists to dig far below the remnants to examine the levels of occupation which may have antedated the cities. We assign the date of 2500 B.C. to the beginning of this Indus Valley civilization because some of its seals—small embossed implements in the shape of disks, cylinders or rectangles, used to impress patterns onto other items for decoration or to authenticate their origin—have been found in Mesopotamia and can be related to Sumerian chronology.

All we know about the Indus civilization has been learned from the remains of two great cities, Harappa and Mohenjo-Daro, which we think were twin capitals. The two cities, located about 350 miles apart, were apparently laid out in geometrically exact patterns on previously unoccupied ground. Lesser cities as far apart as a thousand miles have been found along the Indus and its tributaries, and along the broad delta where it flows into the Arabian Sea.

The Indus civilization drew its strength from the great Indus River, just as Sumer did from the Tigris and the Euphrates, and as Egypt did from the Nile. The products of its thriving agricultural economy were traded as far west as Persia and Mesopotamia, and perhaps even Asia Minor. Bronze was widely used by its people, as was a beautifully painted pottery formed on potter's wheels. Many of its houses had running water and the equivalent of modern sanitation, but seem to have had no windows facing the street. Shops have been unearthed which evidence a familiarity with trade and other commercial processes. There was a uniform system of weights and measures, unknown elsewhere in the ancient world.

Priest-King of Mohenjo-Daro.

Bricks of standard size which were fire-baked were used in construction of the buildings of Mohenjo-Daro. The citadel was raised on a high base, perhaps as a protection from floods. In it were the granary, the public baths and the administration buildings.

As far as we can determine from archaeological comparisons, the total population of the Indus civilization seems to have consisted of about 100,000 people, who were no doubt the ancestors of the brown-skinned Dravidian peoples of southern India today. Like the Egyptians, they were organized into a regimented society tightly controlled by their government, which seems to have been headed by priest-kings.

More knowledge than this about the Indus civilization—its prehistorical development, its true antiquity, its people's thoughts, hopes and fears—will have to await the day when we shall be able to translate its writing, or when archaeology provides new insights into its past.

In China, the legendary Hsia Dynasty is said to have come into being about 2200 B.C. in the Valley of the Yellow River. Although its rulers took the title of emperor, more likely they were tribal chieftains, leaders of Neolithic agricultural tribes. As with the other legendary empires of China, archaeology has found no confirmation of their existence. Yet, as with other legends, this one may prove someday to be fundamentally true.

About 2500 B.C. in what is today Cambodia, a Neolithic society called the Somrong-Sen was developing which has left a variety of artifacts consisting of tools, weapons and ornamentation. Among these are axes, hoes, chisels, knives, fishhooks, shell ornaments and beads.

OCEANIA

The inhabitants of Australia, New Zealand and the other inner islands of Oceania remained in a very primitive stage of technological development. The outer islands, as far as archaeological evidence shows, seem to have been unoccupied at this early date.

AFRICA, except for its Mediterranean Lands

The Saharan agricultural community had been obliterated by desert winds and by lack of rain, and its people scattered to other parts of Africa. About 2350 B.C., according to records of the Egyptian Old Kingdom, noblemen of the Egyptian dynasty made expeditions into the African interior to search for metals including gold, copper and tin.

THE AMERICAS

The climate of North and South America was approaching that of the New World today. By 2300 B.C., permanent villages were scattered throughout both continents, most of them practicing at least a primitive agriculture.

In Mexico's Valley of Tehuacán, located southeast of modern Mexico City in what is now Puebla State, remnants of beautifully styled handmade painted pottery dating from about 2500 to 2000 B.C. have been found.

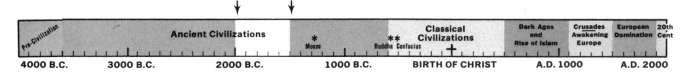

Pre-Civilization	Ancient Civilizations		＊ Moses	＊＊ Buddha Confucius	Classical Civilizations	Dark Ages and Rise of Islam	Crusades Awakening Europe	European Domination 20th Cent

4000 B.C.   3000 B.C.   2000 B.C.   1000 B.C.   BIRTH OF CHRIST   A.D. 1000   A.D. 2000

2000 — 1500 B.C.

**The Code of Hammurabi   •   Luxurious Civilization in Crete   •
The Destruction of the Indus Civilization   •   The Shang Dynasty in China**

By 2000 B.C., agricultural techniques had been so greatly improved that farmers no longer had to confine their efforts to the fertile deltas of the great river valleys in order to realize an abundant crop. By utilizing the plow and the techniques of fertilizing and fallowing (that is, plowing a portion of land and letting it lie idle for one or more growing seasons), they could produce, on rain-watered lands, food well in excess of their own needs. As a result, cities began to spring up in the lands of Asia Minor, in Persia and on the Aegean shores and islands. This was a period of growth for less advanced civilizations.

On the fringes of these new civilizations lived barbarian peoples with whom trade developed. The barbarians quickly learned to use many of the devices of civilized life, being attracted especially to those which could be used in warfare. They employed bronze not so much for tools as for battle-axes, and they converted the four-wheeled cart to the much more maneuverable two-wheeled war chariot. They waited and watched these lesser civilizations, and in times of disorganization or dissension they turned these newly mastered devices against their teachers. The result was a series of conquests of civilized peoples by barbarians. Often the conquerors went on, after overthrowing the lesser cities, to conquer the primary civilizations in the river valleys.

In some instances the conquerors, with barbarian fury, destroyed the cities and their ways of life. More often, however, they adopted the pleasures and luxuries of the civilizations and became the "elite" of the societies they had defeated. When this occurred, the conquerors (or their sons in the next generation) frequently faced uprisings among the subject people, for the memory of the defeated can be long. Always, too, they had to guard against possible attack by the watchful, envious Semitic and Indo-European nomads on their outer fringes.

This power contest between expanding civilizations and the barbarians on their peripheries was to be a basic pattern of history, not only in the current period (2000–1500 B.C.) but for a good part of the next three thousand years.

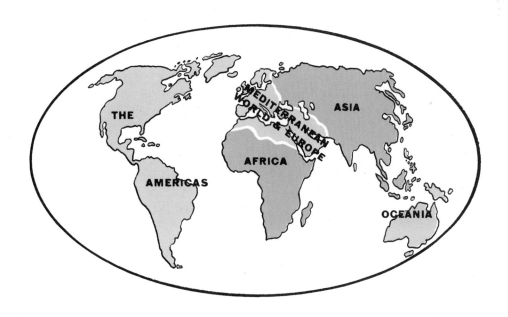

THE MEDITERRANEAN WORLD and Europe

Sumerian rule of Mesopotamia, which was reestablished about 2050 B.C., lasted until 1850 B.C., when an invading semitic people called the Amorites or Babylonians took control. These conquerors were to rule Mesopotamia for less than two hundred years (until 1575 B.C.), but during their ascendancy the cultural level of the Tigris-Euphrates Valleys would rival and even surpass that of the original Sumerian civilization. Archaeologists have found tens of thousands of tablets inscribed with letters, business records, poems and tales, all attesting to Babylonian cultural accomplishments. These were all written in Akkadian cuneiform; by this time the Akkadian language had become the common tongue of all Mesopotamia.

Under the great Babylonian King Hammurabi (1728–1686 B.C.), a code of ethics, morals and law, known as the Code of Hammurabi, was formulated and adopted. It is admired to this day by students of law and government for its frequent good sense, its fairness and its consistency.

King Hammurabi is shown on this commemorative inscribed stone, or stele, receiving from the sun god the 300 laws which comprise the famous Code of Hammurabi.

The Babylonian civilization was surrounded by half-civilized peoples who would, in future centuries, have a considerable impact upon history. For example, the Bible tells of the Hebrews in the old Sumerian city of Ur and of how their leader, Abraham, led his flock out of this worldly, idol-worshiping city in search of a new home in the land of Canaan, roughly the area occupied by modern Israel. In addition, we read in Babylonian records that the Assyrians were living on Babylon's borders. Assyrian merchants in turn left records of their trade with the Hittites in Asia Minor. We hear of the Phoenicians, who at this point were a simple fisher folk living on the Asian coast of the Mediterranean Sea. Each of these peoples in the future would build formidable military states or would contribute in some way to mankind's culture and store of knowledge.

By 1575 B.C., yet another nomadic people had overwhelmed Babylonia. These were the Kassites. Although they ruled Mesopotamia for the next four hundred years,

their leadership and influence were weak, and little or no cultural advancement took place during their reign. In about 1530 B.C., the city of Babylon was razed by Hittites from Asia Minor, who, after the attack, left with their booty, making no attempt to hold the land.

An early Egyptian horse and chariot. The horse and probably the chariot were brought to Egypt by the conquering Hyksos.

In Egypt, the dynasties of the Middle Kingdom which had ruled since 2000 B.C. were increasingly beset by internal strife and dissension. About 1788 B.C., the fierce, nomadic Hyksos, Asian tribesmen of mixed racial stock, invaded the lower Nile Valley. The Hyksos warriors rode across the desert in highly maneuverable war chariots from which they could let loose deadly flights of arrows. This Hyksos weaponry, in combination with Egypt's internal disorganization, doomed the once proud people of the Nile. For the first time in over a thousand years, Egypt came under foreign domination; the Hyksos ruled the lower Nile Valley for more than two hundred years.

In 1580 B.C., native Egyptians led by the King of Thebes rose up and overthrew the hated Hyksos. They then moved the capital from Memphis upriver to the city of Thebes. Thus began the four hundred years (1580 to 1085 B.C.) which are called the New Kingdom. During this period the Egyptians, realizing that the deserts and the sea could no longer protect them from invasion, undertook an aggressive and preventive international policy, attacking other nations in order to prevent attack on themselves. The Eighteenth Dynasty, the first to rule the New Kingdom, was brilliant both militarily and culturally, and under it the Egyptian Empire eventually extended east through Syria-Palestine in Asia and south through Nubia in Africa.

During this period, from 2000 B.C. to 1500 B.C., civilization on the isle of Crete rose to a level of sophistication not unlike that of the court of France at Versailles almost four thousand years later. The main Cretan palace at Knossos was magnificent even by present standards. It was made of finely masoned stone several stories high, and it featured beautiful frescoed walls attesting to the Cretan worship of the great Mother Goddess, the sacred snake and the bull. Its corridors and staircases were supported by handsome tapering timbers. The palace boasted such refinements as a plumbing system, baths, running water and an actual flushing toilet.

Not only the ruling classes, but much of the general population of Crete seems to have led a life of comparative plenty, made possible by the island's control of the enormously profitable Mediterranean sea trade and its monopoly of the sources of tin.

Crete became very aggressive commercially during this era and established trading centers along the coasts of Greece, the most important of them being the cities of Mycenae and Tiryns. Another Aegean city, Troy, located in Asia Minor, may have had a similar relationship with Crete. It is believed that these cities were not garrisoned by Cretans, but rather that they enjoyed a very close commercial and cultural relationship with the mother island.

Various Indo-European peoples were migrating into the European continent. Celts from the Asian Steppes penetrated into Middle Europe, and Greek- and Latin-speaking peoples came across the Balkan Peninsula from Asia via passages both north and south of the Black Sea. Of these, the Hellenic peoples (Greek-speaking) would turn south into the Aegean area, and the Italic peoples (Latin-speaking) would travel farther west before turning south into Italy.

This view of the palace at Knossos is of an entrance showing porticos upon which were painted scenes of "bull-grappling," which may have been a sport or ritual ancestral to modern bullfights.

ASIA, except for its Mediterranean Lands.

In the Indian subcontinent, the great civilization which had prospered for over a thousand years along the Indus River and its tributaries was destroyed about 1500 B.C. by Indo-European nomads coming, probably, from Persia (Iran). These white-skinned barbarians, known as Aryans, reduced Harappa and Mohenjo-Daro to smoking piles of rubble and drove the darker-skinned (presumably Dravidian) people to the southern portions

of the subcontinent, where their descendants live to this day.

In China, according to legend, the Hsia rulers (or tribal leaders) fell to fighting among themselves, causing much misery among their subjects. About 1700 B.C., the Prince of Shang conquered and unified China. He founded the Shang Dynasty, whose beginnings are dated from 1776 B.C. by some historians and from 1523 B.C.

by others. The dynasty remained in power until 1028 B.C., with its capital at the city of Po, in what is now eastern Honan. T'ang, the first king of the Shang Dynasty, is reputed to have been a virtuous and conscientious ruler.

From 1500 B.C. on, Chinese history is substantiated by archaeological findings and inscriptions upon shells, bones and bronze; actual written historical records that have been discovered date back to 1300 B.C. During Shang time, animals were domesticated, and millet and wheat were the basic cereal crops. Warrior chiefs during the latter Shang years carried bronze daggers and rode in chariots with bronze fittings. Some archaeologists think that the Chinese learned of the chariot from the Indo-Europeans, who had been using it since about 2000 B.C. The reason so many centuries passed before the chariot appeared in China, it is thought, is that geographical barriers—the vast deserts, steppes and mountains of northern Asia—between the two areas made the transportation of knowledge extremely difficult.

In Southeast Asia there were migrations beginning about 1900 B.C. (from what is now southwest China) into Indonesia. The descendants of these migrants are the Bataks of Sumatra and the Dayaks of Borneo. Similar migrations took place from south China into Malaysia.

These Shang bronzes were superbly crafted vessels used to hold sacrificial offerings of meat, grain and wine in rites of ancestral worship.

OCEANIA

The peoples of Australia, New Zealand and New Guinea remained in a very primitive state of development. The outer islands are believed to have been uninhabited.

AFRICA, except for its Mediterranean Lands

The early Negroes, Pygmies and Bushmen were living in primitive stages of development throughout the southern deserts and the great savannahs of sub-Mediterranean Africa. Egyptian records tell of trade expeditions about 1500 B.C. to the country of Punt, located in the area of the present-day Somali Republic on the Indian Ocean.

THE AMERICAS

By 2000 B.C., permanent agricultural villages were being established in the highlands of Mexico.

In what is now Peru, agricultural communities with houses of stone and mud-brick flourished. An attractive handmade pottery was beginning to be used about 1600 B.C. There are also evidences that temple worship and a hierarchy of priests existed in Peru at this time. This was six hundred years before similar activities are known to have developed in Mexico or Central America.

Waterfowl and fish were hunted in the rich lake area by Mexican prehistoric highland farmers. Female figurines of clay found with other artifacts in the area may have been used in fertility rites.

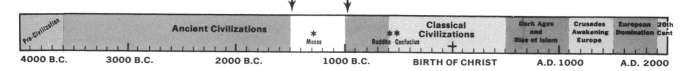

Pre-Civilization	Ancient Civilizations	*Moses	**Buddha Confucius	Classical Civilizations	Dark Ages and Rise of Islam	Crusades Awakening Europe	European Domination	20th Cent

4000 B.C.   3000 B.C.   2000 B.C.   1000 B.C.   BIRTH OF CHRIST   A.D. 1000   A.D. 2000

1500 — 1000 B.C.

**The Iron Age • Moses and the Ten Commandments • Phoenicia and the Alphabet •
The Fall of Crete**

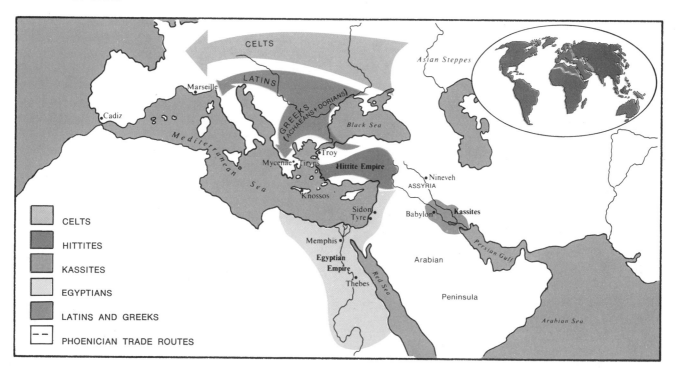

THE MEDITERRANEAN WORLD and Europe.

About 1400 B.C., the Hittites, one of several peoples who had resided in Asia Minor for many centuries and who spoke an Indo-European language, became the first people to learn how to separate iron from its ores by the heating process called smelting. As a result, the Iron Age came to the Mediterranean world, bringing about a revolution in warfare as far-reaching as that caused by the introduction of war chariots in previous centuries and of bronze in still earlier times.

The Hittite armies, well equipped with weapons made from cheap and plentiful iron, carved out an empire that included most of their neighbors in Asia Minor. Later they invaded Syria, added part of it to their empire, and stopped the advance of Egypt's powerful armies there. They also invaded Babylon, but failed to hold it for long. Yet by 1200 B.C. the Hittite Empire was crumbling, attacked from the east by Assyrians and from the west by Achaeans—who had been among the first of several Greek-speaking peoples to migrate into Europe over the preceding several centuries.

The Egyptians' army had extended its conquests east-

Ramses II built the Temple of Karnak, the largest columned hall ever constructed, at his capital city of Thebes. Its columns were 69 feet high and 33 feet in circumference. Ramses II was the spectacular king who, during Egypt's imperial period, fought the war with the Hittites, and who also ruled during the exodus of the Hebrews.

ward from their center on the Nile to Canaan and into Syria, where it was met and contained by Hittite forces. At home Egyptian armies repelled invasions by Libyans and other peoples, but by the middle of the twelfth century B.C. the Nile civilization was weakening and could no longer hold its far-flung empire together.

About 1290 B.C., some Hebrew tribes who earlier had wandered from Canaan into Egypt in search of better pasturage and had been enslaved there by the pharaohs escaped from their long Egyptian captivity. Their exodus from Egypt was led by Moses, the great lawgiver. He is so called because through him the Jews received the

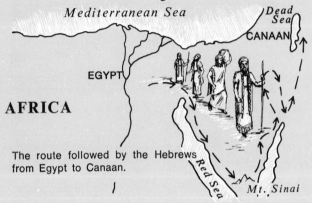

The route followed by the Hebrews from Egypt to Canaan.

Ten Commandments and a code of civil and religious conduct. Moses led the Hebrews across the Red Sea and through the deserts of the Sinai Peninsula back to Canaan, where they formed a loose union with the Hebrew tribes who had remained there during the Egyptian captivity. In the 1000s B.C., Saul became the first king of the Hebrews.

The Minoan civilization of Crete fell about 1500 B.C. to Greek-speaking Achaeans. The great palace and other structures at Knossos, after suffering great earthquake damage, were probably demolished by these Achaeans in 1450 B.C. Three centuries later, a new wave of Greek-speaking people called Dorians obliterated what little remained of Minoan culture on the island.

On the Peloponnese Peninsula of the Greek mainland, the walled city of Mycenae remained a center of Cretan culture and an important commercial center. Over a period of time, however, it was infiltrated by Achaeans, who eventually made themselves its ruling class. About 1184 B.C. these same Achaeans destroyed the city of Troy in Asia Minor, as described in the epic poem the *Iliad* by Homer. About 1100 B.C., Dorian Greeks like those who had wiped out the remnants of culture on Crete attacked and destroyed the mainland

city of Mycenae, and the entire Aegean area reverted to a dark age—a period in which the written word, art, science and the other appurtenances of civilization were abandoned.

As the power of Crete and Mycenae waned, the Phoenicians (about 1200 B.C.) became the chief sea power of the Mediterranean. They operated out of their native island cities of Tyre and Sidon, located just off the coast of what is now Lebanon, and over many centuries they founded daughter trading cities such as Marseilles in France, Cadíz in Spain, and (most important from a historical point of view) Carthage on the coast of Africa. Very important among their trade goods were a purple cloth and lumber obtained from cedar forests in Lebanon. These they traded for pottery in Rhodes, for oil, figs and wine in the Aegean, and for tin in Spain.

The Phoenicians were highly skilled navigators, and their daring explorations in a later time extended north to the Cassiterides Islands near Great Britain and south down the coasts of Africa. Most important, the Phoenicians invented a simplified alphabet which was later adopted by the Greeks and became the basis for the alphabets of the entire Western world.

PHOENICIAN	MODERN
⨯	A
9	B
ヨ	E
Ɩ	L
ɰ	M
ο	O
ſ	S
Ƴ	K
✕	T

The original Phoenician alphabet with its modern equivalents. Phoenician traders spread the use of ink and paper as well as their alphabet throughout the Mediterranean.

The continent of Europe was experiencing a prolonged invasion of Indo-European-speaking peoples. Greeks and Latins continued to cross the Balkan Peninsula and to settle along the Mediterranean coasts. The Celts continued to migrate from the Asian Steppes, penetrating as far as France and Britain, and were followed by Germans traveling much the same route. Slavic peoples would come along a route similar to that of the Celts at a somewhat later time, but would not penetrate far beyond what is today Eastern Europe.

ASIA, except for its Mediterranean Lands:

In the Indian subcontinent, the light-skinned Aryans who had destroyed the Indus civilization were establishing tribal kingdoms under the rule of their rajahs. They felt themselves to be entirely superior to the dark-

skinned Dravidian people whom they had conquered (even though the Dravidians were culturally far more advanced), and they considered it sinful to have any physical contact with them. Their religious beliefs, which at this time were largely a form of nature worship, had been transmitted by word of mouth in the form of poems, songs and hymns from generation to generation. Even minor variations within their recital were forbidden. Toward the end of this period (about 1000 B.C.) these collected hymns and prayers, which were called the Vedas, were beginning to be set down in written form.

After 1200 B.C., the last twelve of thirty Shang rulers are believed to have ruled from An-Yang, a city located in what is now Honan Province. During Shang rule, the first known systematic astronomical studies were made. Eclipses, novas and comets were regularly observed and their paths recorded. Much progress was made in the science of optics and in the mathematics necessary to explore both optics and astronomy. Yet, around 1140 B.C., the Shang rulers were weakening and the feudal state of Chou was growing in power. In despair, the last Shang ruler burned himself to death, and in 1122 B.C. the Chou Dynasty was established under the leadership of Wu Wang, who took the title of emperor and ruled over the group of feudal states which then made up China.

Huge burial pits were dug for royal funerals during the Shang Dynasty, in which live humans as well as pottery, art objects, and even horses and chariots were buried along with the deceased royal personage.

OCEANIA

The peoples of Oceania remained in very primitive stages of development.

AFRICA, except for its Mediterranean Lands

After the dispersal of the Saharan cultures, the people of sub-Mediterranean Africa remained in far more primitive conditions than those of Africa's Mediterranean lands, although several inland city-states were to prosper from time to time. Climatic and geologic conditions were to keep Africa at a great disadvantage compared with more favored areas of the earth until late modern times, while some of its peoples, such as the Pygmies in the Congo, remain in the Stone Age even today.

THE AMERICAS

The temple at Chavin was three stories high, with passages and rooms lined with slabs of stone. Its sculptured cat-god is typical of the Chavin art form's preoccupation with cats and the feline body.

The oldest remains in Yucatán of settlements which were built by the ancestors of the Mayan peoples date from about this time. Near this area, the beginnings of what is called the Olmec art style are found close to the modern cities of San Lorenzo, Veracruz and Tabasco. The Olmec is noted for its colossal heads carved from single blocks of stone and for its catlike figurines. It is believed to have had considerable effect on later Mayan art. At about the same time, a similar art form called the Chavin was developing in Peru. In much of South America, but especially on the Peruvian coast, lima beans, squash and maize, as well as manioc (a root crop), were being cultivated.

In the Southwestern part of what is now the United States (Colorado, New Mexico and Arizona), a group of Indians known today as the Basket Makers were abandoning their nomadic way of life and beginning to settle in agricultural communities.

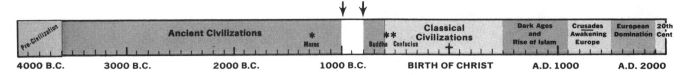

Pre-Civilization	Ancient Civilizations	*Moses		**Buddha Confucius	Classical Civilizations	Dark Ages and Rise of Islam	Crusades Awakening Europe	European Domination	20th Cent

| 4000 B.C. | 3000 B.C. | 2000 B.C. | 1000 B.C. | BIRTH OF CHRIST | A.D. 1000 | A.D. 2000 |

1000 — 800 B.C.

**Expanding Assyria • Two Hebrew Kingdoms • The Aryans Dominate India •
Feudal Rule in China**

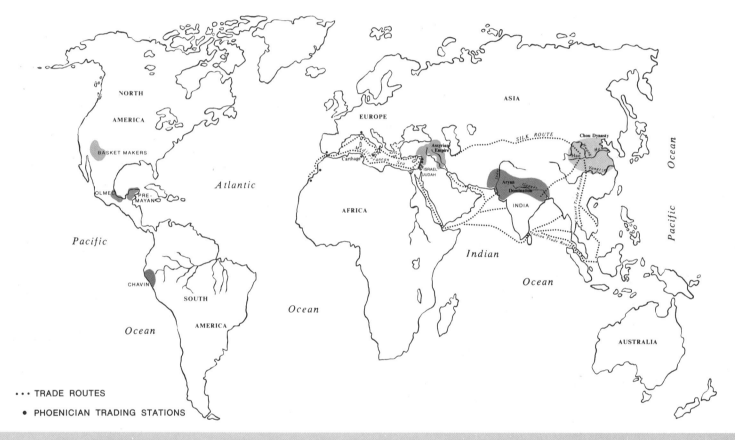

••• TRADE ROUTES

• PHOENICIAN TRADING STATIONS

THE MEDITERRANEAN WORLD and Europe

Late in the 900s B.C. the Assyrians, from their capital city of Nineveh, began the extension of their empire west to the Mediterranean Sea. The Assyrian army was well organized and efficient, and was everywhere dreaded for its extreme cruelty. The terror which the army inspired made it a powerful instrument for the administration of conquered lands, inspiring obedience and conformity throughout the Near East, and extracting tribute from subject peoples.

The Hebrews achieved their greatest temporal power during King David's reign, from 1012 to 972 B.C. After conquering the Philistines and other nearby tribes, they moved their capital from Hebron to Jerusalem, which became their Eternal City. Jerusalem was later to become a city sacred to both Christians and Moslems. During the reign of King David's son King Solomon, the Hebrews made alliances with the Phoenicians and

The Assyrian Army was organized into units of infantry, horse cavalry, charioteers and camel troops. Spears, swords, bows and arrows were the weapons of those exceedingly fierce fighters.

the Egyptians. Solomon was noted for his wisdom and for his furtherance of trade through commercial agreements with other nations, but his economic activities burdened his people with heavy taxes. Upon his death, civil war divided the Hebrews into two nations—Israel in the north and Judah in the south.

The Phoenicians in 814 B.C. founded the city of Carthage on the North African coast, located near the modern city of Tunis.

The Egyptian throne was seized about 950 B.C. by a strong Libyan prince who made himself Pharaoh Sheshonk I, the first in a dynasty of Libyan rulers of Egypt. Sheshonk I ruled aggressively, but under later Libyan pharaohs the line weakened and there was dissension and civil war.

In Mediterranean Europe, the Greek tribes were adopting a settled way of life within small states separated by rugged mountains. Originally these tribal states were ruled by leaders who frequently called themselves kings. These kingdoms would over the years evolve into the city-states of Classical Greece. During these centuries of evolution, trade was expanded and settlements grew into towns. Most of our information from this obscure period in the history of Greece comes from the *Iliad* and the *Odyssey,* believed to have been written around 850 B.C. by a poet named Homer.

Other Greek tribes called Ionians settled along the European coasts, east to Asia Minor, and beyond to the Black Sea. By the late 800s B.C., these Ionian Greeks had gained control of the Aegean Islands and had captured or built a dozen coastal cities. They maintained

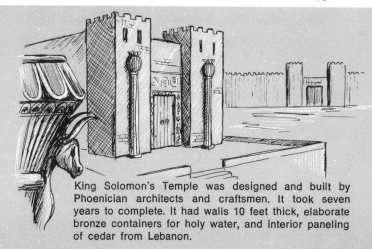

King Solomon's Temple was designed and built by Phoenician architects and craftsmen. It took seven years to complete. It had walls 10 feet thick, elaborate bronze containers for holy water, and interior paneling of cedar from Lebanon.

strong cultural ties with Greek peoples back in the Aegean peninsula and retained Greek as their spoken tongue.

The Etruscans arrived in Italy sometime during the 800s B.C. According to Classical tradition, deriving from the writings of Herodotus, these people were the highly cultured Lydians who were driven from Asia Minor as a result of the collapse of the Hittite Empire, of which they were a subject state. These Etruscans were to play a very important part in the early development of the Italian Peninsula and of Roman civilization and of Italy.

The Celts continued to push their way through Central Europe, advancing by now as far as Britain, conquering the earlier inhabitants. The German-speaking peoples, in addition to inhabiting Central Europe, were working their way into the north as far as Scandinavia.

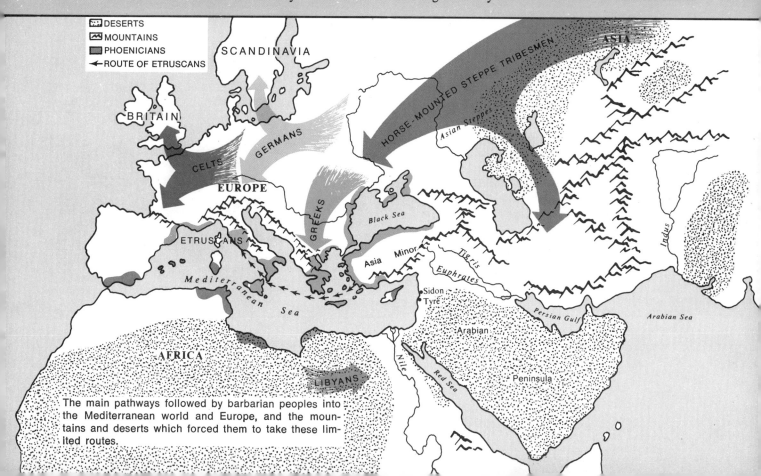

The main pathways followed by barbarian peoples into the Mediterranean world and Europe, and the mountains and deserts which forced them to take these limited routes.

ASIA, except for its Mediterranean Lands

In the Indian subcontinent, the Aryan peoples who had demolished the civilization on the Indus River about 1500 B.C. were now spreading south and east into the valley of the Ganges River, overrunning the darker-skinned Dravidians, many of whom had fled there after the fall of the Indus cities of Mohenjo-Daro and Harappa. The Aryans were organized into small kingdoms which engaged in agriculture and cattle raising. These kingdoms were often at war with one another, so that their rajahs lived within walled cities into which the entire populace could retreat during times of attack.

Aryan society was strongly patriarchal. Monogamy was the accepted practice, and there seems at this early date to have been no belief in reincarnation or related religious doctrines. The population was beginning to be separated into castes based on color of skin and on occupation.

In China, the Chou Dynasty was ruling from its capital, Hao, a city in the Wei Valley. Its control extended into the north Chinese plain as well as south of the Yangtze River. The Chou kings turned over large holdings of land to relatives and nobles in exchange for pledges of loyalty and military aid—a practice which would be used advantageously one thousand years later by medieval kings in Europe.

In Southeast Asia about 900 B.C., in present-day Vietnam, Laos and Cambodia, Chinese influence was being felt as merchants from China began to trade in the area. In a similar manner, the coastal areas of these countries, as well as those of Burma, Thailand, Malaysia and Indonesia, were being contacted and influenced by traders sailing from the Indian subcontinent. This pattern of Chinese influence upon the more inland portions of Southeast Asia and of Indian influence upon its coastal regions would continue into modern times.

OCEANIA

The scattered peoples of Oceania continued to live in a most primitive manner.

AFRICA, except for its Mediterranean Lands

During the 900s B.C., the Phoenicians began establishing trading stations along the Atlantic coasts of Africa, just as they had done in previous centuries along Africa's Mediterranean coasts.

THE AMERICAS

In the Southwest area of today's United States, the agricultural communities of the Basket Maker Indians continued to develop, with maize, beans and squash being the most important crops cultivated.

Mexico and Central America (and especially the Yucatán Peninsula) witnessed continued progress by the pre-Mayan peoples. In the areas of modern Veracruz and Tabasco remains have been found of ceremonial centers using Olmec art forms which date from this period.

In South America, the Chavin art style had spread over much of Peru. Like the Olmec in Mexico, its beginnings date back to about 1200 B.C. Examples of Chavin art dating from as recently as A.D. 200 have also been found. The style is noted for its fine masonry and (like the Olmec) for its stylized sculpture with emphasis on catlike forms.

A massive stone head almost 8 feet high (typical of the Olmec art form) is believed to have played a part in the elaborate rituals of the pre-Mayan peoples of the area which today is called La Venta, in Mexico. Such carvings, which weigh up to 20 tons, are found near sacrificial altars.

In Central Europe, remains of permanent Celtic settlements in which iron tools and weapons were used date back to 800 B.C. or earlier. Germanic tribes continued to come from the east, pushing behind the Celts. Behind the Germans, Slavic tribes were forcing entry into Eastern Europe. All of these peoples—Celts, Germans and Slavs—were speakers of Indo-European languages closely related to the speech of the peoples of Iran and portions of India.

Celtic farming settlements consisted of thatched huts of timber, sticks and clay. Their iron axes helped clear the forest, and their iron-tipped plows enabled them to break up clay soil too difficult for bronze tools to till.

ASIA, except for its Mediterranean Lands

Steppe tribesmen, mostly speakers of Mongol and Turkic languages indigenous to the region, were learning to ride astride their horses in a manner which permitted their hands to be free to handle weapons, principally the bow and arrow. This would in future years introduce a revolution in warfare, comparable in effect to those revolutions caused earlier by the introduction of bronze, then iron, and then the war chariot.

Mounted Mongol-Turkic warrior of the Asian Steppes.

In the Indian subcontinent, Magadha, located in the eastern Ganges Valley, became the first Aryan kingdom of importance.

During these two centuries (800–600 B.C.) important commentaries on the Vedas, the sacred literature of the Aryans, were written. These commentaries (called the Brahmanas and the Upanishads) serve today as a source of information about the life of these times, but when they were written they served to buttress the caste system by giving it almost religious legitimacy. By 600 B.C. there were four distinct castes maintained under the direction of the priests, or Brahmans, who were themselves the first and highest caste. Next came the caste of warrior-nobles, called Kshatriya, followed by the third caste of farmers and artisans, called Vaisya. Light-skinned Aryans made up all of the first three castes. Non-Aryans and slaves of both Aryan and non-Aryan origin composed the fourth caste, which was called Sudra. With the passage of time, many more castes and subcastes would be added and there would be some absorption of Sudra into the higher castes.

In China, as local princes became strong enough to form separate states, the feudal society of the Chou overlords became weaker and eventually Chou rule was in name only. About 771 B.C. an influx of barbarian people of unknown race from the north razed the royal capital, forcing its transfer in 770 B.C. from Hao on the Wei River to Loyang near the Yellow River. Out of the lack of real unified authority emerged five tribes which for almost two hundred years vied among themselves for supremacy. During this time, the emperor in Loyang remained the nominal head of the state, but his authority was confined largely to religious matters. The philosopher Lao-Tse, the founder of Taoism, was born near the end of the 600s B.C. Taoism taught that life should be lived simply and should not be concerned with worldly things, yet should be closely attuned to the cosmos.

Japanese legends tell of Jimmu, the first Japanese emperor, said to have reigned about 600 B.C., but modern authorities feel that this date was chosen arbitrarily almost thirteen centuries later. Japanese legends suggest much about the struggles that must have existed between early tribal leaders for supremacy.

In Southeast Asia, in Indochina during the 600s B.C., bronze weapons and tools, probably obtained through contact with China, began to be used. Influence from the Indian subcontinent grew stronger in the coastal areas of Southeast Asia as small Hindu villages began to develop new ports.

OCEANIA

The peoples of Australia, New Zealand, New Guinea and the hundreds of other islands of the Pacific remained at a very primitive level of technological development.

AFRICA, except for its Mediterranean Lands

The mixture of brown and black peoples of Nubia in the upper Nile Valley had long been influenced by Egypt through trade and other contacts. About 800 B.C., the kingdom of Kush had been established in this upper Nile area and had grown strong enough to conquer Egypt and to rule it in the Twenty-fifth Dynasty. In the 600s B.C., the Kushian rulers were expelled by Assyrian conquerors. The kingdom of Kush was one of Africa's earliest centers of iron smelting and working, its people going directly from the use of stone tools to iron without going through a copper or bronze stage.

THE AMERICAS

Remains of widespread farming centers of the Adena-Hopewell cultures (named after the farms on which the relics were discovered) have been found which date back to 600 B.C. These American Indian peoples lived in the valleys of the Mississippi, Ohio and Kentucky Rivers. Apparently much of their technological and artistic skill was derived from earlier accomplishments of Mexican tribes. The pottery and figurines of the Adena-Hopewell cultures, for example, are definitely patterned after those crafted by peoples of northeastern Mexico.

The Basket Makers of the Southwest United States had by this time completely abandoned their nomadic way of life in favor of an agricultural existence. Their homes were now built partly underground, and were lined with slabs of stone, very much like the pit-house built in earlier centuries in what is now Mexico.

The area in Yucatán occupied in later centuries by the great Mayan ceremonial centers, such as Tikal, was beginning to be populated by what are believed to be early Mayan peoples.

THE ANCIENT CIVILIZATIONS

A Look Back

By 600 B.C., the Ancient Civilizations had either totally disappeared or been so changed as to be almost unrecognizable. The civilizations on the island of Crete and on the Indus River, for example, had disappeared about 1500 B.C., when they were totally obliterated by barbarian invasions. The cultures of Mesopotamia and the Nile Valley had been overrun and infused with foreign blood and foreign ways so often that they bore little resemblance to the original highly creative societies which had once been the center of their respective parts of the ancient world. Similarly, feudal China, despite history's custom of referring to its everlasting continuity, was very unlike the original Shang civilization which had dominated the great Yellow River Valley from 1700 B.C. to 1122 B.C. Feudal China bore even less resemblance to the great society of China that was yet to come.

So, by 600 B.C., history had recorded human experience for almost three thousand years, a period longer than the total of all subsequent human experience. We have spoken in detail of the great accomplishments of the varied peoples of different colors and races who built and destroyed and then built again the cultures in these ancient lands. In total their feats seem to have rivaled those of peoples of subsequent eras. Their art and science, their military accomplishments, their governments, religions and architecture have left examples to inspire awe in men to this day.

Yet what do these tangible remains really tell about the individuals who created them? Certainly the brilliant military organization of the Assyrians, or the massive funereal structures of the Egyptians, or the invention of the wheel, of plumbing devices and even of writing, or the observation of astronomical events and celestial bodies by the Chinese, tell little about the actual lives of human beings.

Fortunately, we are not without some insight into the minds and hearts of the millions of people who lived and died during these three thousand years. Written histories and records of public life have been discovered, along with political speeches, business communications, diplomatic correspondence, and even love letters, which reveal the more private lives of men and women who lived in these ancient times.

Some of these writings were incised into stone tablets, others carved onto walls or brushed onto cloth or papyrus. From them and from legends we learn that people living in 3000 B.C. or 2000 B.C. or 800 B.C. held opposing viewpoints, behaved inconsistently, loved and hated intensely, reasoned logically and illogically. In the times of the ancient Egyptians and Sumerians, of the Babylonians, the Hebrews and the early Greeks, benevolent and ethical behavior existed side by side with the basest cruelty. There was literature. Games were invented and played with eagerness and keen competition. There were laughter, sorrow, despair and hope. Mankind, we know, has changed very little in five thousand years.

IV
THE CLASSICAL CIVILIZATIONS
THE 1,100 YEARS FROM 600 B.C. TO A.D. 500

A Look Ahead

Now mankind was about to enter upon a second period when great societies would develop and oppose each other. These new societies would for the most part be brought into being by peoples of different racial stocks (or, more correctly, by peoples speaking different languages) from those who had founded the Ancient Civilizations.

In China, barbarian tribes that for centuries had hungrily watched the Shang and Chou civilizations from their outer perimeters would now play an important role in forming a new China. In India, the barbarian Aryans who had destroyed the subcontinent's great Indus civilization would devote themselves to building a new civilization, encountering frequent harassment and occasional cooperation from the barbarians who lived on their borders.

Persians would unite all of the Asian and African shores of the Mediterranean Sea into one great empire; later, on the Mediterranean's European shores, first the Greeks and then the Romans would unite the European lands, then cross the sea to incorporate the older coastal civilizations of Asia and Africa into their empires. It is from the "Classical" art and the edifices of the Greeks and the Romans that this period of history takes its name.

From the great city of Carthage, on the African coast of the Mediterranean, the Semitic Phoenicians, one of the more ancient peoples, would first resist, then challenge the might of each of the new empires.

The locales where these new dramas would be played were the same as those where the people of the ancient civilizations had confronted and struggled against each other for three thousand years—the lands of China, India and the shores of the Mediterranean Sea. Toward the end of this period, in lower Mexico, the Mayan civilization—the first civilization in the New World—would come into being.

The eleven centuries of the Classical Civilizations would see the arts and sciences reach new heights in China, India and, most especially, Greece. During this period—actually, during just a very few centuries of it—many of the world's great religions would be founded, and men would examine their souls and their consciences and ask the "why" of life as never before, and perhaps never since, in human history.

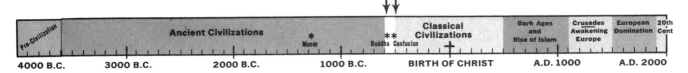

| Pre-Civilization | Ancient Civilizations | | Classical Civilizations | Dark Ages and Rise of Islam | Crusades Awakening Europe | European Domination | 20th Cent |

| 4000 B.C. | 3000 B.C. | 2000 B.C. | 1000 B.C. | BIRTH OF CHRIST | A.D. 1000 | A.D. 2000 |

Moses *   Buddha ** Confucius

600 — 500 B.C.

The Babylonian Captivity • The Century of Persia • The Hebrew Prophets • The Reforms of Solon in Athens • Buddha in India and Confucius in China

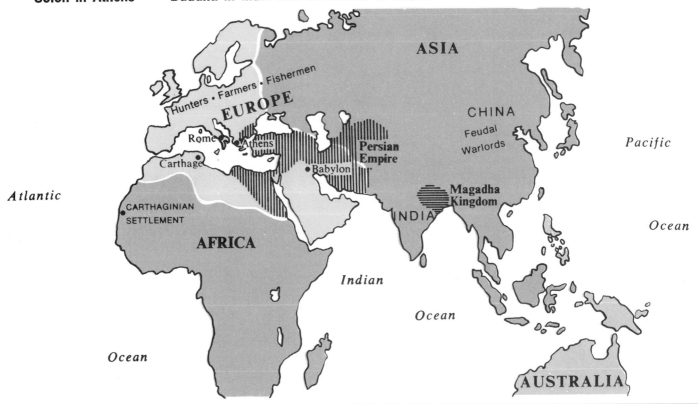

THE MEDITERRANEAN WORLD and Europe

In 597 B.C., the Chaldeans of Mesopotamia, led by King Nebuchadnezzar, destroyed the tiny Hebrew kingdom of Judah and exiled its people to Babylon, the Chaldean capital city. This period is known as the Babylonian Captivity. During it, the captive Hebrews came under the influence of the primitive Chaldean religious practices. Several Hebrew sages known as prophets (foremost among whom were Jeremiah and Ezekiel, and later Zechariah and Malachi) tried through sermons and exhortations to offset this pagan influence and to restore the Hebrew people's sense of personal relationship to God, as well as to impress upon them each individual's responsibility for his own acts. This sixth century before the birth of Christ is, as a result, often referred to as "the Age of the Prophets."

At about the same time, the Persians in Iran under Cyrus were growing in strength, so that by the middle of the century they had overthrown their former masters, the Medes. During the next several decades, the

Babylon during Nebuchadnezzar's reign was famed for its unique structures, among which were the Gate of Ishtar with its surface of glazed blue brick, the Hanging Gardens (one of the Seven Wonders of the Ancient World), and the Ziggurat, which many historians think may have been the Biblical "Tower of Babel."

Persians were locked in combat with a coalition of Mediterranean powers. Of these, the first to fall to the Persians (in 547 B.C.) were the Lydians of Asia Minor, led by their King, Croesus, who is known in legend for his vast wealth. Along with the Lydians, many Greek cities in Asia Minor came under Persian domination and the Persian King was now called Cyrus the Great.

Lydia, a country of Asia Minor which had long been a commercial cross-roads between East and West, became about 550 B.C. the first nation to produce die-stamped coins. This process was adopted by the Greeks and helped them to vitalize trade in the entire Mediterranean world.

In 538 B.C. the Chaldeans fell to Persia, and Cyrus released the Jews from captivity. Some of these Jews returned to their homeland in Judah. In 525 B.C., during the reign of Cyrus' son Cambyses, Persia conquered Egypt.

The next Persian ruler was Darius, who extended the empire to the mouth of the Danube River in what is now Russia, and to the Indus River in what is now Pakistan. Only Carthage, because of its distant location west of Egypt on the African Mediterranean coast, escaped Persian domination at this time. Darius organized the empire into twenty self-governing provinces called "satrapies," linked together by a network of roads and an efficient postal service and financed by a thorough tax-collection system. The Persian Empire, although ruled despotically, was well administered and its laws were just and fair by comparison with its predecessors in the Mediterranean area.

In Athens, in Mediterranean Europe, the great reformer Solon brought about the restructuring of Athens' constitution. Among other important reforms, every citizen had a voice in government. It should be kept in mind, however, that not all Athenians were citizens. Slaves had no voice in government, nor did non-landowners, and only the elite classes could aspire to high office. Even so, this reform brought about the first experiment with democracy in a world that heretofore had been governed only autocratically.

We have already mentioned the Greek poet Homer, who is said to have written the *Iliad* and the *Odyssey* in the 800s B.C. In the 700s, another Greek poet, Hesiod, wrote such outstanding poems as the *Works and Days,* which pictured the life of the peasants of the day. Such men were setting the stage for an explosion of culture in Greece in later centuries which would enable these scattered city-states to affect human thought and art as have no people before or possibly since. From 600 to 500 B.C., the acceleration of activity in the arts and sciences was evidenced in the work of the poetess Sappho, whose love poems and odes have survived only in fragments; of Thales, who founded a new school of philosophy and did important work in astronomy, engineering and geometry; of Pythagoras, a great mathematician and astronomer; of Aesop, who is famed for the collection of fables which bears his name, and of Heraclitus, a philosopher of great genius.

In Italy, the Latin and Italic tribes were struggling to free themselves from Etruscan rule. The city of Rome threw off its last Etruscan king in 510 B.C., and, with this city as its center, the Republic of Rome came into being.

The continent of Europe was populated by hunting, farming, and fishing peoples living in widely varying stages of technological development. We know that iron was used by some Celts in France and perhaps also in England. The Germanic tribes of Northern and Central Europe used iron, too, but their tools and weapons were more commonly made of stone, with perhaps some of bronze.

ASIA, except for its Mediterranean Lands

In the Indian subcontinent, the kingdom of Magadha, after a lengthy struggle with the other Aryan kingdoms of India, became the land's supreme power. The Magadha Empire would survive for almost two hundred years, from about 542 B.C. until 334 B.C. However, the northwest of India came under the hegemony of neighboring Persia. Coinage was probably introduced to northwest India at this time, and Taxila, the capital of the north's prosperous state of Gandhara, became the center of trade between India and Persia. Among Indian products in great demand were jewelry, cloth and rice. Indian metalworkers, carpenters and entertainers had gained a high repute and were often in demand in Persia

and elsewhere.

During this century, two great Indian philosophers were born, both of whom devoted their lives to reforming and elevating the existing Hindu religion. The end effect of both of their lives, however, was the founding of new religions. Siddhartha, the Buddha, was born in 563 B.C. Buddhism, which resulted from his teachings, became very important in India for hundreds of years and spread, as well, to much of the rest of Asia. Buddha taught brotherly love, the dignity of man and the ideals of modesty, self-control and moderation. He ardently opposed the caste system which demeaned many men in India. Today there are approximately 175 million Buddhists in the world, but very few live in India, the country of Buddhism's origin.

Mahavira, born in 540 B.C., is credited with forming the religion of the Jains, although Jainists claim a greater antiquity, contending that there were twenty-three saints of equal rank with Mahavira who preceded him. At its center, the sect is ascetic and strongly monastic, with its practitioners renouncing all worldly goods. The bulk of its adherents, however, are merchant-traders who live in large cities, which prevents their closely following this demanding ascetic life. Today there are approximately one and three-quarter million Jainists, most of whom live in India.

In China, the period of the middle Chou Dynasty was one when feudal warlords controlled the country, when artisans created ornate work in bronze, and when many philosophers and writers lived. The earliest evidence yet found of the use of iron in China is on an iron tripod, dating, it is thought, from about 550 B.C., in which a code of law is engraved. At about this same time, the great Confucius (K'ung Fu-tzu) was born, and proposed his philosophy of high moral standards and of public and personal ethics. Confucius was an early advocate of nationwide education, and of government by civil servants responsible and accountable for their acts. He taught that one must "know oneself to achieve self-perfection." Confucius did not formulate a new religion; many people today are followers of Confucianism as well as being Buddhists or Taoists or Christians.

In Southeast Asia, the ancestral groups of the Siamese, Laotian and Shan peoples were migrating from their original homes in southwestern China to Laos, Thailand and Cambodia respectively, where their descendants live today.

Confucius held several government offices in his native province of Lu. After the Prince of Lu failed to follow his philosophy, Confucius went into exile and wandered through China as a teacher for fourteen years.

OCEANIA

The peoples of Oceania's scattered islands and of its continent of Australia remained in a state of very primitive technological development.

AFRICA, except for its Mediterranean Lands

The Greek historian Herodotus tells of a Carthaginian voyage of colonization to the west coast of Africa about 520 B.C. It was led by Admiral Hanno, whose flotilla of sixty ships and thirty thousand colonists established a settlement on the Río de Oro. The colony lasted fifty years (until 470 B.C.). The area today is part of Spanish Morocco.

THE AMERICAS

In the Yucatán Peninsula of Mexico, religious shrines were being built on platforms of wood or stone and also upon mounds of earth. It is thought that these shrines were forerunners of the great pyramids which would be constructed in later eras as far north as Mexico City by the Mayan people and their successors the Toltecs.

An altar set upon a circular pyramid of clay in pre-Mayan Mexico.

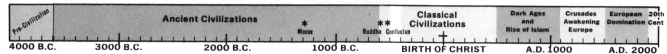

500 — 400 B.C.

War Between Persia and Greece and Between Greek and Greek • Hellenic Art, Science and Literature

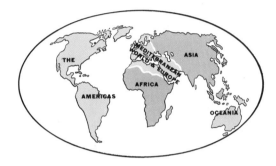

THE MEDITERRANEAN WORLD and Europe

The fifth century B.C. opened with the revolt of the Persian-ruled Greek cities in Asia Minor, and saw their total capitulation to the Persians in 494 B.C. after five years of battle. Persia then turned its wrath against the Greek city-states of Europe which had aided the rebellion of their sister cities in Asia Minor. For twelve years, beginning in 492 B.C. and ending in 479 B.C., Persia hurled her fleets and armies against the Greeks, only to be, in the end, defeated. During the twelve years of this war many notable events occurred: In 492 B.C. a Persian battle fleet heading for Greece was destroyed in a storm at sea; in 480 B.C. a force of three hundred Spartans died to the last man, to hold successfully the narrow pass of Thermopylae and permit the main Greek armies to escape; and, finally, the more experienced seamanship of the Athenians made possible the total defeat of the Persian fleets in the narrow waters of the Bay of Salamis between Athens and the island of Salamis just off the coast of Greece. Final defeat came to the Persian forces in a land battle at Palataea in 479 B.C.

Athens, now the leading city-state of Greece, formed the Delian League as a bulwark against further Persian invasion. The other Greek cities, located on the Greek mainland and the Greek islands and along the coasts of Asia Minor, although members of the League, were subordinate to Athens and were required to pay fees to the alliance in ships and money. These developments, led by Athens but participated in by many Greek cities, took place under the great Athenian statesman Pericles, who was in power from 460 B.C. to 429 B.C. It was during the rule of Pericles, a period known as the Golden Age, that Athens achieved her greatest glory in architecture, philosophy and science. The splendid buildings of the Acropolis and the magnificent statuary which graced the city were built during these years, as well as the "long walls," the parallel fortifications which ran from the city of Athens to its port, located at the town of Piraeus several miles away.

The city of Sparta was envious of Athenian power—though certainly not of Athenian art, science and litera-

The Greeks lured the Persian fleet into the narrow waters of the Bay of Salamis, where King Xerxes watched his more than 1,000 ships rammed and sunk by three or four hundred Greek vessels.

ture, for Sparta cared little for such things—and war broke out between the two city-states in 458 B.C. For fifty-four years they fought, with victory coming first to one, then to the other, in what are known as the Peloponnesian Wars. Final triumph came to Sparta near the end of the century, in 404 B.C., and she replaced Athens as the dominant power of Greece.

Three years later, in 401 B.C., Cyrus the Younger, brother of King Artaxerxes II of Persia, led ten thousand Greek mercenary troops in a revolt against his brother's empire. This bold venture failed when Cyrus was killed near the city of Babylon and his ten thousand Greek mercenaries were stranded in enemy territory. The story of their struggle to return home is told in the *Anabasis* by Xenophon, who was a member of the expedition.

Despite the Greeks' constant involvement in war, Hellenic culture developed a breathtaking grandeur during the 400s B.C. Particularly, the golden years of Athens under Pericles, as previously mentioned, saw attainments in arts, science and letters by men whose works and whose names have been honored by succeeding generations down to the present time.

Phidias (born about 500 B.C.) was the famous Greek sculptor who, in the time of Pericles, created much of Athens' and the Parthenon's statuary, including a gold-and-ivory statue of Athena and a large one of Zeus, also in gold and ivory. Myron (about 500 B.C.) is best known for his statue *The Discus Thrower.*

Greek men of literature created many works during this period. Pindar (522–440 B.C.) excelled in lyric poetry. Aeschylus (525–456 B.C.) is noted for his tragedies and for developing the drama as an art form; his plays include *The Suppliants, The Persians* and *Agamemnon.* Sophocles (486–406 B.C.) is regarded by

many as the foremost Greek dramatist, and is especially renowned for his famous trilogy *Oedipus Rex.* Euripedes (480–406 B.C.) was the writer of tragedies based on Greek myths. Aristophanes (448–388 B.C.) was the author of many comedies and satires. Xenophon (435–355 B.C.) a pupil of Socrates, was a soldier, a scholar and the author of the *Anabasis,* a true account of Greek military history in which he participated.

The historian Herodotus (485–425 B.C.), the "father of history," wrote an account of the Persian Wars which included fables, superstitions and popular opinions as well as verifiable facts. Thucydides (460–400 B.C.), known as the first "scientific historian," wrote an objective account of the Peloponnesian Wars between Sparta and Athens.

In the fields of philosophy and science, Heraclitus, born about 500 B.C., taught that reality could be found only in the flux or change of nature. Democritus (460–370 B.C.) taught that all things are made up of tiny, invisible particles called atoms, which in various combinations or groupings make up the different forms of matter as we know them. Socrates (469–399 B.C.), the first great philosopher of Greece, held that there were absolute standards of truth and conduct, that these standards could be found by careful analysis, and that men would accept these standards once they were clarified. Plato (427–347 B.C.) was Socrates' foremost pupil. He is most famous for his book *The Republic,* a criticism of Greek democracy, and for his recommendation of benevolent autocracy as the best form of government. In addition, most of what we know of Socrates we have learned from Plato's *Dialogues,* in which the great teacher Socrates is the chief speaker. Hippocrates (about 500 B.C.) is known as the father of experimental biology and medicine. He applied a scien-

The Parthenon on the Acropolis ("hill") in Athens, the Discobolus by the famed sculptor Myron, and the colossal statue of Athena epitomize artistic accomplishments in the Golden Age of Greece.

tific, cause-and-effect approach to medicine and believed in careful observation and in nature's power to heal. The "Hippocratic Oath" is taken by all modern physicians as a promise to serve mankind always and to think first of the patient.

Greek temples are considered by many to be the most beautiful buildings of man. Not as large as the Egyptian, not as inspiring as the Gothic, the Greek temples are outstanding for sheer beauty. They employed the column-and-lintel system; the arch was known (the Etruscans had used it in Italy for centuries), but the Greeks did not use it. Their temples employed three styles of columns which epitomized three schools of architecture. The Doric was the simplest of the three. The Parthenon on the Acropolis (hill) of Athens is its best example. The Ionic columns were more slender, and their caps were somewhat more ornate. A fine ex-

ample of the Ionic is the Erectheum, also on the Acropolis in Athens. The Corinthian architectural style was the most ornate of all. Its slender columns had rows of sculptured acanthus leaves encircling their caps. The Temple of Athena Alea Tegea is a beautiful example of the Corinthian school.

In the Italian Peninsula during the 400s B.C., the city of Rome was conquering neighbor peoples such as the Sabines, the Aequi and the Volsci, and thus becoming the center of an expanding state. Since the overthrow of the last Etruscan king (in 510 B.C.) Rome had been governed by her aristocrats, who acted through a Senate chosen from their number. Under Senate supervision, two consuls chosen from the ranks of senators were selected to rule for a year. Friction grew between the government and the mass of Romans, called "plebeians," who complained that they had no voice in their own rule. Finally the plebeians rebelled, and a new office called the tribune (there were as few as one, as many as ten tribunes at one time) was devised to safeguard plebeian rights. Roman law was codified for the first time in 450 B.C.

In Sicily, quarrels between the island's cities gave Carthage an excuse to intervene in Sicilian affairs. By the end of the century, Carthage was entrenched in the western part of the island, but on the eastern end such cities as Syracuse remained in Greek hands under the tyrant Dionysius.

Within the continent of Europe, the Celtic and Germanic peoples still used stone, wood and bone tools and weapons primarily, although bronze had been in some use for many years and iron was known to both peoples. Toward the end of the century, the Celts (called Gauls by the Romans) began to push south toward Italy.

Three styles of Greek columns: Doric, Ionic, Corinthian.

ASIA, except for its Mediterranean Lands

The Persian-ruled provinces of northern India were furnishing mercenary troops to Persia from 486 B.C. to 465 B.C. for the war against Greece. There was considerable trade between northern India and Mesopotamia. In the eastern and southern portions of the subcontinent, the caste system continued to develop and to influence Indian life.

In China, warfare and mutual slaughter had become a way of life among the states of the late Chou Dynasty. The widespread smelting of iron in China gave weapons to greater numbers of people. As a result, Chinese armies grew larger.

OCEANIA

It is possible that the first voyages to the outer islands of Polynesia (including Hawaii) took place as early as the 400s B.C. Some voyages to these sparsely and often unpopulated islands were exploratory, others were probably the accidental result of being caught and blown westward by storms.

AFRICA, except for its Mediterranean Lands

During the 400s B.C., the smelting and forging of iron, which had long existed in the Sudanese kingdom of Kush, was continued and expanded in the nation's capital city of Meroe. Iron tools and weapons found south of the Sahara Desert, along the Niger and Senegal Rivers, were possibly brought there by exploratory and trading expeditions. The Greek historian Herodotus refers to the Senegal River in discussing such expeditions made by Greek and other Mediterranean peoples.

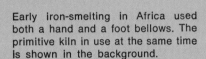

Early iron-smelting in Africa used both a hand and a foot bellows. The primitive kiln in use at the same time is shown in the background.

THE AMERICAS

In the early 400s B.C., farming and fishing cultures developed along the Ecuadorian coasts. Remnants of the Chavin art form with its characteristic feline-like sculpture and finely masoned buildings are found in the same area dating from this period.

Thus, by 400 B.C. there were highly developed agricultural communities in what are now Ecuador and Peru, in Central America and the Yucatán Peninsula, and in other parts of Mexico. There were somewhat less highly developed communities in parts of North America, particularly around the Mississippi River and its tributaries, and also in what are now the Southwestern states of Arizona and New Mexico.

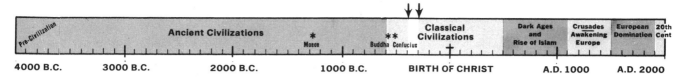

400 — 300 B.C.

Alexander the Great • The Development of Hellenistic Culture • The Maurya Dynasty in India • Horse-mounted Archers in Chinese Armies

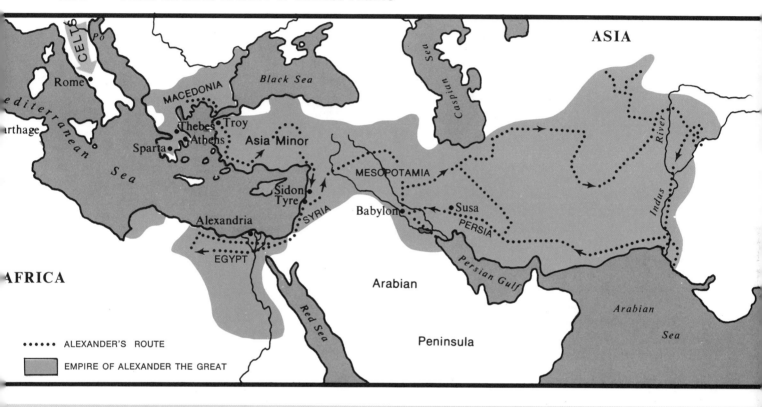

••••• ALEXANDER'S ROUTE

▨ EMPIRE OF ALEXANDER THE GREAT

THE MEDITERRANEAN WORLD and Europe

During the 300s B.C., the Mediterranean world witnessed the meteoric rise of Alexander the Great, while Carthage remained in control of the western Mediterranean and Rome was rapidly growing into the area's third great power. The century began with Sparta as the dominant Greek city-state. However, after the demands of a six-year war with Persia, oppressive Spartan policy drove the other cities to rebel and brought about the rise of Thebes as the most powerful city of Greece. Theban supremacy lasted only a few years, and for a period of time no one city was strong enough to determine a policy for a divided Greece.

This confusion and rivalry enabled Philip of Macedon, king of a mountain country to the north of Greece —in present-day Yugoslavia, Bulgaria and northern Greece—to intervene in Greek affairs. The great Athenian orator and statesman Demosthenes (383–322 B.C.) attempted in vain to alert his people to this danger from the north, in a series of famous speeches known as the

Philippics, after the name of the Macedonian king. By 341 B.C. Philip was at war with Athens and then with Thebes and other Greek cities. The final outcome was a degree of unity among the Greek city-states, but under the hegemony of Philip of Macedon.

During these years of war, rebellion and defeat, Greek art, literature and science continued to flourish as in the previous century.

Praxiteles (about 390 B.C.) was the most highly regarded of all Greek sculptors. His statue *Hermes with the Infant Dionysius* is his only work to have survived into modern times, but ancient writers have left descriptions of other great works by him, among them an *Aphrodite,* an *Eros* and an *Apollo.*

The comic dramatist Menander (343–291 B.C.) wrote plays about life in Athens which presented a delightful mixture of serious and amusing occurrences.

Aristotle (384–322 B.C.) was perhaps the most famous philosopher of all times. His work in logic, ethics, politics, physics and metaphysics had a far-reaching effect upon his contemporaries, later upon the Hindus in India and the Moslems in Arabia, and later still upon the Christian Church. Much of his work was valuable to man in his search for knowledge, but much of it that was carried into posterity as "gospel" was almost without basis in fact.

Three schools of philosophy gained popularity in Greece during the 300s B.C. Of these, the Cynics maintained that virtue, not pleasure, should be the goal of man's existence. This school of philosophy degenerated in later times into a contempt of all knowledge and of all things civilized. The second school, the Epicureans, believed solely in the evidence of the senses. They held that simple living and the absence of pain bring forth an inner peace that should be the true goal of life. Epicureanism, like Cynicism, has been altered in later interpretation into something very different. The third school, the Stoics, maintained that the true aim of man should be to live a life of active virtue. The Stoics held that the universal brotherhood of man (even non-Greeks) should be the foundation stone of human action. This school advocated "justice for all"— a revolutionary idea perhaps in the world of Greece, but an idea that had long been preached by the Hebrews and the disciples of such men as Buddha in India and Confucius in China.

In 336 B.C., Philip of Macedon was assassinated and his nineteen-year-old son, later known as Alexander the Great, ascended the throne. In a series of rapid campaigns, Alexander subdued the Greek cities and other areas which had been under his father's hegemony, but which had revolted after his death. Alexander next turned his now combined Greco-Macedonian armies against the Persian Empire, crossing the Hellespont (Dardanelles) to Troy in Asia Minor. By 331 B.C. he had conquered the Phoenician cities, including Tyre, which fell only after a protracted six-month siege. Next Egypt capitulated, and the city of Alexandria was founded on Egypt's Mediterranean coast northwest of modern Cairo.

Alexander then swept through Babylon into Persia, and the main portions of the Persian Empire fell into his hands. He spent the next four years campaigning in the lands north and east of Persia, so that by 326 B.C. his armies had crossed the Indus River and defeated the ruler of the Punjab area of what is now Pakistan. Here his exhausted armies refused to go farther, and he had to content himself with following the Indus to its delta and then returning by land to Susa in Persia. Expeditions are also known to have been sent by Alexander (or his successors) from the mouth of the Indus River east across the Indian Ocean and then into what are now Indonesia, Malaysia and China.

In his temporary headquarters in the city of Susa, Alexander began to fuse the cultures of Greece with those of such cities of the African and Asian Mediterranean as Alexandria and Babylon. He had grandiose schemes of developing trade between India, Persia, Egypt and Greece, and to this end he advocated intermarriage between Greeks and Persians. He himself married a daughter of Darius, the former Emperor of Persia. Even so, upon his sudden death at the age of thirty-two in Babylon, the great empire he had created in thirteen years could not be maintained. It was divided among his generals, each of whom tried to found a dynasty in his share of the spoils: Antigonus took Greece and Macedonia, Ptolemy took Egypt, and Antiochus took Asia; later, Antiochus' son Seleucus took Mesopotamia and Persia, and still later Syria and Asia Minor.

Out of Alexander's efforts, a tremendous economic and cultural upsurge came to Egypt and the nations of the African and Asian Mediterranean. It represented a blending of Greek competence and energy with native resources and the cultural advantages of these Asiatic and African lands and peoples. This growth was neither wholly Greek nor completely Near Eastern, but a mixture of the two. Its headquarters was the Egyptian city of Alexandria, where scholars and teachers congregated and built a great library and museum. From this focal city it spread all along the African and Asian coasts to the other cities of the Mediterranean. It was to last for

In the siege of Tyre, Alexander's army built a 200-foot causeway to the island city and then pounded its walls with catapults and battering rams.

The lighthouse at Alexandria, a 600-foot marble tower on an island at the entrance to the great city's harbor, was one of the Seven Wonders of the Ancient World.

In the western Mediterranean, Rome and Carthage were still coexisting peacefully, with the aid of treaties covering trade rights.

Within the European continent, the Celtic and Germanic peoples continued their Neolithic farming-hunting-fishing existence. Much bronze and iron were used by these peoples, but some of their tools and weapons were still made of wood, bone and stone. A people from Europe called the Picts invaded and settled Scotland during this century. These people were apparently a mixture of Indo-European-speaking tribes as well as some who were speakers of other, unknown, languages.

several centuries, even under new masters, the Romans. This new burst of creative energy and commerce is called "Hellenistic" to distinguish it from the wholly Greek, or Hellenic, period that preceded it.

In Italy, Rome was invaded and sacked during the 300s B.C. by Celtic barbarians who had earlier left their homes in Gaul and crossed the Alps into the valley of the Po River. After the sack of Rome and after being placated with a heavy ransom, they returned to live in the Po Valley, an area that Romans would henceforth refer to as Cisalpine Gaul ("Gaul on this side of the Alps").

Celtic religious ceremonies were usually held near pools deep in the forests, presided over by priests called Druids.

ASIA, except for its Mediterranean Lands

The luxurious court life in the elaborately ornamented palace of Chandragupta I of the Maurya kingdom was described in detail by the Greek ambassador, Megasthenes.

In the Indian subcontinent, the Magadha Empire came to an end about 350 B.C., the victim of an internecine struggle for the throne which divided it into a group of feudal warring kingdoms. In India's north, however, the area that had been under Persian hegemony broke free about 320 B.C. when its Persian overlords were conquered by Alexander of Macedon. Three years later, in 327 B.C., Alexander's armies entered this part of India and conquered it. Remnants of the resulting Greek influence on Indian culture are apparent even today in statuary, coins and various other artifacts which bear unmistakably the Grecian imprint.

Shortly after Alexander's death in 323 B.C., Greek influence in the Punjab began to weaken, and in 321 B.C. Chandragupta founded the Maurya Dynasty, which united much of northern India into an efficient, well-governed kingdom. Seven years after the founding of the dynasty, the resident Greek ambassador to the Maurya kingdom wrote the first detailed description of India. Near the century's end, a treaty of commerce was signed between Chandragupta and Seleucus, Alexander's successor in neighboring Persia and the Near East.

In China, during the 300s B.C., the philosopher Mencius was born. Mencius (322–288 B.C) was a follower of Confucius and a strong advocate of justice tempered with mercy. Like Confucius, he placed great stress on education and on a government responsive and responsible to the people. This century saw the feudal wars in China at their peak, as the chariot was replaced in warfare by the archer mounted astride his horse— a formidable technique learned from the barbarian Huns, one of the nomadic peoples of the Steppes, who were now always on China's periphery. Yet, during this same period, painting became a revered art form in China, and in mathematics the decimal system was put into general usage for account keeping.

In Southeast Asia, there are evidences remaining of Alexander's expeditions (or his successors') which embarked from the delta of the Indus River and sailed to the coast lands of what are now Burma, Malaysia, Indonesia and China. A Buddha-Apollo-type statue, created a few hundred years later, has been found in the area, and Classical-Greek-type ships still in use attest to these visitors who brought cultural and mercantile influence all the way from the Aegean Sea.

The Viets, a tribe located in south China, migrated into what is now North Vietnam in order to escape hostile neighbors. The Viets subdued the Proto-Malays in the area and formed the kingdom of Nam-Viet.

AFRICA, except for its Mediterranean Lands

About 350 B.C., the kingdom of Kush, which had once ruled Egypt and whose people had for centuries been skilled workers in iron and gold, was reaching its peak of political power and commercialism. Its capital, the city of Meroe, is named in trading records of Indian and Chinese merchant-sailors.

THE AMERICAS

There was a lively trade and exchange between the widely spread agricultural cultures of North America, especially between the Basket Makers of the Southwest and the Adena-Hopewell nations of the valleys of the Mississippi River and its tributaries. In the Arctic, remnants of an old Bering Sea culture are found dating from the 300s B.C. and earlier. These include the sites of permanent villages with houses built partially underground. Harpoons were used to help provide a diet which consisted largely of sea animals.

The development toward an advanced culture by the pre-Mayan and pre-Incan peoples continued in Central and South America.

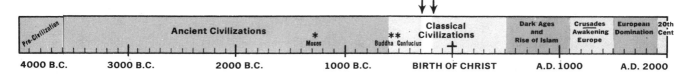

| Pre-Civilization | Ancient Civilizations | *Moses | **Buddha Confucius | Classical Civilizations | Dark Ages and Rise of Islam | Crusades Awakening Europe | European Domination | 20th Cent |

4000 B.C.   3000 B.C.   2000 B.C.   1000 B.C.   BIRTH OF CHRIST   A.D. 1000   A.D. 2000

300 — 200 B.C.

Rome versus Carthage—The Punic Wars • King Asoka in India • The Great Wall of China

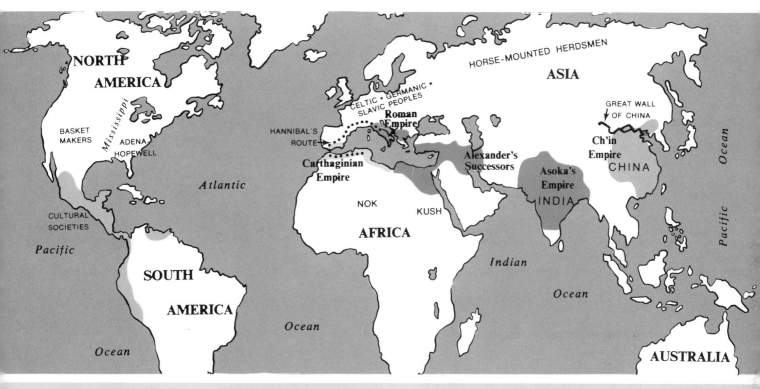

THE MEDITERRANEAN WORLD and Europe

At the beginning of the 200s B.C., control of the Mediterranean world was divided among Carthage, Rome and the former generals of Alexander. Rome was growing so fast from her chief city in the center of Italy that she was in repeated conflict with the other Mediterranean powers, and especially with Carthage, the great commercial center located across the Mediterranean Sea on the African coast.

In 264 B.C., the First Punic War ("Punic" is a derivative of a Latin word meaning Carthaginian) broke out between Rome and Carthage over control of the Strait of Messina, a narrow body of water between the toe of Italy and the island of Sicily. Rome was victorious, but her victory was offset by a maneuver in which Carthage allied herself with the Sicilian city of Syracuse south of the Strait of Messina. Rome now proceeded to build a succession of four war fleets, the first three of which were wholly or partially lost in storm and battle; but the fourth fleet enabled Rome in 241 B.C. to defeat and drive Carthage from Sicily, and to extract an indemnity from her.

In 225 B.C., the Celts who had been living in the Po Valley (the area of Italy called Cisalpine Gaul by Rome) again invaded Roman territory. They were defeated and were henceforth under Roman hegemony.

A new outbreak of war between Rome and Carthage —the Second Punic War—occurred in 218 B.C. when Carthaginian forces in Spain, led by their brilliant general Hannibal, performed the unbelievable feat of crossing the Alps in winter and invading Italy from the north. Hannibal's troops, hundreds of miles from supplies or reinforcements, defeated Roman armies in a series of battles, the most significant being the battle of Cannae in 216 B.C. At this crucial point, Macedonia became allied with Hannibal, and Rome's future seemed in grave jeopardy indeed. Yet, over the next seven or eight years, the military situation was reversed. Hannibal's brother crossed the Alps bringing reinforcements, but he was met and defeated. The Roman general Scipio next drove the forces of Carthage out of Spain, and then crossed the sea to attack them in Africa. Hannibal was urgently recalled from Italy, but he was too late.

Scipio defeated him at Zama, a city southwest of Carthage on the African coast, in 202 B.C., and Rome became master of the western Mediterranean. Although Carthage was able to maintain her hold on her African possessions, the lands immediately to her west and east, Rome now stood as the only really great power left in the Mediterranean area.

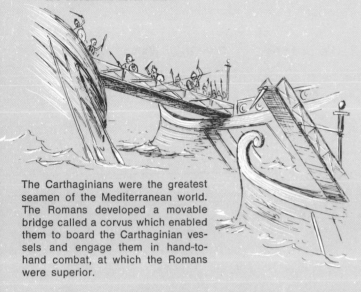

The Carthaginians were the greatest seamen of the Mediterranean world. The Romans developed a movable bridge called a corvus which enabled them to board the Carthaginian vessels and engage them in hand-to-hand combat, at which the Romans were superior.

During the 200s B.C., Greek artists, scientists and men of letters were beginning to be joined by Romans of great talent. It is customary to refer to their joint cultural efforts from this point in history as Greco-Roman, although with certain important exceptions the inspiration remained largely Greek. Outstanding men during this century were Theocritus (310–250 B.C.), a Greek pastoral poet whose description of the peasants and the countryside rank to this day among the best in all literature; Ennus (239–169 B.C.), an early Roman poet and dramatist; Plautius (250–184 B.C.), a Roman playwright whose delightful plays were in some cases sung like modern musical comedies; Euclid (200s B.C.?), the great Greek mathematician, noted most for his *Elements of Geometry;* Eratosthenes (276–194 B.C.), a Greek mathematician and philosopher who measured the earth's circumference with reasonable accuracy considering available instruments, and suggested a method for pinpointing locations on the earth similar to modern longitude and latitude; Archimedes of Syracuse (287–212 B.C.), perhaps the greatest mathematician of antiquity as well as an eminent astronomer and a prolific inventor, whose work in hydrostatics—the physics of liquids and floating bodies—and in inventing military machines and other devices to perform a wide variety of mechanical functions makes a long and impressive list; and Aristarchus (200 B.C.), a Greek astronomer, known as "the Copernicus of antiquity," who taught that the earth revolves around the sun and estimated the distances to the sun and the moon, but whose teachings were largely disregarded by European philosophers for more than a thousand years.

Within the continent of Europe, the Celtic peoples had made probes into Spain and into the Balkan Peninsula, and had penetrated well into Italy, sacking Rome and then withdrawing. The Germanic tribes from their locations in Denmark and in Central Europe were pressing south closely behind the Celts. Other Indo-European-speaking peoples were pressing into the eastern lands of continental Europe from Poland south to the Balkans.

ASIA, except for its Mediterranean Lands

Asoka put the humane and benevolent ideals of Buddhism into practice. His own thoughts and edicts, many of which were derived from Buddhism, he had inscribed on specially erected pillars throughout the realm.

In northern Asia, horse-mounted Hunnish and Turkic peoples (and perhaps some Indo-European peoples as well) drove vast herds of sheep and other grass-eating domestic animals across the steppes, mountains and deserts in constant search of pasturage. These horse-mounted herdsmen were in repeated contact with the civilizations of the Mediterranean world and Europe and with the feudal states of Chou China to their east.

In India, the Maurya Dynasty spread its rule over much of the subcontinent during the 200s B.C. In 269 B.C., Asoka, grandson of Chandragupta, founder of the Maurya Dynasty, ascended to the throne. In the early years of his reign, Asoka ruled tyrannically and was militarily very aggressive; but later he converted to Buddhism and governed his empire with tolerance and humility. Asoka did much to advance the spread of Buddhism both in India and abroad. Yet during these great years of Buddhism within India there was a revival in the north of the more ancient Vedic doctrines, whose complex beliefs would gradually evolve into Hinduism as we know it today. Hinduism, not Buddhism, would eventually become the dominant religion in India and would not be challenged for leadership until a militant Islam entered the subcontinent many centuries later.

In China in 221 B.C., the warring feudal states of the late Chou Empire were finally unified by the Ch'in tribe, a centrally located people who lived in the rich valley of the Wei River. The first Ch'in monarch was Shih Huang Ti, who instituted a complete reorganization of government in China based on strict obedience to the law and severe punishment for all regardless of rank. He attempted to censor art and literature, and to control the thoughts as well as the actions of his subjects. In 214 B.C., Shih Huang Ti linked up existing fortifications and built new sections to form what has come to be called the Great Wall of China, designed to keep the barbarians (as well as all disruptive ideas) out of his kingdom. The nation's unity did not survive his death in 210 B.C., however, and for the next eight years China was torn by wars to determine which member of his family would be his successor.

In the year 202 B.C., Liu Pang, the son of a peasant family, united China under the Han Dynasty. Under Han leadership, China was to experience what is often said to be the greatest age of her history, so much so that for centuries after the end of the dynasty men in China continued to refer to themselves as "the sons of Han." During the 200s B.C., China strongly influenced the kingdom of Chosen, which at the time dominated the Korean Peninsula. Chinese art, religion and way of life were adopted in a somewhat altered form by these proto-Korean peoples.

Chinese influence was spreading, too, into Southeast Asia, into such areas as Tonking, in the northern part of what is now Vietnam, and Annam, in the middle of present-day Vietnam, and from them into what are today Thailand and Cambodia.

There is evidence of the use of bronze in the 200s B.C. by the peoples of the Malay Archipelago and Indonesia.

The Great Wall of China followed a winding course over mountains and valleys and was as long as from New York City to Wichita, Kansas. Its width is about 25 feet at the base and about 15 feet at the top. Thousands of workers died in its construction.

AFRICA, except for its Mediterranean Lands

During the 200s B.C. or perhaps earlier, the first known smelting of iron ore to take place south of the Sahara Desert in West Africa was accomplished at Nok, in what is now Nigeria. The Nok culture is noted for its stylized human figures of clay and its naturalistic animal figurines, which may have an antiquity dating as far back as the 800s B.C. In the north, however, in the Nile state of Kush, a large iron industry had been flourishing for some time. Although the people of Kush had been influenced by Egyptians and Greeks in their early years, and later by Romans and Chinese, they had developed their own language, religion and alphabet.

THE AMERICAS

By the 200s B.C., North America had a highly developed culture (or cultures), with distinct artistic traditions, located in lower Mexico and in Central America. In South America, highly developed societies existed in the highlands of Peru, in Ecuador and along the coast of Venezuela. In addition, both continents had other societies of lesser development, but well above the barbarian level. Outstanding in North America were the Adena-Hopewell societies located along the lower Mississippi River and its tributaries, and the Basket Makers in what are now Arizona and New Mexico.

Outside of these centers of culture, farming was widespread in both continents, but hunting and fishing remained the main means of obtaining food and clothing.

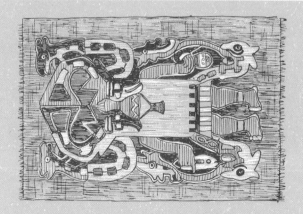

At Paracas, in what is today Peru, weaving became a brilliant art form with intricate designs and patterns.

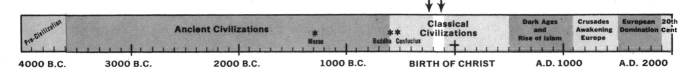

| Pre-Civilization | Ancient Civilizations | * Moses | ** Buddha Confucius | Classical Civilizations | Dark Ages and Rise of Islam | Crusades Awakening Europe | European Domination | 20th Cent |

4000 B.C.   3000 B.C.   2000 B.C.   1000 B.C.   BIRTH OF CHRIST   A.D. 1000   A.D. 2000

200 — 100 B.C.

The Expanding Roman Republic   •   The Maurya Empire Fades in India   •   The Han Dynasty in China

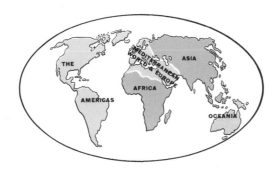

THE MEDITERRANEAN WORLD and Europe

During the 100s B.C., Rome, having secured her position in the west during the previous century by confining Carthage to Africa, now sent her legions into the eastern Mediterranean lands of Europe. Here, in 196 B.C., she overwhelmed Macedonia and formed alliances with the Greek cities liberated from Macedonian rule. From Greece the Roman legions turned to Asia Minor, winning a first Asian victory at the city of Magnesium. In 151 B.C. Rome again turned upon Carthage, and by 146 B.C. she had completely destroyed that city. Thus, by the middle of the century, the city-state from the center of the Italian Peninsula had eliminated all potential rivals in the Mediterranean world except for Egypt, Syria, Mesopotamia and Persia. At about this time, the King of Pergamum, a Greek kingdom in Asia Minor, willed his domains to Rome, and these lands became the first Roman province on Asian soil.

The toga, a large white blanket worn wrapped around the body, was the badge of Roman citizenship. It was worn throughout most of Ancient Rome's one thousand years.

Meanwhile there was trouble for Rome at home, where the sorry condition of her farmers and farm workers was causing unrest and civil strife. Two brothers, Tiberius and Gaius Gracchus, attempted to limit the dictatorial powers of the Senate and bring about agrarian reforms. While their efforts met with some success, eventually both brothers were killed in riots, and the much-needed reforms were abandoned.

There was trouble, too, on Rome's northern and western borders, from restless Celtic and Germanic tribes. The first confrontation with the Germans ended in Roman defeat, but Maurius, a successful general, was hurriedly recalled from Africa and quickly defeated both the Germans in Gaul (France), and the Celts in Cisalpine Gaul (northern Italy). Thus the century ended with Rome's borders secure but under constant threat. This condition of peace maintained by continual military vigilance would later be known as the Pax Romana, or Roman Peace.

During this century of the 100s B.C., two Greek men of science and letters left an indelible mark on man's cultural record. The historian Polybius (205–123 B.C.), in his great *History,* traced the rise of Roman power and attempted to explain the decline of Grecian might. Polybius is noted for his simplicity of style and for his careful regard for detail and accuracy. Hipparchus (160–125 B.C.) has been called the greatest astronomer of antiquity. He estimated with amazing accuracy the sizes of the sun and the moon, and their distances from the earth. In addition, he catalogued over a thousand stars. His work in astronomy led him to invent trigonometry and to elaborate the system of pinpointing locations on the earth by measurements called "longitude" and "latitude."

ASIA, except for its Mediterranean Lands

In the Indian subcontinent, the Maurya Dynasty was weakening and was losing control over its outlying lands. In 190 B.C., two Greek-ruled kingdoms were reestablished in India's northwest, using the ancient names Bactria and Gandhara. Six years later, in 184 B.C., further deterioration of the Maurya rule led to its complete overthrow by Pushyamitra Sunga, who founded a new line of rulers. Under the Sunga Dynasty the empire was loosely knit, and there was a continuation of the revival of the Vedic rites in the northwest which would lead ultimately to modern Hinduism. A land trade route between India and Burma is known to have been in use in this century.

China, under the Han Dynasty, was ruled from 140 to 87 B.C. by Wu Ti, who is considered to have been one of the great kings of that land. Under Wu Ti, Confucianism became the official state doctrine and the study of its precepts was encouraged. He expanded the empire well into what is now Vietnam, annexing the city of Hue in 111 B.C., and thus beginning almost one thousand years of Chinese rule over varying portions of Indochina. About four years later Wu Ti's armies conquered the kingdom of Chosen (Korea). Wu Ti imposed a "Pax Sinica"—that is, a Chinese military peace—over the Far East very similar to the Pax Romana imposed

Han Dynasty architecture is well illustrated in this pavilion with its wooden piers, tiled roof and surrounding wall.

by Rome during the same era. Like the Romans, too, the Chinese of this period built extensive public works and (despite the almost continual wars) provided an atmosphere in which scholarship seems to have flourished. Under Wu Ti's reign, for example, the theory of numbers was extensively explored by Chinese mathematicians. Negative numbers were understood and fractions were utilized in their calculations.

AFRICA, except for its Mediterranean Lands

The African kingdom of Kush had expanded further and become a large and powerful nation with a considerable native culture. Merchants from Kush traveled to India and thence as far as Han China to trade the metalware and other products of their artisans.

THE AMERICAS

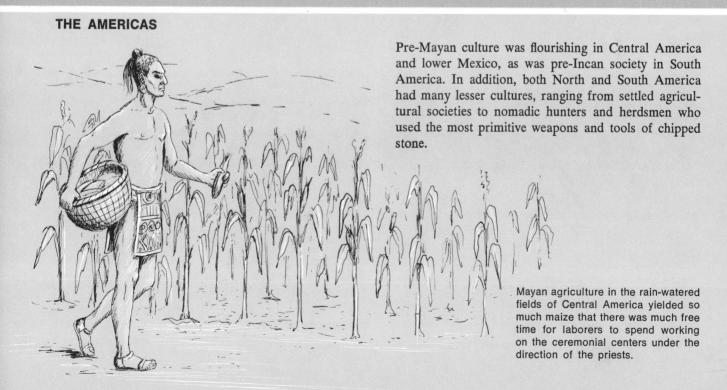

Pre-Mayan culture was flourishing in Central America and lower Mexico, as was pre-Incan society in South America. In addition, both North and South America had many lesser cultures, ranging from settled agricultural societies to nomadic hunters and herdsmen who used the most primitive weapons and tools of chipped stone.

Mayan agriculture in the rain-watered fields of Central America yielded so much maize that there was much free time for laborers to spend working on the ceremonial centers under the direction of the priests.

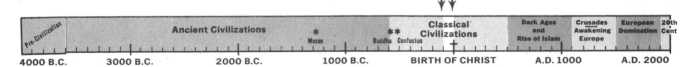

| Pre-Civilization | Ancient Civilizations | *Moses | **Buddha Confucius | Classical Civilizations | Dark Ages and Rise of Islam | Crusades Awakening Europe | European Domination | 20th Cent |

4000 B.C.   3000 B.C.   2000 B.C.   1000 B.C.   BIRTH OF CHRIST   A.D. 1000   A.D. 2000

100 B.C. TO A.D. 1

Civil War and Rebellion in Rome • Hail Caesar! • Divided Rule in India • The Spread of Buddhism • Scientific Progress in Han China

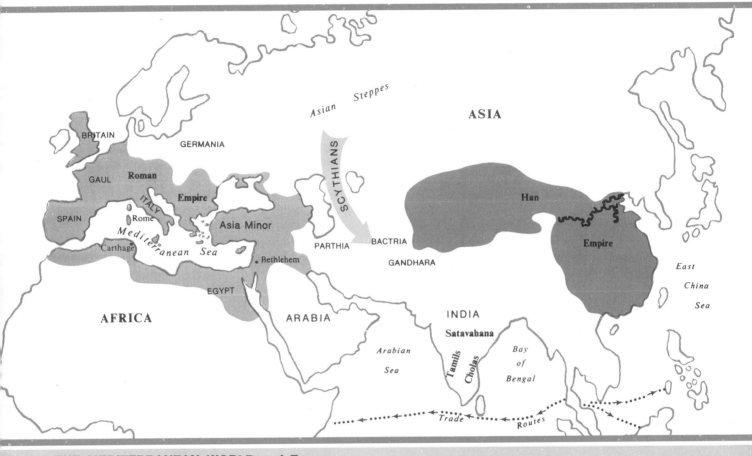

THE MEDITERRANEAN WORLD and Europe

This last century before the birth of Christ saw Rome withstand repeated civil wars and rebellions—by slaves, farm workers and allies—to become an almost invincible power in the Mediterranean world and much of Western Europe. In the last third of the century, Rome's government changed from a republic to a monarchy. In actual fact Rome had never been a true republic, but had been ruled for centuries by a Senate composed of landed aristocrats. As a monarchy and later as an empire, Rome was to be governed for four more centuries by a succession of emperor-generals who would come not only from the Roman homeland but from other parts of Europe and also from Asia and Africa.

The unification of this vast territory into a Roman Empire had significant consequences for the peoples who thus became part of Rome: one allegiance (to Rome)

prevailed throughout the area; one language (Latin) made communication possible throughout the Mediterranean and Europe; a single currency eliminated confusion and encouraged widespread commerce; fine roads (not to be equaled in Europe until the 1800s) linked various parts of the empire; great public works (stadiums, amphitheaters, aqueducts and bridges) were built not just in Italy but to some degree in all the lands around the great sea; and, finally, the peoples had the protection of the Mediterranean world's best armies, which now, under the empire, had troops and generals from Africa and Asia as well as Europe.

Such a complex and farflung empire could not be consolidated without the exercise of great power by the central government in Rome. Grave economic and social problems, both in the city of Rome and in distant colonies, had continually to be solved, and the solutions had to be enforced by Roman armies. Thus, the century leading to Rome's greatest power was marked by a series of titanic struggles among the generals and politicians as to who would wield this power.

Powerful aristocrats, statesmen, and military heroes such as Marius, Sulla, Pompey, and Julius Caesar conspired to take power and were in turn conspired against. Each had his moment of triumph, in most cases brought to a brutal end by murder or suicide. And while, on these upper levels of government, power was passed from Senate to consul to general and back again, the poor, as always, struggled to stay alive.

It appeared that this vying for power had ended when Julius Caesar, after proving his worth against Rome's enemies in Gaul and Britain, marched his legions into the city of Rome and made himself virtual dictator, but

he too was later assassinated. This led to a new contest for supreme rule between Caesar's friend Mark Antony and his nephew Octavian. In this struggle Cicero, the Senate's most skilled and persuasive voice, was murdered, and later Mark Antony, realizing that all was lost to Octavian, committed suicide along with his paramour Cleopatra, the Egyptian Queen.

Octavian was now supreme ruler of all Rome and was named Emperor Augustus by the Senate. Meanwhile the poor still rioted in the streets of the capital, homesick soldiers still languished in barbaric lands as far away as Britain, and the glory that was Rome remained pretty much the blessing of the upper classes.

Augustus Caesar ruled the Roman Empire for almost fifty years, and during that time the imposed Pax Romana stabilized much of the Western world.

In approximately 4 B.C., Jesus Christ was born in

"I came, I saw, I conquered." After his victories in various parts of Europe, Asia and Africa, Julius Caesar returned to Rome in triumph, with these words painted on the lead chariot.

The Senate elected Augustus Caesar *princeps*— "the first." During his reign, he kept the empire in peace and brought prosperity to the land through his governmental reorganization and planning.

Bethlehem, an event that occasioned scarcely a ripple in the Mediterranean and European worlds.

During this century of expansion and turmoil, Roman letters reached great heights with such names as Varro (116 B.C.–27 B.C.), who left writings on subjects as varied as law, science and poetry; Cicero (106 B.C.–43 B.C.), orator, statesman and writer, who created great works on philosophy and political theory, as well as some charming letters on a variety of subjects; Julius Caesar (102 B.C.–34 B.C.), whose commentaries on the Gallic Wars and other political matters rank him as one of the great prose stylists of all time; Virgil (70–19 B.C.), the greatest of Rome's epic poets, who is noted for his perfection of form and whose finest work is the *Aeneid,* dealing with the founding of Rome. Other great poets of the period are Horace and Ovid; and two great dramatists, Plautus and Terence, demand mention. Strabo, a Greek geographer and historian, lived during this century; his seventeen-volume *Geographica* is still in existence.

ASIA, except for its Mediterranean Lands

The rule of the Indian subcontinent was divided among at least four separate empires during this century. In the northwest, the two Greek-ruled nations of Bactria and Gandhara were invaded and conquered about 90 B.C. by the nomadic Scythians from the Asian Steppes. Known in India as the Sakas, the Scythians spoke an Indo-European tongue closely related to Iranian. They were to rule this part of India for almost four hundred years.

Another empire, the Aryan Satavahana, built upon the ruins of the Maurya Empire, came into being about 50 B.C. in the Deccan, the great central section of India. It extended its rule at times from coast to coast in the subcontinent and was powerful for over three hundred years.

South of the Deccan were two great Dravidian peoples, the Tamils and the Cholas, who, from simple agricultural beginnings, had developed complex political and economic structures. These peoples carried on a profitable trade with the Roman Empire via sea routes.

Throughout this last century before the birth of Christ, Buddhism had been spreading from its source in India north into Central and Eastern Asia. At the same time, in India itself, the popularity of Buddhism continued to wane in the face of the widespread revival of Hinduism.

In China, the Han Dynasty rulers were losing effectiveness in the years following the death of the great Emperor Wu Ti. Thus, the Han failed to keep pace with the contemporary empire of Rome, which was just reaching its greatest geographic extent and power. In 87 B.C., the first history of China was written by Tsu-ma Ch'ien, who is sometimes referred to as the "Chinese Herodotus." About 30 B.C., the sundial was developed in China, and during this century sun spots were regularly observed and recorded by Chinese astronomers. Glass was manufactured and used for the first time under Han rule.

About the time of the birth of Christ, seamen-traders of the Malay Peninsula are known to have sailed to East Africa and Madagascar. There is reason to believe that they may even have voyaged to some of the islands of Oceania—if not by choice, then perhaps carried there upon occasion by storms.

The Great Stupa at Sanchi, a memorial shrine built to house the relics of Buddha, is guarded by four gates with beautifully carved scenes from his life.

THE AMERICAS

Sometime during this last century before the birth of Christ, the Cochise, a relatively primitive Indian culture which had existed in southern New Mexico for at least two thousand years, began to make rapid technological progress. It is presumed that the Cochise, who for well over 1,500 years had been familiar with the cultivation of maize, beans and squash, had during this century been stimulated by contact with a more advanced Indian people, perhaps from Mexico, or with the Basket Makers in the northern part of New Mexico, or the Adena-Hopewell cultures of the southern Mississippi. At any rate, these people, who are known to historians from the turn of the millennium on as the Mogollon culture, began to learn new arts and skills. Pottery and pit-houses which were built below ground level began to appear, as did stone, wood and bone tools of better design. The Cochise also learned at this time to weave available fibers into baskets and other domestic items.

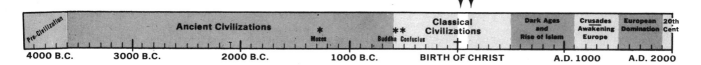

4000 B.C. 3000 B.C. 2000 B.C. 1000 B.C. BIRTH OF CHRIST A.D. 1000 A.D. 2000

A.D. 1 — 100

The Battle of Teutoburg Forest • The Crucifixion of Jesus Christ • The Journeys of Saint Paul • Socialistic Reforms in Han China • The Silk Route

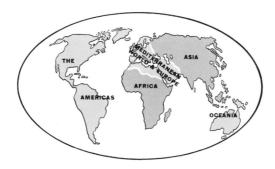

THE MEDITERRANEAN WORLD and Europe

During the first century after the birth of Christ, a number of events occurred which would significantly alter human history. The first of these was a disastrous defeat of the Roman armies in Germany, a defeat which would permit the growth of Teutonic military might and confidence. At the battle of Teutoburg Forest, Rome failed to reinforce its beleaguered legions, which had, therefore, to retreat from their position on the Elbe River to the Rhine frontier, hundreds of miles to the south.

Two other events of this century which continue to affect the lives of men even to the present day were religious in nature: Jesus Christ was crucified in Jerusalem around the year 30, and twenty-one years later Paul of Tarsus began his missionary journeying and the writing of the epistles which would largely determine the substance of Christianity as it is known today.

Both Jesus of Nazareth and Saint Paul, as Paul of Tarsus has come to be known, lived in times of great upheaval. War and threats of war, rebellion, treason and assassination of rulers characterized the Roman world in which they lived.

Paul of Tarsus traveled over the Mediterranean world preaching and organizing Christian churches. His letters (epistles) written to Christian groups were in some cases incorporated into the Scriptures.

The first Roman emperor, Augustus, died in A.D. 14 and was succeeded by his stepson Tiberius. It was during the latter's reign, when Pontius Pilate was governor of Judea, a part of Palestine under Roman rule, that Jesus was crucified in Jerusalem. The next emperor of Rome was Caligula, a tyrant who was murdered in the year 41. During Caligula's reign, the Parthians of Persia occupied the Roman territory of Armenia.

In the year 41, the Praetorian (palace) Guard, the only powerful military group in or near the capital, proclaimed Augustus' stepgrandson Claudius emperor, and their choice was accepted by the Senate. Under Claudius' thirteen years of able rule, a continuing war was fought with the Parthians over Armenia; advances were made in the conquest and pacification of Britain; and many public works were started in Rome, including the dredging of the Tiber River to Rome's new port at Ostia. It was during Claudius' reign also that Paul began the journeys to the cities of the Near East which spread Christianity to the Gentile world.

On Claudius' death in A.D. 54, his stepson Nero was chosen emperor by the Praetorian Guard. War with Parthia, as Persia was now called, broke out again, and a revolt in Britain had to be quelled by Roman legions. In the year 64 a devastating fire in the city of Rome was blamed on the Christians, and many of them died in the first persecution of the Church by Rome. The Christians were persecuted because the Romans feared their different attitude toward religious matters and frowned upon their lack of loyalty to the Empire. In A.D. 66, a rebellion in Jerusalem spread throughout Palestine, and about the same time Rome was confronted with rebellion in Gaul. After these revolts were controlled, the Praetorian Guard declared Galba emperor, and, as a result, Nero committed suicide in the year 68. In this same year Emperor Galba was murdered, and two other emperors set up by the guard died violent deaths, one by execution, the other by murder. It was apparent that the military could make and break Roman rulers at will.

Vespasian, who ruled from 70 to 79, restored order and, by demanding strict loyalty to himself and disbanding questionable units, did much to limit the power of the military. He fostered further pacification in Britain. Also during his reign, Rome destroyed the rebellious city of Jerusalem and suppressed revolt in Gaul. In 79, Vespasian was succeeded by his son Titus, during whose reign the cities of Pompeii and Herculaneum in southern Italy were buried by a catastrophic eruption of the volcano Vesuvius.

In the year 81, Domitian became emperor. He advanced the Roman frontiers in both Europe and Britain, and built a line of fortifications along the empire's Danube border. The second great persecution of Christians occurred during Domitian's rule. On his death in the year 96, an elderly senator named Nerva was appointed emperor. Nerva designated Trajan as his co-regent, a political move intended to enable Nerva to choose his successor, and Trajan was declared emperor in 98 at Nerva's death.

Roman architecture and engineering of this era employed the beauty of the Greek column and lintel, but depended for structural strength on the Etruscan arch. The Colosseum in Rome, which was built in about A.D. 75, is a vast, elliptical amphitheater whose walls are a series of such arches joined and supporting one another. In later years, the Romans would construct vast domes over buildings (such as the Baths of Caracalla), using a series of arches in what is called barrel-and-groin vaulting.

During this century, a dozen or more Roman men of letters and science made important contributions to the store of human culture. Among the writers of prose were Seneca (4 B.C.–A.D. 65), statesman and philosopher; Pliny the Elder (A.D. 23–79), a contributor to practically every field of science and philosophy, and his nephew Pliny the Younger (62–114), whose writings give an accurate picture of Roman social life; Flavius Josephus, Roman soldier and historian of Jewish birth who wrote of Jewish antiquities and history; Quintilian, Roman educator and rhetorician; Plutarch (46–120), a biographer of Greek birth, noted for his books comparing parallel events in the lives of outstanding men of Greece and Rome (for example, the political orators Demosthenes and Cicero); Tacitus (55–120), Roman historian and orator; Epictetus (60–140), great Stoic philosopher; and Suetonius (70–160), Roman historian especially noted for his *Lives of the Caesars.*

Among Roman poets were Lucan (39–65), of Spanish birth, the author of the *Pharsalia,* considered second only to the *Aeneid* among Roman epics; Martial (40–104), also of Spanish birth, noted for his books of epigrams; and Juvenal (55–140), Roman satirical poet, noted for his irony and invective and for his attacks on the baser attributes of contemporary Roman life.

In science, Hero, a Greek of Alexandria, Egypt, is considered to be one of the great inventors and technicians of all time. In addition to many ingenious devices, such as a water clock and the plans for a steam engine, he made substantial contributions to the fields of optics, geography and music.

All of these men, whether of Roman, Greek, Spanish or Jewish birth, owed allegiance to Rome.

Roman engineering and architecture in various parts of the empire:
The aqueduct at Segovia, Spain
The Colosseum at the city of Rome
The Maison Carrée (a Roman temple) at Nîmes in France

ASIA, except for its Mediterranean Lands

In the Indian subcontinent, the Greek-influenced cities located in the Punjab (the area in the northwest along the Indus River and its tributaries) continued to flourish during this century. Its sculpture, called the Gandharan School, shows strong Greek influence, while its architecture seems to have drawn inspiration more from neighboring Persia. About the year 50, Christianity was introduced into the Punjab by missionaries and tradesmen.

Also in the middle years of this century, a horse-mounted people from Central Asia known as the Kushan tribes (unrelated to the North African kingdom) invaded and conquered a large portion of India. During the two hundred years of Kushan rule, their peak of power was achieved during the reign of King Kanishka, which began in A.D. 62 and lasted until approximately the year 96 (although some historians place Kanishka's reign as much as fifty years later).

Indian merchants became very active during this century. They established trade routes out of their city of Taxila to Rome, Greece and Ethiopia. Sea routes by Dravidian traders from southern India east to Malay and Indonesia and west to what is now called the Arabian Peninsula and to Africa had, of course, been in use for centuries.

In China the first Buddhist missionaries arrived, most likely from India, and the first Buddhist community was established about the time of the birth of Christ. Buddhism, however, enjoyed only minimal success in China during the four hundred years of the Han Dynasty (from 200 B.C. to A.D. 200).

Beginning in A.D. 8, Wang Mang usurped the throne for fourteen years from the Han rulers. He abolished slavery, attempted to nationalize the land and established many socialistic programs. Civil-service examinations were given for the first time to all candidates for government office, as had been recommended by Confucius some five hundred years earlier. Wang Mang's death was followed by more than a decade of war before China returned to Han rule.

In the year 97 China subdued the states of Turkestan, located between China and the Caspian Sea, and sent envoys to establish trade with the Parthians of Persia and with Rome, in order to clear a trans-Asia trade passage later called the Silk Route. About the year 100 the first reference to the manufacture of paper appears in Chinese writings.

The Parthians of Persia guarded their end of the "Silk Route" with a special force of horses and riders —both armored against the arrows of horse-mounted barbarians of the Steppes.

In Southeast Asia, beginning about the end of this century and continuing over perhaps the next two hundred years, migrants from the Indian subcontinent were settling in what is now Cambodia, conquering the peoples already there and founding the kingdom of Funan, which would become the area's first independent state. Funan would become noted for its commercial activities and for its elaborate drainage and irrigation canals. To the north, much of what is now North Vietnam had been virtually a Chinese province since 111 B.C., and would be under Chinese hegemony for a total of almost one thousand years.

AFRICA, except for its Mediterranean Lands

In the highlands of northeast Ethiopia, the kingdom of Axum, apparently founded by Asian emigrants from the Arabian Peninsula, was approaching a high cultural level. About the year 50 it had established extensive trade with neighboring Kush, and had become the center of the ivory market, linked by trade to other African communities as well as to the Arabian Peninsula.

References to Roman expeditions of about A.D. 50 into the interior of Africa speak of a General Paulinus who crossed the Atlas Mountains (in what is now Morocco) and the Sahara Desert to reach the headwaters of the Niger River.

THE AMERICAS

During the first century A.D., the Mayan people of Central America began a very rapid cultural advance. They developed the beginnings of a system of writing and numbering and a more elaborate religion and government. Their culture was fast approaching civilization level.

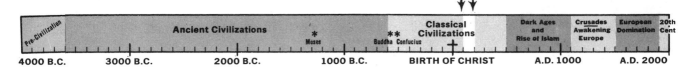

| Pre-Civilization | Ancient Civilizations | | Classical Civilizations | Dark Ages and Rise of Islam | Crusades Awakening Europe | European Domination | 20th Cent |

*Moses   **Buddha Confucius

4000 B.C.   3000 B.C.   2000 B.C.   1000 B.C.   BIRTH OF CHRIST   A.D. 1000   A.D. 2000

100 — 200

The Dispersal of the Jews • The Persecution of Christians in Rome • Indian Scholarship • Development of the Lands of Southeast Asia

THE MEDITERRANEAN WORLD and Europe

This second century after the birth of Christ was in many ways Rome's last period of greatness, a century in which Rome was still expanding and still creating. During the century's first eighty years four outstanding emperors headed her government. Trajan, who reigned from A.D. 98 to 117, expanded Rome's frontiers and maintained a much needed internal calm, but under him the fourth persecution of the Christians took place. Hadrian, who ruled from A.D. 117 to 138, strengthened weak points at home and built fortresses along the frontiers, enlarging the empire to perhaps its greatest extent. Yet, about A.D. 133, Hadrian's armies exterminated a major portion of the population of a rebellious Jerusalem and exiled the rest. Antoninus Pius governed creditably for twenty-three years, from A.D. 138 to 161. And Marcus Aurelius, the philosopher-emperor, valiantly attempted to defend Rome's borders against attacks from all directions, and finally died in a campaign in Central Europe against the Germans.

Marcus Aurelius was succeeded by his son Commodus in A.D. 180. Commodus ruled for twelve years and proved to be a braggart and a fool. He was murdered in the year 192, and the Senate appointed Pertinax emperor. Pertinax reigned a brief three months before being assassinated. His successor, General Severus (who had been born in Africa), seized power and ruled until the year 211, when he was executed. Severus gave a greater voice in government to the non-Roman peoples of Italy, a move which made it possible for his son and successor, Caracalla, to grant the franchise to all citizens of the empire in the 200s. Yet under Severus also, conversions to Christianity were forbidden and the persecution of the Church continued.

During this century in Central Europe, Germanic tribes were consolidating into ever larger and stronger tribal groups. The Slavs, another Indo-European people, had been moving in force into European Russia and Eastern Europe for centuries. In the British Isles, the Scots and the Irish were emerging as distinct peoples—amalgams of the Picts, the Celts and the other tribes who had earlier invaded and settled those islands. In England, Rome was consolidating her position against

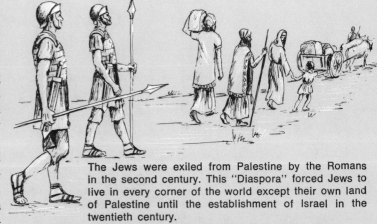

The Jews were exiled from Palestine by the Romans in the second century. This "Diaspora" forced Jews to live in every corner of the world except their own land of Palestine until the establishment of Israel in the twentieth century.

the English and the Scots. During the reign of the Emperor Hadrian, walls were built across northern England against the fierce Scots from the north.

Important men of letters and science worked in the Roman Empire in this century. Lucian (117–180), who was born in Mediterranean Asia, on the Euphrates River, and wrote in Greek, is best known for his essays and satirical dialogues on a wide variety of subjects; his writing greatly influenced French and English satirists 1,700 years later, in the nineteenth century. The philosopher Apuleius, a North African who wrote in Latin, is best known for his romance *The Golden Ass,* which gives a keen insight into the mores and customs of his century. Marcus Aurelius (121–180), the emperor and philosopher, was the author of *Meditations,* written in Greek; the work reveals the philosophy of a discouraged and disillusioned leader who yet believed in self-mastery and stoicism. Tertullian (160–230), born at Carthage in Africa, was one of the great early Christian theologians and defenders of the Church. Ptolemy (90–168), Greek astronomer and geographer, elaborated the cosmic system long favored by the Greeks, which pictured the heavens as "earth-centered," with the sun and the planets revolving about it; this view was accepted for almost 1,400 years, until the Polish monk Copernicus corrected it in the late 1500s. Galen (130–201), a Greek of Pergamum in Asia Minor, was the most honored and respected writer on anatomy, biology and medicine of Classical times.

ASIA, except for its Mediterranean Lands

The vast central area of the Indian subcontinent called the Deccan had been governed loosely since the middle of the first century B.C. by the Satavahana Empire, which rose to a powerful position during this century. Most important, the Satavahana served as a trade and cultural link between the Greek-influenced Saka kingdoms to the north and the dark-skinned Dravidian kingdoms to the south. The Indian nations had regular contact during this century with the lands of western Asia, with Africa and with Rome, as well as with China and the developing countries of Southeast Asia. Indian scholars made many advances in astronomy, medicine and literature which were exported to other countries along with Indian trade goods.

China's dominion spread to include the Tarim Basin of Sinkiang and its oasis, an area China wanted to control in order to insure the safe passage of her caravans along the Silk Route to the west. Paper was invented and manufactured in China early in this century (about the year 105) and soon began to replace more expensive silk and bamboo writing surfaces.

Along the Pacific coasts of Asia, vast areas of land with millions of inhabitants were continuing to organize into political units, adopting the basic cultures and ways of life which would characterize them for the next two thousand years. Such cultural and political divisions were occurring in the peninsula to the north of China now known as Korea, in the islands of Japan off Korea's shores, and in the areas to the south which today are called Vietnam, Laos, Thailand, Burma and Indonesia. All of these lands had been populated originally by Mongol nomads from the Central Asian land mass, as well as by peoples from China. Each new nation included some Indian blood in its racial mixture, a heritage from earlier voyagers who had come from the Indian subcontinent.

It is likely that some of these peoples of mixed Mongol, Chinese and Indian blood sailed out to the islands of Oceania during this century and much later returned to the continent as the "Island Peoples." Their religions were mixtures of Buddhism and Confucian ethics from China, and Buddhism and Hinduism from India, all combined with primitive forms of nature worship remaining from their early tribal days.

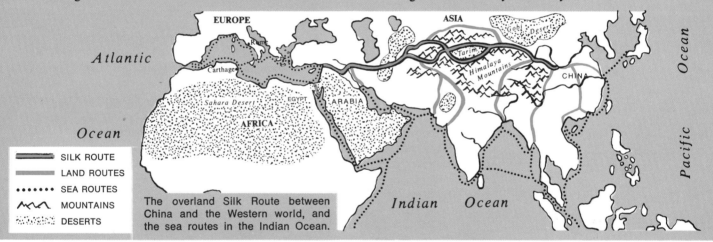

SILK ROUTE
LAND ROUTES
SEA ROUTES
MOUNTAINS
DESERTS

The overland Silk Route between China and the Western world, and the sea routes in the Indian Ocean.

AFRICA, except for its Mediterranean Lands

Previously isolated areas in Africa's interior were now being influenced by contact with more civilized sections of the continent. In Nigeria, however, the Nok culture which had existed since early historic times began to decline.

THE AMERICAS

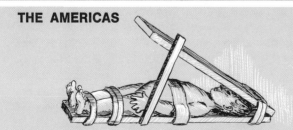

Mayan babies were placed in cradles with their heads held between flat boards to obtain the long and rather flat-shaped skulls seen in Mayan sculpture and murals.

In North America, along the northern Pacific coasts, many maritime societies were developing, the most notable being the Bering Sea culture. These were culturally far less advanced than the societies of the Southwest and of the lower Mississippi and would remain so for centuries. The Mayans of lower Mexico and Central America continued their advancement toward civilization. The Incas of Peru in South America apparently were progressing at a slower pace than the Mayans.

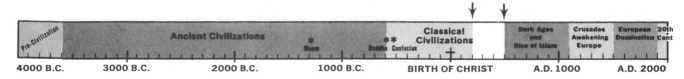

| Pre-Civilization | Ancient Civilizations | Classical Civilizations | Dark Ages and Rise of Islam | Crusades Awakening Europe | European Domination | 20th Cent |

4000 B.C.   3000 B.C.   2000 B.C.   1000 B.C.   BIRTH OF CHRIST   A.D. 1000   A.D. 2000

200 — 500

The Rise of Christianity and the Fall of Western Rome • The Glories of the Gupta Civilization in India • The Fall of the Han Dynasty in China • The Mayan Civilization in Central America

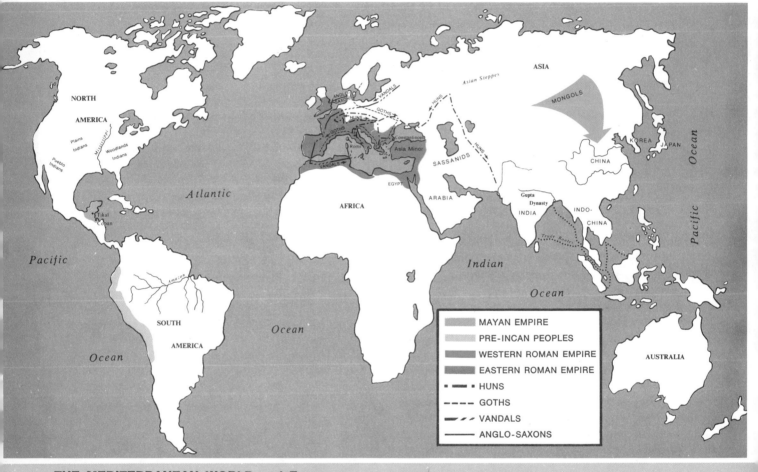

MAYAN EMPIRE
PRE-INCAN PEOPLES
WESTERN ROMAN EMPIRE
EASTERN ROMAN EMPIRE
— · — · HUNS
— — — GOTHS
— ⁄ — ⁄ VANDALS
———— ANGLO-SAXONS

THE MEDITERRANEAN WORLD and Europe

During the next three centuries (the 200s, 300s and 400s) Rome's control at home and abroad was so weakened by internal conflict and by repeated barbarian attacks that by the middle of the 400s the European and African portions of the Roman Empire had collapsed and fallen to invading Germanic tribes such as Visigoths, Astrogoths, Vandals, Lombards and Franks, to name but a few.

The first of these three centuries, the 200s, saw Rome torn by border wars, by revolt in the provinces, by famine and by plague in the cities. During one 49-year period (A.D. 235–284), sixteen puppet emperors were set up and pulled down by the troops. Near the century's end, the Emperor Diocletian, who ruled from 284 to 305, restored order by placing all of the empire under mili-

tary law and dividing its lands into two administrative sections—the western one headquartered in Milan, Italy, and the eastern one in the city of Nicomedia, Asia Minor. During this period, Roman citizenship was extended to all free persons living in the empire, although persecution of Christians continued.

In this same century, in A.D. 230, the Parthian rulers of Persia were replaced by a family called the Sassanids. The Sassanid Dynasty brought Persia to a high point in art, science and engineering, and created a system of fine roads and efficient communications throughout the nation. Rome had not been able to overcome Persia under the Parthians, and she fared no better against the Sassanids.

In the next century (the 300s), Constantine, who succeeded Diocletian to the throne, reunited the two divisions of Rome under one rule. He then (313) issued the Edict of Milan granting freedom of worship to the Christians, and he himself joined the Church. Constantine later moved the Roman Empire's capital to the ancient Greek city of Byzantium, in Asia Minor at the point where the continents of Europe and Asia meet, and changed Byzantium's name to Constantinople. Today, as part of Turkey, this city is known as Istanbul.

Increasing pressure from the Goths in the Danube River area, along with intermittent struggle with Sassanid Persia, added greatly to Rome's difficulties.

After Constantine's death, his successors divided the empire into two permanent administrative sections, with the main capital in the city of Constantinople and the lesser capital in the city of Rome.

Theodosius became emperor in A.D. 379 and by decree made Christianity the official religion of all Romans, outlawing all other religions. In many parts of the empire, German generals were appointed as governors by a succession of helpless emperors. Thus, Stilicho, a Vandal, ruled in the west, and Gainas, a Goth, in the east, while Alaric, a Visigoth, after ravaging Roman lands from the Danube River south to Greece and almost to Constantinople, was appointed governor of the Balkans.

Beginning about the middle of the 300s, a new form of architecture developed known as Byzantine, which drew its inspiration from the eastern half of the Roman Empire—that is, from Constantinople rather than from the city of Rome. This architecture was far more ornate than that of the West, and was noted for cathedrals with magnificently decorated domes covering square understructures. The best examples of Byzantine architecture are to be found today in the cathedrals of Istanbul (Constantinople), and in such Italian cities as Venice. An altered form of Byzantine architecture was later used in most Russian churches.

The next century, the 400s, saw the final collapse of the European and African sections of the Roman Empire to a combination of Germanic peoples who were themselves being driven westward by horse-mounted Huns from Asia. One of the Germanic peoples, the Visigoths, sacked the city of Rome in 410 and withdrew

at once with their booty. About the year 439, another Germanic tribe called the Vandals crossed the Mediterranean and captured Rome's African provinces. In 450, the Huns from Asia under their ferocious leader Attila were turned back from the city of Rome by a combination of desperate former enemies, composed of Roman troops and Visigoths who banded together against a far more dangerous and savage enemy.

By 476 the last emperor of Western Rome was deposed by the Germanic chieftain Oddacer. After the fall in Europe and Africa of Western Rome, the Eastern half of the empire, whose capital city was Constantinople (sometimes still called by its Greek name, Byzantium), would survive for an additional one thousand years.

In Gaul, Clovis (481-511), leader of the Franks, defeated rival Germanic tribes such as the Alemani and the Visigoths and founded the Frankish Empire. From the Frankish Empire would evolve over the centuries many of Western Europe's most important modern nations. Clovis became a Christian in 496, and thus took a great step toward determining that, in future, Europe would be Christian.

By converting to Christianity, Clovis gained the support of the Christian bishops of Rome against the other Germanic leaders, most of whom, although Christians, had embraced the Arian heresy, which denied the divinity of Christ, a position contrary to that taken by the Christian hierarchy in Rome, in the Near East and elsewhere.

The city of Rome, although now in an inferior political position to that of Constantinople, struggled to remain as head of the Church. Her initial task was to make the bishop of Rome superior to all the other bishops of the Church, and to determine that her bishops, or popes as they were called, be chosen only by the other bishops of the Church (in later centuries by its cardinals) and not by popular franchise or by lay rulers.

Rome then felt impelled to eradicate the various "heresies" which tended to blunt and weaken Christian doctrine as conceived by the popes. There were hundreds of these, including the Arian heresy mentioned above; the Manichean heresy, which explained evil by the dual nature of light and darkness; the Nestorian

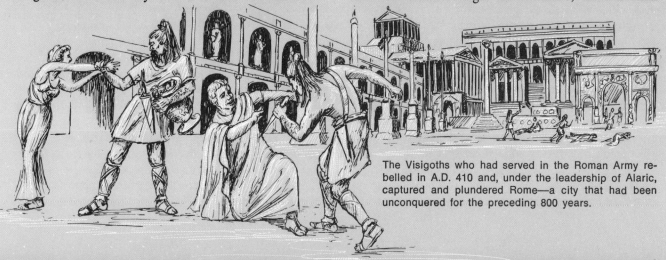

The Visigoths who had served in the Roman Army rebelled in A.D. 410 and, under the leadership of Alaric, captured and plundered Rome—a city that had been unconquered for the preceding 800 years.

heresy, which made a distinction between Christ as a divine and as a human being; and—perhaps the most dangerous to Rome—the heresy of the iconoclasts, who opposed the making of religious images or the worship of them. This heresy would, over the centuries, divide Christianity into two irreconcilable portions. By the middle of 1,000s, as we shall later see, that portion of the Christian Church whose center was the city of Constantinople and that portion of the Christian Church whose center was the city of Rome would arrive at an irreparable breach and become, in effect, two competing faiths.

The first monastery in Europe was founded in this century by Saint Benedict (480–543). The monks in Europe's monasteries played a key role in preserving the culture and knowledge of past centuries during the "Dark Ages" that followed the collapse of the western half of the Roman Empire.

Clovis the Frank, by marriage to a Christian princess and baptism in the Christian faith, promoted pro-Frankish support in the Church, which helped him to rid Gaul of rival Germanic leaders and tribes.

ASIA, except for its Mediterranean Lands

In the Asian Steppes and Asia's great central land mass, vast groups of horse-mounted nomads continued to coalesce into loosely defined ethnic groups under military leadership. One of these, the Mongols, had been pressing eastward into northern China for some years. The Huns, a second ethnic group, had been raiding northern India and were driving into Europe, stampeding the Germanic and Slavic tribes that had settled along the way. In the middle 400s, as previously noted, these Huns had advanced into Italy and threatened the city of Rome before being forced by combined Roman and German forces to turn back.

The Indian subcontinent had for several centuries been divided into three main areas and ruled about as follows: in the northwest by Greco-Persian kingdoms sometimes self-ruled, sometimes dominated by steppe peoples; by descendants of the original Aryan conquerors of the ancient Indus civilization in the east and in portions of the Deccan; and, finally, in the deep south, by descendants of the founders of the ancient Indus civilization. Exact geographical outlines of the lands of these peoples varied from century to century, and all three groups had been subject over centuries to invasion and conquest by steppe peoples, such as the Sakas.

About A.D. 320, all northern India was united under the Gupta Dynasty, led by Chandragupta I (not to be confused with the Chandragupta who founded the Maurya Dynasty in the fourth century B.C.). His son and successor, Samudragupta, ruled for fifty years and extended the Gupta Empire east and south into what is today Bengal, Assam and Nepal, and then into the Deccan. Further Gupta expansion was limited by resistance from the Dravidian kingdoms in the south.

During the late 300s, and continuing into the 400s under Chandragupta II, ancient Indian culture approached its greatest heights. Its literature, architecture, and sculpture were noted for their delicacy, dignity and restraint. Great progress was made in the sciences and in mathematics. In astronomy, for example, parallax was understood, as was the fact that planetary orbits were elliptical instead of spherical. Aryabhata, a noted Indian astronomer, taught a cosmology based upon the fact that the earth rotated on its axis. He approximated the value of pi and calculated the length of the solar year.

During these three centuries, Buddhism continued to lose ground in India, the land of its founder, and the more ancient Hinduism, or Brahmanism, expanded further and gained many adherents.

Indian sculpture during the reign of Chandragupta II reached its greatest refinement, as seen in this classical bust of Buddha.

In China, the Han Dynasty collapsed in the year 220, more than a century before the fall of its counterpart, Rome, in the far west. Upon the disintegration of the Han Empire, the government of China was divided among three kingdoms, Wei in the north, Wu in the middle and lower Yangtze Valley, and Shu in the Szechwan area, each of them claiming the right to rule the entire land. The northern areas of the empire were victims of repeated invasions by horse-mounted Mongols.

Buddhism in China made great gains in the numbers of its devotees during this period of political confusion. Similarly, Chinese culture continued to expand. In the 400s, the compass was invented and put into use in navigation, and the accuracy of the Chinese calendar was improved. Much prose and poetry of outstanding merit were written during this century.

The ancient kingdom of Chosen in what is now Korea had been intruded upon and for centuries ruled at least in part by Chinese from the south and various nomadic peoples from the north and the northwest. By about A.D. 300, the last of the Chinese had been eliminated and three native kingdoms, Korguryo in the north, Paekche in the southwest, and Silla in the central section, evolved and ruled independently. All three were prosperous and had close economic and cultural rela-tionships with China.

Japan too was in frequent contact with Chinese mer-chants, scholars and teachers. The evolving Japanese culture would gain much from the more ancient civiliza-tion of China.

In Southeast Asia, Chinese influence decreased greatly with the collapse of the Han Dynasty. Two kingdoms of Indochina, Funan and Champa (the latter a semi-piratic group which preyed upon neighbor states and their ships), formed an alliance against declining China and attacked Tonking. The importance of mer-chant-traders from both the northern and the southern parts of India grew throughout Indochina and Indonesia as the strength of China waned. Many autonomous trading states were established by these Hindu traders during the 300s and 400s.

AFRICA, except for its Mediterranean Lands

By the third century, the people of large areas of con-tinental Africa—including the country of Axum in what is now Ethiopia, the Nok culture along the Niger, the kingdom of Kush in the Sudan, and Nigeria—had learned how to smelt and forge products of iron. There was at this time considerable population growth, and the Bantu-speaking peoples spread to the nondesert grasslands south of the Sahara.

In A.D. 325 the armies of Axum attacked and cap-tured Meroe, the capital city of the ancient African kingdom of Kush. Shortly thereafter, Axum became a Christian state, but neighboring African peoples re-mained pagan. In later centuries many of them would turn to Islam, the religion which would be founded by the Arab Mohammed. The kingdom of Ghana was founded on the Atlantic coast of Africa, presumably about A.D. 400 by a Semitic-speaking people, but most of its populace would be black.

THE AMERICAS

During the 300s, the Mayan society of Central America and southern Mexico blossomed into the Western Hemi-sphere's first full-fledged civilization. Although there is strong indication of earlier high development (the first three centuries after the beginning of the Christian era mark the Mayan protoclassic or developmental period), the early 300s are generally regarded as the time during which Mayan government, religion, arts and sciences together reached that society-wide development to which the word "civilization" can be properly applied. From this time on, the Mayan lowlands were dotted with more than one hundred ceremonial centers which were places of religious activity, scientific research and commerce, but which were not residential. The peasants lived in villages surrounding these centers.

The Mayan city of Copan in the Honduras is thought to have been the capital of what is known as the Old or Classical Empire. Copan is also believed by some archaeologists to have been the center of Mayan intel-lectual society. Here much of the mathematical and astronomical research was carried out. Other major cit-ies were Tikal, noted for its pyramids and vast cere-monial centers; Yaxchilon and Piedras Negras, famed for their sculpture and other works of art; Palenque, esteemed for its beautiful "low relief" tablets; and Uxmal in Yucatán, for its fine buildings.

The many temples of the separate Mayan ceremonial centers were built of limestone covered with white plaster. Here the priests studied as-tronomy, astrology and mathematics, and performed religious ceremonies and sacrifices.

In South America, the pre-Incan peoples of what is now Peru, Venezuela and Ecuador had attained high levels in agricultural practices and in certain of the arts and sciences. However, their overall cultural level dur-ing these Old Empire years of the Mayans had not yet reached civilization status.

In what is now the United States, the Adena-Hope-well cultures which had flourished for centuries along the lower Mississippi River and its tributaries declined during the 300s. The pottery and figurines left by these people, as well as their ceremonial burial grounds, are the chief sources of our knowledge of their high state of development—of their agriculture and trade and their dress, social customs and religious practices.

THE CLASSICAL CIVILIZATIONS

A Look Back

How can we evaluate these eleven centuries of human experience which began six hundred years before the birth of Christ and ended five hundred years after his death? What kinds of people were the Persians, the Greeks and the Romans, the Hindus and the Chinese of Classical times? In what ways were their problems similar and how were they different from those of men who had lived before them on the earth? What legacies did they leave for the men who were to come after them?

To begin with, it is notable that the peoples who founded the Classical Civilizations faced in essence the same problems as had their predecessors thousands of years before them in ancient Egypt, Crete, Mesopotamia, the Indus Valley, and China. Barbarians, still menaced the borders; the quarreling of city-states and petty princes still inhibited internal organization; and powerful and ambitious leaders still rose up to compel the submission of other men to their will.

Each nation of Classical times was limited, although somewhat less so than those of ancient times, by geography—by the fertility of lands, by the abundance of water supplies, and by the degree of accessibility to invasion, as well as the suitability of a location for trade. Each of these civilizations of the Mediterranean, the Indian subcontinent and the Far East was limited, too, by its "national character," which was to some degree a product of its prehistory and of its early experiences as a nation.

Thus, when Greeks were pushed out of the Greek mainland and forced to live elsewhere along the Mediterranean shores by successive invasions of other Greek tribes, the Greek people as a whole became so geographically dispersed that it was inevitable that their cities (like those of Phoenicia in a preceding era) would never be united. Perhaps also the freedom enjoyed by Greek sailors out of their home ports in Athens and Corinth and Byzantium, as well as the variety of their contacts with the cultures of many other peoples of the Mediterranean world, was a prime contributor to Greek creativity and to Greek devotion to individual freedom.

Rome, on the other hand, was unified geographically and historically. It was one city—*the* City—from which, like the spokes of a wheel, the Romans moved out to conquer and rule, first the Italian Peninsula and then the rest of the Mediterranean world. All roads led to Rome and out, the hub and center of every Roman citizen's life. Romans could admire and use Greek art and science and philosophy, but at the same time despise the Greek character for its seeming lack of discipline and respect for order.

India too seems to have been a product of both her geography and her beginnings. How much of the restricting social and political caste system of the Hindu world can be attributed to the prehistoric Aryans, who in earliest times (as conquering barbarians) had refused to mix with the dark-skinned peoples who had populated India before them? How great a part did India's beginnings play in fragmenting the subcontinent into sometimes three, sometimes many more divisions? How much of India's rejection of the philosophy of her own great Buddha can be attributed to her devotion to the collection of myths and customs called the Veda, which these early Aryans brought with them and which later formed the beginnings of the Hindu religion?

As for China, how much of her isolation from the mainstream of human progress can be attributed to the vast mountains, deserts and plains of Asia which isolated her from India and the Mediterranean world? Could not the Great Wall of China have been as much a symptom of China's geography and its effect on her national character as it was of her fear of the Mongol and Hun barbarians along her borders?

Questions such as these intrigue the student of history, and his answers, too, are often a product of his own early experiences and the kind of world in which he grew up.

V

THE DARK AGES AND THE RISE OF ISLAM

THE 600 YEARS FROM A.D. 500 TO 1100

A Look Ahead

The greatest years of Rome, from about 200 B.C. to approximately A.D. 200, corresponded roughly to China's great years under the Han Empire. True, the Roman Empire lasted more than two hundred years after the collapse in A.D. 200 of the Han Dynasty, but these last centuries were years of decline and struggle to survive, rather than years of attainment.

India enjoyed two outstanding periods during the Classical era. The first occurred under King Asoka from 269 B.C. to 236 B.C., during the Maurya Dynasty. Under Asoka's rule, the worship of Buddha and concern for human welfare came to be foremost in the thinking of India's leaders. The second great Indian period was under the Gupta Dynasty from A.D. 320 to 534, when students from all Asia came to study in Indian universities and libraries.

All of the empires of the Classical Age—the Han in China, the Asokan and Guptan in India, and the Persian, Greek and Roman in the lands around the Mediterranean Sea—eventually succumbed to a combination of internal weaknesses and external attacks, and all came to an end, leaving behind them chaos and voids of leadership. Into these voids for the next several centuries were to pour barbarians of every race and color. These barbarians would hear tales of the accomplishments of the defunct empires and see the remains of their buildings, roads and aqueducts; and they would dream of building new empires to replace them.

Here and there in the remnants of the empires, bright spots of culture survived. After the fall of the Han, for example, several enclosures of civilization remained in China. Each would claim to be heir to the Han scepter, and each would aspire to reunite the entire kingdom under its rule. A similar situation would exist in India, while in the Asiatic Mediterranean the Byzantine Empire, claiming the mantle of all Rome, would try (almost successfully) to pick up the pieces of the shattered empire in Africa and Europe. Sassanid Persia, while it had never been a part of Rome, would try to bring parts of that fallen empire under its aegis, casting lustful eyes especially upon nearby Mesopotamia, Palestine and even Constantinople itself.

Various Teutonic peoples, first the Franks under Charlemagne and later the kingdoms of Germany, would make pretense that they were Rome and, often aided by the popes, would form and reform something called the "Holy Roman Empire," which Voltaire in a later era was to point out was not holy, not Roman, and not an empire.

Finally, the Christian Church, headquartered in the city of Rome and acting through its missionaries to princes and commoners, would bring a real unifying force to Europe, a unity that was sometimes spiritual, sometimes military, and often both.

But while all this happened, a new political and spiritual giant would arise in the Arabian Peninsula, where Mohammed, its leader, was born in A.D. 570. Islam, the militant religion which he founded, would conquer all of Mediterranean Africa and Asia, then spread into India and eventually into the lands of Southeast Asia. It would cross the Mediterranean into Spain, where only the desperate resistance of Frankish troops under Charles Martel would prevent it from crossing the Pyrenees and conquering all Europe.

By the end of this six-hundred-year period, from A.D. 500 to 1100, which we have called "The Dark Ages and the Rise of Islam," Christianity and Mohammedanism would have probed at each other several times across the Mediterranean, and their enmity would be well established.

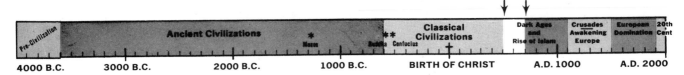

500 — 700

Justinian Codifies Roman Law • 100 Years of Moslem Conquests • The Golden Age in T'ang China • Buddhism Introduced into Korea and Japan • The Mayan Civilization at Its Height

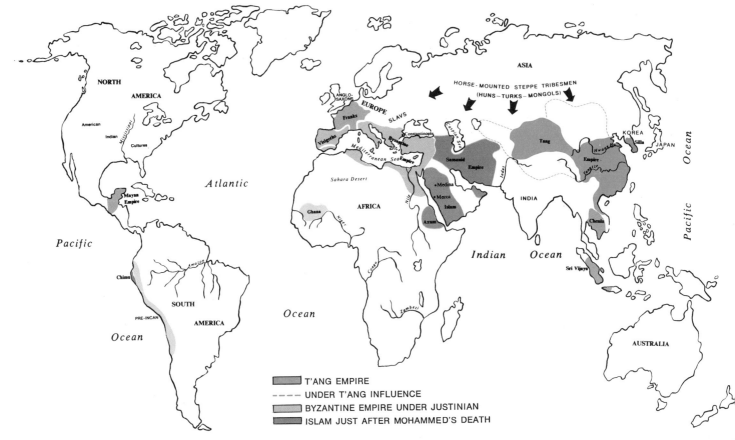

T'ANG EMPIRE
- - - - UNDER T'ANG INFLUENCE
BYZANTINE EMPIRE UNDER JUSTINIAN
ISLAM JUST AFTER MOHAMMED'S DEATH

THE MEDITERRANEAN WORLD and Europe

The fall of Rome left the European and African portions of the empire in chaos. During the 500s, Europe broke up into localized villages largely out of contact with each other and with the rest of the world. Trade between them was virtually nonexistent. The empire's roads and aqueducts fell into disrepair. Science and literature were forgotten.

Byzantium, as the surviving eastern portion of the Roman Empire was now called, was the first of several powers which, over the centuries, would try to fill the void of leadership in Europe and in Mediterranean Africa. The Byzantine Emperor Justinian, with his capital established at Constantinople, directed a series of battles to reunite the eastern and western segments of the Roman Empire. He won back Africa, Italy and a part of Spain, as well as various Mediterranean islands,

During the Dark Ages, scholarship was nonexistent except in the Christian monasteries, where priests and monks spent long hours preserving and copying manuscripts which embodied the accumulated culture of Europe.

and he forced the Franks in Belgium and France to recognize his authority. The reunification, however, was short-lived, and the European and African portions of the empire soon returned to chaos, with many separate parts and many warring rulers. Today Justinian is best remembered for the codification of Roman law which was done under his guidance, and which proved of inestimable value to jurists of later centuries.

The Persians, under the Sassanian Dynasty, continued prosperous and strong, conquering the former Roman territories of Egypt and Armenia. During the next century Sassanid Persia became a serious threat to Byzantium, overrunning Byzantine-ruled Damascus and Jerusalem in 614 and 619, and gravely endangering the imperial capital, Constantinople. In 627, however, the Persians were defeated by Byzantium, and the city of Jerusalem was recovered by the Byzantine Empire two years later.

The large dome, lavish gold and colored mosaics and lacelike carvings of Constantinople's Cathedral of St. Sophia (built in A.D. 523-537) make it an outstanding example of Byzantine art and architecture.

During the 500s, Indo-European Slavic peoples were settling in Poland, in west Russia and in the Balkans.

Various Germanic tribes vied to control the European remnants of the Roman Empire: Visigoths in what is now Spain, Vandals and Lombards in Italy, and Franks in France and Belgium. All were intermarrying with and blending into existing populations. The Franks, who had adopted Christianity under King Clovis in the previous century (A.D. 496), were emerging during the 500s as Europe's dominant people. In the late 600s rivalry among Frankish princelings threatened the kingdom, but Pepin II gained ascendancy over what is now Austria and began reuniting the dissident Frankish leaders.

In England, the legendary King Arthur is said to have died in the battle of Camlan in the year 532. Most of England was under the rule of Anglo-Saxons, Germanic tribes which had earlier crossed the Channel. Among the many small regions into which England was divided, the kingdom of Kent, ruled by Ethelbert (560–616), was becoming predominant. It was to Kent that Pope Gregory I sent Saint Augustine on his mission to convert the Anglo-Saxons, a goal the latter successfully achieved. In the year 616, upon the death of Ethelbert, Kentish supremacy declined and Northumbria became the leading Anglo-Saxon state. Christianity was gradually accepted as missions were established throughout the land.

Beowulf, a poem of about three thousand lines composed in Anglo-Saxon, dates back to the middle 500s. It is the oldest extant poem in a non-Classical European language. Two English men of letters who lived around the end of the following century are worthy of mention: Caedmon, a poet, and Bede, the first known English historian.

In the year 571, Mohammed was born—in the city of Mecca, deep in the Arabian Peninsula. Mohammed never learned to read or write, but he listened to the Jews and the Christians tell about their religions, and, after receiving several revelations from God, he conceived a new religion which he called Islam ("submission"), adopting much of the basic theology of Judaism and Christianity but adding much that was original and distinctly Islam's own.

In 622 Mohammed was forced by nonbelievers to flee from Mecca to the city of Medina, where he continued to preach and to convert the Arabian people to the new religion. This flight is known as the Hegira in the Koran, the sacred book of Islam. Mohammed later returned to Mecca in triumph, converting its people to Islam. After his death in 632, the militant religious state he had founded began one hundred years of conquests in Africa, Asia and Europe. By A.D. 650, Islam, with its capital city in Damascus, had conquered and converted Egypt, Mesopotamia, Persia and much of Byzantium, but not the city of Constantinople or its nearby lands in Asia Minor. By the end of the century, civil war had divided the Moslems into two rival groups called the Shi-ites and the Sunnites. The Sunnites would eventually establish their supremacy and extend Islam's rule eastward into north India and Turkestan, and westward through North Africa to what is now Tripoli.

Fanatic Moslem warriors rode into battle with a ferocious fearlessness based on the Koran's promise that every believer who was killed fighting the infidels would be granted a place in Paradise.

ASIA, except for its Mediterranean Lands

Horse-mounted Mongol, Turkic and Hunnish peoples continued to leave the vast Asian Steppes periodically and to invade the more civilized lands, such as India, Europe and China, on their outer perimeters.

By the middle 500s, the Gupta Empire of India had declined, due to a combination of Hun attacks and internal weaknesses. At the same time, within the Indian subcontinent, wide movements of various peoples were bringing about a variety of new ethnic combinations and languages. In India's deep south, smaller Dravidian kingdoms such as those of the Pallava and Andhra dynasties were vying with Gupta and other Dravidian kingdoms for control of the area called the Deccan. These peoples of south India were wide-ranging seafarers and were responsible for many of the colonies established in Southeast Asia in areas that are today Thailand, Burma, Indonesia and Malaya.

By the end of the century, Indian mathematicians had originated the system of arithmetical notation introduced to the West at a later time by the Arabs and known therefore as "Arabic numerals." The symbol for zero was in wide use in India, as was the decimal point.

In 606 the lands to the north of the city of Delhi came under the rule of King Harsha, who established an empire which included much of northern India. A famed tourist and diplomat from China, Hiuen-Tsang, wrote of Indian accomplishments under Harsha and made keen observations about the land and its people. In 664 a Moslem incursion against the city of Multan in the Punjab took place. The Moslems would keep probing and penetrating into India for almost three hundred years.

All China was reunited and returned to its position of dominance in Asia in the year 589 under the autocratic rule of Sui Wen Ti, the first ruler of the Sui Dynasty. Under Sui rule a new and totally preplanned capital, the city of Ch'angan, was built and more than a million workers were employed to connect existing waterways into a transportation system called the Grand Canal, which carried passengers and freight between China's key cities and its industrial and farming areas. Yet during the early 600s the Sui Dynasty, despite its domestic achievements, was destroyed by its foreign diplomatic and military adventures and failures. On the collapse of the Sui, T'ai Tsung, the first of the T'ang rulers, came into power and inaugurated a golden era in China which was to rival China's previous great years under the Han Dynasty. Under the T'ang, a complete reorganization of government took place. All officials were appointed by and were directly responsible to the emperor. The Confucian system of civil-service examinations was brought back into use. China again extended her hegemony over Korea, Manchuria and the lands to the west as far as the borders of India.

In Korea, by the year 668, the kingdom of Silla had achieved supremacy over the other nations in the peninsula. Buddhism, spreading from China, was becoming the predominant religion.

In Japan, Buddhism was introduced from China during the middle years of the sixth century. China's cultural influence was growing in Japan. Chinese script was adopted, and by the 600s a code of laws with many reforms based upon the Chinese model was introduced. The code put more power into the hands of the emperor

King Harsha traveled continually throughout his empire, supervising his government administrators and giving particular encouragement to artists and scholars.

and imposed a separation between civil and military authority.

In Southeast Asia, two new kingdoms developed during the 500s and 600s. One, the kingdom of Chenla, came into being north of the already established country of Funan in Indochina. Its people called themselves the Khmers, which is what the inhabitants of the area (now Cambodia) call themselves to this day. Chenla would grow into a great land empire. A second Southeast Asian kingdom developed on the island of Sumatra in the Indonesian archipelago and was called Sri Vijaya. During the 600s Sri Vijaya became the most important trading center of Indonesia and Malaya.

Sturdy outrigger canoes, designed to hold up to twenty men, are known to have carried Indonesian traders as far as Africa.

AFRICA, except for its Mediterranean Lands

The kingdom of Ghana, located in West Africa along the "Gold Coast," was growing in commercial power based largely on gold and salt mining, and on trade with other nations of Africa and the peoples of India and the Mediterranean.

In the late 600s, African peoples were being exposed to Islam. Later, many would adopt it as their religion.

THE AMERICAS

By this time Mayan society had developed rigid and seemingly immutable social classes. The priests and other rulers were the elite. Below them was a large and somewhat vaguely defined class of peasant-commoners. Finally, at the lowest level were slaves. Mayan religion was polytheistic—worshiping more than one god. It professed a mystical concept about time, including a belief that the future could be foreseen. Mayan art, as with most early civilizations, was largely concerned with the representation of religious ideas and the glorification of the priestly class. There was a belief in immortality and in an afterlife. Monogamy was practiced.

Mayan science was primarily involved with astronomy and mathematics. The Mayan calendar was more accurate than that then used in Europe, and Mayan mathematics included the concept and use of zero.

In South America, the pre-Incan peoples of the kingdom of Chimú in Peru and that of Quito in Ecuador were making cultural progress. Their agricultural practices were quite sophisticated, and they were producing a handsome pottery and attractive sculpture and architecture connected in some way with their religious worship.

In North America, there are today findings of an American Indian culture that was beginning to develop in that period along the Mississippi River and the river systems of what is now the southeastern United States, built in the locations of the extinct Adena-Hopewell cultures. Houses were made of mud and wattle. The bow and arrow were in use, and primitive cultivation of plants was practiced. Two kinds of pottery have been found in the area, apparently not related to the earlier and more advanced Adena-Hopewell pottery.

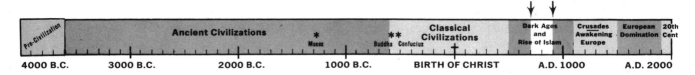

| Pre-Civilization | Ancient Civilizations | *Moses | **Buddha Confucius | Classical Civilizations | Dark Ages and Rise of Islam | Crusades Awakening Europe | European Domination | 20th Cent |

| 4000 B.C. | 3000 B.C. | 2000 B.C. | 1000 B.C. | BIRTH OF CHRIST | A.D. 1000 | A.D. 2000 |

700 — 900

The Golden Age of Islam • Charlemagne • Viking Incursions Throughout Europe • The Mayan Empire Vanishes

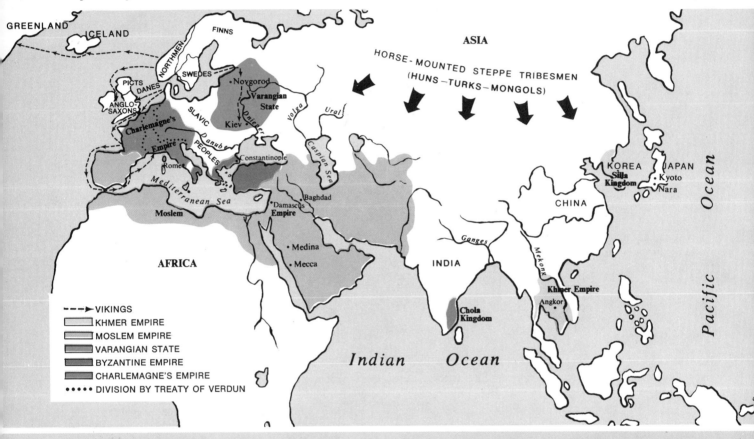

THE MEDITERRANEAN WORLD and Europe

By the end of the 600s, the militant Moslem empire had been extended by conquest eastward from the Arabian Peninsula through Afghanistan into Asia, and westward through Egypt and the other lands of North Africa. In 711 a Moslem army of Arabs and Berbers—a people of North Africa living in what is now Libya—crossed the Straits of Gibraltar from Africa into Spain, where the Visigothic government retreated from the invaders' fierce onslaught and eventually collapsed. By 714 the entire Iberian Peninsula was in Arab hands and the rest of Europe was gravely threatened.

The Moslems also extended their frontier eastward again during this era, wrenching Turkestan from China in 751, thereby cutting China's land access to India.

The 700s became the Golden Age of Islamic culture. The capital was moved from Damascus in Syria to Baghdad in Iraq. Here, under Caliph Harun al-Mansur

The marketplace in Baghdad during the reign of the Abbasid Caliph Harun al-Mansur attracted trade from China, India, Africa, Russia and even Scandinavia.

and later under Caliph Harun al-Rashid—famous in the collection of short stories called *The Arabian Nights*—the art, science, mathematics and literature of Islam reached heights equaled at the time perhaps only in T'ang China. The racial composition of the Moslem peoples now included Semites from the Arabian Peninsula (the original Moslems), peoples from Persia and the Indian subcontinent, and most of the other racial strains of the Mediterranean lands. In addition, a considerable number of Mongol, Hunnish and Turkic peoples had become Moslems as a result of conquests and conversions by the Arabs in Asia. These Asiatic peoples would play an increasingly important part in Islam with the passage of time.

Beginning in 867, Byzantium, the eastern remnant of the Roman Empire, enjoyed a resurgence of power under a group of Macedonian emperors. However, Byzantium and its capital of Constantinople continued to be menaced by militant Islam. In addition, the Christian Church (which linked Rome and Byzantium) was racked by a bitter internal struggle over the issue of "image worship." The eastern portion of the Church, centered at Constantinople, contended that the material picturization of Christ, the saints and the Virgin was wrong and should be forbidden. A contrary position was taken by Rome. The widening schism between the eastern and western branches of Christianity resulted eventually in several separations and reunions of the east and west branches of the Church. At one time, for example, Nicholas, Pope of Rome, excommunicated Photius, the Patriarch of Constantinople; and Photius, in turn, anathematized Nicholas.

In Europe, the Frankish ruler Charles Martel, son of Pepin II, was aiding Saint Boniface in his mission to convert the Germanic peoples to Christianity. Later, Martel (whose name means "hammer") led Frankish troops in victory over the Moors (Moslems) at Tours in 732, preventing the Moslems from moving out of Spain into Central Europe and thereby probably preserving Christianity in the Western world. From this time, the Arabs in Europe were confined to Spain, where their brilliant Omayyad Dynasty ruled from the city of Cordova.

Charlemagne, the grandson of Charles Martel, tried, like Justinian of Byzantium before him, to rebuild the Roman Empire. He conducted fifty-four campaigns to unite and bring into Christianity such peoples as the Lombards, the Saxons, the Danes, the Avars, the Slavs, and the Moslems. He succeeded in all of his campaigns except the one in Spain against the Moslems, and in A.D. 800 he was crowned "Emperor of All the Romans" by the Pope for his services on behalf of the Church and against the enemies of Rome.

Along with his military activities, Charlemagne tried also to inspire a rebirth of culture in the "Roman" Empire, but his accomplishments, like Justinian's before him, were few and short-lived.

The great Charlemagne, illiterate himself, founded a palace school which he attended along with his wife and children and the children of his government officials.

Charlemagne died in A.D. 814, and there was never again the same concert of feeling between the emperors and the popes. Charlemagne's son Louis the Pious attempted to maintain the empire, but he lacked his father's leadership and strength for this monumental task. In 843 A.D., Louis' sons (Charlemagne's grandsons) agreed to the Treaty of Verdun, which divided the empire into three parts. This act laid the foundation for most of the major nations of Europe and for their separate languages. The western section would one day become France, the center section would develop into Italy, and the eastern section would become, first, the "Holy Roman Empire," made up of a conglomeration of German states and baronies, and, later, modern Germany, Austria, Switzerland and northern Italy.

England, France and Ireland were repeatedly attacked and invaded by fierce Danes and other Norsemen during these two centuries of the 700s and 800s. The Anglo-Saxon King Alfred the Great (849–899) is noted for his defense of his country of Wessex in England and for England's eventual survival as a Christian and non-Danish nation. At the same time, Swedes (called Varangians, a variation of "Viking") crossed the Baltic Sea and invaded what is now Russia, following the rivers and streams southeast to an area then populated heavily by Slavic peoples. Here, in 862, the Swedes established a powerful state, centered first around the city of Novgorod. About the year 900, the city of Kiev became their capital.

The great sailing vessels of the Vikings carried bands of marauders who ravaged the coasts of Europe and even sailed up the River Seine (in 885) to lay a ten-month siege to the city of Paris.

ASIA, except for its Mediterranean Lands

Moslem incursions into northern India (especially into the lower Punjab and Sind) occurred repeatedly. To the east of this area, about the year 725, the Pala Dynasty began what would be almost four hundred years of rule of the Bengal and Magadha regions, while in India's deep south the Pallava kingdom declined throughout the 700s and came to an end in the year 888. At about the same time, the nearby Chola kingdom became extremely aggressive after centuries of inactivity. Chola kings built a great commercial empire, and their merchant vessels traveled the Indian Ocean and traded with much of Southeast Asia, establishing colonies in the Malay Peninsula and in Indonesia. In addition to Hinduism, Indian merchant sailors were now bringing the Moslem religion to the ports where they traded and to the colonies which they established.

In China, in the year 712, Hsuan-tsung became emperor. Under this brilliant and vigorous leader, the T'ang Empire reached a peak of cultural activity and accomplishment. China's two great lyric poets, Li Po and Tu Fu, lived during his reign; painting flourished, and Wu Tao-tzu was the outstanding painter in a time of hundreds of great painters. Block printing was beginning to be widely practiced. The oldest extant printed book, which was found in China, dates to A.D. 868.

During the period 753–763, civil war disrupted Chinese life and decisively weakened the T'ang Dynasty. There followed one hundred years of decline, culminating in a peasant revolt in the year 874, after which China suffered fifty years of anarchy.

In Korea, the Silla kingdom reached its pinnacle of power after bringing the entire peninsula under its control. China's influence, however, was still very strong.

The city of Nara became capital of Japan in the year 710. Nara was modeled after the T'ang capital, as were most things in Japan during this period. In 794, the capital was moved to the city of Heian-kyo, later called Kyoto. The 800s are known as the Heian Period in Japan, during which there was a transition from a strong central government to a feudal society with many small baronies and many leaders, and the gradual development of a military class. Less and less power remained in the hands of the emperor. By the year 880, the regent Fujiwara Mototsune had become the first civil dictator in Japanese history, and the succeeding members of the Fujiwara family completely dominated the royal family for centuries.

Most of the nations of Southeast Asia during the 700s were at least in part Buddhist, due to the strong influence for many years of traders and colonizers from India.

Entertainers at the T'ang court were chosen from the students at a training center established by the T'angs in the palace at Ch'ang-an to teach young girls the arts of music and dancing.

Late in the century, however, Moslem influence began to make inroads into the area.

The first decade of the 800s saw the Funan and Chenla kingdoms of Indochina united into the Khmer kingdom, today known as Cambodia. Their capital, Angkor, a city of intricate canals and elaborate irrigation systems, was founded about A.D. 810.

Throughout the entire Southeast Asian area, by the late 800s, influence from the Indian subcontinent was decreasing. Although Moslems kept trying to penetrate the area, resistance to them was growing as well. It is generally believed that the first immigrants from Southeast Asia arrived in Hawaii sometime during the middle of this eighth century A.D.

AFRICA, except for its Mediterranean Lands

During the 700s and 800s, remote areas of the African continent began adopting some of the agricultural techniques of the ancient Ethiopian kingdom of Axum. Such devices as hillside farming which used stone terraces and water channels were to be found in portions of even the deep-southern jungles. By the end of the 800s, iron was being smelted and forged in all but the most isolated areas. The kingdom of Ghana, generally regarded as Africa's first modern state, continued to prosper on the "Gold Coast." Ghana developed a wealthy yet peaceful empire with an intricate and centrally controlled government.

THE AMERICAS

The Mayan Empire reached magnificent cultural and economic heights during the 700s A.D. Trade existed between its centers and also, by land and sea, with foreign peoples as far away as South America. There were more than one hundred economic and religious centers in the Mayan Empire, and around them artistic and scientific activities flourished. Each new building was commemorated with a stela, or carved stone, marking the building's date of construction. The earliest known such stela, located at Tikal, bears a date corresponding to A.D. 292.

During the 800s, one of the most puzzling phenomena of human history occurred. One by one the Mayans abandoned these great cities. Until recently, no natural catastrophe, no human cause seemed to account for these strange events. The cities were not destroyed, but were left intact. Archaeologists and historians had postulated several possible causes: invasion, climatic change, plague, soil exhaustion. None seemed to satisfy the known facts. Today it is generally believed that the overworked peasants rose up in revolt against their priest-rulers and drove them from the ceremonial centers. After that, only minor activity seems to have occurred within the abandoned cities. The most recent stela was dated 889. After that, no new buildings were built for almost two hundred years. The magnificence of the Mayan civilization seemed to have vanished from the earth.

Mayan trade caravans, traveling overland with packs upon their backs, or by waterways in large dugout canoes, carried such goods as feathers, jaguar skins, woven textiles, beans, pottery and even chewing gum.

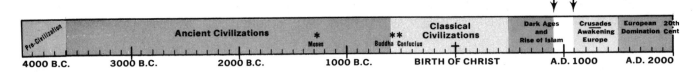

| Pre-Civilization | Ancient Civilizations | *Moses | **Buddha Confucius | Classical Civilizations | Dark Ages and Rise of Islam | Crusades Awakening Europe | European Domination | 20th Cent |

4000 B.C.   3000 B.C.   2000 B.C.   1000 B.C.   BIRTH OF CHRIST   A.D. 1000   A.D. 2000

900 — 1100

Holy Roman Emperors versus Popes • William the Conqueror • The First Crusades • The Sung Dynasty in China • The New Mayan Empire in Yucatán

DOMINANT RELIGIONS
☐ MOSLEM
■ ROMAN CATHOLIC
■ ORTHODOX
▬ ROUTE OF CRUSADE—1096-1099

THE MEDITERRANEAN WORLD and Europe

During the 900s, the German portion of what had been Charlemagne's empire was repeatedly attacked by Magyars, an Asiatic nomadic tribe who were later to found the kingdom of Hungary, and by Slavs. These barbaric peoples in turn were each defeated and subjugated by Otho the Great, the Germanic king, who forced them to embrace Christianity and to become part of his growing empire. This powerful and ambitious ruler was attempting to revive the old Roman Empire, following the example of Justinian from Constantinople in the 500s and Charlemagne the Frank in the 700s. Otho imposed his will upon the other German barons, intervened in the affairs of France (the western portion of what had been Charlemagne's empire) and, finally, crossed the Alps into Italy, where the Pope, who would have preferred a less formidable adversary in the struggle for power, reluctantly anointed him "Holy Roman Emperor."

For centuries the successors of Otho the Great were selected by the many German barons and were called emperors of the Holy Roman Empire. Nominally, at least, they were the rulers of a unified and reincarnated Rome, but in actuality it was the popes who were the real rulers of whatever was left of the western portions of Ancient Rome, and the real creators of European unity.

During the next century (the 1000s), quarrels between popes and Holy Roman emperors became particularly intense. The "investiture" question—whether pope or emperor should choose bishops of the Church—gave rise to two rival groups: the Ghibellines, who supported the emperors, and the Guelphs, who aligned themselves with the popes. The struggles between these two groups would disrupt the peace of Europe for more than two centuries.

This investiture discord reached a climax in 1077

when Emperor Henry IV was excommunicated and had to come to Pope Gregory VII as a humble penitent dressed in sackcloth in order to preserve his position as Holy Roman emperor and avoid rebellion among his subjects. Later Henry was to have his revenge, but subsequent popes and Holy Roman emperors were to battle back and forth in the contest between Church and State.

While emperors, popes and kings contested for control of Europe, the peasants, who had been plunged into the Dark Ages by the fall of Ancient Rome, saw the situation from an altogether different point of view. After the lapse of Roman law and the withdrawal of Roman arms, their lives had been chaotic and full of uncertainty, subject to the whims of passing conquerors, with no authority to turn to for protection or redress of wrongs, and with precarious sources for the barest livelihood. Now, beginning in the early years of the 1000s, a feudal system began to evolve in Europe whereby thousands of individual baronies which were strong, self-contained economic units offered at least a modicum of protection to the peasants.

European feudalism was similar to that which had developed centuries earlier in China and India, and more recently in Japan, when strong central governments had broken down. The peasants were tied to the land (although technically they were not slaves), and they gave to the baron or duke a portion of their labors and their produce, as well as military service and a sworn oath of allegiance called fealty. In exchange, the baron gave his peasants protection and, presumably, justice in his court. For the peasants of Europe, the world ended at the borders of their overlords' land.

Fairs held in the marketplaces of small towns of medieval Europe not only provided a wider exposure for the goods of the peasant but also brought him entertainment and glimpses of a larger world outside his own feudal manor.

England was again subjected to fierce Viking attacks during the late 900s and early 1000s. In the year 1016, Canute, a Dane, became the ruler of all England. Three years later, in 1019, on his brother's death, he inherited the kingdom of Denmark, and eight years after that he conquered Norway, so that his Scandinavian empire included much of the lands around the North Sea.

In the French portion of what had once been Charlemagne's empire, Hugh Capet, the ruler of Paris, became the first in the line of Capetian kings. His descendants, the Capetian family, by a combination of marriage and chicanery, would one day weld France into Europe's most powerful state.

During this century, France, like England and Ireland, was repeatedly attacked by Norsemen. These Norsemen carved out of France a barony which would come to be known as Normandy. Knights from Normandy would later go as mercenaries to Sicily, where they would develop yet another powerful Norman state, extending from Sicily north past Naples.

In 1066, a group of Normans led by William the Conqueror crossed the English Channel and subjugated all of England. These former Norsemen had lived in France long enough to consider it their home and to speak French rather than their original Norwegian tongue. As conquerors they were to form the ruling elite of England. While the conquered people continued to speak Anglo-Saxon, French became the language of the English court. William, the Norman leader, ordered the compilation of the Domesday Book, an exhaustive economic survey of England which was used for taxation, appropriation, and other governmental purposes. Later these anglicized Normans would gain control of French Normandy (through a combination of inheritance and marriage) and would then vie with the French kings to control the rest of the French nation.

The Swedes, who in the late 800s had traveled across Russia from the Baltic and settled in Russia's southeastern section, were now threatening the Byzantine city of Constantinople. One Swedish tribe, the Rus, was to give its name to the entire nation of Russia. The Slavic kingdoms of Poland, Bohemia and Serbia were being formed and reformed in Eastern Europe, as was the Magyar kingdom of Hungary.

The final schism between Christian Rome and Christian Constantinople came during the middle of the 1000s. In 1054 each side took an uncompromising attitude toward the doctrines of the other, and the resulting rift became permanent.

The Arab countries in Mediterranean Asia and Africa were as divided by religious and political controversy during these two centuries as were their Christian counterparts in Europe and Byzantium. Into the weakness caused by their dissension came a new power, the Seljuk Turks from Turkestan. These Asiatics had been infiltrating the Arab lands for several centuries. By the middle of the 1000s they had adopted the religion of Islam and conquered the Moslem territories of Persia, Syria and Jerusalem, and had defeated opposition coming from both Christian Byzantium and Moslem Egypt.

By the end of the century, the growing enmity between the Moslems and the Christians had reached explosive proportions, and had the temporary effect of healing dissensions within both Islam and Christianity.

In 1077, the Christians were beginning to win back the Iberian Peninsula from the Moors (as the Moslems were called in Spain). The northern Spanish states of Aragon and Castile were early recovered to Christian rule, and the former Christian capital of Toledo was regained in 1085. The exploits of the Spanish hero El Cid against the Moors have become part of Spanish legend.

The Byzantine Emperor Alexius appealed to the Christian nations of Europe for aid against the Turkish Moslems who were pressing on his lands to the east. In answer to his appeal, and further inspired by the impassioned words of Pope Urban, the first of several Crusades set out to aid their Christian brothers in Constantinople and to free the Holy Land—a vaguely outlined area including Jerusalem—from the Moslem infidels. The Crusades were made up of people from various nations of Europe and were led by German, French and English kings. They took place over an unbelievably lengthy period of about two hundred years. The First Crusade, consisting of a motley rabble of dreamers,

Of 30,000 Crusaders who marched out of Constantinople to take Jerusalem from the Moslems, only 12,000 survived the hardships of the Syrian desert and the battles along the way to actually take part in the capture of the Holy City.

adventurers and pious Christians, passed through the city of Constantinople in A.D. 1096 on its way to Jerusalem. It was destroyed by the Seljuk Turks at their capital city of Nicaea. The Second Crusade, an official army made up of well-equipped and well-led knights and men, wrested Jerusalem and the Holy Land from the Turks in A.D. 1099 and set up several feudal Christian states in the lands and islands at the eastern end of the Mediterranean Sea.

Omar Khayyam, the Persian poet-mathematician-astronomer, lived during the late years of the eleventh century when Persia was under Seljuk Turkish domination. He is most famous for his *Rubaiyat,* a collection of poems widely admired throughout the Western world, and for his treatise on algebra which contained the first exposition of the binomial theorem.

In Europe, the developing philosophy called Scholasticism gave a new direction to religious thinking, as men such as Saint Anselm (1033–1109) and Pierre Abélard (1079–1142) tried to apply the test of reason to questions of faith, using the techniques of the ancient Greek philosopher Aristotle. Also during these years, a French poet, Chrétien de Troyes, set down in poetry the legends of King Arthur. At about the same time, other French poets were telling in the *chansons de geste* ("songs of deeds") the story of Charlemagne and the heroic men close to him. The most famous of these *chansons* was *The Song of Roland,* composed about the year 1080.

Byzantine architecture still dominated the lands of Eastern Europe, which remained under the influence of the Eastern Church; but in the west, Romanesque architecture, a series of variations on Roman structures, was evolving. The beginnings of modern musical notation were developed by an Italian, Guido d'Arezzo, in the early 1000s.

ASIA, except for its Mediterranean Lands

In 985 in the southern portions of the Indian subcontinent, Rajaraja the Great ascended the throne of the Chola kingdom. Under his efficient administration, a society favorable to the arts developed, and as a result much beautiful sculpture and architecture were produced. By the early 1000s the Cholas had conquered the island of Ceylon, and in 1025 they mounted a series of unsuccessful expeditions against the kingdom of Sri Vijaya more than two thousand miles across the Indian Ocean on the island of Sumatra.

In northern India's Punjab and Sind areas, the long series of plundering invasions by Moslems continued. Originally the Moslem raiders had been Arabic, but, beginning about A.D. 1000, Turkic and Afghan converts to Islam destroyed and pillaged Hindu temples and massacred whole settlements, establishing a period of Turkish authority in the Punjab area. Present-day enmity in India between Moslems and Hindus is not, it can be seen, of recent origin.

China, during the early years of the 900s, still consisted of the numerous kingdoms which had resulted from the breakup of the T'ang Empire. About the year 960, the

Sung porcelains often displayed a combination of incised and painted designs which brought to them the utmost in delicate beauty.

Sung Dynasty was founded. Under its leadership, cultural progress seems to have been vastly preferred to imperial expansions. More than two hundred years of philosophical revivals took place, with much retrospective examination into China's past. Painting was greatly diversified and not restricted primarily to Buddhist subjects, as it had been during the T'ang years. The greatest Chinese painters under the Sung are considered to be Li Lung-mien and Kuo Hsi. The Sung years are also noted for magnificent porcelain figurines and vases, and for the fact that around the year 1041 printing from movable type was invented. This was about four hundred years before Gutenberg developed a similar process in Germany.

In the Korean Peninsula in the year 918, the state of Koryo became the dominant power, but was harassed over the next century by continuous raids from the north by Mongol and Turkic peoples from Manchuria. These raids caused a defense system to be built (completed in the year 1044), consisting largely of a great wall across the northern extremity of the peninsula.

Japan continued to be dominated by the Fujiwara clan, whose members occupied the key posts of both regent and civil dictator. Although the emperors, who were basically their captives, made occasional attempts to depose them, the Fujiwara remained the real rulers of the Japanese islands.

In Southeast Asia, in the year 906, Annam (the Chinese name for what is now North Vietnam) broke away from China, ending over one thousand years of Chinese domination.

On the island of Sumatra, the state of Sri Vijaya, after sustaining several attacks in the year 1025 from the Chola kingdom of southern India, was able to maintain its integrity and make a satisfactory peace with the invaders, whose sources of supply and reinforcement were more than two thousand miles away in southern India.

In the year 1044, in what is present-day Burma, the Mons and the Burmese, two rival peoples who long had vied for control of the area, now were united into the kingdom of Pagan.

AFRICA, except for its Mediterranean Lands

During the 900s, the coastal peoples of East Africa were engaged in a thriving sea trade with merchants from India and China. Beginning about A.D. 1000, Moslems began to dominate this trade and to influence the culture and the religion of the African peoples.

In 1076, a Moslem sect from Morocco called Almoravids invaded the kingdom of Ghana and conquered this Sudanese nation, which, since the 300s A.D., had been a prosperous and independent nation on the main caravan route to the north. The Almoravids, however, soon fell to fighting among themselves, and Ghana regained its independence. It was unable to recover its former trade position, however, and soon began to disintegrate into tribal units.

THE AMERICAS

Sometime during the 900s, a warlike tribe called the Toltecs entered the valley of Mexico, coming probably from the north, and established over the peoples of the valley an overlordship which they maintained for more than two hundred years. They built their capital, Tollán, near present-day Tula, about fifty miles north of modern Mexico City. The Toltec Empire seems to have been composed of many small kingdoms of diverse language and race. Toltec technology and much of its culture undoubtedly derived from the peoples whom they conquered, and thereby indirectly from the Mayan peoples to their south, with whom they had long traded.

The Mayan cities of Yucatán were apparently stimulated into a cultural renaissance by contact with the aggressive new Toltec Empire. Toltec legend tells of one of their great leaders, named Quetzalcoatl (also the name of a Toltec god and later of an Aztec deity), who in the year 999 was driven from Tollán and with his followers invaded the Yucatán Peninsula. There he either conquered or in some other way strongly influenced such Mayan cities as Chichén Itzá and Uxmal into activities reminiscent of the old empire of the Mayans. It is noteworthy that after this renaissance Mexican and other religious motifs were intermingled with the old

Mayan motifs in the religious and ceremonial decorations of these cities.

In South America, although none of the varied kingdoms and nations located from what is modern Ecuador to Chile had achieved what can properly be called civilization status, high culture and great technological skill continued to develop, as evidenced in the agriculture, weaving, sculpture and architecture produced. The great organizing influence of the Incas, which was to unite the vast area into one great empire, was still centuries away.

About A.D. 1000, a Norwegian colonizer named Leif Ericson told of being blown off course while returning from his homeland of Norway to his colony in Greenland. He was driven onto what is now believed to have been the American mainland, probably at Newfoundland. Ericson called the area where he landed Vineland. Here he constructed a temporary settlement. Recent archaeological expeditions to this area of Newfoundland have excavated nine buildings which, by carbon-14 dating, are calculated to have been built about the year 1000 (five hundred years before Columbus). Their style and method of construction indicate that these buildings were Norwegian in origin.

THE DARK AGES AND THE RISE OF ISLAM

A Look Back

How can we evaluate the six hundred years which we have called "The Dark Ages and the Rise of Islam"? Certainly not all of the earth was in the chaotic condition of Europe. China, for example, during these six hundred years enjoyed two eras of glorious cultural attainment, first under the T'ang Dynasty and later under Sung leadership. As a result, Chinese influence upon the cultures of the other nations of Asia (and particularly upon Korea and Japan) was very great, setting patterns in them that have lasted to this day.

Likewise, the Mayan civilization, located in southern Mexico and Central America, reached a cultural peak during Europe's Dark Ages; then, for some unknown reason, its cities were mysteriously abandoned, only to spring up with new and vigorous life in Mexico's Yucatán Peninsula a few centuries later.

These six hundred years were not among the Indian subcontinent's most progressive, except for the attainments of the Chola kingdom in its deep south. Actually, the events during this period that had the most significant consequences for the subcontinent were a series of raids by marauding Moslems, first by Arabs, later by Afghans and Turks.

The Arab Moslems enjoyed a Golden Age during the early years of the Dark Ages, creating great centers of learning at Cairo, at Gundeshapur in Persia, at Baghdad and in Spain. They made a great contribution to human knowledge by translating Indian and ancient Greek works which later were transmitted to Europe in Arabic. Moslem achievements in medicine also were outstanding, and hospitals were established throughout the Middle East. Arabic research into chemistry and mathematics was thorough and original (although "Arabic" numerals and the concept of zero were Indian rather than Arabic in origin and were simply transmitted by the Arabs from India). Arabic architecture, with its magnificent use of the arch, its lacelike design, and its lovely secluded gardens, is to be found wherever the Moslems lived—in Cordova and Granada, in Istanbul, in Damascus and in Baghdad, to name just a few places out of many. The Moslems created exquisite mosaics and were in the forefront of the attempts to reconcile monotheism with ancient Greek philosophy, particularly with the philosophy of Aristotle. Most important, the Arabs gave Mediterranean Africa and Asia the common religion, language and heritage which they share today. Yet, by the early 900s, this Arabian Moslem empire was crumbling through an inability of the various states to get along with each other and to accept common leaders. Their internecine warfare, together with attacks from the Moslem Turks from Asia, undermined the strength of the empire and made possible the ascendancy of the Moslem Turks in their place.

VI
THE CRUSADES AND THE AWAKENING OF EUROPE

THE 400 YEARS FROM A.D. 1100 TO 1500

A Look Ahead

The eleventh century had seen the Moslem and Christian worlds erupt into a series of conflicts with each other which would flare up again and again over the next two centuries. The first of these conflicts was the opening of the Christians' campaign to regain the Iberian Peninsula from the Moslems. The second was a tragicomic unofficial Crusade in which a motley army of thousands of Christians was annihilated in 1096 by the Turks. The third conflict was the "official" First Crusade—a campaign in which a well-led and adequately equipped Christian army captured Jerusalem in 1099 and established Christian kingdoms in Jerusalem and elsewhere on the African-Asian shores and the islands of the eastern Mediterranean.

Altogether there were to be at least six more Crusades during the next two hundred years. At first, Christian armies would take the land route through the Balkans and across Asia Minor to Constantinople and thence to Jerusalem. Later, they would cross the Alps to the Italian port cities of Venice and Genoa and Pisa, and from there sail to the Near East.

In the beginning, the Crusaders appear to have been motivated by a sincere religious zeal to free the Holy Land. All too soon, however, more worldly ambitions began to lure men into the ranks of the "holy" armies, until, in time, the religious aims were all but supplanted by such motivations as the desire for adventure and the chance to plunder and gain free land. Perhaps no mass acts of human history compare to the Crusades as demonstrations of the good and evil which intermingle in men's affairs—of the almost unbelievable combination of self-sacrifice, cruelty and greed of which men are capable.

After Jerusalem was successfully recaptured from the Turks during the official First Crusade, subsequent Crusades made possible the achievement of all kinds of personal ambitions. Otherwise, for both Christianity and Islam, they were a sad waste of human life and property. The hatred which they inspired between Islam and Christianity as well as between Christian and Christian divides the Western world to this day.

In some respects, however, the Crusades were eminently productive: they made Europe aware of the superior cultures of Islam, of Byzantium, of China and of India; and they opened up the Mediterranean Sea to trade between Europe and the East. Out of this awareness and trade there emerged in Europe, as we shall see, a wholly new view of life, a rebirth or "renaissance," which began in Italy and spread to the rest of the continent.

This reawakening of Europe began in the 1100s and 1200s, the two centuries in which all but the first two Crusades occurred. During these two centuries, and the two that followed them, both England and France were developing national identities. Their people would have a mixture of Celtic, German, Frankish and Norman blood, but they would become distinctly English or French.

During these four hundred years the power of the Papacy to control the destinies of the peoples of Europe would lessen gradually, as nations began to develop leaders and systems of government sufficiently strong and stable to replace the popes as the rulers in temporal matters, and (in some cases) in religious matters too. England and France, where hereditary monarchies became established quite early, would have more secure and effective governments than areas where the continuity of government came later.

In a sense, these centuries we have chosen to call "The Crusades and the Awakening of Europe" could just as appropriately be named "The Years of the Mongols and the Turks." During much of this period, these barbarian nomads would gallop out of the vastness of Central Asia and at least three times overrun vast portions of the earth. In the 1200s, for example, Mongols, led first by Genghis Khan and later by his descendants, foremost of whom was Kublai Khan, would conquer Asia from China to Asia Minor and then thrust deep into Europe. In the next century, the 1300s, other nomads, this time of a mixture of Turkic and Mongol blood and led by the ruthless Tamerlane, would lay waste the lands from northern India through Persia to Asia Minor and into parts of present-day Russia. In the 1300s and 1400s, still other Turkic peoples, the Ottomans, would build a great empire containing the ancient lands of Mediterranean Asia and Africa and a portion of Eastern Europe from the Balkan Peninsula north through Hungary. This Ottoman Empire would last well into modern times.

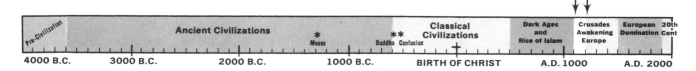

1100 — 1200

Christian Crusades or Moslem Holy Wars? • **Frederick Barbarossa Expands the Holy Roman Empire** • **Turkish Rule in Northern India** • **The First Shoguns in Japan** • **Aztec Beginnings**

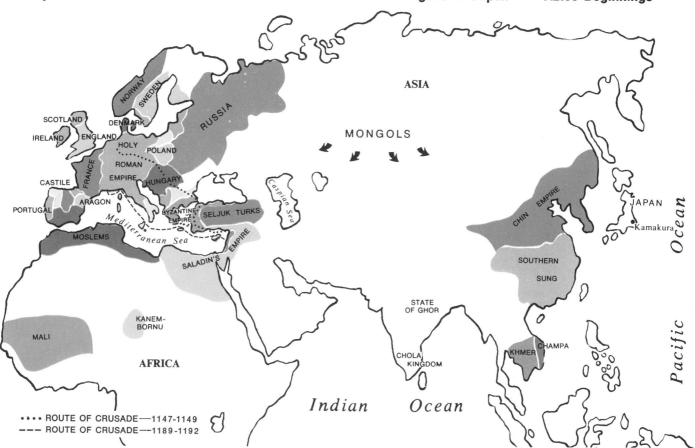

•••• ROUTE OF CRUSADE—1147-1149
--- ROUTE OF CRUSADE—1189-1192

THE MEDITERRANEAN WORLD and Europe

During this century two problems that had long troubled the popes and the Holy Roman emperors were at least partially solved. In 1122, in the Concordat of Worms, it was agreed that in the future the popes had the power to invest bishops and abbots, although the emperors held the power to veto any choices they did not like. Further, it was agreed that the emperors should invest clergymen with land, which they would hold as the emperors' vassals. Thus the areas of power between Church and state were delineated. In 1123 the First Lateran Council confirmed this agreement and, in addition, passed decrees against simony (the selling of holy office) and against marriage of the clergy.

In Asia Minor, Christian Byzantium paid huge tributes to the Seljuk Turks, who now controlled Arabia and Persia. In 1147–1149 a Third Crusade (actually the second official Crusade), made up of forces from many countries and led by Louis VII, King of France, ended in total failure. The French leaders of the Crusade received no help from the Christians in Constantinople and the Near East whom they had come to aid; the German contingent under Holy Roman Emperor Conrad III was destroyed in a battle in Asia Minor; and the Flemish and English troops turned away from the journey to Jerusalem, going instead to Moslem-ruled Portugal, where they founded a Christian kingdom with Lisbon as its capital.

In Europe, the Guelphs (the Pope's partisans) and the opposing Ghibellines (the Emperor's supporters) were united under Holy Roman Emperor Frederick I (1152–1190), who claimed and for a time received the right to select the Pope and very nearly succeeded in reuniting the European lands of ancient Rome as had Otho, Charlemagne and Justinian before him. Frederick, a man of tremendous energy, was determined to control the lesser barons of Germany and to make the clergy responsible to him rather than to the popes. He fought five separate Italian campaigns to bring the cities of northern Italy into his empire, and finally, by marrying his son to Constance, heiress to the Norman throne of southern Italy and Sicily, brought the rest of Italy under Germanic Holy Roman hegemony.

Henry the Lion, like other European rulers, was subdued by Barbarossa and was forced to surrender his German duchies into the control of the emperor.

But Frederick (nicknamed Barbarossa, or Red Beard) was unable to secure succession to the imperial throne for his heirs, as the German barons refused to cooperate or to subordinate themselves, and for this reason Germany failed to achieve the continuity of rule which would have united the Holy Roman Empire under her rule. Instead, the Empire remained a collection of independent German baronies and Italian city-states. Soon the Italian cities broke away, and in the not too distant future the German baronies too would revert to independence. The Holy Roman Empire would become again little more than a name.

While these events were taking place, France and England were being unified into nations by means of strong kings who established hereditary monarchies. The Norman rulers of England were reorganizing the government, and the French tongue they spoke was blending with the Anglo-Saxon spoken by the majority of the inhabitants to become what is now the English language. The struggle between Church and state was evident also in England, where the quarrel of King Henry II of the House of Plantagenet, with Thomas à Becket, Archbishop of Canterbury, over the matter of whether king or Church had final jurisdiction in

Church matters, led to the murder of Becket—an example of the pattern of the king's domination of the clergy which would lead to a complete break between England and the Church of Rome at a later date.

In 1171, Henry landed at Waterford in Ireland in response to a request for aid from the deposed Irish King, Dermot MacMurrough. Henry was greeted as "Lord of Ireland," and he claimed the land as his own. He gave huge estates of Irish land to English nobles, but with the passage of time the nobles became more Irish than English and were disloyal to King Henry and his successors.

Back in the Near East at this time, a remarkable Moslem leader from Mesopotamia named Saladin was rallying around him both Turkish and Arabic Moslems. After a series of successful campaigns against the Fatimite rulers of Egypt, Saladin became sultan of Egypt and established the Ayyubite Dynasty. He began a vigorous "Holy War" against Christian states in the Near East such as Syria, Byzantium and Palestine. Saladin's Moslem forces recaptured Jerusalem in A.D. 1187, just about ninety years after the Second Crusade had wrested it from the Moslems. Thus began more than seven hundred years of Moslem rule of the Holy City of Jerusalem.

In 1189 the "Crusade of Kings" led by three European rulers, Frederick Barbarossa of the Holy Roman Empire, Richard I the Lionhearted of England (son of Henry II), and Philip II of France, was defeated by Saladin's armies. During this Crusade, Frederick Barbarossa lost his life in a river in Asia Minor. Richard and Philip quarreled incessantly, and Philip eventually sailed back to France. Richard, after a victory over the Moslems at the port of Jaffa, in Palestine, negotiated a peace with Saladin that reestablished the Christian kingdoms on the coast and granted Christians freedom to make religious pilgrimages to Jerusalem.

The two Crusades of this century and the Holy Wars mounted by the Moslems to expel the invading Christian infidels illustrate how differently the same conflict can be viewed by opposing interests. The Moslems considered the Christians to be crude barbarians who, when they attacked Islam, were attacking religion and civilization at their peak of greatness. To the Christians, however, the Crusades were justified wars against defilers of the most holy places. Each felt they were serving God and earning for themselves a place in heaven. Ironically, however, neither the Christians nor the Moslems allowed religious zeal to prevent them from making treaties, trade pacts and other agreements with one another when it was to their worldly advantage to do so.

In Spain there remained only scattered groups of Moslems. Two Spanish Christian kingdoms, Castile and Aragon, contended for control of the entire peninsula.

The 1100s were noted for the founding of a number of military-religious organizations to accomplish various purposes. The Knights Templar, for instance, were established to protect pilgrims to Jerusalem. Among other orders founded at the turn of the century or shortly thereafter were the Cistercians, the Gilbertines, and the Carmelites.

Among prose and poetry worthy of mention during this twelfth century were several spoken and written accounts of the life of the legendary King Arthur in both French and English. *The Anglo-Saxon Chronicle,* a collection of manuscripts covering events in England from the 800s through the middle 1100s (and said to have been assembled at the inspiration of King Alfred) was an important historical document of the period. *Everyman,* a famous morality play written in Anglo-Dutch, was perhaps the twelfth century's most important dramatic writing, and is typical of the kinds of plays which were performed by members of trade guilds on holidays and during fairs in medieval Europe. Walther von der Vogelweide (1170–1230), perhaps Germany's greatest lyric poet except for Goethe, wrote poems of love which display brilliant form and great delicacy of feeling. His strong German nationalism seems almost prophetic.

At the height of Islam's prosperity, the sons of wealthy Moslem families were prepared for leadership at seminars on poetry and the classics held in the libraries of mosques.

ASIA, except for its Mediterranean Lands

In the Indian subcontinent, the Chola kingdom continued to rule much of the peninsula's deep south and to send trading expeditions by sea to Africa, Southeast Asia and China. The northern portions of India came under a long period of Moslem Turkish rule, beginning about 1151 when the small Turkish state of Ghor began a militant expansion. By 1177, Muhammad of Ghor had spread his rule throughout the Punjab and eastward through much of the plain of the Ganges River.

In China, a Manchurian people known as the Chin established dominance over northern China, forcing the Sung rulers to move to China's southern reaches, where they were henceforth known as the Southern Sung. Even as a diminished power, the Southern Sung governed efficiently and its people were prosperous. Its cities had fortified walls; there were well-developed irrigation systems, an efficient postal service, and high attainment in the arts. The Sung left fine examples of landscape paintings, as well as many delicately wrought items of porcelain ware. The first known use of gunpowder as an explosive was under Sung rule about the year 1150; gunpowder was not used in Europe until the middle 1300s, when it was also first used in warfare.

Japan had been ruled, in effect, since the middle 800s by the Fujiwara family, which had dominated and subordinated the emperors to its will. By the early 1100s, Fujiwara control declined as other military families from the provinces grew in power. Civil war broke out between two of these provincial families and tore the fabric of the nation until 1185, when Yoritomo, a general of one of the warring families, gained ascendancy. Yoritomo reorganized the government and made the city of Kamakura his capital. In 1192, he appointed himself shogun, which means "barbarian-subduing great general." He was the first of a long line of hereditary military rulers of Japan to bear this title. The shogun was to be the real center of power in Japan, although the illusion that the imperial family governed was carefully maintained.

Yoritomo, the first Japanese shogun, established control over most of the productive lands of Japan by installing his loyal followers as constables in the provinces.

In Southeast Asia, the kingdom of Pagan (located in what is now Burma) fell victim to poor administration and to the internal quarrels betwen the Burmese and the Mons, its component peoples.

Similarly, in 1177, internal weakness in the kingdom of Cambodia permitted the neighboring Champa nation to invade and capture the city of Angkor. Four years later, Cambodia reorganized its forces and drove out the Champa forces.

The magnificent temple of Angkor Wat was built by the Khmers of Cambodia prior to the Champa invasion in the twelfth century.

AFRICA, except for its Mediterranean Lands

Mali, a black Moslem nation, succeeded the kingdom of Ghana as the area's gold producer. Ghana had disintegrated into separate tribal groups after being conquered by the Almoravids in the preceding century. Mali, located in the northwest section of Africa, originally an agricultural and trading society, became deeply involved in organized mining and eventually became the most important producer of gold in Africa.

In the Sudan, the kingdom of Kanem-Bornu began to dominate lands in north-central Africa agriculturally enriched by the periodic overflow of the rivers draining into Lake Chad.

THE AMERICAS

During the early years of this century, the Aztec Indians entered the valley of Mexico from the north and settled near the Toltecs. Here, apparently, they underwent a considerable period of tutelage and subservience to the Toltecs, learning much of the agriculture and irrigation practiced by these people. No doubt they were exposed to such Mayan developments as the calendar and writing as well.

In 1168 the Toltecs were weakened by internal religious and political conflicts and, as a result, were overrun by waves of barbarian peoples. The Aztecs are not thought to have been among them. After the fall of the Toltecs, the Aztecs found themselves surrounded by hostile peoples and began more than a century of wandering in search of a place to settle.

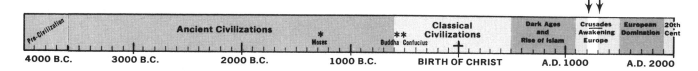

	Ancient Civilizations		Classical Civilizations	Dark Ages and Rise of Islam	Crusades Awakening Europe	European Domination	20th Cent
Pre-Civilization		* Moses	** Buddha Confucius				

4000 B.C. 3000 B.C. 2000 B.C. 1000 B.C. BIRTH OF CHRIST A.D. 1000 A.D. 2000

1200 — 1300

Genghis and Kublai Khan • Magna Carta • The Crusaders Sack Constantinople • Marco Polo in India and China • The Mayapan Period in Yucatán

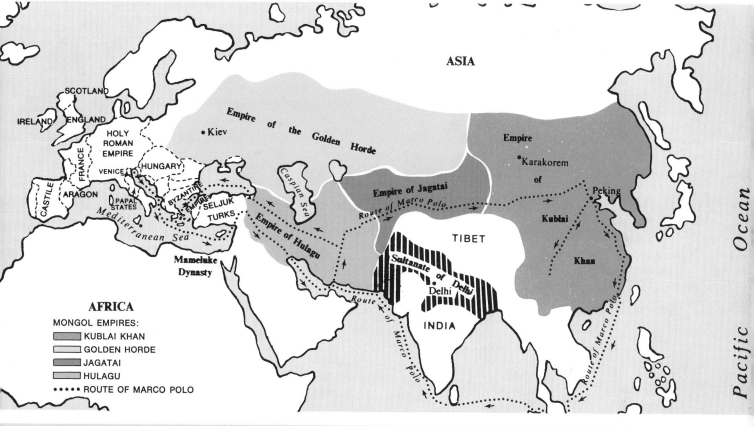

MONGOL EMPIRES:
- KUBLAI KHAN
- GOLDEN HORDE
- JAGATAI
- HULAGU
- •••• ROUTE OF MARCO POLO

THE MEDITERRANEAN WORLD and Europe

In this century of the 1200s, civilization was subjected to the fiercest and most widespread attack by barbaric peoples that the world has ever known. In these attacks, led by Genghis Khan and later by his sons and grandsons, vast armies of Mongolian barbarians poured out of the great plains of Central Asia. The great Mongol leader Genghis Khan first led his savage followers into China, in 1211. Then, beginning in 1216, he invaded the Near East, where sixty thousand of his Mongol horsemen destroyed ancient centers of civilization, ruined great irrigation works, and laid waste every living, growing thing in their path. By the time of his death in 1227, Genghis Khan was the conqueror of lands from the Yellow Sea off China's Pacific coast to the Caspian Sea and to the Dnieper River in Russia.

Genghis Khan's successors led victorious Mongol armies into Russia, where they later established a great

Tatar state called the Golden Horde. From Russia they poured into the heart of Europe through Slavic Poland and Magyar Hungary, and crushed the German armies in Silesia. Western Europe was reprieved only by deaths among Mongol leadership which caused a withdrawal, and also by its great distance from the center of Mongol population, the capital city of Karakorum in Asia.

Egypt too was spared by its distance from the Tatar capital. It alone of the Moslem lands of the Near East escaped being overrun by a great wave of Mongols which swept into that area in 1245. In the year 1250, Egypt came under the rule of a new dynasty of former slaves called Mamelukes, who were to govern the ancient Nile lands for the next three hundred years. Indeed, these Mamelukes, through the military skill of their leader, Baybar, saved Egypt from another great wave of Mongols, which was led by Genghis Khan's grandson Hulagu. In the year 1258 this avalanche of Tatar horsemen—to select just one almost unbelievable example—destroyed Baghdad and its surrounding lands in what is now Iraq, slaughtering tens of thousands of people in a single week. All of the Arab Islamic lands except Egypt fell to this new wave of Mongols. However, these conquerors too were eventually converted to the Moslem faith, thus giving even greater strength to the religion.

A tribe of Turks called the Ottomans were spreading into the Mediterranean world between the Mongol incursions, overcoming the Seljuk Turks who had preceded them in that area. It is customary to date the beginning of the Ottoman Empire from around 1288, the time of the accession of Osman I to leadership of the Ottomans who were occupying parts of several Near East nations.

While all this was happening on Europe's borders and to her neighbors in Asia and Africa, the peoples of Central and Western Europe continued to live and act much as they had in the previous century, almost ignoring the Mongols who threatened their very existence. Popes and emperors still battled for Europe's lands and the souls of Europe's peoples. The Guelph and Ghibelline factions set up rival emperors and rival popes in Italy, France and Germany. Eventually, a disunited, frustrated Germany chose as Holy Roman emperor a Swiss nobleman of little importance, Rudolf of Hapsburg, and thus the Hapsburg Dynasty, which would

become one of the most powerful in Europe, came into being, almost, it would seem, by happenstance.

From 1202 to 1300, the last five Crusades—the Fourth through the Eighth—took place. The Fourth, in 1202, was led mainly by French nobles in partnership with merchants from the city of Venice. It is most memorable for its cruelties, for its corruption, and for the damage done in it by Christian to Christian when, in one of the acts of human history most difficult to understand, Crusaders sacked the Christian city of Constantinople. Retribution came sixty years later, in 1261, when Constantinople Christians, led by the Palaeologi family, drove out the French and Venetian usurpers who had remained to rule Byzantium after their sack of Constantinople. The Palaeologi family was then to govern Constantinople for the last two hundred years of its existence as a Christian city—that is, until its fall to the Ottoman Turks in the fifteenth century.

The Fifth, Sixth, Seventh and Eighth Crusades, like all of the preceding ones except the First, failed in their aim to recover holy places from the so-called infidels. Furthermore, during the Eighth Crusade, in 1291, the Moslems regained the Palestinian port city of Acre, the last of the Christian strongholds in the Near East, which had been in Western hands for almost two hundred years—since the First Crusade, in 1099. It was at Acre that the Order of Teutonic Knights (which would later become a military power in Europe) had been formed one hundred years earlier, to protect pilgrims en route to the Holy Lands.

Moslem power in Spain continued to decline, so that by 1266 only Granada remained in Moorish hands.

In Italy, the city-state of Venice, due in good part to its ideal location for dominating Mediterranean Sea trade, became a great and rich power. During these same years, the Inquisition, a Roman Catholic tribunal for the seeking out and punishing of religious heresy, was established by the Church in Italy. It was also in Italy in the thirteenth century that the poet Dante, the theologian Saint Thomas Aquinas and the Florentine painter-sculptor-architect Giotto all lived. And it was from Venice that Marco Polo, in about 1271, set out with his father and uncle on his fabulous journey across Asia into the Chinese Mongol kingdom of Kublai Khan. Marco Polo later wrote the famous book of his travels in French, but he was an Italian, a member of a family of Venetian merchants.

In France, the Capetian kings began more than one hundred years of fighting to win from England's Plantagenet kings the lands they held in France through marriage, inheritance and conquest. Louis IX of France (Saint Louis, canonized in 1297) was the most highly regarded European ruler of his time. His high standards of ethics and justice made him the arbiter of awakening Europe and his reign the golden age of medieval France. During this century, French became the spoken and written language of most of the courts of the world. The

Many medieval towns prepared to withstand attack and siege by enclosing agricultural areas and livestock, as well as the town itself, within high walls and battlements.

University of Paris, the greatest university of medieval times, was formally chartered about 1200.

In England, the Magna Carta, or Great Charter, a guarantee of certain fundamental rights wrested by the English barons from King John, was signed in 1215. It was an agreement made originally only with the nobles, but eventually it would be extended to the entire British people. This document was an important step toward democracy in England, as was the first Parliament, which met in the 1260s.

Oxford University was founded in the early 1200s, probably as an offshoot of the University of Paris, and Roger Bacon, the great English philosopher and scientist, lived and worked at both of them during the thirteenth century. English kings, through their heritage of such duchies as Normandy, continued to control almost three fourths of France.

Two great religious orders were founded during the thirteenth century, the Franciscans and the Dominicans. Members of both monastic groups traveled about teaching and helping the needy rather than living in monasteries as was customary in other orders.

Gothic architecture, with its lofty naves and stained-glass windows, developed in France from the Romanesque during the 1200s. Notre Dame Cathedral in Paris and the cathedrals of Reims and Chartres in France and of Milan in Italy are outstanding examples of Gothic architecture, as are certain public buildings such as the Town Hall of Brussels.

Reims Cathedral, in which many of France's medieval kings were crowned, took more than one hundred years to build. With its elaborate carvings and stainedglass windows, it is a superb example of Gothic architecture.

ASIA, except for its Mediterranean Lands

In the Indian subcontinent, a Moslem dynasty of former slaves ruled from the city of Delhi between the years 1206 and 1266. The Moslem ruling class was, however, greatly outnumbered by the Hindu population, out of which the military and clerical classes were necessarily composed. Religious tolerance on the part of both Moslems and Hindus was vital under these conditions.

Islamic architecture introduced to India a style of open and spacious prayer chambers covered by arches, vaults and domes of concrete and mortar, and richly ornamented with both Moslem and Hindu motifs. In 1290 the ex-slave dynasty at Delhi ended and was replaced by the Moslem Khaljis Turks, who ruled until the year 1320.

The rivalry between the Hindu and Moslem religions and cultures continued to fester within Indian society. The Moslems believed that any non-Moslem was an infidel, whereas the Hindu devotion to a caste system based on race, color and birth was repulsive to the Moslems. The dogmatism expressed by both groups about these issues made them enormously intolerant of each other.

Mongol warriors overran country after country until, by 1300, the descendants of Genghis Khan ruled from the Pacific Ocean west to Poland, Hungary and Syria.

China was invaded by Mongols led by Genghis Khan in 1211. Six years later, Genghis razed Peking, the great city which a few decades later would be rebuilt as his grandson's capital. By 1231 Korea too was subjected to Mongol attack, and by 1234 all of northern China had fallen to the Mongols. The Korean Peninsula, however, was not to be conquered until 1259, by other Mongol leaders who were descendants of Genghis.

In 1279, Genghis' grandson Kublai Khan overran the lands of the highly cultured Southern Sung, and for the first time all of China fell completely under foreign domination. Fortunately, Chinese civilization captivated Kublai before he conquered the Chinese people. Like others who conquered China before and after him, he was soon more Chinese than Mongol, and he set out to rebuild and expand the nation in the tradition of his Han and T'ang predecessors. He instituted welfare for the aged, built great public works, repaired the imperial highways and created an efficient postal system.

Kublai's attempts to conquer Japan in 1274 and 1281 were unsuccessful, as were his attempted invasions of Indochina. He sent an army into Champa in Indochina in 1282, but his rugged horsemen were unable to adjust to the rigors of the tropical climate, and his fine land troops were not good enough sailors to cross the Sea of Japan.

From 1275 to 1292, the brothers Nicolo and Maffeo Polo, and Marco, Nicolo's son, lived and worked in China and other lands of the East under the Emperor Kublai Khan.

Marco Polo wrote of his service in the court of Kublai Khan, whose Yuan Dynasty was the first non-Chinese dynasty to rule all of China.

THE AMERICAS

In Yucatán, the Mayan cities of Chichén Itzá and Uxmal were destroyed, apparently by their own rebellious, overworked peasants, who lived in the cities' outskirts and did most of the work for the priests and the political leaders. With their fall, Mayapan became the leading city of Yucatán. From this time on, Mayapan and the other Mayan centers became real cities rather than ceremonial centers, with the people living within them instead of on their peripheries. This change was accompanied by a sharp decline in the quality of the architecture and also in the general art and technology of the Mayan people.

The Aztecs paused in their wanderings and made an attempt to settle where Mexico City now stands. They fortified Chapultepec Hill (now a park in modern Mexico City), but were driven out by hostile neighbors and forced to resume their nomadic life.

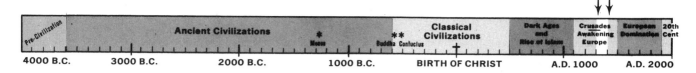

| Pre-Civilization | Ancient Civilizations | | Classical Civilizations | Dark Ages and Rise of Islam | Crusades Awakening Europe | European Domination | 20th Cent |

4000 B.C.   3000 B.C.   2000 B.C.   1000 B.C.   BIRTH OF CHRIST   A.D. 1000   A.D. 2000

1300 — 1400

The Second Babylonian Captivity • **The Hundred Years' War** • **The Birth of Switzerland** • **The Black Death** • **Tamerlane** • **The Aztec Civilization**

THE MEDITERRANEAN WORLD and Europe

Although the Mamelukes continued to rule in Egypt, as did the Christian Palaeologi family in Constantinople, a new threat to the future of the Mediterranean peoples was evolving out of the expanding activities of the Ottoman Turks. These conquering Asiatics made incursions into Asia Minor at several points, capturing the city of Adrianople there, and then took the city of Thessalonica on the Greek mainland in Europe. Once again a semi-barbaric people was on the rampage in the Mediterranean world.

In Europe many changes were brought about by the Crusades, particularly in Italy, through which many of the Crusaders had passed on their way to and from the Holy Land. The city-states of Venice and Genoa reached pinnacles of sea power and financial influence during this century, and, also stimulated by sea trade, the more inland cities of Pisa and Florence were expanding rapidly.

Trade with the East required that the produce of the feudal baronies of Europe reach these port cities of Italy, where it could be put aboard ships to be exchanged for the spices, silks and other products of Africa and Asia which were coming to be so highly prized in Europe. It also meant that commercial travelers from the East were coming to Europe to bargain, trade and sell. An unexpected consequence of this trade and travel was the dread plague, the Black Death which is believed to have originated in Asia and to have been brought into Europe by these travelers from the East. During the years 1347 to 1350, the continent lost at least a fourth of its population to this dread disease.

The Hanseatic League, a union of north-German cities, was formed during this century to defend and control Baltic trade; early commercial cooperation among these cities dates back to the late 1100s. The League established trading branches from Novgorod to London. It defeated its Danish rivals and was able successfully to dominate the fur trade with Russia, the fishing industry of Scandinavia, and the cloth trade with Holland. However, by the early 1400s the Hanseatic League began to decline, and its trade centers were replaced eventually by trade centers such as Paris, London and Brussels which had better access to the Atlantic sea lanes.

The political peace of Europe continued to be disturbed by repeated disagreements among the German barons over the election of the Holy Roman emperors. In 1291 three Swiss principalities, wishing to be free of the Empire's control over their economic and political activities, formed a union called the League of the Three Cantons. Other baronies were shortly to join the Swiss union, so that eventually, by the end of the 1300s, there were eight cantons. Final Swiss independence was not assured, however, until the next century.

The struggle between Church and state continued, due in some part to the insistence by the state that it had the right to tax the clergy, but the focus shifted from Germany, which was disunited and weak, to France, which had a powerful centralized government. From

All Venice was in a festive mood on Ascension Day when the Doge left the palace on his royal barge to join in reenacting the ritual marriage of Venice and the sea.

1305 to 1377, popes lived in the city of Avignon, under the domination of the French monarchy. This period is known in Church history as the Babylonian Captivity, in memory of the time the Hebrews were held captive (in the 500s B.C.) in the city of Babylon. Later, from 1378 to 1418, a period known as the Great Schism, there were two popes—one in Avignon, the other in Rome. This struggle for power and for domination of the Church saw at one time as many as three popes, each with his own College of Cardinals and his own centers of administration.

England and France continued their intermittent struggle over the lands held in France by English kings. The series of battles fought largely over this question are collectively labeled the Hundred Years' War, usually dated from 1337 to 1453. During these many years of battle, the weapons changed considerably. British archers with their longbows proved conclusively at Crécy (1346) that the heavily armored knights of France were outmoded. During the early years of this century, England also fought with Scotland over control of the Scottish throne. This problem, however, was to await later times for solution.

In England, Geoffrey Chaucer wrote *The Canterbury Tales,* and the first translation of the Bible into English was made by John Wycliffe. Wycliffe, an Englishman, and John Huss, a Bohemian follower of his who also lived in the 1300's, were two of the earliest churchmen to attempt basic reforms within the Church. Both men were strongly opposed by the Pope. Huss, in fact, was executed because of his outspoken views.

Two great Italian writers lived and worked in this century. The lyric poet Francesco Petrarca, known to us as Petrarch (1304–1374), began to explore Europe's Greek and Roman heritage and to revive interest in Classical subjects. Petrarch tried to make Latin the language of the literary world, but he is best remembered for the lovely sonnets he wrote in his native Italian. Many historians think that by stimulating interest in Classical subjects Petrarch laid the basis for the Renaissance, which came into full flower more than one hundred years after his death. The other great Italian writer of the century, Giovanni Boccaccio (1313–1375), is remembered today for his *Decameron,* a series of tales which, while reflecting contemporary life, have a universal and timeless appeal.

Toward the end of the fourteenth century, in 1380, a new Mongol invasion into Russia was stopped by Dimitri Donskoi, Grand Duke of Moscow. In the battle, the Golden Horde (the state established by the first Mongol or Tatar group to invade Russia), whose khans had ruled much of Russia since the middle of the previous century, was defeated by the invading Mongols, making possible the rise to power of a Russian state under the grand dukes of Moscow.

Timur, or Tamerlane (the latter name an English corruption of "Timur the Lame"), was a descendant of Genghis Khan who made himself Khan of an area in Asia now called Turkestan. From his headquarters city of Samarkand, he set out on a career of destruction and killing unrivaled in history. About 1380 he led a Mongol Turkic attack into Persia, and in 1381 into Russia as far as Moscow. He captured Baghdad in 1393, and in the later 1390s his armies overran much of the lands held by the Ottoman Turks in Asia Minor and other parts of the Near East.

ASIA, except for its Mediterranean Lands

The northern portions of the Indian subcontinent were under Turkish-Moslem rule for the better part of this century. A dynasty bearing the name Tughluk ruled from the year 1320 with an attitude toward its Moslem and Hindu subjects which fluctuated between kindly paternalism and such appalling brutality as the wholesale massacre of 400,000 Hindus from southern India.

In 1336 the southern portions of the Indian subcontinent became the Vijayanagar kingdom, a well-run military state which was at continual odds with the Turkish Moslems in the north. The city of Vijayanagar was handsome and prosperous; its people were skilled seamen and traders.

In the year 1398, Tamerlane, who had already conquered Persia, Mesopotamia and parts of Asia Minor, invaded India's Moslem north and massacred 100,000 Hindu prisoners at Delhi; then, after sacking the city itself, he turned and fought his way back to the Indus River.

In the Far East, in 1368, the Mongols were driven out of China. Beginning with the Ming Dynasty, which came to power in that year, China was once again governed by its own people. Although the Ming Dynasty did not elevate China to the peaks of power or creativity attained by its Han or T'ang predecessors, it governed well and the nation maintained high standards in the arts and sciences.

The Hindu temples being built in southern India consisted of a central courtyard surrounded by massive stone walls with heavily carved gates in the form of monumental pyramids.

In Korea, the kingdom of Koryo, which had rebelled against Mongol rulers in 1356, submitted willingly to Ming Chinese overlordship in 1369. A new dynasty of Koryo kings, the Yi Dynasty, was established in Kyong-song (modern Seoul) in 1392. The Yi Dynasty was to rule more than five hundred years, until 1910, and it too was consistently loyal and subservient to China.

Japan was ruled by the Ashikaga shoguns during the 1300s, a time in which there was continual political disruption and almost incessant warfare, along with remarkable economic development and expansion. New industries and trade guilds flourished, despite heavy taxes and war. Kyoto was once again Japan's capital.

In the early 1300s in the Indonesian archipelago, the kingdom of Majapahit rose to a position of supremacy. Its lands included most of present-day Indonesia and Malaysia, and it dominated trade in Southeast Asia.

In Thailand, several kingdoms vied for power, with the nation of Ayutthaya becoming the most powerful during this century.

OCEANIA

About 1359, the Maoris, who are thought to have been living theretofore on scattered Polynesian islands, began a series of emigrations to their present homeland on the island of New Zealand.

AFRICA, except for its Mediterranean Lands

In the Moslem kingdom of Mali, the mining of gold had reached great proportions. This kingdom, which had replaced Ghana after it had been destroyed by the Almoravids, was ruled by King Manasa Musa. The King, recently converted to Islam, made a historic pilgrimage to the holy city of Mecca, leading a caravan of sixty thousand troops and twelve thousand slaves dressed in silk. Five hundred of the slaves carried six-pound staffs of solid gold. There were eighty camels, each bearing three-hundred-pound bags of gold dust on its back. Musa became famous in Africa, Asia and Europe for his magnificent pilgrimage, and also for his flamboyance and his generosity. The gold he brought into the Near East depressed the money market there for several decades.

Manasa Musa, king of Mali, made his famous pilgrimage to the Moslems' sacred city of Mecca in 1324.

THE AMERICAS

In 1325 the Aztec Indians again forced an entrance into the valley of Mexico, and they were successful finally in overcoming its other inhabitants. Near the location of modern Mexico City they built their capital of Tenochtitlán, and around it the military empire that would one day occupy most of the lands of present-day Mexico. The Aztecs were the last people to establish a great civilization in North America and were among the most warlike. They built their civilization upon much that they had learned from the Toltecs and indirectly from the Mayans through the Toltecs. Although the Aztecs' picture writing was less complex than Mayan hieroglyphics, and their astronomy less advanced, their skill as weavers and makers of jewelry and pottery was unexcelled. Their medicine and surgery achieved heights attained by no other people of the Western Hemisphere prior to the coming of the Europeans.

In South America, late in this century of the 1300s, the Incas, who were one of the west coast's many highly advanced peoples, began to expand and to dominate neighboring peoples.

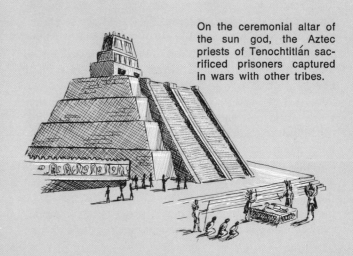

On the ceremonial altar of the sun god, the Aztec priests of Tenochtitlán sacrificed prisoners captured in wars with other tribes.

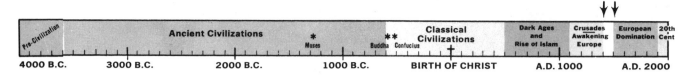

| Pre-Civilization | Ancient Civilizations | *Moses | **Buddha Confucius | Classical Civilizations | Dark Ages and Rise of Islam | Crusades Awakening Europe | European Domination | 20th Cent |

4000 B.C.　　3000 B.C.　　2000 B.C.　　1000 B.C.　　BIRTH OF CHRIST　　A.D. 1000　　A.D. 2000

1400 — 1500

The Renaissance—Leonardo, Michelangelo, Gutenberg • Constantinople Falls to the Turks • Columbus Discovers America • Vasco da Gama Sails Around Africa to India • The Incas of South America • Spaniards and Portuguese Divide the New World

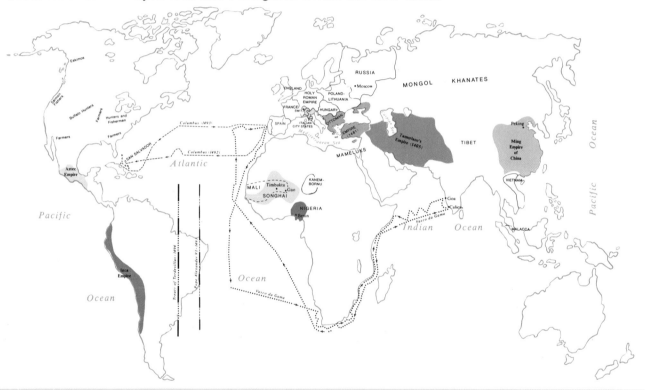

THE MEDITERRANEAN WORLD and Europe

The full impact of Europe's contacts with the East, so greatly stimulated by the Crusades, was most evident in the economic and cultural activities of the Italian cities.

Venice, Genoa, Pisa and Florence, because of their locations on trade routes between Western and Central Europe and the Mediterranean, flourished as the exciting trade with China and India expanded. These Italian cities were in the forefront also in the great reawakening interest in life called the Renaissance—interest in human beings as people with both strengths and weaknesses, interest in the arts and sciences; interest, in fact, in the whole world past and present, but most particularly the Mediterranean world's Greek and Roman past. The city most important in this upsurge of cultural activity was Florence, where the ruling Medici family fostered the most brilliant intellectual and artistic outpouring since the Golden Age of Greece; but other Italian cities too produced great painters, thinkers, writers and sculptors.

A complete listing of all the great men of Italy in this century is beyond the scope of this book, but the most rudimentary list would include the following names: Leonardo da Vinci (1452–1519), artist, scientist, engineer-inventor and anatomist; Michelangelo Buonarroti (1475–1564), sculptor, painter, architect and poet, who ranks along with Leonardo and the poet Petrarch (of the 1300s) as one of the three symbols of the complete Renaissance man and the essence of its genius; Niccolò Machiavelli (1469–1527), political writer and statesman, whose book *Il Principe (The Prince)* to this day is a subject of controversy due to its instructions as to how to seize power ruthlessly and rule a state as a despot; the sculptors Donatello (1386–1466) and Ghiberti (1378–1455); the architect Filippo Brunelleschi (1377?–1446); and the painters Fra Angelico (1387–1455), Masaccio (1401–1428), Sandro Botticelli (1444–1510), and Giovanni Bellini (1430–1516). Such a listing is useful, of course, only if it is recognized that many names of renown have been omitted.

Among the countless achievements of the Italian Renaissance:

A hydraulic system designed by Leonardo da Vinci, who is said to have been the first man to use modern scientific methods;

The Pietà, a world-renowned sculpture created by Michelangelo when he was only 25; and

The dome of the Cathedral of Florence, designed by the famed Renaissance architect Brunelleschi.

The Renaissance, although essentially Italian in spirit, spread quickly to the other nations of Europe. In this century, a German, Johann Gutenberg (1397–1468), invented printing with movable type. (Printing with movable type letters was never really successful in China, Korea and Japan—countries in which the method first appeared—because of the thousands of ideograph letters which had to be cut and stored, as opposed to the Western alphabet of twenty-six letters. Rather, Far Eastern printing was done with an entire page cut out and used as block printing and reproduced over and over. The individual-letter method was invented in China or possibly Korea, but was not really used.) The Flemish school of art, outstanding practitioners of which were Jan van Eyck (1387?–1441) and Hugo van der Goes (1440–1482), to mention just two among at least a dozen great painters, was second only to the Italian. The Dutch theologian Desiderius Erasmus (1466–1536) became the intellectual leader of his time, and his English colleague Sir Thomas More (1478–1535) achieved fame, too, for his philosophical writings. François Villon (b. 1431) became the first great lyric poet of France.

In Central Europe, a divided Germany was preyed upon by selfish rulers and churchmen. During this century the Hapsburgs were acknowledged as the first hereditary emperors over the hundreds of states (mostly German but also sometimes Spanish, Italian and French) ruled by barons and kings which together were called the Holy Roman Empire. In 1499 Swiss independence from the Empire was guaranteed in the Peace of Basel.

The Hundred Years' War between France and England ended in A.D. 1453, with England driven finally from France. The French troops had been inspired and led by a young girl, Joan of Arc, who later became a prisoner of the English and, in 1431, was condemned as a witch by an ecclesiastical court and burned at the stake. Her martyrdom unified and strengthened French resolve against the English.

England next became involved in the War of the Roses (1455–1485 A.D.), a civil war in which two powerful families, the Lancasters, whose symbol was the red rose, and the York family, of the white rose, fought for the throne of England. Henry Tudor, of the Lancasters, finally defeated Richard III and began the reunification of the English nation under the aegis of the Tudor family.

By the early 1400s, English control of Ireland had been reduced to little more than the area around Dublin, but toward the century's end Henry VII, the new Tudor King of England, reestablished control over a major part of the island.

In Russia, Ivan III, after driving the Mongols and their satellite Russian princes from Moscow in 1471, entered the city of Novgorod sometime between 1475 and 1478 and declared himself czar (Caesar) of all Russia, making Moscow his capital.

At the beginning of this century the Mamelukes were ruling in Egypt, as was the Palaeologi family in Constantinople, capital of Byzantium. By this time, however, Byzantium had been reduced by constant Ottoman attrition to little more than the city of Constantinople. In 1453, Constantinople too fell to the Turks, and two years later, in Europe, the city of Athens and most of Serbia fell. The city-state of Venice then went to war with the Ottomans (for thirteen years, from 1463 to 1476) in a frantic effort to contain the rampant Turkish forces who were now pushing hard into Europe.

The fall of Byzantium to the Ottoman Turks is usually taken by historians to mark the end of the "Middle Ages" between the fall of Ancient Rome and the beginning of modern times. Certainly an era of history ended with the fall of the eastern half of what had been the Roman Empire, headquartered at the city of Constantinople. Byzantium was conquered one thousand years after the disintegration of the western portion of the empire, which had had its capital at the city of Rome. For a considerable part of this one-thousand-year period, Byzantium's city of Constantinople had been the repository of the documents sacred to Christianity and much of the culture of the West. Moreover, during her years of power Byzantium stood as a barrier to Europe for Asian Huns, Magyars, Mongols and Turks, forcing them to take the more rigorous and much longer route through Russia. In the same way, trade with India and China remained open to Europeans as long as Constantinople guarded the sea route to the East.

As Byzantium fell, and as the Ottoman Turks pressed into the Balkan lands of Eastern Europe, from them into Hungary, and thence toward Vienna and the very heart of Western Europe, the merchants of Europe began to look for new routes to the riches of India and China—routes which would be less hazardous than the remaining land routes. The Portuguese and the Spaniards, favorably located on the Atlantic Ocean, were the first of many nations to attempt to find these routes. Both were aided greatly by improvements in ship construction fostered by the Portuguese Prince Henry the Navigator (1394–1460). Spain and Portugal would become rich, and eventually, during the 1500s, Spain would become the most powerful of all European states because of her control of the Atlantic Ocean, just as the Italian cities had become rich and powerful in the 1300s and 1400s because of their locations on the Mediterranean trade routes.

Granada, the last stronghold of the Moors in Spain, fell in 1492 to the Christian Spaniards. King Ferdinand and Queen Isabella jointly ruled their combined Spanish kingdoms of Castile and Aragon during this period and are credited with uniting Spain into one nation. They also are noted for encouraging the early explorations which led to the centuries of Spanish world domination.

Both Portuguese and Spaniards crossed the Mediterranean and established themselves in North Africa. It was the Portuguese, most notably Vasco da Gama, who would explore Africa's west coast and sail around the Cape of Good Hope to India. The Spaniards were more interested in discovering a route to India across the Atlantic Ocean. In the course of this search, the magnificent Italian seaman Christopher Columbus, while on a sailing expedition for Spain, landed in the islands of the Caribbean and discovered what would later be known as America.

The great Genoese sailor Christopher Columbus landed in the New World under the sponsorship of the Spanish crown. It was in Queen Isabella's name that he claimed the islands of the Bahamas, and it was to her that he returned bearing strange gifts from across the Atlantic.

ASIA, except for its Mediterranean Lands

The century of the 1400s can be viewed as an interim period in India in which Turkish military power declined in the north and was replaced by several small Moslem kingdoms.

The southern areas of the subcontinent had been governed almost consistently by Hindus. Between the Hindus who dominated the south and the Moslems who ruled the north there had been continuous enmity and, very often, bloody war. Yet Islam, the Moslem religion, had great attraction for Hindus of the darker-skinned "untouchable" classes because it welcomed all colors and classes. At the same time, it repelled devout Hindus because Islam professed to be the only true religion.

Nanak, founder of the Sikh religion, was born in India in the year 1469. The Sikh faith in its early years was monotheistic and professed high regard for both Moslems and Hindus. It was, however, openly opposed to the Hindu caste system, as well as to Islam's contention that it, and only it, was the true religion. Thus, in its basic tenets, the new Indian faith opposed both of India's dominant religions, although it proposed that Moslems and all castes of Hindus should unite into one great brotherhood.

In 1498, the Portuguese explorer Vasco da Gama sailed south from Europe to Africa's Cape of Good Hope and then proceeded north and east to India. The effect of his voyage was to open a safer route to Europe for the spices, jewels and other trade items of the East.

The formerly used route through the Red Sea and then overland to Europe through Arab-Turkic country had always been open to attack and demands for tribute. After the Byzantine Empire collapsed, as mentioned, trade was more dangerous than ever before.

In China, Yung Lo, the third in the line of Ming rulers, moved his capital from the city of Nanking back to Peking, which had been the capital of Kublai Khan. Yung Lo attempted to reconquer the lost territories of China's empire, to restore it to the size it had been at its greatest extent. He also sent expeditions to India, Southeast Asia and the islands of Indonesia, demanding that tribute be paid to the Emperor of China. The coasts of China, meanwhile, were under constant attack by Japanese pirates who conquered several coastal cities and preyed upon Chinese seagoing vessels.

In Korea, the Yi Dynasty's efficient administration brought prosperity and economic development to the peninsula. About 1446, a Korean alphabet was developed.

The Champa kingdom in Southeast Asia was conquered by Vietnam about 1407, and Vietnam, reconquered in turn by Ming China, did not regain its independence until 1428.

The Indonesian kingdom of Malacca adopted the Islamic religion during this century, and from Malacca the faith spread throughout the rest of the Indonesian archipelago.

AFRICA, except for its Mediterranean Lands

The Songhai, at one time a district of the Mali kingdom in West Africa, broke away from Mali overlordship and eventually, under the leadership of a chieftain called Sonni Ali, conquered its former rulers. The city of Gao became the capital of Songhai, and salt its most important product on the trans-Saharan caravan routes. In 1464, the city of Timbuktu on the Niger River was incorporated into the Songhai Empire.

In West Africa during the 1400s, an intricate maze of trading routes extended between key cities and

sources of raw materials. In Nigeria, the city of Benin became a sizable manufacturing center of cotton goods and an important trade link on the caravan routes.

During this century, the Bantu-speaking peoples migrated from just south of the Sudan to the rain forests of Central and West Africa at about the same time as other African primitives were also moving to the south, perhaps to avoid attacks and appropriation of their produce by the Moslems of North Africa.

THE AMERICAS

In the year 1492, Christopher Columbus made his first voyage to the New World, probably landing on the island which he named San Salvador, in the Bahamas off the coast of Florida. In the century of his historic voyage, the Mayan cities of Chichén Itzá, Uxmal and Mayapan had been either abandoned or destroyed. The Toltec Empire had been gone since the late 1100s. Thus, both the Mayan and the Toltec civilizations were extinct or dormant prior to the arrival of Spaniards in the New World.

The Aztec Empire was at its peak of power and size, although there is strong evidence that great internal po-

litical disruptions existed, which would help account for the ease with which it was later conquered by the Spaniards. It is estimated that the Aztec Empire consisted of about five million persons.

During this century of the 1400s, the Incas of South America completed their conquest of a vast area which they ruled under the best-organized political and social structure of pre-Columbian America. The highly regimented Inca state at its greatest extent covered what is now Ecuador, Peru and Bolivia, as well as parts of Chile and Argentina. Throughout this vast area, a network of highways permitted the Incas to exercise tight military and economic control over their empire. Although the Inca Empire never reached the heights of astronomical knowledge and mathematical skill achieved by the Mayans of Central America and the Aztecs of Mexico, it equaled them in engineering and architecture. In addition, Inca woven textiles were unsurpassed.

The Inca emperor was unquestioned ruler over an enormous area of South America, an empire as rigidly controlled and stratified as that of ancient Egypt.

Until recently it was believed that the Incas had no system of writing, but new discoveries have indicated that hidden in their intricate fabric patterns may have been a form of written communication. Quipu, a system of colored strings arranged in a designated order so as to convey a message, was also used as a kind of writing.

In what is now the United States and Canada, there were several distinct areas of human development. The most primitive group were the Eskimos of the Far North, whose existence was based on the hunting of sea mammals. The most advanced peoples were the comparatively highly developed agriculture societies living in the American Southwest, in the valleys of the Mississippi and its tributaries, and in the Southeast. In between these extremes of development were a wide variety of hunting, fishing and food-gathering peoples, ranging from the salmon fishers of northern California, Oregon and Washington to the buffalo hunters of the Great Plains and the hunter-fishers who inhabited woodlands everywhere.

The Indian peoples of North America spoke more than three hundred distinctly different languages. They lived in housing as varied as portable tents (the tepee, made of skins supported by sticks), blocks of ice or snow (the Eskimo igloo), community wooden homes that housed several families (the Iroquois long houses placed behind protecting stockades), and houses made of earth and rocks (the hogan of the Navahos).

All North American Indians lived in the Stone Age. That is to say, they employed tools made only of wood, bone and shell, and did not know the use of metal tools.

In the year 1493, Pope Alexander VI, at the request of the King and Queen of Spain, granted to their Catholic majesties all lands to the south and west of Spain in the direction of India which were not held by Christian rulers prior to Christmas Day 1492, with the exception of the Portuguese-held Azores and Cape Verde Islands. In 1494 the Treaty of Tordesillas, drawn between Spain and Portugal, moved the line of demarcation 270 leagues farther west, thus enabling Portugal to claim the lands comprising modern Brazil. It is a consequence of this treaty that Brazil is the only nation in the Western Hemisphere which claims Portuguese as its native tongue.

THE CRUSADES AND THE AWAKENING OF EUROPE

A Look Back

Beginning with the First Crusade in A.D. 1096, Europeans in great numbers crossed the Mediterranean Sea to war upon the Moslem "infidels." In the process, they learned that the "barbarian" Arabs and even the Turks were far less barbaric and possibly far more cultivated than they had ever imagined. What was perhaps a greater surprise, they learned that their fellow Christians in the city of Constantinople were more cultured than they themselves. These discoveries may have provided a temporary shock to European self-esteem, but their long-term effect was to create strong appetites for the products and the life style of the East, as well as for its science, literature and art, much of which had had its beginnings in Classical Greece and Rome.

Out of these increasing contacts with the Oriental lands grew, at least in part, the European Renaissance—a rebirth of interest in government, art, science and religion, and a new humanistic attitude of man toward himself.

Strangely enough, when toward the end of this four-hundred-year period the Ottoman Turks cut off Europe's contacts with the East, that too had the effect of furthering the Renaissance. There were two reasons for this: first, Europe's merchants were compelled to discover new routes to India and China, an effort which in turn led to important discoveries in the sciences of geography, navigation and shipbuilding; and, second, with the fall of Constantinople to the Ottomans, thousands of Byzantine Greek scholars fled the city to the Italian coasts, taking with them records of the accomplishments of the Greeks and Romans which had been preserved in that great Byzantine city.

The stage was set: Europe was ready to rediscover her own past and move forward into a brilliant, but troubled and uncertain, future.

VII
THE CENTURIES OF EUROPEAN DOMINATION

THE 400 YEARS FROM A.D. 1500 TO 1900

A Look Ahead

At the time America was discovered, Europe was little more than a multitude of nations and principalities loosely held together by a common religion, Christianity, and a common cultural background from Ancient Greece and Rome, and by some experiences shared in the years of the Dark Ages and the Crusades. Yet one or another of these diverse nations of Europe would dominate much of the earth during the next four hundred years. From 1500 to 1900, first Portugal and Spain, then France and Holland, and finally England would rule empires far larger than their homelands and often larger than Ancient Rome's. They would do this by an amazing display of energy, ambition and military skill, augmented by an outpouring of scientific and artistic creativity.

It is noteworthy, and difficult to explain, that as the nations of Europe were rising to world power and becoming increasingly productive in the arts and sciences, the old centers of civilization in Egypt, Babylon and Persia, as well as India and China, were sinking into a period of economic and cultural lethargy from which they have not fully recovered to this day.

But to say that these four centuries from 1500 to 1900 were characterized by the rise of European nations and the decline of the nations of the East is to tell only a small part of a much greater story, a story which paints a magnificent panorama of the strengths and weaknesses of humankind. Most important, such limited statement would fail to reveal what happens when a people begins to question portions of its own long-accepted dogma, religious, moral, intellectual or political; for, to some degree, this is what happened to Europe during these centuries. Abroad, during this period, Europe's strength seemed overwhelming, but on the Continent and in England there was much confusion and self-doubt. Ideas as to the nature of man's relationship to God and to his fellow man caused confusion. Institutions thought to have been inspired and maintained by divine power were questioned and often attacked. In the light of a new "freedom to question," previously held convictions were reevaluated and sometimes replaced.

A series of revolutions, rebellions, and evolutions swept across these Christian lands, beginning in the 1500s and lasting almost until the twentieth century. The history of this four-hundred-year period which we are about to detail—the rise and fall of nations, the wars, the personalities and their accomplishments—must be read against this background of revolution and change. The most important of these revolutions were the following:

The Reformation

Beginning in the 1500s and lasting for at least three hundred years (some historians contend that it is still going on today after five hundred years), Europeans brought into question every phase of established Christian doctrine. Wars were fought over religious details. The outlines of whole nations and even empires shifted with changes in the fortunes of one point of view or another.

The Age of Reason

In the 1600s and 1700s, an intellectual revolution which had its origins in part in the Renaissance and in the Reformation swept over Western Europe. Traditions and principles which had stood for thousands of years were discarded.

Philosophers insisted that reason was the only worthwhile test of truth. Modern scientific methods grew out of this intellectual ferment, as scientists and philosophers in the 1600s and 1700s applied the test of rational thought to their observations of nature. The accuracy of these observations was greatly increased by the development of such instruments as the microscope, the slide rule, the adding machine and the sextant.

The Enlightenment

In the 1700s a wave of self-criticism accompanied by a review of its own institutions swept across Europe. The Enlightenment, as this wave of self-criticism was called, reconsidered much that, in the past, had been too readily accepted. Many things in philosophy, in art and in science were replaced with more humanistic points of view. Both the Enlightenment and the Age of Reason played parts in bringing about the French Revolution.

The English Revolution

In the late 1600s, Englishmen began a new series of successful attacks to limit and restrict the powers of their rulers and to question such long-held beliefs as the divine right of kings. The attacks were led by men who had been inspired and emboldened by ideas arising during the Age of Reason. Out of earlier rebellions Englishmen had evolved the Magna Carta (in 1215). Now in England the Bill of Rights (in 1689) proclaimed a widened agreement as to the prerogative of man to rebel against established order and government.

The American Revolution

The American colonies, in turn, seized upon this "right to rebel" which had been formulated by the English, and turned it back against them. The Revolutionary War (1775–1783) set a pattern which would be followed by most of the nations of South America and many nations in Europe in establishing governments of their own choosing.

The French Revolution

The French Revolution (1789–1799) differed from the American Revolution in that it was a great social upheaval in addition to being a rebellion against an existing government. It violently eradicated from French society many privileges of birth, and it attempted to correct long-standing evils and injustices. Its Declaration of the Rights of Man became the bill of particulars to be used against injustice over all the earth.

The Industrial Revolution

The Industrial Revolution was in fact not a revolution at all, but a slow evolution which took place over 150 years, from 1750 to about 1900. During this evolution, machines replaced the hand tools which had been used by civilized man for thousands of years. As a result, vast quantities of goods could be produced with less effort. Out of the Industrial Revolution developed the production line and, later still, the economic system called capitalism.

The Revolution in Transportation and in Communication

In some ways, the most important of all of these revolutions—the ones that affected human life the most—were the revolutions in the means to travel from place to place on the earth, and in the means to communicate with other men. Great advances in road building, such as were developed by the Scotsman McAdam, contributed greatly to this revolution and were adopted throughout the entire world. Iron railroad tracks were first used in England and soon spread to all of Europe and to the United States. Where transport of men and goods had previously been limited to speeds of ten or fifteen miles an hour, the new steam-driven locomotives could travel fifty miles per hour. Soon gasoline engines would propel vehicles at even greater speeds.

Mechanical power came to the seas also. Prior to its development, sailboats had taken weeks to cross the ocean. Now steam-driven vessels reduced the journey to a matter of days.

Telegraph and submarine cables were laid linking England and Europe to the United States, making possible almost instantaneous communication between the two continents.

The English physicist James Clerk Maxwell and the German physicist-inventor Heinrich Rudolf Hertz did the preliminary work which was to enable the Italian Guglielmo Marconi to make possible instantaneous communication by radio over all the earth. Finally, in the late 1850s, the first power-driven airplanes were designed and flown, and earth distances and travel time were diminished even more.

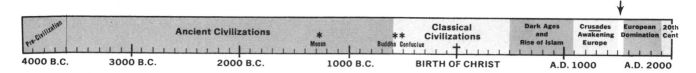

Pre-Civilization	Ancient Civilizations	*Moses	**Buddha Confucius	Classical Civilizations	Dark Ages and Rise of Islam	Crusades Awakening Europe	European Domination	20th Cent

4000 B.C.   3000 B.C.   2000 B.C.   1000 B.C.   BIRTH OF CHRIST   A.D. 1000   A.D. 2000

1500 — 1550

Martin Luther and the Beginnings of Protestantism • The Growth of Spanish Power under Charles V • England Breaks with the Church of Rome • Mogul Conquests in India • Destruction of American Indian Civilizations • Black Slavery in the New World

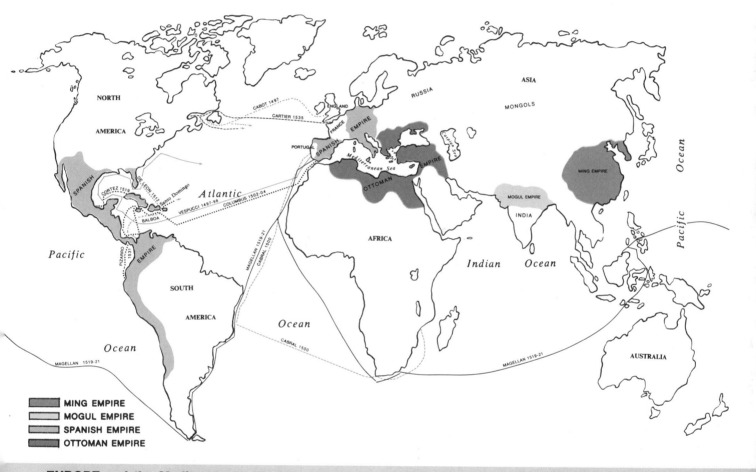

MING EMPIRE
MOGUL EMPIRE
SPANISH EMPIRE
OTTOMAN EMPIRE

EUROPE and the Mediterranean World

The Ottoman Turks followed up their conquests of the previous century by sweeping through Egypt, Syria and most of the other former Arab Moslem lands. Under Suleiman the Magnificent, the Ottomans assumed leadership of the Moslem world and also absorbed ever larger portions of eastern Europe. Hungary and the Balkan Peninsula became a part of the Moslem empire, but Vienna, to which the Turks laid siege in 1529, was saved when valiant resistance by its garrison, combined with miserable weather, caused the Ottomans to withdraw.

Sweden had been occupied by the Danes prior to 1520, when Gustavus Vasa drove them from the land. He was crowned king of Sweden in 1523, and pledged himself to eliminate lawless elements that had long preyed on the nation, and to free the Swedish people from economic oppressions which still remained as a vestige of the old Hanseatic League.

In Germany, Martin Luther, an Augustinian monk, had been greatly disturbed by abuses and corruption within the Church. In 1517 he nailed to a church door his Ninety-five Theses for Church reforms, the most important being elimination of the misuse of indulgences, a means by which a sinner could achieve remission of punishment for his sins. Luther's action precipitated the schism in the Christian Church which divides it to this day. Luther was excommunicated—that is, deprived of his rights of Church membership—and condemned as an outlaw in 1521. The issues he raised split Germany into warring Catholic and Protestant states, and later divided much of the rest of the Christian world.

Martin Luther's translation of the Bible into German, accomplished during the year he remained in hiding in Wartburg Castle, safely out of the reach of Holy Roman Emperor Charles V's men, was so brilliantly done that it became the basis of the modern German language.

In 1536 Martin Luther was joined in his attack on the Roman Catholic Church by another reformer, John Calvin, a Frenchman whose views, while critical of the Church, were less emotional than Luther's and presented a more rigid and systematized theology. The differences between Luther and Calvin would divide the Protestant portion of Christianity. Calvin settled in the city of Geneva, Switzerland, in 1536, and eventually came to rule that city with both a temporal and a religious rule as strong and inflexible as the popes had been accused of exercising in Rome.

King Charles I of Spain, a Hapsburg and grandson of Ferdinand and Isabella, inherited Castile and Aragon from his grandparents, as well as Naples and Sicily in Italy. To him came also by inheritance those lands which are now Holland, Flanders, Austria and Hungary. When, in 1519, he was chosen to head the Holy Roman Empire as Emperor Charles V, he ruled much of Europe as well as Spain's colonies in North and South America. Indeed, his empire at this time was more vast than Ancient Rome's at its greatest extent. However, his reign, despite the treasure that poured in from the New World, was beset with increasing problems. As Holy Roman emperor, Charles V was protector of Rome and the Catholic Church, but in 1527, while fighting the French to retain his lands in Italy, he allowed his troops to sack Rome, the city sacred to Christianity. This affront to the Church and the Pope could only add further strain to the already uncertain relationships within the embattled Church. Spain was eventually to triumph over France in Italy and retain her possession of Naples, Milan and Sicily, but only at great expense of blood and treasure to both nations.

England too was torn by conflict within the Church hierarchy. King Henry VIII had been a loyal Catholic and defender of the faith. He spoke and wrote against the heresies of Martin Luther and other Protestants. In 1535, however, when the Pope refused to dissolve Henry's marriage to Catherine of Aragon, of the powerful ruling family of Spain, Henry had himself declared head of the Church of England by Parliament. He thus, in effect, became "Pope" of the English Church and was able to allow himself a divorce and sanctify his marriage to Anne Boleyn, the second of his six wives and the mother of Queen Elizabeth. His action also freed English Catholics from the authority of Rome, although it was many years before the rifts among the English people caused by Henry's high-handed move were healed.

Henry had been aided by his favorite churchman, Cardinal Thomas Wolsey, in the early years of this maneuvering, but Wolsey's scruples caused him to delay in attaining the results Henry desired and eventually brought about Wolsey's fall from the King's good graces. Wolsey died in disgrace in 1529. Many other outstanding British churchmen protested Henry's action and were executed. Among them were Bishop Fisher and Sir Thomas More, who replaced Wolsey as Henry's favorite. The unscrupulous Thomas Cromwell was next elevated to the position of Henry's chief adviser, and he proceeded to persecute and pillage the Roman Catholic monasteries. Henry died in 1547, survived by his sixth wife, Catherine Parr, and three children—Mary, a Catholic, daughter of Catherine of Aragon; Elizabeth, a Protestant, daughter of Anne Boleyn; and Edward, a Protestant, son of Henry's third wife, Jane Seymour.

As monastery schools were forced to close during the reign of Henry VIII, due to the break between the King and Rome, schools were founded to provide lessons in hunting, hawking and musical instruments, as well as the usual academic subjects, to children of all social classes.

The people of Ireland strongly protested Henry's action in breaking with the Church of Rome, and remained Catholic despite any persuasion or any action he took. As a consequence, the English under Thomas Cromwell destroyed many monasteries and other Church properties in Ireland as in England.

ASIA, except for its Mediterranean Lands

Beginning in 1526, northern India came under the domination of the Moguls. The Moguls (the word, which is sometimes spelled Mughal, is derived from "Mongol") had been headquartered in Kabul, Afghanistan, which they had conquered in the year 1504. Under their leader Babar, a fifth-generation descendant of Tamerlane, these former nomads made a series of raids into the Indian subcontinent and then, in 1525, invaded in force. They conquered northern India as far south as and including area around the city of Agra, south of the city of Delhi. The Mogul Dynasty would dominate India or portions of it for more than three hundred years, from 1526 to 1858, at which date the British Crown would assume formal rule of India. Babar died in 1530 and was succeeded by his son Humayun, who proved to be a weak and indecisive ruler.

A great Indian poet, Tulsi Das (1532–1623) lived and worked under the Moguls during the sixteenth century. His poetry is considered to have been unsurpassed in his time anywhere on earth.

The Portuguese had acquired the city of Goa on the west coast of the Indian subcontinent in 1510 and made it their chief port and trading headquarters. Portuguese ships after 1510 began making regular voyages from Lisbon around Africa to Goa.

In China, the Ming dynasty continued its orderly rule despite the looting of its coastal cities by Japanese pirates. Portuguese traders first arrived in China in the year 1514. The Mings looked upon them as little better than the Japanese pirates. The Portuguese arrived in

Japan twenty-eight years later. In 1549, Christianity was introduced into Japan by the Spanish missionary Saint Francis Xavier.

In the Korean Peninsula, no one faction among those contending for control of the country was strong enough to subdue its rivals and unify the Korean people under its rule. Confucian scholars attempted to settle disputes between local rulers and bring order to the land, but their efforts were largely fruitless.

In Southeast Asia, the Moslem state of Malacca was conquered in 1511 by the Portuguese, who used its strategic location in the chain of islands called the archipelago to control trade. The Portuguese attempted to displant the religion of Islam and replace it with Christianity, but with little success.

In 1521, the Portuguese explorer Ferdinand Magellan, sailing westward under the aegis of Spain, died in the Philippine Islands. His crew continued on, reaching Spain and thus accomplishing the first round-the-world voyage.

In the 1500s civil unrest led to the breakup of Vietnam into several smaller states. The land had been politically unstable for many years, with leaders of various areas vying to impose hegemony over the whole. By the mid-1500s the Trinh family ruled the north; the Nguyen family, the south.

A war between the Burmese and the Tai to gain control of the area that is now Burma began about 1530, and would continue for almost one hundred years, bringing little but suffering to all concerned.

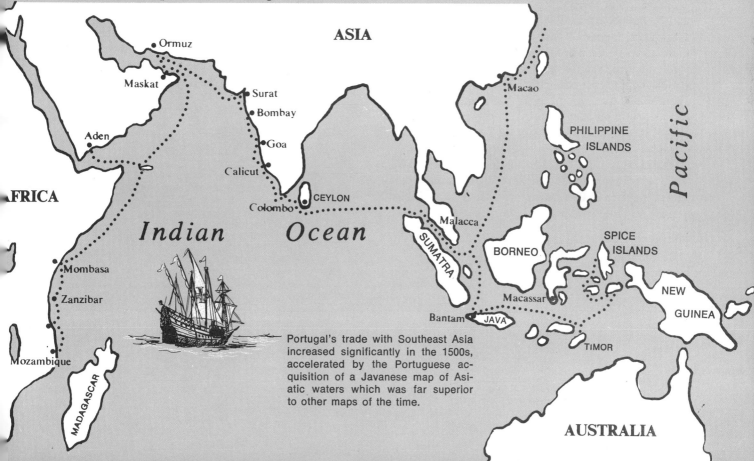

Portugal's trade with Southeast Asia increased significantly in the 1500s, accelerated by the Portuguese acquisition of a Javanese map of Asiatic waters which was far superior to other maps of the time.

AFRICA, except for its Mediterranean Lands

In the 1500s, European nations began to make explorations into Africa with the thought of establishing trading colonies for slaves, ivory and gold. At this time the most prevalent forms of religion in Africa were worship of nature and idols, except in limited areas which had adopted Islam through Arabic or Turkish influence. Christianity was confined to what is now Ethiopia.

THE AMERICAS

During this half century many Spaniards made important explorations and conquests in the New World: Ponce de Leon explored Florida; Vasco Nuñez de Balboa reached the Pacific Ocean by making a land crossing at the Isthmus of Panama; Hernando Cortez invaded and destroyed the Aztec civilization in Mexico; and Francisco Pizarro conquered the Inca civilization of Peru in South America. The remnants of the Mayan civilization fell to the Spaniards shortly thereafter. In less than fifty years, all the great Indian civilizations of the New World had been destroyed. The Spaniards justified their acts by the argument that the Indians were barbarians and pagans and that they brought to them the blessings of Christianity. In exchange, the Spaniards took back to their native land tons of gold and silver.

Other, non-Spanish Europeans also were actively exploring the New World from Newfoundland south to Brazil at this time. John Cabot, a Genoese by birth, in the service of England, and later his son, Sebastian, had probed the northern reaches of North America at the end of the previous century; Pedro Alvares Cabral, a Portuguese, claimed Brazil; Amerigo Vespucci, a Florentine, explored much of South America in the service first of Spain, then, on a later voyage, of Portugal. He had two continents named for him. Jacques Cartier, a Frenchman, discovered the St. Lawrence River. Europeans eagerly probed this newly discovered world, looking for land, treasure and glory for themselves and their royal sponsors.

In the year 1501, the first black slaves from Africa were introduced into the Americas at the Spanish colony on the island of Santo Domingo. Shortly thereafter, black slaves were imported into Central and South America.

Although Francisco Pizarro received a fortune in gold from the Incas, he nonetheless murdered the captive Inca ruler and set up a Spanish government in the city of Lima, which he founded in 1535.

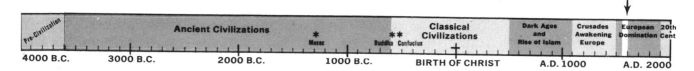

1550 — 1600

The Counter-Reformation • The Defeat of the Spanish Armada by England • The Birth of Holland and Belgium • Copernicus, Galileo, Shakespeare • Europeans in China and Japan • Colonial Activity in the Americas

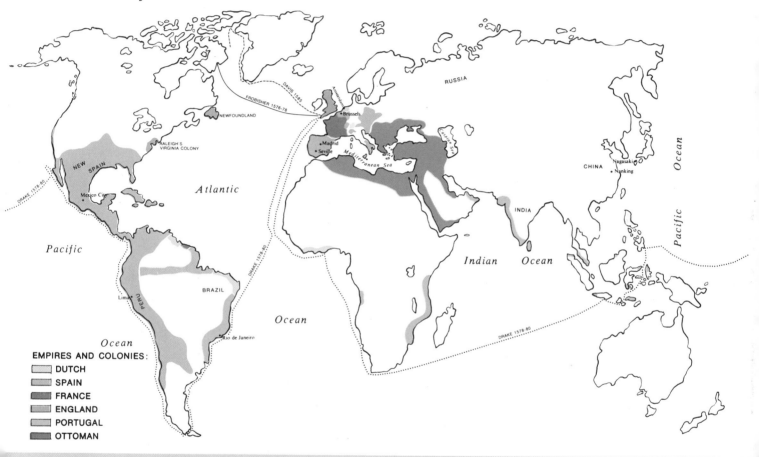

EUROPE and the Mediterranean World

The Ottoman Turks suffered a severe defeat in 1552 at the city of Kazan in Russia at the hands of Ivan the Terrible, one of the last in a line of rulers known as the house of Ruric the Swede. The Turks, however, continued to control much of Eastern Europe, as well as much of the Mediterranean lands of Asia and Africa. In 1565, the Mediterranean island of Malta rebelled and successfully resisted Turkish counterattacks. Subsequently, in 1571, the Ottomans were decisively defeated in the battle of Lepanto by a combination of Spanish, Papal and Venetian ships. This significant victory eased Turkish pressure on Western Europe, but Turkish control of Eastern Europe (Hungary, Greece and the other Balkan lands) and of Mediterranean Africa and Asia continued.

Economically and culturally, the Spanish cities of Seville and Madrid in Europe and of Mexico City in the New World became the most important cities of the earth. Brussels, Antwerp and Amsterdam, Spanish-owned cities of the Lowlands, became great financial centers whose people were very productive in the arts and sciences. The Portuguese line of rulers ended in 1580 with the death of King Henry. Philip II, King of Spain (who had some family claim to the Portuguese throne) sent an army into Lisbon, joined Spain and Portugal under his rule and proclaimed himself King Philip I of Portugal as well as King Philip II of Spain. Thus the two great empires became one.

Spain's art, literature and theater flourished, and its dress and manners were copied throughout Europe.

Within Europe, the voices of reform would not be silenced. A Spaniard, Michael Servetus, in rebellion against Roman Catholic doctrine, denied the existence of the Trinity. There were reformers who wished to burn all religious images and others who desired to establish a church without priests. Huldreich Zwingli, a Swiss reformer in the city of Zurich, protested against the veneration of saints and against such Church practices as the selling of indulgences, or pardons for sins, given (often without the knowledge of Rome) in return for gold or services.

John Calvin, although born in France, had set up in Geneva, Switzerland, as previously noted, a variety of reforms which rested on his own interpretation of the Gospels. The "Pope of Geneva," as he was sometimes called, more than rivaled the Pope of Rome and the Spaniards in their application of the Inquisition, the tribunal formed to investigate heresy. Like them, he used spies and informers in his own inquisition to seek out heretics, and, like them also, he meted out punishments to discourage others from following their example.

Spain and Italy, by and large, held fast to Roman Catholic dogma, but elsewhere, particularly in parts of Germany, the reformers brought about great religious upheavals and even civil wars. Northern Germany became Lutheran, and western Germany Calvinist, but Austria remained steadfast in its adherence to Rome.

Spain, as the champion of Roman Catholicism, unleashed during this half century the ruthless ferocity of the Inquisition in the lands under her control, in order to bring Protestants and dissenters to heel. She also took to the field against all nations or parts of nations which had adopted or had sheltered reform, and against non-Christian allies of Protestant states, such as the Turks, to whom these nations turned for help.

Ultimately, Spain found that she could not suppress the forces of religious revolt, forces which were often thinly disguised political upheavals. Religious rebellion in the Lowlands became political rebellion by means of which Holland and Belgium eventually wrenched themselves free of Spain. Out of these revolts the Dutch Republic was founded, and the Dutch Navy grew strong enough to compete with the navies of Spain and England; however, Spain did not officially recognize Dutch independence until the next century.

In 1545 the Papal Council of Trent was convened by Pope Paul III, to formulate a counterblow at the Reformation. Through the Council, the Roman Church tried to reestablish control over the peoples of Europe. The Council, which met intermittently until 1563, attempted to reunify the Church and to reaffirm Catholic dogma, and it reconfirmed the Inquisition's powers to punish heresy.

The reformed church in England, which was called the Anglican Church, differed little from the Roman Catholic Church in practice and belief. The Anglican Church, however, was headed by the English king or queen, not by the Roman pope. Roman Catholicism was restored briefly in England by Queen Mary, who succeeded her Protestant half brother Edward VI on the throne in 1553. During her reign there was much persecution of Protestants, and at her death in 1558 both she and her religion were unpopular. She was succeeded by her half sister, Elizabeth, who restored Anglican Protestantism as the official religion of England.

France remained largely Catholic, but French kings occasionally supported Protestant nations, despite their religious heresies, if they were anti-Spanish politically. Within France, roving bands representing Catholic or Protestant points of view fought what amounted to a terrible civil war. In the Saint Bartholomew's Day Massacre, which began in Paris on August 24, 1572, thousands of French Protestants known as Huguenots were killed by Catholics. In the name of religion and Christ, Europe had entered upon a century-long madness of mutual condemnation and slaughter among individuals, families and nations.

The Protestant Henry of Navarre became King Henry IV of France in 1589 and then became a Catholic in order to gain control of the city of Paris. Under Henry's excellent rule, the Edict of Nantes was formulated in 1598 to guarantee religious toleration to the Protestant Huguenots and to give them control of many fortified towns.

Many Catholics thought that Mary Stuart, Queen of Scots, Catholic granddaughter of Henry VIII's older sister, had a better claim than Elizabeth to the throne of England. When Mary Stuart fled to England after having been forced to abdicate the throne of Scotland, her presence was looked upon as a threat to the peace

The reign of Elizabeth I in England was marked not only by widespread exploration and extension of empire, but by a flowering of the arts which saw the great William Shakespeare performing in his own plays in the theaters of London.

of the realm. As a result, she was kept virtually a prisoner for many years and was finally executed. During Elizabeth's reign, the English defeated the supposedly "Invincible" Armada of two hundred Spanish ships which were sent in 1588 to invade England, depose Elizabeth and reinstate Catholicism. England's victory and Elizabeth's capable and wise rule made possible the nation's future rule of the seas and its subsequent rise to world power.

A rebellion in Ireland during Elizabeth's reign was put down, and the Irish people were severely punished. The (Protestant) Church of England was designated the official church of Ireland. Catholics were denied the right to hold office, and Catholic lands were given, in many cases, to English nobles.

Poland, in 1577, became an elective monarchy when, on the death of Sigismund II, its ruling dynasty came to an end.

In Russia, after the reign of Ivan the Terrible and that of his son Fedor I, the Ruric Dynasty ended. Boris Godunov seized the throne in 1598 and ruled until 1605.

During the 1500s, the Renaissance in Europe continued in the midst of war, colonization and church reform. Again, just a listing of great writers, artists and scientists of this one-hundred-year period requires selections which will leave out many names as noteworthy as those included. In the sciences three great astronomers, Nicolaus Copernicus of Poland (1473–1543), Tycho Brahe of Denmark (1546–1601), and Johannes Kepler (1571–1630), laid the basis for modern astronomy and for the theories of Isaac Newton which were to follow in the 1600s. Galileo of Italy (1564–1642) developed the experimental method which based its conclusions on careful experiment and observation rather than solely upon intellectual examination; Galileo could well have been included with the above triumvirate of great astronomers, but his contributions in

other areas of science were so many that his fame cannot be confined to any one field. Gerhardus Mercator of Flanders (1512–1594) made immense contributions to mapmaking and founded modern cartography. William Harvey, an Englishman (1578–1657), demonstrated the fact that the blood circulates within the body rather than "ebbing and flowing," a hypothesis which had previously been accepted.

Galileo, the Italian scientist who was the first to examine the heavens through a telescope, cast doubt upon theories about the moon, the planets and the Milky Way which heretofore had satisfied men for hundreds of years.

In the fields of letters, the Italian autobiographer Benvenuto Cellini (1500–1571), the Italian epic poet Torquato Tasso (1544–1595), the German songwriter Hans Sachs (1494–1576), the great Portuguese poet Luis Vaz de Camoëns (1524–1580), two great French prose stylists, François Rabelais (1495–1553) and Michel de Montaigne (1533–1592), the great Spanish novelist Miguel de Cervantes (1547–1616), the prolific Spanish dramatist Lope de Vega (1562–1635), and, of course, the incomparable William Shakespeare (1564–1616), poet and dramatist whose appeal has extended to men and women of all nations and all classes for the past four hundred years—all these must be included on any list, no matter how brief.

The printing press and movable type made possible the production of books in large quantities, thus accelerating the spread of knowledge throughout Europe.

In the visual arts, at least a dozen great Italians must be represented here by the painters Titian (1490–1576) and Tintoretto (1518–1594), and by the sculptor and goldsmith Benvenuto Cellini (1500–1571), who also wrote a famous autobiography. The paintings of the German Hans Holbein the Younger (1497–1543), of the Flemish Peter Paul Rubens (1577–1640), and of El Greco (1541–1614), who was born in Crete but did his best work while living in Spain, all give an idea of the universality of European art during this sixteenth century.

Renaissance architecture saw much of Classical Greece and Rome combined with the Gothic style of the preceding period. That the great Italian Andrea Palladio (1508–1580) did much research into the Classical past is evident from his own work and also from that of later architects who learned from him. This century's outstanding building must be St. Peter's Basilica in Rome, begun by Bramante just prior to his death in 1514, and furthered by Michelangelo in the sixteenth century.

ASIA, except for its Mediterranean Lands

In India in 1556, Akbar, grandson of Babar, the founder of the Mogul Dynasty, ascended to the throne. He reorganized the government into efficient administrative units, redesigned the tax structure along more equitable lines, and instituted many social reforms. Akbar also became renowned as a patron of the arts and as an able and tolerant emperor.

In 1580, during Akbar's reign, the first Jesuit mission was established at the Mogul city of Agra. Christianity, Hinduism, Islam, Jainism all were given friendly receptions by this remarkable ruler, who was an ardent student of all religions. In 1582, Akbar decreed a new religion of his own design to be the official faith of his empire, but it won only limited support which faded away upon his death.

In China, during the second half of the sixteenth century, Ming rule survived despite attacks in 1550 from the north by steppe people known as the Ordos, and by Japanese pirates who became audacious enough to attack even the city of Nanking in 1555, and also, in 1592 and 1597, to invade Korea, which was under the hegemony of China. The Ming rule, although greatly weakened during this period, survived the efforts of Christian missionaries to proselytize the Chinese people and of Europeans to dominate Chinese trade. In 1557, however,

Portuguese merchant-sailors conquered the island of Macao, located just off China's coast.

Japan went through a forty-year period of national reunification, beginning in 1560 under Oda Nobunaga, who made himself dictator of the central part of the nation. By 1590 Nobunaga's successors had welded Japan into a unified whole, although the Emperor as always remained the nation's nominal ruler.

Japan began to evidence great expansive energy. Japanese naval pirates continued to be active in Chinese, Siamese and Philippine waters. The Japanese twice attempted to invade Korea, and thereby came into close contact with both Chinese and European traders. In the year 1570, the Japanese fishing village of Nagasaki was opened to foreign trade and soon became a great port. There was an exuberant spirit of progress within the land—almost a renaissance of cultural and intellectual activities. Christianity was introduced into Japan during this half century by Saint Francis Xavier and others. These missionaries were well received at first, but the missionaries' rigid intolerance of other religions inspired a bitter reaction from the government and the usually friendly Buddhists. Eventually these frictions, plus highhanded treatment of the Japanese by European sailors, led to persecution of the Christians in Japan.

OCEANIA

The city of Manila on Luzon Island in the Philippines was founded by Spanish colonists in the year 1571. By 1595 the first Dutch trading vessels began visiting the other islands and coasts of Oceania and Southeast Asia.

AFRICA, except for its Mediterranean Lands

The empire of Kanem-Bornu came into the peak of its power in the Lake Chad region in the years between 1571 and 1603. The empire had been in existence since the last decades of the 1100s. In 1591 Moslems from Morocco invaded the Songhai kingdom, and this last Negro-ruled empire of West Africa, along with its great city of Timbuktu, came under foreign domination.

In 1595, Dutch settlements were founded on Africa's Guinea coast.

THE AMERICAS

After the destruction of the Aztec and Inca civilizations, the Spaniards proceeded to colonize the vast lands of Central and South America. They brought their culture to the New World and attempted to convert the natives to Christianity.

Two great universities were founded in the Americas in the second half of this century: the University of Mexico in New Spain, as Mexico was then called, and the University of San Marcos in Lima, Peru. Shortly thereafter, the city of Rio de Janeiro was established in Brazil by the Portuguese.

Exploration of the world by Europeans continued in the second half of the century. Voyages were made to seek out a northeast passage to India by Richard Chancellor and to locate the northwest passage by Martin Frobisher and John Davis, all of England. Sir Francis Drake, also of England, made the second voyage around the world. An English colony was founded in Newfoundland in 1583, and in 1584 a short-lived colony was founded in Virginia by Sir Walter Raleigh. In 1586–1588 Thomas Cavendish, an Englishman, made the third circumnavigation of the globe, and in 1591 James Lancaster made the first English voyage to the East Indies, which led to the formation of the East India Company by British merchants-speculators.

Europeans learned about the New World from copies of artists' drawings such as this one of an Indian village in Virginia.

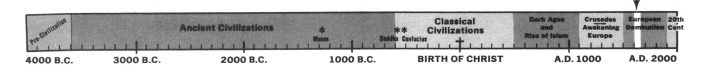

Pre-Civilization	Ancient Civilizations	*Moses	**Buddha Confucius	Classical Civilizations	Dark Ages and Rise of Islam	Crusades Awakening Europe	European Domination 20th Cent

4000 B.C.   3000 B.C.   2000 B.C.   1000 B.C.   BIRTH OF CHRIST   A.D. 1000   A.D. 2000

1600 — 1650

The Thirty Years' War • Oliver Cromwell: "Lord Protector of the Commonwealth" • The Romanov Dynasty in Russia • European Nations Compete for World Trade • The Manchu Dynasty in China

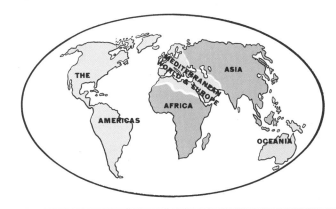

EUROPE and the Mediterranean World

The Thirty Years' War began as a continuation of the religious strife in the Holy Roman Empire. It ended with an alliance of Catholic and Protestant nations fighting a coalition of still other Catholic and Protestant nations. At the war's start in 1618, the Empire was again attempting to suppress Bohemian Protestants. By 1635, however, the conflict had broadened into a general European war, with Sweden (Protestant), France (Catholic) and Holland (Protestant) aligned against a coalition of Germans (Protestant) and Austria and Spain (both Catholic). It ended in 1648 with the Treaty of Westphalia. Germany was reduced to a weak federation of about three hundred states, Spanish power was beginning to decline, and France was well on the way to being Europe's strongest nation. Sweden's militarily brilliant King Gustavus Adolphus was killed in battle in 1632, after which France's wily minister, the great Cardinal Richelieu, led his nation to military predominance and made important territorial acquisitions, the most important of which was the province of Alsace, formerly a German barony. Richelieu fostered commercial development in France and built up the state by weakening the power of the nobles.

Prior to the war, in 1610, France had come under the rule of a nine-year-old, Louis XIII, with Cardinal Richelieu serving as the boy king's all-powerful chief minister. Louis XIII was succeeded in 1643 by five-year-old Louis XIV, who would rule until 1715, a period of seventy-two years comprising the longest reign in modern European history and, in many ways, one of the most successful. During the early years (even after the

King had reached his majority) the government was conducted by Cardinal Mazarin, who served in a position similar to Richelieu's under the preceding king.

Cardinal Richelieu used his great influence to rally the people of Paris to support the King of France's armies when German and Spanish troops marched through France to make an attack upon Paris itself.

In Britain, the accession to the throne in 1603 of James I (son of Mary Queen of Scots) joined England and Scotland under one monarch, but left their governments and churches separated. James firmly believed that he ruled by divine right. He was in constant conflict with his Parliament, often ruling without it and imposing his will as he saw fit. His quarrels with a Protestant group called Puritans drove many of them to emigrate to the Netherlands in 1608, and later, in 1620, to the New World, where they founded what came to be called the New England colonies.

James I had Sir Walter Raleigh executed after a Raleigh-led expedition up the Orinoco River in Venezuela ended in failure, and after Sir Walter disobeyed orders and became involved in battle with the Spaniards in Guiana.

In 1625 James I was succeeded by his son, Charles I, who attempted to continue his father's high-handed policies. Parliament rebelled, however, and by 1642 there was open civil war between the Crown and Parliament which led to royal defeat at the hands of Parliamentary forces commanded by the Puritan Oliver Cromwell, and eventually to the beheading of Charles in 1649. England now became a republic and was called the Commonwealth. Beginning in 1653, however, Cromwell ruled as a virtual dictator, with the title "Lord Protector."

Repression of Irish Catholics became very severe under James I, Charles I and Cromwell. During these periods, northern Ireland was colonized by Scotsmen. Most of the land was held by Protestants, but most of the people were Catholic. The Irish rebelled time and again, and each time the rebellion was crushed and the leaders were punished.

During this half century, Spain finally recognized Dutch independence, and gave halfhearted acquiescence (but not recognition) to that of Portugal and of Catalonia (Barcelona), both of which were under Spanish hegemony. In Russia, Michael Romanov was elevated to the throne in 1613, thus founding the great Romanov Dynasty which was to rule Russia for three hundred years, until its collapse in 1917 in the midst of World War I.

ASIA, except for its Mediterranean Lands

The English "East India Company" was given a charter by Queen Elizabeth in 1600. Its purpose was to promote trade and to colonize India and other parts of Asia. By the end of the century it had established or gained control of trading cities along the coasts of the subcontinent, most important of which were Calcutta on the east coast, Madras on the southeast coast, and Bombay on the west coast. Similar companies to promote trade in India and the Far East were formed by France, Holland and Portugal.

Akbar, the Mogul Emperor of India, died in 1605 and was succeeded by his son Jahangir, who managed to maintain the empire in the north. However, as a result of his addiction to drink and opium, he permitted power to pass into the hands of Nur Jahan, one of the women of his harem. The entire empire was swept by a serious epidemic identified later as bubonic plague.

In 1628, Shah Jahan became Mogul emperor and ruled with seeming indifference to his subjects' welfare. The famed Taj Mahal was built by Shah Jahan as a tomb for his wife.

In the Far East, the Manchus, a group of tribes of eastern Manchuria, combined their military might and began to expand into neighboring lands. By 1627 the Manchus had conquered Korea. By 1644 they had begun a campaign which would destroy Ming resistance in China. The Manchu Dynasty was to last until 1911 and was to bring China to new heights of culture, economy and population.

About 1600, at the request of the Emperor, Japan came under the rule of the Tokugawa shogunate, with the shogun no longer a puppet ruler but in a position of real leadership, and established its capital at the city of Edo, later called Tokyo. The city quickly became the nation's economic and cultural center as well as its political headquarters. The Tokugawa shogunate led Japan into a period of internal prosperity. It developed a very conservative political outlook which was both anti-Christian and strongly isolationist. In the year 1633, foreigners were being expelled from Japan; by the late 1630s only a few Chinese and Dutch merchants were permitted to remain. As in all previous shogunates, the

The Taj Mahal, constructed entirely of white marble and said to be one of the world's most beautiful buildings, was designed by Mogol Emperor Shah Jahan as a tribute to his wife.

prestige of the imperial family was carefully preserved.

In Southeast Asia, companies formed by the British, the Dutch and the French were competing for the trade in the Indonesian area, with Dutch merchants and colonizers gaining the ascendancy. By 1619, Dutch merchants had established the city of Batavia (now called Jakarta) as their headquarters and were driving the British out of the area.

By 1641, the strategically located Malacca Straits were in Dutch hands, and in 1642 Abel Janszoon Tasman, an adventurous Dutch sea captain, reported sighting the west coast of what would later be called New Zealand.

Dutch art benefited greatly from the painting of family portraits of wealthy Dutchmen who had made enormous fortunes in trade with Southeast Asia.

AFRICA, except for its Mediterranean Lands

The slave trade, which was to send millions of black people from Africa to the New World, was expanding rapidly during this half century. During this period, black African dealers lured or captured their fellow blacks from the interior and sold them to Christian and Moslem merchants. Most of the transporting of the slaves to the Americas to be resold was done, however, by white Europeans.

THE AMERICAS

By the middle of the 1600s, the Portuguese had established their supremacy in Brazil and had driven out French and Dutch colonists. Much of Latin America had already been colonized when, in 1607, the first permanent English settlement was established in America at Jamestown, Virginia. A few years later, in 1619, a Dutch warship brought the first black slaves to North America and sold them in Jamestown; but, as previously noted, Negro slaves had been used by the Spaniards in the Spanish colonies as early as 1501.

In 1608, just one year after the founding of Jamestown, the city of Quebec was established by the French explorer Samuel de Champlain. Shortly thereafter, in 1620, the English Puritans founded Plymouth in New England, and five years later, in 1625, the Dutch built New Amsterdam, afterward to be renamed New York by the British.

Harvard, the first college in what was to become the United States, was established in Massachusetts in 1636.

The Dutch merchants of New Amsterdam, unlike the British who later took over their colony, were primarily interested in the fur trade with the Indians rather than in Colonial settlement and development.

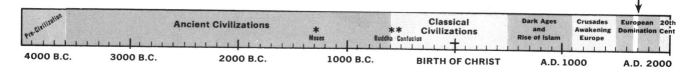

Pre-Civilization	Ancient Civilizations	Classical Civilizations	Dark Ages and Rise of Islam	Crusades Awakening Europe	European Domination	20th Cent

4000 B.C.   3000 B.C.   2000 B.C.   1000 B.C.   BIRTH OF CHRIST   A.D. 1000   A.D. 2000

1650 — 1700

The Decline of Spain and the Rise of France • The Westernization of Russia • William and Mary Rule Britain • Newton, Milton, Molière, Rembrandt • The Manchu Dynasty at Its Height • The French Explore the Mississippi River System

EUROPE and the Mediterranean World

Beginning about 1650, the Ottoman Turks renewed their campaigns against the Christian countries to the west. They attacked Poland, but were decisively defeated in 1673 by Polish armies led by a nobleman, General Jan Sobieski. The General became king of Poland in 1676, and during his reign much of the territory previously captured by the Ottomans was restored to Poland.

The Turks moved against Vienna, but in 1683 were defeated here also, this time by Polish and imperial troops headed by Sobieski and Duke Charles of Lorraine. In 1697 another Turkish drive was defeated by imperial forces under Prince Eugene of Savoy at the battle of Zenta, in what is now Yugoslavia. The Treaty of Karlowitz (1699), in which Austria, Poland, Venice and the Turks participated, gave Turkish-held Hungary and several Slavic states to Austria, the Ukraine and other nearby lands to Poland, and southern Greece to Venice.

At this time, Brandenburg-Prussia (later known simply as Prussia) was consolidating its several ducal states into a centralized realm under Elector Frederick William. (The title "elector" was given to German princes who had the right to take part in choosing the Holy Roman Emperor.) Frederick William maintained a standing army so powerful that Prussia became a force in Europe to be constantly reckoned with. His son Elector Frederick III, who succeeded him in 1688, continued with brilliant success the work of building an efficiently organized military state. The rest of Germany remained weak and divided. Only Austria appeared capable of withstanding Prussia's drive to dominate the other German peoples.

Peter the Great, Czar of Russia from 1689 to 1725, began the gigantic task of converting his country, with its historical and cultural ties to the Near East, into a modern European nation. Every facet of Russian life—economic, political, educational, financial, military—

came under the Czar's demanding scrutiny and energetic determination to Westernize his heretofore backward realm.

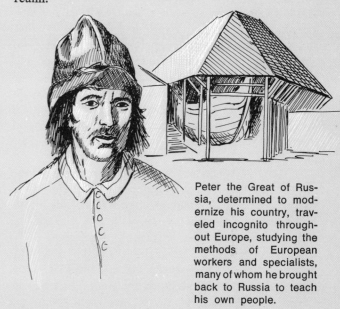

Peter the Great of Russia, determined to modernize his country, traveled incognito throughout Europe, studying the methods of European workers and specialists, many of whom he brought back to Russia to teach his own people.

Sweden's throne, after Gustavus Adolphus' death in the Thirty Years' War, had passed to his daughter, Christina, and then to Charles X. Between 1660 and 1697, Charles XI, a strong and competent ruler, solved many of Sweden's domestic and foreign problems, leaving upon his death a well-organized nation with a steady flow of needed revenue, protected by a competent army. At this time, Sweden controlled the Baltic seaports and stood as a barrier there to Russia's natural outlets to the sea.

The Dutch merchant fleet aroused growing concern in England for the prosperity of British carriers. As a result, the Navigation Acts were passed in 1651 by Parliament, prohibiting the shipment of goods into British ports in vessels other than those of Britain or of the nation producing them. The issue of mercantile supremacy preoccupied the two countries for many years, leading to intermittent warfare.

England was ruled, beginning in 1653, by a form of government called the Protectorate, headed by Oliver Cromwell, who was called "Lord Protector." The Protectorate functioned under a written constitution and enjoyed strong support from a standing army of thirty thousand men. In 1654, Parliament quarreled with Cromwell, who then proceeded to dissolve it, as provided in the constitution. The Lord Protector did not call for new Parliamentary elections, however. Cromwell died in 1658 and his son, Richard Cromwell, became lord protector. A new Parliament met in January of 1659, but, following a dispute with the army, it too was dissolved. In May 1659, however, the Parliament came together unofficially and induced Richard Cromwell to resign. The following year a "Convention Parliament" of 556 members invited Charles II, son of the executed Charles I, to return from exile and proclaimed him king.

The new King governed much as his father had done, but managed to avoid open breaks with Parliament. Major points of contention between Charles II and Parliament were that Charles appointed Catholics to office and also strongly favored support of France's European policy, which aimed at French domination of Spain and at French control of Spain's former lands of Holland and Flanders. Parliament, on the other hand, wanted to go to war with France in opposition to this policy.

In 1665, the dread plague (which periodically had decimated parts of the Continent) swept across England, killing as much as a fourth of the population. A year later, in 1666, fire devastated large areas of the city of London. St. Paul's Cathedral and many other churches and public buildings were rebuilt later by the architect Sir Christopher Wren, who also planned the wide avenues which characterize London today.

Charles II's brother, James II, succeeded him in 1685. James had strong Roman Catholic leanings. His autocratic actions aroused so much antagonism that he was forced to abdicate three years later. As a result, the English people, through their Parliament, again had an indirect voice in selecting their own ruler. James's Protestant elder daughter, Mary, was in Holland, married to William of Orange, also a Protestant, who was leading the Dutch people in their effort to repel the attacks of Louis XIV of France on the Low Countries. An invitation was sent by Parliament to William and Mary, proposing that they be the joint sovereigns of England. The abdicated King James fled to France, and William and Mary (1689–1702) assumed the throne without bloodshed in what has been called the Glorious Revolution. England and Holland, now united through a common sovereign, joined forces in a war against France that lasted from 1680 to 1697, and William of Orange and Mary ended the attempts by Louis XIV to make Holland a part of the French kingdom.

Despite such occasional setbacks as her defeat by England and Holland in 1697, France had become the most powerful nation of Europe and would remain so throughout the 1700s. This was due in part to her renowned King, Louis XIV, who had succeeded to the throne in 1643, at the age of five, and had assumed personal control of the government in 1661. The reform of the French administrative system, the abolition of tariffs on domestic trade, the building of canals and roads and the development of a well-disciplined army were among the accomplishments of this monarch's reign.

The Palace of Versailles, lavish setting for the extravagant court of King Louis XIV, became the cultural center of Europe and a model for palaces in other European capitals.

France's geographic location on both the Mediterranean Sea and the Atlantic Ocean was also a significant factor in her climb to power, as was the decline of Spain, her old enemy. In fact, as Spanish power waned and France was freed from the danger of attack along her entire southern border, Spain became so subordinated to France that Spanish strength at times could be manipulated to augment that of France. By the end of this period even the throne of Spain was occupied by a Bourbon, a member of the French ruling family, when the Duke of Anjou was crowned King Philip V of Spain in the year 1700. All of Europe now became concerned about the overwhelming power which could result if the two nations should unite under one crown.

During this period, France was the most populous nation of Europe, with approximately nineteen million persons, as compared to six million in England and Scotland combined, and perhaps five million in Spain. What is more, France was to suffer no revolutions and see no war fought on her own soil for more than 150 years—a singular blessing indeed. Just as Spain's culture and way of life had spread to every European and many non-European nations in the 1500s and early 1600s, so now French culture, language and dress would spread over much of the civilized earth. The French tongue, for a second time (the first was in the 1200s), would become the spoken language of the courts of Europe as well as of diplomats everywhere. In addition, French replaced Latin as the writing vehicle of men of letters, just as Latin in its day had, to some degree, replaced Greek.

The spread of French culture was given a special impetus in the late 1600s when almost a quarter of a million French Huguenots fled their native land to avoid persecution. Their exodus resulted from the repeal by Louis XIV of the Edict of Nantes, which had heretofore guaranteed Protestants freedom of worship. With them the Huguenots took from France to Holland, Germany, England and other countries not only a great deal of material wealth, but much of French culture and technological competence.

The 1600s saw a continuation of the explosion of scientific and artistic activities called the Renaissance. Two giants of philosophy and science, a Frenchman residing in Holland, René Descartes (1596–1650), and an Englishman, Isaac Newton (1642–1727), originated methods of mathematical analysis and new approaches to the basic understanding of the physical sciences which would place them in the front ranks of significant contributors to man's store of knowledge. Other giants in these fields were the philosopher-mathematicians Gottfried Wilhelm Leibniz of Germany (1646–1716) and Blaise Pascal (1623–1662) of France, and the physicists Robert Boyle (1627–1691) of Ireland and Evangelista Torricelli (1608–1647) of Italy.

In the field of letters, dozens of truly fine writers achieved lasting renown. In prose one must include the pioneer in international law Hugo Grotius (1583–1645) of Holland, whose *De Jure Belli et Pacis* (*On the Law of War and Peace*) is outstanding; the philosopher Baruch Spinoza (1632–1677), also of Holland, whose *Tractatus Theologico-Politicus (Treatise on Theology and Politics)* is a good example of his several important works; three prose stylists of England, John Bunyan (1628–1688), noted for his *Pilgrim's Progress,* Daniel Defoe (1660–1731), author of *Moll Flanders* among other fine works, and Samuel Pepys (1633–1703), noted for his *Pepys Diary;* and two outstanding French writers, the great orator Jacques Bossuet (1627–1704), whose *Oraisons Funèbres (Funeral Orations)* are good examples of his work, and François de La Rochefoucauld (1613–1680) whose *Maximes* epitomize his wit and profundity.

Among poets there were John Milton (1608–1674) of England, whose *Paradise Lost* dominated poetry in the seventeenth century, and Jean de La Fontaine (1621–1695) of France, whose *Fables* are noted for their satire and their tolerance. In drama there were the French poet-playwrights Pierre Corneille (1606–1684), whose *Le Cid* and *La Mort de Pompée* illustrate his originality and skill, and Jean Racine (1639–1699), noted for his *Andromaque* and his *Britannicus* among other works, and the Spaniard Pedro Calderón de la Barca (1600–1681), also a poet-dramatist, many of whose more than one hundred plays are still performed. Molière (1622–1673), of France, is renowned for his many comedies, outstanding of which perhaps are *L'École des Femmes (School for Wives)* and *Tartuffe,* the latter a satire on religious hypocrisy.

In art, two Spaniards, Diego Velázquez (1599–1660) and Esteban Murillo (1618–1682), three Hollanders, Rembrandt van Rijn (1606–1669), Frans Hals (1580–1666) and Jan Vermeer (1632–1675), and the Flemish-born Anthony Vandyke (1599–1641) all demonstrated again that the cradle of great art was no longer confined to Italy.

Modern ballet developed in France in the 1600s, built upon ancient Greek, Roman and Italian foundations. Professional dancers, musicians and dramatists performed at court during the years of Louis XIV. Ballet reached a peak in Paris when the Sun King, as Louis was called, founded the Royal Academy of the Dance.

Isaac Newton, hailed as the greatest genius of his time, set forth in his *Principia* the three laws of motion and the mathematical formula describing gravitation, the attraction that exists between all forms of matter.

ASIA, except for its Mediterranean Lands

Aurangzeb, one of the four sons of Shah Jahan, became the head of the Mogul Empire in India in 1658. Under him the Mogul power and the empire's stability were greatly undermined, due to his almost pathological distrust of subordinates and his persecution of Hindus and other non-Moslems. Hindu uprisings as well as conflicts with the Sikhs (who had come full cycle from extreme tolerance to great militancy) tore at the empire's unity.

Aurangzeb made attempts also to expel the British from their strongholds in the subcontinent, but, when he succeeded, the decline in the once profitable trade caused an abrupt reversal of this policy. Indeed, the spread of British power was further augmented by the vacuum left by lessening activities of the Portuguese in the rich Bengal area of northeast India and in Bombay on the west coast—a vacuum which English merchants quickly filled. These expanding activities brought British rivalry with French traders in India to a critical point.

In China, a great ruler of the Manchu Dynasty, the Emperor K'ang-hsi (who reigned from 1662 to 1722), made determined efforts to elevate the general level of prosperity of his subjects, and to eliminate such customs as the binding of women's feet. The emperor was responsible for the construction of many public works and the sponsorship of many artists and writers. In 1689 the Treaty of Nerchinsk, the first pact between China and a

Western nation, was concluded. It fixed the Sino–Russian boundary and made a beginning of trade arrangements between the two empires. Yet, despite these progressive attitudes, some distrust of foreigners persisted in China, and European merchants were confined to the Portuguese-held city of Macao on an island just off the coast. However, Jesuit scholars were widely admired and were welcomed to the Emperor's court.

Japan's Tokugawa shogunate continued to rule from the city of Edo. Japanese cultural activities were largely free of Chinese influence under the Tokugawa. A new form of poetry called haiku became widespread, as did the kabuki theater and a wide variety of puppet plays. All are still popular in Japan today. In 1657, a great fire destroyed most of the capital city of Edo, including the palace and surrounding buildings.

In Southeast Asia, European powers continued to vie for commercial advantage, with the Dutch seemingly gaining a predominant position. The interaction between European and Asian peoples and between their religions was both having a profound cultural influence on Southeast Asia and causing ill-feelings and rifts that are unhealed to this day.

Emperor K'ang-hsi, despite his distrust of most Europeans, so encouraged Jesuit missionaries, even using them as tutors for his own children, that by 1700 there were approximately 200,000 Chinese Catholics in China.

AFRICA, except for its Mediterranean Lands

There was continuing activity by English, Dutch, Italian and French merchants along the coasts of Africa in locations suitable for the establishment of trade with the interior. In 1652, Capetown was founded by the Dutch on the continent's southeastern tip, and in 1697 French colonists led by André de Brue completed the conquest of the Senegal River on Africa's westernmost bulge, near modern Gambia.

THE AMERICAS

The Frenchmen Jacques Marquette and Louis Jolliet were exploring what today is called the Midwest of the United States. In 1673 they followed the Fox and Wisconsin Rivers westward to the Mississippi River, and then explored the Mississippi south to its confluence with the Arkansas River. Another Frenchman, Robert de La Salle, reached the mouth of the Mississippi River in 1682 and claimed the entire area in the name of the King of France. His attempts to found a colony in this area (named Louisiana after Louis XIV) ended in failure due to difficult climatic conditions and to the hazards of bringing supplies into the area.

The Navigation Acts passed by the English Parliament in the years 1651, 1660, 1663, 1673 and 1696 were designed primarily to control trade and shipping to and from the New World. These acts, which often were to the economic disadvantage of the English colonists, are felt to have been a major cause of the American Revolution a century later.

In the year 1681 William Penn founded the colony of Pennsylvania, and in 1692 the notorious witchcraft trials in which more than twenty persons were hanged as witches were held in Salem, Massachusetts. William and Mary College, named after the British sovereigns (the second college in what is now the United States), was founded in Virginia in the year 1693.

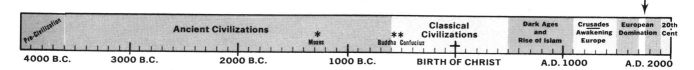

| Pre-Civilization | Ancient Civilizations | *Moses | **Buddha Confucius | Classical Civilizations | Dark Ages and Rise of Islam | Crusades Awakening Europe | European Domination | 20th Cent |

4000 B.C.   3000 B.C.   2000 B.C.   1000 B.C.   BIRTH OF CHRIST   A.D. 1000   A.D. 2000

1700 — 1750

The War of the Spanish Succession • Frederick the Great of Prussia • French and British Rivalry in India • Restrictive British Colonial Policy in North America • Expanding American Frontier Life

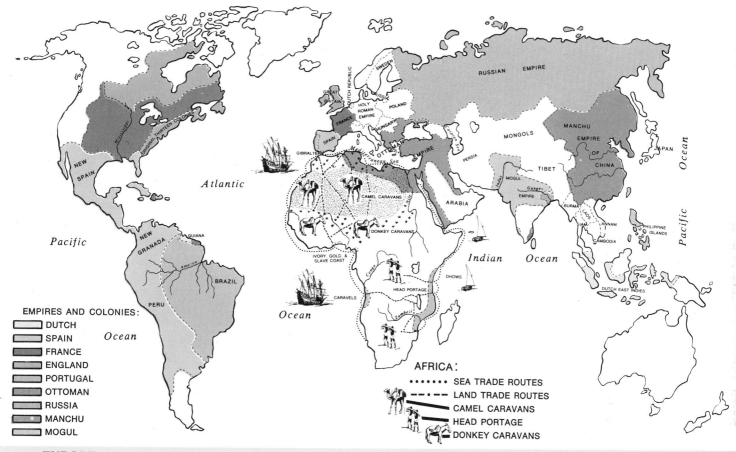

EMPIRES AND COLONIES:
- DUTCH
- SPAIN
- FRANCE
- ENGLAND
- PORTUGAL
- OTTOMAN
- RUSSIA
- MANCHU
- MOGUL

AFRICA:
- •••••• SEA TRADE ROUTES
- – – – LAND TRADE ROUTES
- CAMEL CARAVANS
- HEAD PORTAGE
- DONKEY CARAVANS

EUROPE and the Mediterranean World

The decline of the Ottoman Turkish Empire continued throughout the 1700s. The empire's losses of territory in the previous century to Russia, Poland and Austria were blows from which it never recovered. The once invincible Turks would never again be a threat to Europe.

Sweden, under Charles XII, was to enjoy a last dream of empire in this half century. Charles won a series of brilliant victories over the combined forces of Denmark, Poland and Russia, but the Swedish victory was to be short-lived. The Russian Army, reorganized by Peter the Great, crushed Swedish forces at Poltava in 1709. This victory opened former Swedish ports on the Baltic to Russia and by 1715 ended Swedish ambitions.

After the death of Czar Peter in 1725, Russia had a succession of four sovereigns within twenty-five years.

Peter's wife, Catherine I, reigned from 1725 to 1727, Peter II ruled for the next three years, Anna Ivanovna governed from 1730 to 1740, and Elizabeth Petrovna from 1741 until 1762, when Catherine the Great became empress.

The Italian Peninsula was divided during the 1700s into as many as nine separate states. The north was an unstable group of republics and small realms, some of which came under the hegemony of the Austrian Hapsburgs; the peninsula's center was ruled by the Church (the Papal States); and the south after 1738 was governed by a Spanish Bourbon and known as the Kingdom of the Two Sicilies (Naples and Sicily).

King Charles II of Spain willed his domains to a grandson of King Louis XIV of France, Philip of Anjou, who became King Philip V of Spain in 1700. This bequest, which stipulated that the French and Spanish thrones should never be united, led, on Charles's death, to the War of the Spanish Succession, due to the fact that Louis XIV of France ignored the stipulation and tried to lay the basis for a French-Spanish empire. The Holy Roman Empire (at the time, Germany, Austria and part of northern Italy), whose Emperor also claimed the throne of Spain, joined with Holland and England to prevent a union of France and Spain under Bourbon rule. From 1701 to 1713, France, virtually alone, fought the combined armies of the rest of Europe, which were led by British generals. Despite her tremendous military power, France was finally defeated. In the resultant treaty in 1713, called the Peace of Utrecht, Philip was recognized as the ruler of Spain, but it was also agreed that Spain and France should never be united under one ruler.

Disposition of Spanish and French colonies in the Mediterranean and in the Americas in this same Peace of Utrecht brought additional colonial power to Great Britain (as England and Scotland were now called). Among Britain's acquisitions were Gibraltar, which she had occupied since 1704 and now agreed to purchase from Spain, and Nova Scotia and Newfoundland, which she received from France.

In 1715, Louis XV succeeded to the French throne. It was during the reign of this absolute monarch that the French political philosopher Montesquieu was to write his famous treatise *The Spirit of Laws,* in which he pointed out the wisdom of separating government into executive, legislative and judicial divisions. This concept of separation of governmental activities was later embodied in the United States Constitution. The political writings of Montesquieu are thought to have played an important part in inciting the French Revolution.

Also during Louis XV's reign, the writings of François-Marie Arouet, best known by his pen name of Voltaire, the dominant literary and intellectual figure of the century and leader of the Enlightenment, were having a tremendous impact on the social, political and scientific thinking of all Europe.

The growing power of Prussia reached a new peak in the 1700s, primarily as a result of the military genius of Frederick II, commonly known as Frederick the Great, who came to the throne in 1740. Frederick's most disruptive campaign was directed against Europe's other great Germanic power, Austria, and was mounted to keep the imperial throne from the Austrian Archduchess Maria Theresa, who, although a woman, was the rightful Hapsburg heir. The War of the Austrian Succession, as it became known, lasted eight years from 1740 to 1748. France and Spain supported Prussia, and Britain and Holland fought on the side of Austria. The war ended in 1748, and the Treaty of Aix-la-Chapelle gave recognition to Maria Theresa's sovereignty, but permitted Frederick of Prussia to retain certain cap-

tured Hapsburg Austrian lands, most important of which was Silesia. After the treaty, France, wary of growing Prussian strength, changed sides and formed an alliance with Austria, while Britain, always concerned about French power, also changed sides and became an ally of Prussia.

Frederick the Great owed his easy conquest of Austrian Silesia to the inheritance of a Prussia in sound financial condition with a standing army of 100,000 of the best trained and appointed soldiers in Europe.

Queen Anne came to the English throne in 1702. During her reign the Parliaments of England and Scotland were united into one legislative body, thus further unifying the two nations which a century before (in 1603) had come under the rule of the same king. On the death of Anne in 1714, George I, a Protestant of the German house of Hanover who was descended from James I, was brought to the British throne. The new King's lack of interest in politics and governmental

During the reign of George I, Robert Walpole became Britain's first prime minister and headed the government for 20 years, guiding the formation of England's two-party system.

affairs, as well as his limited knowledge of English, helped bring about the development of a strong prime minister and fostered the growth of two political parties—the Whigs, who represented Britain's great mercantile middle classes, and the Tories, who represented the landed gentry and the church hierarchy. In 1715 a group known as Jacobites attempted unsuccessfully to regain the crown for the Stuart family in the person of "James III" (Catholic son of James II), who later became known as the Old Pretender. George II succeeded to Britain's throne in 1727. In 1745, Charles Edward, the Young Pretender (son of the Old), led the last Jacobite uprising. It failed, and its army, composed mainly of Scotsmen, was destroyed.

ASIA, except for its Mediterranean Lands

India was troubled, after the death of Aurangzeb in 1707, by two related problems: (1) the disintegrating Mogul Empire, and (2) French and British rivalry for control of the lands and trade of that failing kingdom. At one point during the War of the Austrian Succession, French forces took the city of Madras from England, but in 1748 the city was returned to Britain by the Treaty of Aix-la-Chapelle, which covered disputes in the colonial lands as well as in Europe.

The Persians, under Nadir Shah (1736–1747), moved into Afghanistan and, turning south, invaded and sacked Delhi and other parts of the dying Mogul Empire. Nadir Shah also defeated Ottoman Turkish opposition in this area.

Ch'ien Lung ascended to the Manchu throne in 1736. During his reign, which lasted till 1795, China enjoyed a considerable increase in wealth and population. The Emperor continued his predecessors' policy of sponsoring artists and scholars, and the empire extended its influence into Burma, Tibet and Nepal.

In Japan, Yoshimune, a member of the Togugawa family, became shogun in 1716. He tried to make the government more stable financially and to eradicate corruption. Although he was not very successful in aiding the economy, he did succeed in furthering the military-like culture of the nation. He encouraged the importation and study of all European books except those on religion. Thus Western science and medicine were intensely studied in Japan during his shogunate.

In the years 1732 and 1733, Japan was troubled by a widespread famine which was at length relieved by positive action on the part of the Shogun.

Southeast Asian nations were plagued by wars and instability in the first half of the 1700s. Laos was torn by civil war; Cambodia was invaded by several neighboring peoples, among whom were the Vietnamese; and Burma was divided in 1740 by a war between its two component peoples when one of these, the Mons, threw off the yoke of the other, the Burmese, and installed their own ruler at their city of Pegu. The Dutch and English East India Companies both were trading in Burma in the early 1700s, followed by the French in about 1729. Suspicion of European motives continued throughout Southeast Asia.

AFRICA, except for its Mediterranean Lands

The growing slave trade in Africa was causing serious conflicts among the competing Europeans and also among native tribes, who would raid one another to obtain slaves for sale to the whites. Black traders from the African interior continued to supply the Europeans and the Moslems with gold and ivory as well as with slaves.

The camel caravans which crisscrossed the African deserts were replaced by donkey trains in northern Africa, by human porters in the great forests and by African dhows and European sailing vessels along the coasts.

THE AMERICAS

In Paraguay, in 1730, an attempt of the people to free themselves from Spain ended in failure, but it was a forecast of the series of rebellions which within one hundred years would free most of the New World from European rule. The wars of Europe had their counterparts in the New World, with the colonists tending to take the sides of their countries of origin. In North America the War of the Spanish Succession was called Queen Anne's War (1702–1713), and the War of the Austrian Succession was known as King George's War (1743–1748).

During the first fifty years of the 1700s, Yale University was founded in Connecticut, followed shortly by Princeton University in New Jersey. Thus, Harvard (1636), William and Mary (1693), Yale (1701) and Princeton (1746) were America's first colleges. It is interesting to note that the University of Mexico City and the University of San Marcos in Lima, Peru, had preceded the earliest university in non-Latin countries of North America by more than fifty years.

In 1733, the colony of Georgia, the last of the thirteen original British colonies to be founded, was established as a haven for English debtors and for Protestant refugees from Central Europe.

Benjamin Franklin began to publish *Poor Richard's Almanac* in Philadelphia in 1732.

In the year 1733, the Molasses Act was passed by the British Parliament, placing prohibitive duties on any sugar and molasses imported into the colonies from other than British possessions. It represented another misguided attempt by England to control trade in its American colonies.

During the early decades of the 1700s, American settlers, largely of British, French and German ancestry, were shaping an entirely new way of life on the wooded frontiers of North America. Under extremely primitive conditions and in constant danger of Indian attack, these men and women cleared the land, built their own log cabins, often made their own tools and their own clothing and even spun the cloth or worked the skins of which the clothing was made. The prize, of course, was free land, an unheard-of reward for the immigrants from Europe's crowded cities and overworked farms.

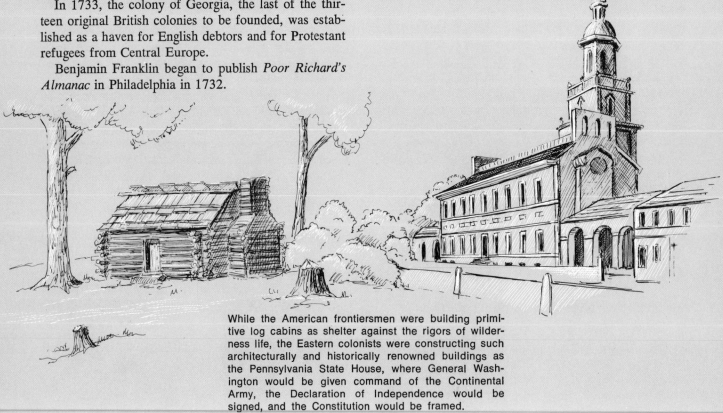

While the American frontiersmen were building primitive log cabins as shelter against the rigors of wilderness life, the Eastern colonists were constructing such architecturally and historically renowned buildings as the Pennsylvania State House, where General Washington would be given command of the Continental Army, the Declaration of Independence would be signed, and the Constitution would be framed.

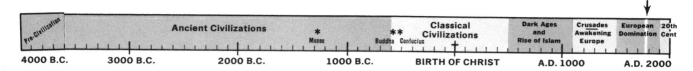

| Pre-Civilization | Ancient Civilizations | * Moses | ** Buddha Confucius | Classical Civilizations | Dark Ages and Rise of Islam | Crusades Awakening Europe | European Domination | 20th Cent |

4000 B.C.   3000 B.C.   2000 B.C.   1000 B.C.   BIRTH OF CHRIST   A.D. 1000   A.D. 2000

1750 — 1775

The Seven Years' War • The First Partition of Poland • Explorations of Captain Cook • Clive of India • Rebellion in Colonial America

EUROPE and the Mediterranean World

Prussia, led by Frederick the Great and allied with England, fought the Seven Years' War (1756–1763) against most of Europe, including France and Russia. The war originated in a territorial quarrel between Prussia and Austria over Saxony, and in boundary disputes in North America between France and England. Spain and England subsidized Prussia, since it was to their interest to keep France occupied with a European war, while they could at the same time act with a free hand in the New World and in Southeast Asia. The war ended with no border changes in Europe, but England was enabled to take over France's colonies in North America.

In 1772, Austria, Prussia and Russia jointly participated in the first of three partitions of Poland. Russia, whose ruler at this time was Catherine the Great (1762–1796), ruthlessly expanded her borders at the expense of Poland, as did Austria and Prussia.

The Ottoman Turkish Empire continued to control much of the Balkan area of Europe, as well as much of Asia Minor and Mediterranean Asia. Ottoman hold on North Africa was weakening, however, as the internal strength of the empire waned.

In 1774, Louis XVI succeeded to the French throne. He came to the head of a nation whose great wealth and power had been eroded in the last several decades by almost constant warfare and by unrestrained extravagance, epitomized by the luxurious court at the Palace of Versailles. France's colonial empire had largely fallen, or was shortly to fall, into the hands of England and other nations. The social and economic condition of France's common people, to which the nobility was largely indifferent, was appalling. In 1762, in France, Jean-Jacques Rousseau wrote in his book *The Social Con-*

tract, "Man is born free, but everywhere he is in chains." Rousseau's works, like the earlier writings of Montesquieu and the writings of Voltaire, are thought to have contributed greatly to the revolutionary movement in France.

England was about to replace France as the most powerful nation of Europe and of the entire world. Command of the seas, which she had enjoyed for many decades, and the protection which the Channel gave to her (enabling her to choose whether or not to involve herself in Europe's affairs) were about to bring her an era of prosperity and power perhaps not seen before in human affairs.

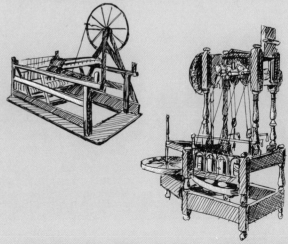

The tremendous expansion of England's textile industry in the second half of the 18th century stemmed from James Hargreaves' invention, the "Spinning Jenny," which increased production of yarn, and Arkwright's spinning machine, which improved the quality of the yarn. Both ran on either water or animal power.

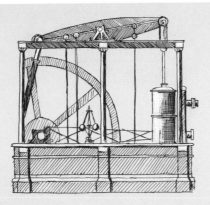

Power to run the machines of the Industrial Revolution was provided by the steam engine, invented by James Watt. The inventor sold his machine to the industrialists, most of whom had been farmers, by describing its ability to work in terms of "horsepower."

ASIA, except for its Mediterranean Lands

Increased rivalry between France and Britain for control of India marked the beginning of this twenty-five-year period, with French power reaching its zenith in 1751. From this time, British fortunes in India would be in the ascendancy, and French fortunes (as at home and in the Americas) would be on the decline. Robert Clive, or Clive of India, as he became known, was the military and administrative leader largely responsible for eventual British supremacy in the Indian subcontinent. In order to persuade Britons at home to permit the East India Company to absorb ever larger portions of India, he capitalized on incidents such as the deaths of many English prisoners who were held overnight in suffocating heat in a tiny guardroom, the "Black Hole of Calcutta." In 1757, after an Indian force had taken

Robert Clive, through shrewd use of small British naval units, managed to control the seas around India, reinforcing and supplying his own troops while at the same time preventing the French from doing the same.

Bengal to aid the French, a British expedition led by Clive and Admiral Charles Watson defeated these Indian forces at the battle of Plassey. Two years later, Dutch armies were defeated by Britain, and in 1761 a decisive victory over the French at Pondicherry left Britain in virtual control of India, with France and Portugal in possession of only scattered locations. The Dutch were left with the island of Ceylon only.

In the year 1773, Warren Hastings was appointed the British East India Company's first governor general, a position which gave him control over the entire company in the subcontinent. Hastings instituted reforms, improved coinage, and simplified the revenue system. These and other methods which were rather high-handedly imposed

kept British interests solvent during the troublesome times when Britain was at war with other European trading companies as well as with native Indian rulers. Hastings also placed salt and opium manufacture under government control, took strong action to reduce the ravages of robber tribes called dacoits, and required British officials to acquire a knowledge of both Moslem and Hindu law. In 1773, Parliament passed a Regulating Act limiting the British East India Company's directors and the private acts of its employees. It set up a supreme court for British subjects in the company's territories, prohibited private trade by company officers and imposed limitations on the acts of governors general.

In China, Emperor Ch'ien Lung's pacification efforts along his frontiers were particularly successful in the far-northwestern area that is now Sinkiang. Ch'ien Lung also subdued Burma and ventured out on inspection trips throughout his empire, observing the nation's vast resources and demonstrating his concern for the land and the people. He took strong action to control the acts of the Dalai Lama, the high priest of Tibet, whose people had for some time been guilty of violence against Chinese residents of that area.

European merchants in Canton were restricted to the area outside the city walls known as "the factories." They were permitted to deal only with officially designated Chinese merchants and were forced to pay, in lieu of a fixed tariff, whatever bribe the Chinese official chose to extort.

The quarrel in Burma between its two component races, the Mons and the Burmese, which had split the kingdom into separate states, was settled in this quarter century with the aid of China's Emperor Ch'ien Lung, and the land was reunited as one kingdom.

In 1773 an insurrection in Vietnam led by two brothers of the Tay-Son family overthrew both the Trinh government, centered in the north at the city of Hanoi, and the Nguyen government of the south, centered at the city of Hue.

OCEANIA

In 1771, Captain James Cook of England (having previously made a survey of the St. Lawrence River and the Newfoundland coast in the Americas) returned from an exploratory trip around the world on which he made the first reliable map locating many of the islands of the Pacific. On this voyage, Cook went first to Tahiti, sailed around New Zealand and then charted the east coast of Australia. He traveled thence around the Cape of Good Hope and north to England. On a second voyage lasting from 1772 to 1775, he explored the New Hebrides Islands, New Caledonia, and Norfolk Island.

AFRICA, except for its Mediterranean Lands

In 1770, a Scotsman, James Bruce, explored the area of Africa that is now Ethiopia and also the area of the Blue Nile River.

THE AMERICAS

The French and Indian War (1754–1763) was the final phase of a long struggle between France and England to win control of North America, and it was also a phase of the greater war taking place in Europe called the Seven Years' War. After the British General James Wolfe took Quebec from France in 1759, the war in America quickly moved toward total British victory. At the war's end, the Treaty of Paris (1763) determined that Canada and the French holdings east of the Mississippi River went to England, while French territory located west of the Mississippi went to Spain. French holdings in the Caribbean were now reduced to a few islands.

In 1759, at the end of the French and Indian War, the British government began rigidly to enforce the Navigation Acts passed in the previous century, in order to raise funds to pay for British troops which, Parliament claimed, had to be stationed in the colonies to protect the citizenry there. The American colonists were forced to lodge these soldiers in their homes and complained bitterly against this billeting of troops, contending that it imposed a needless financial burden upon them. Two acts of Parliament, the Molasses Act (1733) and the Sugar Act (1764), which were passed to limit colonial trade in these products with other than British colonial producers, evoked particularly strong opposition in America. A third act, the Stamp Act (1765) provided that stamps must be purchased from the government and affixed to all legal documents, newspapers, pamphlets, playing cards and dice. It caused such bitter reaction that the colonists convened a special committee called the Stamp Act Congress to draw up memorials to the King and to Parliament. The congress also adopted a "Declaration of Rights and Liberties."

In 1770, colonial hatred for the British troops stationed in Boston erupted into a brawl between colonials and soldiers in which five citizens were killed and several wounded, and to which the Americans gave the name "Boston Massacre."

In 1773, in what was called the "Boston Tea Party," Bostonians dressed as Indians boarded English ships in the harbor and dumped 342 chests of tea into the bay as a protest against a tax placed on tea imported into the colonies.

Benjamin Franklin, American author, publisher, scientist and statesman, was building the international reputation which would make him the colonies' most valuable diplomat during its war with England. In 1757, the Philadelphia assembly sent Franklin to England to act as liaison between the colonies and the mother country. He remained in Europe for nearly all of the ensuing eighteen years, largely in England and France, returning in 1775 at the beginning of the Revolutionary War.

In 1774, French Canadians (largely Roman Catholics and therefore deprived, under British law, of the right to vote) were awarded both political and religious liberties in what was called the Quebec Act.

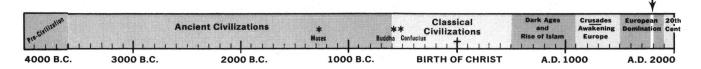

| Pre-Civilization | Ancient Civilizations | *Moses | **Buddha Confucius | Classical Civilizations | Dark Ages and Rise of Islam | Crusades Awakening Europe | European Domination | 20th Cent |

4000 B.C.   3000 B.C.   2000 B.C.   1000 B.C.   BIRTH OF CHRIST   A.D. 1000   A.D. 2000

1775 — 1800

The French Revolution • Poland Destroyed in the Second and Third Partitions • The Industrial Revolution in England • Voltaire, Montesquieu, Rousseau, Adam Smith, Gibbon, Goya, Goethe, Bach, Mozart, Beethoven • Britain Rules India • The American Revolution

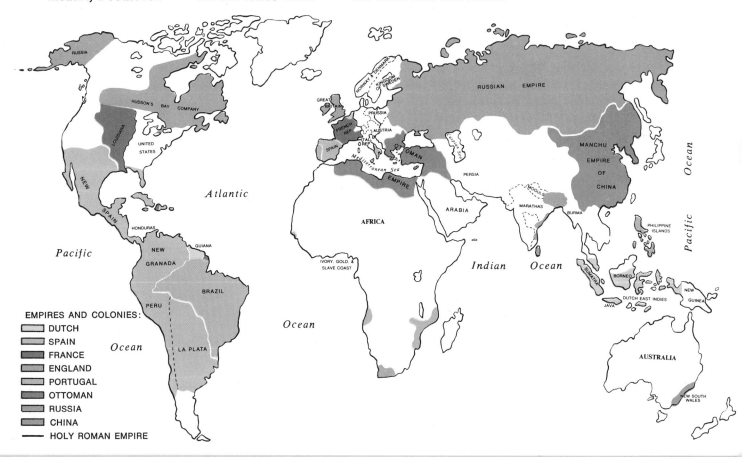

EMPIRES AND COLONIES:
- DUTCH
- SPAIN
- FRANCE
- ENGLAND
- PORTUGAL
- OTTOMAN
- RUSSIA
- CHINA
- — HOLY ROMAN EMPIRE

EUROPE and the Mediterranean World

The Ottoman Turkish Empire continued to weaken during the last twenty-five years of the eighteenth century. The empire's subject peoples in Europe and in the Mediterranean lands of Asia and Africa were increasingly restive, and neighboring states eyed Turkish lands with growing acquisitiveness. The Turkish rulers countered the threats to their empire with cruel and repressive treatment of their subjects and especially with persecution of Christians.

In the Treaty of Jassy in 1792, Catherine the Great of Russia acquired from Turkey the northern Black Sea coast as far west as the Dniester River, thus further reducing Ottoman lands. Russian arms were now threateningly close to Istanbul, the capital city of the Ottoman Empire.

Catherine the Great of Russia took the lead in the Second and Third Partitions of Poland, which finally broke the spirit of the Polish resistance and divided the nation's remaining lands among Russia, Austria and Prussia.

Poland was partitioned for a second and a third time during this twenty-five-year period. In 1793, Prussia acquired the Baltic city of Danzig and the area west of Warsaw, while Russia took most of Lithuania and the Ukraine, reducing Poland to less than half its former size. In 1795, after the third partitioning, in which Prussia, Austria and Russia divided Poland's remaining lands among themselves, Poland ceased to exist as a nation.

In France, the condition of the common people had worsened and the nation itself was near bankruptcy. In 1789, Louis XVI, in desperation, decided to call the Estates General for the first time in well over a hundred years. This was the national assembly, in which representatives of the three classes, or estates—nobles, clergy and commoners—each had a voice. Even while this assembly was drawing up a new constitution abolishing class privileges, the mobs of Paris were storming the Bastille, the ancient prison which symbolized to the people their years of privation and neglect. The royal family was brought forcibly to Paris from Versailles, and later the King and the Queen, Marie Antoinette, were guillotined—along with countless others—by the "Jacobins," the extremist group headed by Maximilien Robespierre.

For ten years, from 1789 to 1799, France was torn and bloodied by this rebellion, which is called the French Revolution. During this time, despite her desperate internal state, France fought a war against a coalition of European nations, among them Holland, Prussia, Austria, Britain and Spain, all of whom were apprehensive that the revolution might spread to their own lands.

The coalition against France was defeated by the brilliant generalship of Napoleon Bonaparte. Only England, safe behind the waters of the English Channel, was able to hold out against the troops led by this general from the French island possession of Corsica.

In 1798, Bonaparte led French forces across the Mediterranean in an expedition to conquer Egypt and gain control of the route to India. Although he was cut off from France when the brilliant British Admiral Horatio Nelson destroyed the French fleet in the battle of the Nile, Bonaparte's army won several important victories and was in control of Egypt until 1801. Meanwhile, in 1799, Bonaparte returned to France and, by a *coup d'état,* made himself the preeminent ruler of the French with the title "First Consul."

During these same twenty-five years Britain became tremendously wealthy. True, she lost all her American colonies except Canada and a few islands, and at the same time she endured tragic warfare against the French armies in Europe; nonetheless, she was able to consolidate her rule in India and strengthen her control of the sea. By 1800 she had no peers in wealth and power. Throughout the latter part of the eighteenth century, the Industrial Revolution began to change the English countryside. Busy and appallingly dirty mills and factory towns blighted the countryside. Many farm people were forced by economic need to move to these towns, and even very young children were required to work in factories under conditions which kept them little more than slaves. The schism between capital and labor that divides most nations even today first developed during these years in England. Trade became the hallmark of the British way of life. *The Wealth of Nations,* a book

After the storming of the Bastille, the great prison in Paris, and the liberation of the prisoners held there, the French peasants freed themselves from the tyranny of the nobility by destroying the legal records of their obligations and servitude.

by the Scots economist Adam Smith, epitomized the philosophy that would bring unheard-of wealth to the English middle class. Smith was a strong advocate of *laissez-faire,* or non-interference by government in the affairs of business. This, he wrote, would make possible "free trade," a "free economy" and great prosperity.

In 1782, after the disastrous policy which led to the loss of the American colonies, King George III appointed as prime minister of Great Britain the twenty-four-year-old William Pitt the Younger. Pitt followed a strong independent policy, often at odds with the King. Under Pitt, French ambitions in Egypt were thwarted, and a beginning was made to reform the abuses of the East India Company in India.

Pitt was confronted, as had been previous English leaders, with pressing Irish economic and political problems, and with frequent Irish rebellion.

The 1700s saw no lessening of the amazing productivity of Europeans in the arts and sciences. Britain replaced France as Europe's wealthiest and most powerful nation, and her people became the most productive in intellectual and artistic pursuits. Yet, despite English and Scottish leadership in the literary arts and the sciences, for reasons not readily explicable Britain at no time took the lead in the fine arts (such as painting or sculpture) as had Italy, Spain and France in their years of leadership.

German-speaking peoples too began to make outstanding contributions in the 1700s, especially in philosophy and music; but German eminence in science and technology would not come into being until the next century.

The following necessarily limited listing of outstanding Europeans of the 1700s is presented to give the reader some perspective of this remarkable century.

In the social sciences, Adam Smith (1723–1790), the Scot whose *Wealth of Nations* founded political economy in Britain, Charles-Louis de Secondat de Montesquieu (1689–1755), whose *Spirit of Laws* is a landmark in governmental study, and Jean-Jacques Rousseau (1712–1778), whose *Social Contract* inspired men all over the earth to rebel against injustice, all had an effect on their own times and a continued impact on the thinking of later generations.

The philosophers of the Enlightenment, the Scots logician and historian David Hume (1711–1776), noted for his *History of England* and his *Political Discourses,* and two Germans, Immanuel Kant (1724–1804), whose *Critique of Pure Reason* is highly regarded, and Georg Wilhelm Friedrich Hegel (1770–1831) esteemed for his *Philosophy of History* and his *Science of Logic,* as well as the Frenchman Voltaire mentioned below, made long-standing contributions to man's thinking about himself and his place in the cosmos.

In prose literature, the contributions of men writing in the English language—with a notable exception—

dominated the century. The exception, a giant of his times, was the prolific Voltaire (1694–1778), poet, philosopher, critic, historian, playwright and letter writer. The list of English, Scottish and Irish writers of this century is breathtaking. Many were giants of literature; all had somethng to say for their own times, many for all times. Among them were Jonathan Swift (1667–1745), Irish novelist and essayist, thought by many to be preeminent among writers of English prose of the 1700s; Henry Fielding (1707–1754), a great novelist, whose *Tom Jones* is considered among the half-dozen finest novels of all time; Samuel Johnson (1709–1784), writer, lexicographer and critic, and James Boswell (1740–1795), who wrote a biography of Samuel Johnson which is considered to be one of the finest in the English language; Edward Gibbon (1737–1794), whose masterpiece, *The Decline and Fall of the Roman Empire,* presented 1,300 years of history (from about three hundred years before the fall of Western Rome to the fall of the city of Constantinople to the Turks in the fifteenth century), written with a clarity of scholarship and language that is unique among historical writings; and Jane Austen (1775–1817), English novelist whose books (among which are *Sense and Sensibility, Pride and Prejudice* and *Persuasion*) show the power of a fine mind aided by a delightful sense of humor in developing her characters and portraying contemporary society.

Poetry, like prose, was dominated in the 1700s by outstanding Britons, among whom were Alexander Pope (1688–1744), noted for his wit and satire and for the precision of his verse; William Blake (1757–1827), poet, artist and mystic; and Robert Burns (1759–1796), who wrote his earthy poetry in Scots rather than in English. Of comparable stature were the German lyric poet Friedrich Hölderlin (1770–1843) and the renowned French poet André Chénier (1762–1794).

The scope of drama was broadened during the 1700s by Italian, French, English and German playwrights. Among Italians, Pietro Metastasio (1698–1782) wrote dramatic poems to be recited to music, melodious dramas or "melo-dramas," as they came to be called; Carlo Goldoni (1707–1793) wrote sparkling comedies in which women were more honestly represented than had been the custom of the times, some even depicted in rebellion against masculine domination; Vittorio Alfieri (1749–1803) wrote tragedies, often with the aim of inspiring his fellow Italians to strive for freedom from the foreign powers that divided and ruled their country.

Two French dramatists belong on any list of eighteenth-century playwrights: Pierre de Marivaux (1688–1763) who wrote comedies based on psychological motifs and complications, and Pierre-Augustin Caron de Beaumarchais (1732–1799), who wrote *The Barber of Seville,* later made into an opera by Rossini, and *The Marriage of Figaro,* used as the basis of an opera by Mozart.

The English playwright Richard Brinsley Sheridan (1751–1816) wrote comedies of manners with superb character studies and sparkling dialogue, among them *The Rivals* and *The School for Scandal*.

German theater in the 1700s was dominated by what is known as the "Sturm und Drang" (Storm and Stress) movement, which voiced an impatience with the stolid factualism of the Germanic literature of the past and attempted to replace it with a new, more exciting and human approach to literature and to life itself. An important dramatist of this period was Gotthold Ephraim Lessing (1729–1781), who wrote plays of German middle-class life and plays which dealt with problems arising from class oppressions. Of far-reaching importance also was his work of literary criticism. Johann Christoph Friedrich von Schiller (1759–1805) wrote dramas of political and social protest, yet suggesting a philosophical analysis and adjustment to political and social problems. Johann Wolfgang von Goethe (1749–1832) is considered to be by far the most important writer in the German language of the 1700s, perhaps of all time. He was a poet of tremendous stature, a powerful dramatist, and a philosopher of great penetration and wisdom. His works stand above those of all other German writers and, in the eyes of some critics, rank second to Shakespeare's in world importance.

Notable painters of Italian, French and English birth graced the 1700s. Yet perhaps none but the Spaniard Francisco Goya (1746–1828) approached the heights achieved by artists of the preceding three centuries, which include the Renaissance years of the 1400s and 1500s. Antonio Canaletto (1697–1798) of Italy was a master of perspective and color whose accuracy of detail is remarkable. Jean-Antoine Watteau (1684–1721) of France opened new vistas in French painting, and Jacques David (1748–1825), court painter in France under Napoleon, is noted for his paintings of Greek and Roman Classical themes. In England, two portraitists, Joshua Reynolds (1723–1792) and Thomas Gainsborough (1727–1788), and the mystic illustrator and engraver William Blake (1757–1827), previously mentioned as a poet, achieved fame.

Music in the eighteenth century was dominated by German-speaking composers. Johann Sebastian Bach (1685–1750) wrote instrumental music (mostly for the organ and the clavichord), as well as group compositions featuring the violin, the flute, the oboe, and other instruments. His inventiveness in the use of counterpoint and polyphony, particularly in religious choral works, is unequaled. His massive creative output was extraordinary. Franz Joseph Haydn (1732–1809), an Austrian, originated the symphony and the string quartet. Wolfgang Amadeus Mozart (1756–1791), also an Austrian, was one of the great musical geniuses of all time, whose over six hundred works include, just to skim the surface, violin sonatas, symphonies, operas, operettas, oratorios, church music, chamber music, litanies

and hymns; some of these he composed as early as age six.

Other composers of high merit of the 1700s were the German-born George Frederick Handel (1685–1759), who lived and worked in England, the Italian Alessandro Scarlatti (1660–1725) and the German Christoph Willibald Gluck (1714–1787).

Ballet had reached a peak in France in the early eighteenth century and then virtually came to a halt with the French Revolution. However, it was to reach new heights in later times in Russia due to its early encouragement and sponsorship by Russian monarchs. Both Czar Peter the Great and Empress Catherine the Great brought to Russia the finest French and Italian ballet artists.

Architecture in France in the 1700s developed the highly ornate Rococo style. In Germany a Baroque architecture developed that was remarkable for its very large, heavily ornamented buildings. Architecture in England in the early 1700s continued in the Renaissance style developed by Sir Christopher Wren and others in the preceding century. English and Irish country houses developed a style called Georgian, in which symmetry and formal layout of grounds and buildings predominated. The buildings were constructed largely of brick, with stone trim.

Science and technology reached unheard-of heights in the 1700s. The Industrial Revolution began in England, accelerated by the research and inventions of men of many nations of Europe.

Following in the tradition of Isaac Newton of the previous century were a long list of Britons whose efforts virtually changed the face of the earth. Among these,

The lighter-than-air balloon, made possible when Henry Cavendish discovered hydrogen in 1776, was taken aloft successfully in 1783 by the Montgolfier brothers.

doing original work in the basic sciences, were Henry Cavendish (1731–1810) and Joseph Priestley (1733–1804), two founders of the science of chemistry; John Dalton (1766–1844), who evolved the modern theory of the atomic structure of matter; Humphry Davy (1778–1829), who did important research in chemistry and was to invent the carbon-arc lamp and the miner's safety lamp; William Herschel (1738–1822), who laid the groundwork for new theories in astronomy; and Edward Jenner (1749–1823), who developed vaccination against smallpox.

During these same years, English inventors made important contributions: John Kay (1704–1764?) designed mechanical means of weaving; James Hargreaves (1745–1778) invented the spinning jenny; Edmund Cartwright (1743–1823) designed the power loom; and the Scotsman James Watt (1736–1819) made the first practical steam engine.

Men of other nations also made great contributions to science and technology in the 1700s. Foremost among these were the Frenchmen Jean-Baptiste Lamarck (1744–1829), a naturalist who did basic work in the classification of both living and fossil creatures; Antoine Lavoisier (1743–1794), a pioneer in chemistry who did important work in explaining the nature of combustion; André Ampère (1775–1836), whose work in electricity presaged the development of the electromagnet and who was to formulate the important "Ampère's rule"; and Charles Coulomb (1736–1806), who organized the accumulated knowledge of electrical behavior into a useful scientific order. The Italian Luigi Galvani (1737–1798), who was actually an anatomist at the University of Bologna, did pioneer work in electrochemistry. Another Italian, Alessandro Volta (1745–1827) furthered the work of Galvani in electrochemistry and invented the battery.

Two Swedish scientists contributed immensely to basic knowledge in the 1700s. Emanuel Swedenborg (1688–1772) did important research in a wide variety of fields including mathematics, physics, paleontology and physiology. He was also a noted philosopher. Carl Linnaeus (1707–1778) worked out the first classification tables and charts for plants and animals and thus laid the foundation for the work of future biologists. A Danish scientist, Hans Christian Oersted (1777–1851), did fundamental work in electricity and, most important, would later demonstrate the relationship between electricity and magnetism.

ASIA, except for its Mediterranean Lands

The last quarter of the eighteenth century found the British in India almost constantly at war with native rulers of such kingdoms as Mysore and Maratha. The situation was complicated by the fact that the French supplied both money and troops to the rebel potentates. In 1778 there was a direct confrontation between French and British forces, and two French-controlled territories, Pondicherry and Mahé, fell into British hands.

In 1784 the British enacted what is called Pitt's India Act, to limit further territorial expansion on the part of the practically autonomous East India Company and to make the company answerable to a board of control appointed by the Crown. Two years later, Lord Cornwallis (of American Revolutionary fame) was selected by the company with strong pressure from the Crown to become both governor general and commander in chief of British India. He established a code which reformed the judicial system of India along British lines, but which excluded native Indians from all high posts. Regrettably, too, it failed to prevent the continuing exploitation of the peasantry by tax collectors and assessors. In the year 1793, Sir John Shore was appointed governor general. Within his time of leadership, in 1796, the Dutch, weakened by war at home with France, were driven from the island of Ceylon. For the next few years Ceylon would be administered jointly by the company and the Crown, but in 1802 the Crown alone assumed control. In 1798, Lord Mornington (later Marquis Wellesley), was appointed governor-general.

In China, Ch'ien Lung ruled until his abdication in 1795. During the last twenty-five years of the 1700s, the Manchu government of China was beset with rebellion in Kansu province, in Nepal, in Hunan and elsewhere. Although corruption was widespread within the government, all revolts were suppressed and the Manchu hold on these lands remained firm. In 1784 the first Americans began to participate in the profitable China trade through the port city of Canton.

Christianity came to Korea in the late 1700s, but shortly thereafter Korea closed its ports to foreigners.

Rice riots in Japan's capital city of Edo in 1787 followed the double tragedy of a disastrous eruption of Mount Asama in 1783 and a widespread famine in the north.

In Vietnam a counterrevolution was organized by a fifteen-year-old member of the Nguyen family of the city of Hue, against the Tay-Son brothers, who had conquered Vietnam in 1773. The young leader, who took the name Gia-Long, was aided by French missionaries, money and officers. After reconquering the city of Hue, Gia-Long marched north to Hanoi, where he defeated remnants of Tay-Son forces and set himself up as emperor of both northern and southern Vietnam. He rewarded his French allies with a treaty giving them a monopoly of trade between Vietnam and other nations.

In the year 1782, Rama I became king of Thailand, and later he secured part of the neighboring kingdom of Cambodia.

OCEANIA

After the late-eighteenth-century explorations of the Pacific waters by Captain James Cook, which included charting much of the coasts of Australia and New Zealand and the discovery of the Hawaiian Islands, Britain assumed control of Australia and began to use it as a place of exile for convicts, many of whom were political prisoners. The first shipload of these convicts arrived in Australia's Botany Bay in 1788, ten years after Cook's last voyage.

AFRICA, except for its Mediterranean Lands

The British Crown acquired Sierra Leone from its native owners in 1788 with the express purpose of developing it as a home for freed slaves.

In 1796, Mungo Park, a Scottish explorer, made his first expedition to the Niger River.

THE AMERICAS

For six years, from 1775 to 1781, the American colonies fought the British in the War of American Independence, commonly called the Revolutionary War. The war began in 1775 with battles at the towns of Concord and Lexington in Massachusetts. The peace treaty was signed in 1783. Among the war's key events were:

The Declaration of Independence in 1776, and the appointment of George Washington as commander in chief.

The entry of France, then Spain, into the war against the British. Both had revenge in mind as well as territorial acquisition.

Surrender of an entire army to Washington by Cornwallis at Yorktown in 1781.

Adoption of the Articles of Confederation by the colonies in 1781.

Negotiation of the peace with the British by Benjamin Franklin, John Adams and John Jay, followed by the signing of a preliminary peace treaty in Paris in 1782, and a final treaty in 1783.

On December 7, 1787, Delaware became the first state to ratify the United States Constitution, which was destined to be the supreme law of the land. The Constitution was subsequently adopted by the vote of each of the states-to-be, but it was not ratified by North Carolina until the Bill of Rights was added to it in 1789. George Washington became the United States's first president in 1789, John Adams its first vice-president, and Alexander Hamilton its first secretary of the treasury.

In 1797, John Adams was elected the second president of the United States, and Thomas Jefferson its second vice-president.

After much debate and editing, and following a considerable parliamentary struggle, the Declaration of Independence, drafted by Thomas Jefferson, was approved by the Continental Congress on July 4, 1776.

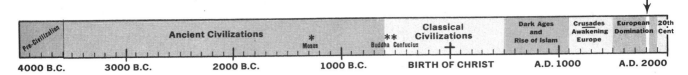

Pre-Civilization	Ancient Civilizations		*Moses	**Buddha Confucius	Classical Civilizations	Dark Ages and Rise of Islam	Crusades Awakening Europe	European Domination	20th Cent
4000 B.C.	3000 B.C.	2000 B.C.	1000 B.C.		BIRTH OF CHRIST		A.D. 1000		A.D. 2000

1800 — 1825

Emperor Napoleon I • The Battles of Trafalgar, of Russia and of Waterloo • The Repressive Metternich Philosophy • Liberia Founded in Africa • The Louisiana Purchase • The War of 1812 • The Monroe Doctrine

▮▮▮ SPAIN
▮▮▮ ENGLAND
▮▮▮ LOUISIANA PURCHASE
••••• ROUTE OF LEWIS AND CLARK

EUROPE and the Mediterranean World

This was the quarter century of the rise and the fall of Napoleon. After the terrors of the French Revolution, the people of France looked for a leader who could bring order out of chaos. They found him, they thought, in the little Corsican General Napoleon Bonaparte, who, like Augustus Caesar and Charlemagne before him, made himself first consul, then, in 1804, emperor. Like certain of his predecessors, Napoleon codified the law (the Napoleonic Code is the basic law for many modern

nations in addition to France) and tried also to inspire a renaissance in the arts and sciences. He revised the French system of education and improved the economic structure of the nation. In 1800, he obtained Louisiana back from Spain, to whom it had been awarded after the Seven Years' War.

Napoleon readied a tremendous army on the French side of the Channel, poised to invade Britain, but his fleets were defeated in 1805 by England's Admiral

Horatio Nelson in the battle of Trafalgar off the coast of Spain. Britain thus maintained her control of the seas and ended the likelihood of a French invasion of England. Napleon turned, instead, against England's European allies. In a series of masterful blows, he defeated Prussia, Austria and Russia. His power was now at its peak. France, Italy, Holland, Belgium and much of Germany were ruled by Napoleon or his appointees. The Holy Roman Empire had ceased to exist. Napoleon formed an alliance with Czar Alexander I of Russia, and it was agreed between them that the Czar was to rule east of the River Niemen and Napoleon was to rule in the rest of Europe.

Perhaps the most awesome ingredient of Napoleon's military genius was his ability to make a swift and accurate analysis of a military situation, followed by rapier-like military decisions.

Napoleon now attempted to strangle British trade by what was called the Continental System, in which he attempted to close all European ports to British vessels and British goods. Instead of bringing England to her knees, this device was to lock Napoleon and the nations of the Continent into Europe, cut off from sorely needed trade goods. To make matters worse, Portugal refused to go along with Napoleon's Continental System. To close this opening Napoleon sent French troops to occupy Portugal, whose royal family fled to Brazil.

In 1808, some 100,000 French troops were sent into Spain on the pretext of guarding the coasts from the British, and Napoleon's brother Joseph was made Spain's king. The campaign in Spain became known as the Peninsular War. It dragged on for more than five years, until well into October 1813, draining France of men and treasure. Yet, in the midst of this war, Napoleon was still able, in 1809, to deal a crushing blow to a rebellious Austria. However, when he followed this victory with an invasion of Russia in June of 1812, the death knell of his empire was sounded. Each French victory in Russia lured the French armies deeper into a vast land where every bit of food and fuel had been obliterated by czarist troops in a "scorched earth" re-

treat. The exhausted French troops finally arrived on September 14 in Moscow, only to find it abandoned. They then had to withdraw more than a thousand miles through the snow and ice of a terrible Russian winter. The magnificent French Army was virtually destroyed, with more than half a million men lost out of six hundred thousand invading troops.

A new coalition of European powers defeated the remaining French forces at a battle near Leipzig, Germany, and in 1814 Napoleon abdicated and was banished to the island of Elba in the Mediterranean. In less than a year, however, he was back in Paris reorganizing French troops for a new campaign. His new Grande Armée was totally vanquished on the plains of Belgium in 1815, at the battle of Waterloo, by a pincers composed of two armies, one led by British Field Marshal Wellington, the other by Prussian Field Marshal von Blücher. Napoleon was now exiled to the island of St. Helena in the South Atlantic, and the French throne was restored to the Bourbon Louis XVIII.

With Napoleon deposed, the nations of Europe met at the Congress of Vienna in 1814–1815 to bring order to lands torn by almost a quarter century of war. The decisions they made were largely to restore the conditions, the rulers and the boundaries which had existed prior to the French Revolution. For example, Germany and Italy, which Napoleon had consolidated into a few large states, were again subdivided. In addition, Austria (now known as the Austrian Empire) picked up several areas in Italy; Prussia got Saxony and territory along the Rhine River, besides Danzig and the part of Poland that she had won in the first two partitions; Holland and the former Austrian Netherlands were joined into one "Kingdom of the Netherlands," to form a barrier on France's northeast against a possible revival of French ambitions; a Germanic Confederation was organized to replace the cohesive force that the Holy Roman Empire had once exerted in Germany; and there were various territorial shifts to Russia, Denmark, Britain and other states.

Intermittently during these years, the Austrian diplomat Prince Klemens von Metternich wielded great influence in his own country and in many other European states. Extremely conservative and opposed to constitutional government and all forms of liberalism, he intervened with secret police and troops whenever he deemed it necessary. His was the strongest voice at the Congress of Vienna, a body which ignored the growing nationalism and demands for individual liberty of European peoples.

A ruling group called the Concert of Europe, consisting of Austria, Prussia, Russia and Britain, was set up to meet periodically and settle European problems, but the extreme conservatism of the Continental powers due to Metternich's influence and to fear of revolutions caused them to be in constant disagreement with Britain. After 1822 the Concert of Europe existed in name only.

From 1801 to 1825, Alexander I was czar of Russia. His early reign had brought a degree of enlightenment and increased freedom to Russia's oppressed people, but in later years he, like many other European rulers, came under the influence of Metternich and he withdrew the benefits he had previously given Russia's serfs. Two years after the expulsion of Napoleonic troops from Russia, Alexander became an active participant in the Congress of Vienna, which eventually allotted to Russia most of the grand duchy of Warsaw. Alexander reorganized the duchy as the kingdom of Poland, in permanent union with the Russian Empire and with the Czar of Russia as its king.

The Italian writer Giuseppe Mazzini (1805–1872), who spent much of his life in exile, began by means of his writing to foster a spirit of independence in Italy, and to inspire its people to rebel against foreign domination. In 1821, the first of several attempts to expel Austria from north Italy ended in failure.

In France, in the year 1824, Louis XVIII was succeeded by his brother, Charles X.

England made important strides in the development of a democratic and parliamentary government. In 1807, for example, the British Parliament abolished the slave trade which had long troubled the British conscience. In a more conservative mood, Parliament in 1801 passed an Act of Union which abolished the Irish Parliament and made Northern Ireland a part of the United Kingdom of Great Britain.

The Ottoman Empire, continuing to deteriorate during the 1800s, became a growing burden to the rest of Europe. The Ottoman Turkish situation was referred to as the "Near East Problem," due to the empire's almost explosive instability and to the danger that its problems might ignite the rest of Europe into a general war.

Years after Parliament abolished the slave trade, British children were laboring long, wearisome hours in the factories of Britain's overcrowded slum-ridden industrial cities.

ASIA, except for its Mediterranean Lands

By 1825, much of the southern two thirds of the Indian subcontinent was in British hands. In this vast area there were a few small enclaves still retained by Portugal and France, as well as scattered areas still native-ruled. Along the northern borders, however, the Sind and the Punjab would not be British-ruled until later in the century. In 1813 the East India Company's charter was renewed by Parliament, but stipulations were written into it assuring free trade within the subcontinent, as well as the free admission of missionaries and the sovereignty of the Crown over the company.

The First Burmese War was fought between Britain and Burma in 1824, and Rangoon (the great Burmese seaport and capital) was captured by British forces. A treaty guaranteeing British trade rights, which also provided for the transfer of Assam and certain coastal areas to British India, was negotiated with Burma in the year 1826.

China resisted continuing pressure from Europeans for increased trade rights within her lands. Opium was smuggled into China's interior, worsening the already bad relationship between China and the Western na-

tions. In the year 1805, a Catholic priest was strangled for violating the government's edict against foreign religious presence on the Chinese mainland, and all European literature and periodicals were banned. Japan and Korea too were largely closed to Europeans.

By 1800, most of Southeast Asia had come under European economic influence. In addition, various nations of the West were vying for political control of these Southeast Asian lands. There was greatly increased Christian missionary activity. In Vietnam, Emperor Gia-Long, who had recaptured the nation from the Tay-Son insurrectionists at the end of the 1700s, began building a strong centralized government. He permitted some French traders and missionaries to live and work within his lands. In 1820, Minh-Mang succeeded Gia-Long as emperor. He was a devout Buddhist as well as a Confucianist, very much opposed to Christianity and very suspicious of European motives. In 1824 he ordered all Europeans, most of whom were French, expelled from the nation.

Dutch-held Java was invaded and captured in 1811 by the British, who proceeded, under Thomas Stamford

Raffles, to modernize its legal system, while permitting administration to remain in native hands. In later treaties (1814 and 1816), Java was restored to Dutch rule.

In the year 1819, Raffles founded the city of Singapore on an island located just off the southern extremity of the Malay Peninsula. The island had been virtually abandoned for years, but its strategic location caused it quickly to dominate the entire area, both commercially and militarily.

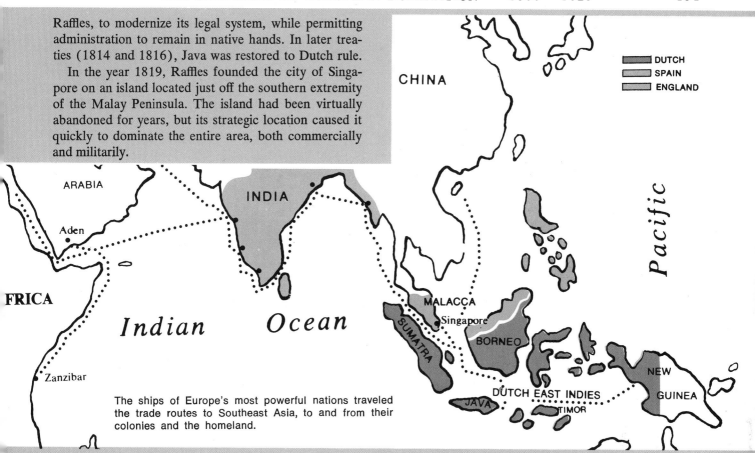

The ships of Europe's most powerful nations traveled the trade routes to Southeast Asia, to and from their colonies and the homeland.

OCEANIA

English and French sailors continued the exploration of the Pacific islands and Australia during the early years of the 1800s. Trade kept pace with this exploratory activity, as did missionary work. Australia, New Guinea, New Britain, the Gilbert, Marshall and Marianna Islands, and Hawaii were visited and studied by such men as Matthew Flinders of Britain and Louis-Claude de Freycinet of France. Trade goods consisted of sandalwood, trepang (a sea cucumber used especially by the Chinese for soup stock) and coconut oil. The Europeans brought with them diseases to which the natives had little or no resistance. Island populations declined sharply because of these diseases and also because many natives were kidnapped and sold into slavery.

AFRICA, except for its Mediterranean Lands

In 1805 the Scotsman Mungo Park made a second expedition (this time at the request of the British government) to the Niger River in Africa. He led a party of twenty-four men, most of whom died from fever or at the hands of belligerent natives. Park himself was last seen as he plunged into the Niger River, apparently to escape an attack by natives.

The Dutch-held Cape of Good Hope fell to the British in 1806.

Liberia was founded in the year 1820 as a refuge for freed American slaves.

THE AMERICAS

Thomas Jefferson was the third president of the United States. His administration is perhaps best remembered for the Louisiana Purchase, a transaction in 1803 by which a vast territory stretching from the Mississippi River to the Rocky Mountains was obtained from Napoleonic France, doubling the size of the United States. These were lands which had been returned to France by Spain in 1800. Jefferson's administration also sponsored the Lewis and Clark Expedition, which left from St. Louis in 1804 to explore the headwaters of the Missouri River and from there to blaze a trail across the continent to the Pacific Ocean.

Haiti gained its independence from France in 1804 and became the world's first black republic.

From 1808 to 1825, the remaining Spanish and Portuguese colonies in North and Central America (led primarily by the revolutionist Simón Bolívar in the Spanish-speaking lands) gained their independence. Bolívar, for whom the country of Bolivia is named, is known in South America as "the Liberator." In 1822 Brazil declared itself permanently separated from Portugal, and Dom Pedro, son of the Portuguese King, was crowned Pedro I, Emperor of Brazil.

From 1812 to January of 1815, the United States battled England in the War of 1812 over the complicated issue of "freedom of the seas"—in essence, the right of the ships of all nations to have equal right of passage in all international waters. In this war, in 1814, the British captured and burned the city of Washington. The final battle, in which American forces under Andrew Jackson prevented a British attack on New Orleans, was fought fifteen days after a treaty ending the war had been signed at Ghent (in what is now Belgium), but before news of the peace had crossed the Atlantic.

James Monroe, the fifth president of the United States, formulated the Monroe Doctrine, which stated that European colonization in the Americas was at an end. This doctrine, which meant that European nations must stay out of Western Hemisphere affairs or face U.S. wrath, would become a mainstay of U.S. foreign policy.

In 1820 the Missouri Compromise was enacted by Congress. It resulted from strong differences of opinion as to whether new states, especially those formed from portions of the Louisiana Purchase, should be admitted to the Union as "slave" or "free." The legislation stipulated that Missouri was to be admitted as a slave state, but that thereafter no portion of the Louisiana Purchase north of 36° 30′ north latitude should be slave.

In 1825, the Erie Canal began carrying passengers and freight across New York State to and from the Great Lakes in the nation's Midwest.

Simón Bolívar led the South American nations in their struggle to win independence from Spain. But he was unable to persuade them to join into one republic, which he felt would spare them from social and political turmoil.

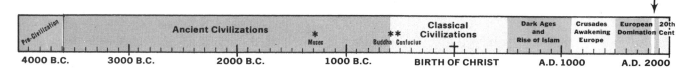

| | Ancient Civilizations | | *Moses | **Buddha Confucius | Classical Civilizations | Dark Ages and Rise of Islam | Crusades Awakening Europe | European Domination | 20th Cent |

4000 B.C.   3000 B.C.   2000 B.C.   1000 B.C.   BIRTH OF CHRIST   A.D. 1000   A.D. 2000

1825 — 1850

Revolutions in Europe • The Near East Problem • Queen Victoria • The Opium Wars • The Instability of South American Governments • The Republic of Texas • War Between Mexico and the United States

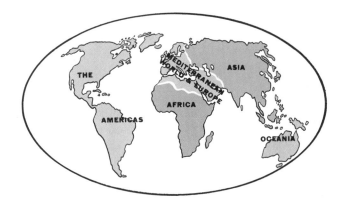

EUROPE and the Mediterranean World

Two underlying problems disturbed Europe's peace during this quarter century. The first was the continuing decay of the Ottoman Empire; the second was the hostility of Europe's rulers to the craving for freedom and national unity of Europe's peoples.

The first of these—the Near East Problem, as it was called—saw the component states of the Ottoman Empire agitating to break free and ambitious neighbors plotting to take advantage of the situation. For instance, the Greeks revolted in 1820 and, after one severe defeat by the combined forces of the Turks and the Egyptians, gained their freedom in 1829. When the Egyptians, angered at having received nothing for their pains, subsequently turned on Turkey, Russia intervened on the side of the latter. In return, Russia in 1833 demanded and won in the Treaty of Unkiar Skelessi the right for her fleet to use the Straits of the Bosporus and the Dardanelles—the strategic narrows leading from the Black Sea past the Turkish city of Istanbul to the Aegean Sea and the Mediterranean—in time of war. In 1842, however, by the Convention of the Straits, the passage was once again closed to the warships of Russia and all other nations.

The second of the problems endangering Europe's peace was the failure of the great powers to recognize the urgency of the drive for national unity and freedom of the peoples of Europe, and to understand that it stemmed in some part from tensions similar to those

which had brought about the French Revolution. As a result of this failure of understanding, the European powers at the Congress of Vienna had attempted to impose on the nations of Europe political arrangements which proved quite unacceptable to the peoples involved. An example of this was the Kingdom of the Netherlands that the Congress had created by joining Holland and what is now Belgium, under a Dutch king, William I. The union lasted little more than a decade; in 1830 Belgium rebelled at Dutch domination and gained her independence. Belgian neutrality and independence were later guaranteed by the other powers of Europe in a treaty signed in 1839 at London.

Similarly, the Congress of Vienna had divided the German peoples into a multitude of small states. This error was in part rectified later by a customs union called a "Zollverein" which commercially joined all the German states of Europe except Austria. The latter was excluded by adroit Prussian maneuvering. Thus, the Zollverein was a device to unify Germany and also an expression of Prussian–Austrian rivalry.

France too still suffered from the social ills which had caused the Revolution, as well as from the actions taken by the Congress of Vienna to force her into the pre-Napoleonic past. The Bourbon Louis XVIII, who became king after the exile of Napoleon, was not indifferent to his people's needs, but his successor, Charles X, adopted a repressive policy limiting free speech and voting rights, among other things—a policy which, in 1830, led France again into revolution and forced Charles to abdicate. His throne was assumed by Louis Philippe of the Orléans branch of the Bourbon family. Louis Philippe encouraged the new and wealthy middle class which had arisen out of France's Industrial Revolution, but ignored the appalling conditions of France's class of factory workers which had also come into being as a consequence of the industrialization of the nation.

In Italy, in 1830, a rebellion against Austrian domination of Italian lands in the north (the first had occurred in 1821) was crushed by the Austrian military. But Italy's division into many states, some independent, some ruled by Austria, some by the Papacy, remained a disruptive problem.

In the year 1848, all of these problems came to a head at once. A series of revolutions and rebellions seeking national unity and individual liberty swept across Europe—France, Germany, Italy, Austria, Hungary. In France, Louis Philippe was overthrown and the Second Republic was declared, with Prince Louis Napoleon Bonaparte (nephew of Napoleon I) later becoming its president. In Germany, the princes yielded without bloodshed to demands for reforms, and even encouraged the convening of a national assembly at the city of Frankfurt to draw up a democratic constitution for all of the German people; but the convention's prolonged deliberations provided time for the panic of the princes to subside, and by 1850 absolute control had been reasserted. In Italy, a series of revolutions against Austrian, Bourbon and papal rule was crushed. In Austria and Hungary, repressive government survived when Franz Josef became emperor in 1848, as it did in Russia under Czar Nicholas I (1825–1855).

In the same year of 1848, two German writers, Karl Marx and Friedrich Engels, published the now famous *Communist Manifesto,* a paper which was to loom large in the future history of Europe and the rest of the earth.

The first railroad was built and operated in England in 1825. From 1825 to 1850, Great Britain enacted a series of great social and political reforms, which included giving Catholics and members of the middle classes the right to vote, to sit in Parliament and to hold public office. Parliament also abolished slavery throughout Britain's worldwide empire. Queen Victoria came to the throne in 1837 and reigned until 1901—a long and fruitful period of industrial growth and prosperity at home, along with colonial expansion abroad. The period became known as the Victorian era.

Famine in Ireland in 1846 precipitated repeal of Great Britain's Corn Laws, thus allowing grain not grown in England, especially grain from Ireland, to be shipped into England duty-free. This enactment was a significant step by Britain toward free trade and toward the ascendancy of her industrial establishment over her agricultural interests. This, as well as many other progressive developments, owed much to the leadership of Sir Robert Peel during his prime ministry (1841–1846).

The French Revolution inspired the poverty-ridden and repressed people of Austria to rebel against the dictatorial acts of Prime Minister Metternich. In 1848 they took to the streets of Vienna, stormed the royal palace, and forced Metternich into exile.

ASIA, except for its Mediterranean Lands

In 1833 the British Parliament renewed the charter of the British East India Company for an additional twenty years, but stipulated that all new laws imposed on India by the company be subject to Parliamentary review. British power and British standards of morals and ethics had spread through ever-widening areas of the subcontinent and into neighboring Burma as well.

A number of Indian practices repugnant to British morality were outlawed: suttee, the tradition of the wife immolating herself on her deceased husband's funeral pyre; thuggee, murder by hired thugs to accomplish social, economic or political ends; and infanticide, the controlling of population and of family economics by the killing of infants. In 1835, English became the official language of all India, and thus, for the first time, a common language was available to the varied population of the vast subcontinent. However, despite the unifying influence of a common language, bitterness between Moslems and Hindus and other racial and religious groups remained.

During the period from 1831 to 1881, the state of Mysore came under British rule. Wars with the Sikhs between 1845 and 1848 led to annexation of the Punjab area. Between the years 1839 and 1842, Britain fought the First Afghan War to block Russia's expansion into Afghanistan, a land bordering India on the north.

Although opium trade in China was forbidden by Manchu leaders, British merchants and those of other nations continued to ship the drug into China illegally at enormous profit. In 1840, a Manchu official's seizure and destruction of a large supply of British-owned opium precipitated the Opium War, which ended in 1842 with Britain victorious. In the resulting treaty, no mention was made of the opium trade, and the Chinese were forced to pay reparations to Britain and to open five port cities to British trade. British merchants in these cities did not come under Chinese law, so that in effect the British merchants operated their own government on Chinese soil. The United States, France and Russia were quick to take advantage of a weakened China and to demand and obtain similar "most favored nations" status for their own merchants.

In Japan, increasing pressure was exerted by both Japanese and Western merchants upon the Shogun to open his nation's ports completely to trade with the West.

In Vietnam, the policy of friendship toward the French had long been abandoned by the successors of Emperor Gia-Long. Between 1825 and 1850, Christian missionaries suffered terrible persecution as the government attempted to drive all Christians from the land. About 1845, after years of dispute, the Vietnamese and the Thais agreed upon a joint rule of neighboring Cambodia.

In the Indonesian archipelago, there was a strong revival of Islamic worship, due in some part to a reaction against Christian activities in the area.

The Opium War was fought over Britain's practice of paying for Chinese export goods with opium, which was contrary to Chinese law. The war was quickly over, for China's junks were no match for the powerful British warships.

OCEANIA

European powers, especially Britain, France and Holland, continued to vie for control of the Pacific islands. In 1840, the city of Wellington was founded by the British on the New Zealand coast in an area possessed of a magnificent natural harbor.

AFRICA, except for its Mediterranean Lands

In 1841, David Livingstone, the Scots explorer, made the first of his missionary journeys into Africa.

In 1847, after some thirty years of work by Americans and others, Liberia became an independent republic—the first black republic of Africa.

THE AMERICAS

The early governments of the new nations of Latin America continued to be very unstable. Dictatorships, military juntas, rule by the landowning elite, and a host of other nondemocratic governments were imposed upon the new republics. In 1825, war between Argentina and Brazil over disputed land led to a treaty which created in 1828 the independent nation of Uruguay. In 1831, Dom Pedro I, Emperor of Brazil, abdicated in favor of his five-year-old son, who in 1840 was declared of age and crowned Emperor Pedro II.

Andrew Jackson became the seventh president of the United States in a time when many American statesmen were struggling to articulate the basic problems of the growing nation and were taking sides on issues, many of which would continue to trouble the nation to the present day. Jackson's election is considered to have been a victory for Western frontier democracy. The new president made the "spoils system"—whereby the victors in an election reward their supporters with political jobs—a nationally accepted policy. He struggled mightily with John Calhoun (the nation's outstanding spokesman for states' rights) over such issues as the tariff, and he objected so strongly to the political activities of the Second Bank of the United States that he vetoed the bank's application for renewal—this despite (or perhaps because of) the support given the renewal by two outstanding statesmen, Henry Clay and Daniel Webster.

The abolitionist movement is considered to have begun during Jackson's administration, with the formation of several anti-slavery societies.

During the Jackson years, Cyrus McCormick patented the first American reaping machine, a revolutionary step in agricultural technology; two states, Arkansas and Michigan, joined the Union; and construction of the Baltimore and Ohio Railroad was begun.

In 1837, Martin Van Buren became the eighth president of the United States. An economic depression, the Panic of 1837, resulted in good part from the wave of speculation that had swept the country from 1833 to 1837, and from poor crops for several years in the Western states.

The Republic of Texas was established in 1836, out of Mexican territory. It was founded by non-Mexicans who came from the United States. Ten years later, during the presidential administration of James K. Polk, the United States and Mexico were at war, largely over the Mexican contention that the American government had supported the Texans' battle for independence in order that Texas could be annexed to the United States as a slave state—which had in fact come to pass in 1845. At the war's end in 1848, Mexico gave up claims to Texas and ceded the territories of New Mexico and California to the United States. The U.S. paid Mexico an indemnity of $15 million. The Compromise of 1850 stipulated that California should come into the Union as a free state, and that the remainder of the territory ceded by Mexico to the U.S. should be divided into two territories, New Mexico and Utah, which would be admitted to the Union later as slave or free states according to the provision of their constitutions at the time of admission.

In 1848 gold was discovered in California at Sutter's Mill near Sacramento, and a great gold rush to the West Coast began.

In 1837 and again in 1838, there were brief rebellions in Canada against the British government. These rebellions startled the Crown into sending the eminent liberal statesman Lord Durham to Canada on a fact-finding mission. Lord Durham's report, published in 1839, urged the Parliament to grant increased self-rule to Britain's colonies in Canada.

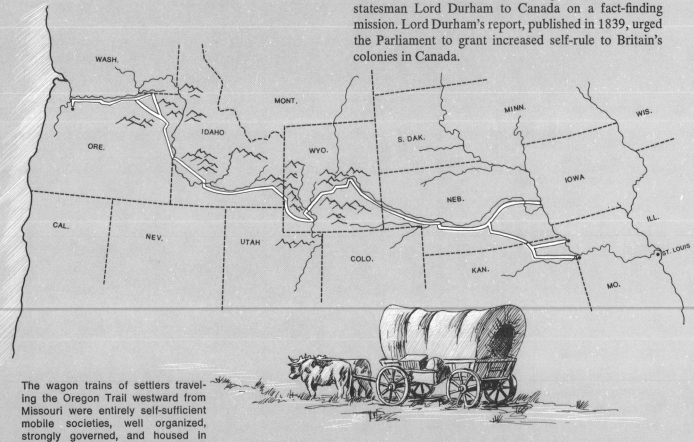

The wagon trains of settlers traveling the Oregon Trail westward from Missouri were entirely self-sufficient mobile societies, well organized, strongly governed, and housed in sturdily built covered wagons called prairie schooners.

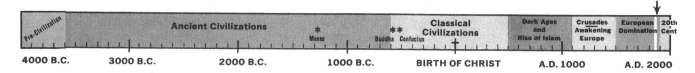

| Pre-Civilization | Ancient Civilizations | *Moses | **Buddha Confucius | Classical Civilizations | Dark Ages and Rise of Islam | Crusades Awakening Europe | European Domination | 20th Cent |

4000 B.C.   3000 B.C.   2000 B.C.   1000 B.C.   BIRTH OF CHRIST   A.D. 1000   A.D. 2000

1850 — 1875

The Crimean War • Bismarck Unifies Germany • The Suez Canal • Charles Darwin and Karl Marx • Civil War in the United States

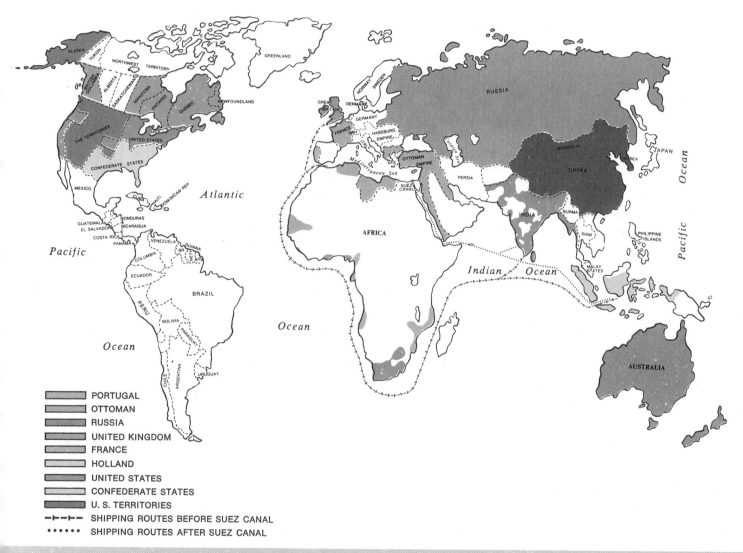

PORTUGAL
OTTOMAN
RUSSIA
UNITED KINGDOM
FRANCE
HOLLAND
UNITED STATES
CONFEDERATE STATES
U. S. TERRITORIES
–•–•– SHIPPING ROUTES BEFORE SUEZ CANAL
•••••• SHIPPING ROUTES AFTER SUEZ CANAL

EUROPE and the Mediterranean World

The Near East Problem continued to disturb Eastern Europe and, in 1854, caused an outbreak of open hostility when Czar Nicholas I proclaimed Russia's right to protect Christians under Ottoman Turkish rule who, the Czar alleged, suffered oppression. The Czar's actions against Turkey were opposed by both France and Britain in what was called the Crimean War. Russia's underlying objective in the war was to obtain access from the Black Sea to the Mediterranean, which her ships could

accomplish only by sailing through the narrow Straits (the Bosporus and the Dardanelles), past the Turkish capital of Istanbul. France and Britain, on the other hand, hoped to contain Russian expansion.

In the Treaty of Paris signed in 1856, a defeated Czar Nicholas bowed to terms that forbade Russian passage through the Straits, left the Turkish Empire intact, and forced Nicholas to agree that no nation should have the right to intervene in the domestic affairs of Turkey. Yet, alleged persecution of Christians within Turkey continued, and small Ottoman states repeatedly attempted revolts, which were put down by the sultans.

In 1855, Czar Nicholas I of Russia was succeeded by Alexander II, who, despite strong opposition from Russian nobles, made a serious effort to improve the lot of the downtrodden serfs of his realm.

In France, Prince Louis Napoleon Bonaparte had limaxed a lifetime of scheming by having himself elected president of the fledgling Second Republic which had risen out of the Revolution of 1848. Then, in 1852, by a military coup, he had himself proclaimed Emperor Napoleon III. The same year saw slavery abolished throughout the French Empire as it had been previously in the British Empire. Napoleon III did much to secure France's domestic prosperity, but he proved quite inept in foreign affairs. He bungled an attempt to aid the Italians in their drive for unity, as well as an attempt to establish and maintain Maximilian, brother of the Austrian Emperor Franz Josef, as ruler of Mexico.

During this same period, Otto von Bismarck was scheming to join the separate German states into one nation under the kingdom of Prussia. Bismarck was elected minister-president of Prussia and began the formation of a Germanic coalition, keeping Austria, the only rival for German leadership, outside the union. He built a fine military machine which he brought to razor-edge sharpness in small wars, the first of them against Denmark, the second against Austria. In the latter, the Seven Weeks' War (1866), Austria was forced to cede to Italy the province of Venetia, including the city of Venice—a first step toward Italian unity.

In 1870, Napoleon III's France and Bismarck's Prussia met head on in the Franco–Prussian War, with France suffering humiliating defeat. As a result of this war, Germany emerged in 1871 as an empire, with Bismarck its prime minister. Napoleon III's empire collapsed, and the French Third Republic came into being out of the wreckage. Bismarck forced France to surrender Alsace-Lorraine to Germany and to pay huge reparations.

During the year 1867, Karl Marx, who was living in London, published the first volume of *Das Kapital (Capital)*, a book which was to become the fundamental written work of world socialism. The second volume was published in 1894.

Italy finally attained national unity in this quarter century, under Victor Emmanuel II of Sardinia (as the ruler of Piedmont, Savoy and Sardinia was called). This came about largely as a result of the prolonged efforts of the patriots Mazzini, Cavour and Garibaldi, and through the aid of France and Prussia, both of whom stood to gain by seeing Austria deprived of her Italian possessions. In 1859, Milan and much of the Italian north were freed from Austrian rule in a war that aligned Piedmont and France against Austria. In that same year, the peoples of Tuscany and other Italian states overthrew their rulers and voted for annexation to Piedmont. In 1860, Sicily and Naples were taken from their Bourbon ruler by an expedition led by Garibaldi and were united with the others by plebiscite. In 1861 the Kingdom of Italy was proclaimed, with Victor Emmanuel—now known as Victor Emmanuel I, King of Italy—as its constitutional ruler. In 1866, as previously noted, Austria ceded Venetia to Italy after being defeated by Italy's ally Prussia in the Seven Weeks' War. In 1870, when French troops guarding the Papacy were withdrawn to fight in the Franco–Prussian War, Italian troops entered Rome. The entire peninsula was now under Victor Emmanuel's rule, with Rome as its capital.

Garibaldi, the fiery Italian patriot, fresh from his capture of Sicily and Naples, marched north to pledge his conquests and his allegiance to King Victor Emmanuel. When the two leaders met and collaborated, the Italian Peninsula was united into one nation for the first time since the days of Ancient Rome.

In Great Britain, during this twenty-five-year period, Charles Darwin wrote the revolutionary *Origin of Species,* propounding his theory of evolution by natural selection. This book was viewed by some as an attack on the authenticity of the Bible's account of the Creation, but was greeted by others not as an attack on religion, but as one of the great advancements in man's understanding of the development of life. Also during this period, England built the world's first underground railway system, or subway, and established what is believed to be the first compulsory-education system. The right to vote was guaranteed to most workers in the Reform Bill of 1867. The secret ballot was instituted in 1872, and important judicial reform was effected in 1873.

Victoria was queen during this very progressive period, and William Gladstone was prime minister. However, when Gladstone supported the Irish in their bid for home rule, he lost favor among Britons who thought he was endangering the empire, and he was replaced as prime minister by Benjamin Disraeli in 1874. Disraeli is best remembered for his part in Britain's acquisition in 1875 of controlling shares in the Suez Canal Corporation (a product of French engineering and promotion) and for his maneuvering with France to frustrate Russia's efforts to win access to the Mediterranean Sea past the Turkish city of Istanbul.

Austria and Hungary, under Emperor Franz Josef, enjoyed an upsurge of creativity in the arts and sciences during this quarter century. Johann Strauss the Younger was but one of the many great Austrian musicians who were composing and performing; Peter Mitterhoffer invented the first typewriter; the Augustinian monk Gregor Mendel, working with sweetpeas, discovered the laws of heredity. In 1867, Austria and Hungary were organized as a dual monarchy, each a separate nation but both ruled by the same king, Franz Josef, and enjoying the same rights.

The opening of the Suez Canal in 1869 revolutionized world trade by eliminating the hazardous voyage around the stormy and pirate-frequented southern tip of Africa and thus reducing the distance between Europe and India by almost 4,000 sea miles.

ASIA, except for its Mediterranean Lands

Between 1850 and 1875, Britain took over the government of India from the East India Company, and proceeded with the modernization of education and transportation in the vast subcontinent. In 1853, for example, a telegraph line was installed from the city of Agra to Calcutta, and in 1857 universities were founded in Calcutta, Bombay and Madras. Although the East India Company's charter was renewed in 1855, its continuing existence was threatened almost at once by a series of rebellions in northern India by both Moslems and Hindus. This outbreak of rebellions was called, collectively, the Sepoy Mutiny. After the rebels were suppressed, Parliament passed the Government of India Act, which dissolved the East India Company and transferred government to the British Crown. A series of reforms and public works followed this transfer of government; the-

oretically all offices were now open to native Indians. The commercial activity of the Indian subcontinent was increased many times over in 1869 by the opening of the Suez Canal, and in 1870 by an underwater telegraph line linking India and Egypt.

China was torn by a series of rebellions during this period. Between the years 1850 and 1864, a revolt called the T'ai P'ing Rebellion, led by Hung Hsui-chüan, came close to overturning the Manchu Dynasty. Failure by the rebels to provide conquered territory with protection or administration caused their rapid decline. Between 1855 and 1873, Moslems of Yunan province near Indochina revolted and set up an independent state. From 1855 to 1881, Miao tribesmen were in almost constant rebellion in Kweichow province in southern China.

In 1858, the Treaty of Tientsin, between China and Great Britain, the United States, France and Russia, opened eleven more Chinese ports to trade and legalized the importation of opium. In 1860, British and French troops occupied the city of Peking. Representatives of the Western powers exploited the Chinese people and treated them as inferiors, but at the same time missionaries introduced modern medicine into China, and telegraphic cables were laid in 1871 from Vladivostok in Russia via Nagasaki in Japan to Shanghai in China. Between 1872 and 1881 over one hundred Chinese students were sent to the United States, and many were also sent to Britain and France for technical training.

In 1874, a Japanese expedition invaded the Chinese island of Formosa, or Taiwan, using as justification the claim that the occupation was punishment for alleged criminal acts of Formosa's citizenry against foreign residents and foreign-owned shops.

Japan in 1853 signed a treaty with the United States in the person of Commodore Matthew Perry, opening

The British began setting up new industries in India such as mills to process cotton and factories to extract indigo for dye. These products became the basis of India's new industrialization, and were among the important products transported through the Suez Canal to Europe.

two of her ports to trade for the first time since 1192. The Emperor was restored as supreme ruler in Japan in the year 1867, thus ending almost seven hundred years of rule by the shoguns. In 1872, universal military service was introduced into the nation.

Vietnam between 1847 and 1883 was ruled by Tu Duc, who, like his predecessors, attempted to keep foreigners from his lands. The persecution of Christians continued until a joint French and Spanish expedition occupied Saigon in southern Vietnam in 1858. In the Treaty of Saigon, signed in 1862, Emperor Tu Duc ceded the southern portions of Vietnam to the French. In 1863 Cambodia became a French protectorate, and by 1874 French soldiers had captured Hanoi in the north. The French returned Hanoi to the Vietnamese as part of an agreement that guaranteed freedom of Christian worship in Vietnam and a strong French voice in Vietnamese affairs. Emperor Tu Duc at this time began a series of appeals to the Chinese asking that Vietnam again be put under Chinese protection.

OCEANIA

In 1850 the Parliament of Great Britain granted self-government to Australia in what was called the Australian Colonies Act. The discovery of gold in Australia the following year, 1851, drew a great influx of population to the land. A similar gold strike in New Zealand in 1861 brought in thousands of fortune-hunting Europeans.

The discovery of gold in Australia drew immigrants in great numbers and forced the development of Australia into a modern nation, with country villages such as Melbourne developing rapidly into busy commercial cities.

AFRICA, except for its Mediterranean Lands

In the period 1858–1859 two English explorers, Richard Burton and John Speke, penetrated deep into East Africa and discovered Lake Tanganyika. When Burton became ill with fever, Speke went on to discover Lake Victoria, which he concluded was the source of the White Nile and the principal source of the Nile River itself.

In 1866, the discovery of diamonds in Africa sparked a rush of Europeans to the Dark Continent.

THE AMERICAS

From 1861 to 1865 the United States was enmeshed in its bitter Civil War—the War Between the States—in which the North fought the South, and, in many cases, brother fought against brother. The war was a clash between two different ways of life, between the industrial North with its large cities and factories and the agricultural South with its great farms and plantations which were operated with slave labor.

Such questions as slavery and states' rights had tended to drive the North and the South apart almost from the nation's earliest days, and by the early 1800s these issues had reached explosive proportions. In 1854 the Kansas-Nebraska Act, sponsored by Senator Stephen A. Douglas of Illinois, reopened the question of whether slavery should be permitted in the vast new territories of the West. The act permitted "popular sovereignty"—that is, the new states were granted the option to permit or forbid slavery as they saw fit.

Abraham Lincoln, running on a platform that opposed any further extension of slavery in the territories, was elected president of the United States in November 1860. Within the next seven months, eleven Southern states seceded from the Union and joined together as the Confederate States of America. On April 12, 1861, the Confederate attack on Fort Sumter in the harbor of Charleston, South Carolina, plunged the nation, which was still less than one hundred years old, into a civil war whose cost would be incalculable. More than half a million lives were lost in battles which laid waste cities, towns and croplands, mostly in the South. Public and private moneys were expended in amounts beyond reckoning, and in the end the victory of one part of the nation over the other could not compensate for the damage done to the whole.

In the midst of the war, on January 1, 1863, President Lincoln's Emancipation Proclamation freed all the slaves in the areas in rebellion. (Slaves in other areas were freed after the war's end.) Two years later, on April 9, 1865, the Confederate forces capitulated and the war was over. Within a week Lincoln was dead, assassinated at the Ford Theater in Washington by an actor embittered by the Southern defeat. The extremity of this act was symptomatic of the bitterness which divided the country at the close of the war.

This was a quarter century of dramatic technological advances. The first transatlantic cable reduced to a matter of minutes the time required for a message to be sent between Europe and America, and the first transcontinental railroad reduced to a few days the time for a journey from one coast of America to the other.

In Mexico, Benito Juárez assumed national leadership in the year 1858 in the midst of a civil war in that country between liberal and conservative factions. Juárez became president of the liberal government and established its capital first at Veracruz, later in Mexico City. He bent earnest efforts to the improvement of his people's economic condition and to the lessening of the Church's political influence. In the midst of Juárez' rule, France, Britain and Spain broke off relations with Mexico over financial payments owed them by Mexico, and invaded and occupied Veracruz. Napoleon III of France installed the Archduke Maximilian (brother of the Austrian Emperor) as "emperor of Mexico." The new Emperor and his Empress, Carlota, had been deceived by Napoleon, in the latter's attempt to gain strong influence in Mexican politics, about the willingness of the Mexican people to have them as their rulers, and about the support they could expect from France. Maximilian, after being deserted by Napoleon III, was captured and executed in Mexico while Carlota was in Europe pleading for aid for her husband.

In 1867, the British Parliament passed the British North America Act, which established Canada as a self-governing dominion within the British Empire.

Abraham Lincoln, President of the United States during the years of the bitter Civil War was assassinated shortly after the war's end. His humane counsel was thus lost to those whose difficult task it was to heal the breach and restore the South to full fellowship in the nation.

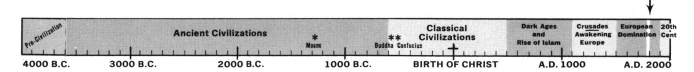

| Pre-Civilization | Ancient Civilizations | Moses | Buddha Confucius | Classical Civilizations | Dark Ages and Rise of Islam | Crusades Awakening Europe | European Domination | 20th Cent |

4000 B.C.   3000 B.C.   2000 B.C.   1000 B.C.   BIRTH OF CHRIST   A.D. 1000   A.D. 2000

1875 — 1900

Origins of the Anglo-French-Russian Alliance • The Worldwide Empire of Britain • Edison, Marconi, Curie, Darwin, Pasteur, Freud, Marx, Dickens, Tolstoy, Mark Twain, Mann, Ibsen, van Gogh, Rodin • French Rule in Indochina • The Partition of Africa by European States • The Spanish–American War

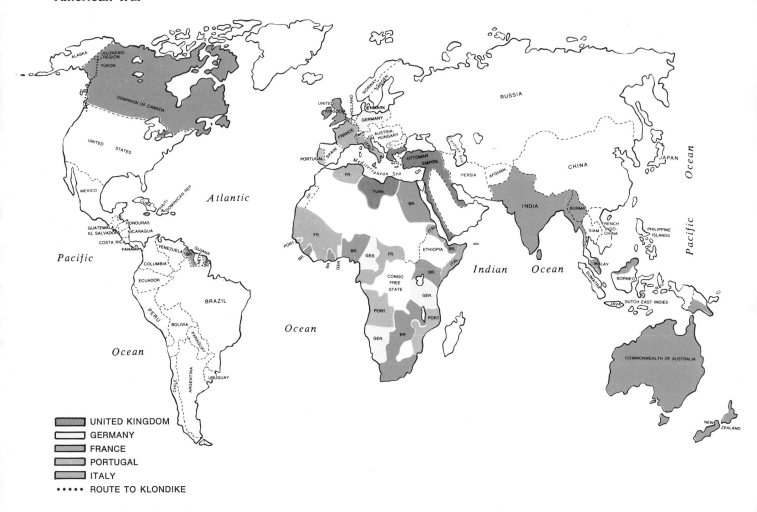

UNITED KINGDOM
GERMANY
FRANCE
PORTUGAL
ITALY
•••• ROUTE TO KLONDIKE

EUROPE and the Mediterranean World

Events in the last quarter of the nineteenth century tended to bring about alliances between long-standing former enemies. Germany and Austria, for example, after years of contention for leadership of the German-speaking peoples of Europe, were now drawn together by common interests, as were France and Russia, the old enemies of the Napoleonic Wars. Even Britain and France were tending toward an alliance, pulled together by common interests and common anxieties after centuries of warring against each other.

The first of the events which brought the new alliances into being was the accession in 1888 of Wilhelm II to the throne of Germany. Kaiser Wilhelm was to rule until the end of World War I in 1918, and would be Germany's last emperor. Shortly after he came to the throne, he dismissed Bismarck as his prime minister and vigorously assumed the reins of government himself, working through various prime ministers. He led Germany to great industrial and military development and, at the same time, toward inevitable conflict with the other European powers. For example, the treaty which Bismarck had so skillfully negotiated with Russia was allowed to lapse, and, as Bismarck had warned, Russia formed an alliance with France, Germany's old adversary. Wilhelm enlarged the German Navy to a size which aroused apprehension in the British government, and he supported Austria's "Drive to the East," which included a proposed Berlin-to-Baghdad railway. Not surprisingly, unrest and suspicion grew in the nations of the Balkan Peninsula when it was realized that the new rail system would pass through that unstable area of the deteriorating Ottoman Turkish Empire.

The Balkan Peninsula had become a powder keg. Its component states, such as Macedonia, Serbia, Rumania and Montenegro, were struggling to break free of Turkey; Russia was trying to gain control of the area by appealing to fellow Slavic peoples there under Turkish rule; and Germanic Austria was trying to do the same thing with an appeal to Balkan residents of Germanic background. The lines were drawn between what was called Pan-Slavism and Pan-Germanism.

France, as previously noted, had become allied with Russia. Britain, despite a long history of enmity with France, was moving toward joining this Franco-Russian alliance, hoping to counter German activities in the Balkans and elsewhere.

Anglo-French cooperation first came into being when Britain and France intervened in Egyptian affairs in the 1870s—acting, they contended, in the interest of French and British creditors of Egypt. Britain became even more deeply involved in Egypt in 1881 when British troops were sent into Cairo to quell a local disturbance which the British government asserted endangered Euro-pean residents there. The troops remained as "aides" to the Khedive, or governor of Egypt. Later in the century, British troops were used to quell a revolt in the Egyptian colony of the Sudan, thus involving Britain even more deeply in African-Egyptian affairs.

The problems of Ireland also troubled Britain in the last quarter of the nineteenth century, with the Irish people struggling for home rule, and British leadership unwisely rejecting the advice of Gladstone and entering into a bitter struggle to retain control of the country.

Within Britain itself, the industrial development of the nation continued, as did the degraded condition of the British working classes. Toward the end of the century, however, Parliament acted to improve the lot of labor, and, as a result, British labor unions were the first anywhere to be permitted to operate legally and to have a voice in government. Britain also pioneered in social legislation aimed at slum clearance, public education and child welfare. In Germany, Bismarck had instituted extensive similar social reforms prior to being dismissed as prime minister by Kaiser Wilhelm.

In France, the Dreyfus Case, a scandal within the Army in which a Jewish army officer, Captain Alfred Dreyfus, was falsely accused and convicted of treason, shocked the nation and much of the Western world. The bitter controversy which ensued involved questions of anti-Semitism, military justice and French national honor.

In 1899 the world's first peace conference was held in The Hague, Holland. It was widely hoped that the conference might be a beginning of the elimination of the use of war as a means of settling political differences.

Artists, Writers and Scientists of the 1800's

By the end of the 1800s, the output of European artists, writers and scientists had accelerated to the point where it dwarfed even the productiveness of the amazing 1700s. This upsurge in productivity was especially evident in science and technology, which during this century literally transformed Western man's way of life. Practically every ethnic group of Europe and the Americas contributed to these technological advances. During the early years of the century, George Stephenson (1781–1848) of England designed steam engines which made travel by rail a practical reality. Other Englishmen such as Michael Faraday (1791–1867) and Charles Wheatstone (1802–1875) made investigations into electromagnetism which laid the foundations for the modern electrical industry. They were followed by two other Britons, James Joule (1818–1889), who did quantitative measurements in the relationship between friction, heat and electricity, and William Thomson (1824–1907) whose accomplishments, among other things, led to the improved ship's compass and the transatlantic cable. During these same early years of the century, a German, Robert Bunsen (1811–1899), did work which led him and his associate Gustav Kirchhoff (1824–1887) to develop spectrum analysis. Bunsen also invented many practical devices, the best known of which is the Bunsen burner, a familiar tool in every chemistry laboratory.

The work of these pioneers in electrical-chemical theory led to the invention of the telegraph by an American, Samuel F. B. Morse (1791–1872), and to that of the telephone by the Scots-American Alexander Graham Bell (1847–1922), as well as to the work of yet a third American, Thomas Alva Edison (1847–1931), who was probably the most prolific inventor of all times; his more than one thousand patents covered inventions in telegraphy, in incandescent lighting, in power production (a version of the dynamo), in transportation (an electrical railway), and in photographic and motion picture equipment.

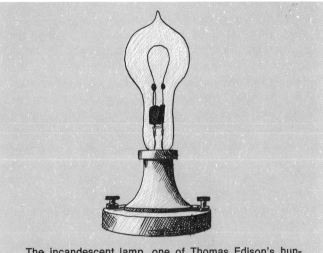

The incandescent lamp, one of Thomas Edison's hundreds of inventions, caused significant changes in the living conditions of mankind, eventually bringing inexpensive and reliable light to homes, farms, factories and city streets.

The gasoline (internal-combustion) engine, which was to be the power source of the automobile and later of the airplane, was the result of the efforts of many men of French, German, English and American origins. Somewhat later a German engineer, Rudolf Diesel (1858–1913), invented the diesel engine, which burned low-cost fuel oil instead of gasoline, and which operated much more economically and simply than the internal-combustion engine.

Around the middle of the century, a Scotsman, James Clerk Maxwell (1831–1879), engaged in revolutionary investigations into electrical phenomena, using mathematical analysis. His work explained many of the previous discoveries in electricity. Most important, Maxwell's work indicated that light is but one form of electronic wave. Further, it predicted that there must be a whole range of similar electronic waves, most of them invisible to the human eye, but all obeying the same laws as visible light and differing from it largely in their "wavelengths." Heinrich Rudolf Hertz (1857–1894), a German physicist, using Maxwell's theories as a guide, produced "long" electronic waves suitable for "radio," or wireless, telegraphy. An Italian inventor, Guglielmo Marconi (1874–1937), used the theories and discoveries of both Maxwell and Hertz to develop wireless radio transmission. By 1898, Marconi had developed his equipment so as to be able to send messages from ship to shore and later as far as from France to England. Wilhelm Roentgen (1845–1923), a German scientist, discovered electronic waves at the extreme "short" end of the wavelength spectrum, which he called X rays and which he found could penetrate most forms of matter and could be used for "seeing" into opaque objects.

In 1869, a Russian, Dimitri Mendeleev (1834–1907), devised a chart of the known chemical elements, which he called the "periodic table." The table arranged the elements in ascending order of their atomic weights, the lightest element first, then the second lightest, and so on. Mendeleev discovered that within this arrangement heavier elements with like characteristics were apt to appear at regular intervals; where this pattern did not occur, he suggested, a yet undiscovered element must exist which would fill the gap in the table's pattern. In every such case the missing element was eventually found. In this way, Mendeleev's periodic table led scientists to discover several previously unknown elements and eventually led to a broader understanding of chemistry and of the very structure of matter itself.

During the second half of the nineteenth century, a number of discoveries were made which cast doubt upon the long-held belief that matter was indestructible, and the conviction grew that the atom (the basic unit composing all forms of matter) could be broken down into smaller or simpler components. An early hint of this divisibility of the atom came from the discovery of the Frenchman Antoine-Henri Becquerel (1852–1908) that the element uranium emitted radiations which were later found to be fractions of uranium's own atoms. The work of the Polish expatriate Marie Curie (1867–1934) and her French husband, Pierre Curie (1859–1906), in isolating from uranium two new elements, polonium and radium, which were products of the breakdown of the uranium atom, made great strides in further demonstrating that atoms could decompose into other atoms of lesser weight or often into combinations of atoms-of-lesser-weight plus energy particles. This process of breaking large atoms into lesser-atoms-and-energy came in a later time to be known as "atomic fission."

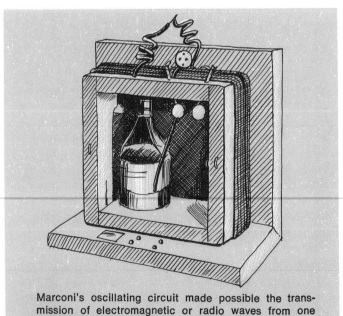

Marconi's oscillating circuit made possible the transmission of electromagnetic or radio waves from one location to another. It became the heart of the network of inventions around which the radio industry was built.

A German scientist, Max Planck (1858–1947), evolved the quantum theory, which proposed that light and other forms of energy were emitted as units called "quanta" rather than a steady flow. Planck's theory became the basis upon which very important work in the physical sciences was built in later decades.

The 1800s produced giants in the biological sciences as well as in physics and chemistry. Of great importance was the work of the English naturalist Charles Darwin (1809–1882), whose research offered evidence of the operation of natural selection by which individuals most fitted to the environment were likely to survive and thereby determine future evolution of plant and animal species. Darwin's work precipitated the bitter controversy over human evolution (did man evolve from the ape?) which troubled many sincere people of his time and later.

Important, too, was the work of the Austrian monk Gregor Mendel (1822–1884), who, working with sweetpeas, made the first scholarly studies of heredity and genetics. The Frenchman Louis Pasteur (1822–1895) did vital work in the study of fermentation and decay, and explored the role played by bacteria in human disease. Two of Pasteur's many achievements were the Pasteur treatment to prevent rabies in humans and the treatment to prevent anthrax in cattle. The Englishman Joseph Lister (1827–1912) demonstrated the connection between bacteria and wound infection and founded modern antiseptic surgery.

The nineteenth century saw the beginnings of psychoanalysis and attempts to understand and treat mental illness. The Viennese physician Sigmund Freud (1856–1939) was the founder of psychoanalysis. His countryman and associate Alfred Adler (1870–1937) later developed his own theories in the field, as did the Swiss psychologist Carl Jung (1875–1961). The previously mentioned discoveries of Wilhelm Roentgen in the field of X ray enabled physicians to "see into" human bodies, and X ray became a most important diagnostic device. Anesthesia was first used in dentistry and surgery in the United States in the middle years of the 1800s, and shortly thereafter it began to be used in England.

Important contributions to philosophy came from every corner of Europe. The German Arthur Schopenhauer (1788–1860) and his countryman Friedrich Wilhelm Nietzsche (1844–1900), writing fifty years apart in the same century, could not have been more separated in their attitudes toward their fellow men, although both were essentially pessimistic as to man's future and both had great influence on the thinking of their times. A third German, Karl Marx (1818–1883), writing on political and economic subjects, had a tremendous impact on future world developments through his *Communist Manifesto,* written in conjunction with Friedrich Engels, and his book *Das Kapital (Capital),* published later.

Two Frenchmen exercised important influence on nineteenth-century thought. The first, Auguste Compte (1798–1857), abandoned the religious approach and espoused scientific attitudes toward sociology and all studies of life; the second, Henri Bergson (1859–1941), challenged and rejected the materialistic and mechanistic conception of the universe. A Dane, Sören Aabye Kierkegaard (1813–1855), a religious and social philosopher, founded modern existentialism.

Two English philosophers were among the great thinkers of the 1800s: John Stuart Mill (1806–1873), writing on economics and political economy with the objective of improving the condition of the laboring classes; and Herbert Spencer (1820–1903), who took all human endeavor and all branches of learning as his province.

The entry of the New World into philosophy and psychology was heralded by the work of two Americans: William James (1842–1910), who formulated pragmatism and who is felt by many to have prepared the way for the conviction, espoused later by Albert Einstein and by Bertrand Russell, that the relationships between things are as real as the things themselves; and John Dewey (1859–1952), whose chief interest was in the reform of education.

The quantity of fine prose, poetry and drama produced in the 1800s by writers of the Western world rose to so great a volume as to be almost unreportable in the limited space of a book such as this. Yet an attempt must be made if the reader is to acquire an understanding of the 1800s beyond simply the politics, economics and wars of the period. The style known as Romanticism came into full flower in the literature of the period, as men of letters turned from the restraints of the Neoclassicism of the preceding centuries and reached out instead to the strange, the mysterious and even the grotesque.

Writers from both Russia and the United States for the first time challenged nations such as France, Germany and Britain for preeminence in the literary arts. Among the great Russian writers of poetry and prose, several names must be included. The great lyric poet Alexander Pushkin (1799–1837) was known not only for his magnificent poetry, but also for his pioneering work on the novel in Russia; his novel *The Captain's Daughter* painted a vivid picture of several strata of Russian society. Mikhail Lermontov (1814–1841) was second only to Pushkin among Russian nineteenth-century poets. Leo Tolstoy (1828–1910) wrote *War and Peace* and *Anna Karenina,* which are considered to be among the greatest novels ever written in any language. Fedor Dostoevsky (1821–1881) was an important influence upon later novelists; his most famous novels, *Crime and Punishment* and *The Brothers Karamazov,* have tremendous scope, covering the range of human emotions from the meanest to the divine. Anton Chekhov (1860–1904) was a master of the short story, as was Maxim Gorki (1868–1939). Chekhov also achieved international fame as a dramatist; *Uncle Vanya* and *The Three Sisters* are among his most admired plays.

Among American writers in the 1800s, Washington Irving (1783–1859) early gained an international reputation for fine prose. James Fenimore Cooper (1789–1851) wrote tremendously popular historical novels, many of which had leading characters who were American Indians, an exciting departure in the reading of Europeans and Americans of the day.

Ralph Waldo Emerson (1803–1882) was a much respected essayist, scholar and lecturer, who seemed oblivious to the widespread controversy aroused by his writings. Henry David Thoreau (1817–1862), another American essayist of the early nineteenth century, also became the subject of much debate and discussion for his ideas about nature and the desirability of the simple life. His book *Walden* gave an account of his two years as a recluse at Walden Pond, located on the estate of his good friend Emerson.

Several American writers made important contributions to the novel in nineteenth-century America: Nathaniel Hawthorne (1804–1864), whose novels include *The Scarlet Letter* and *The House of Seven Gables;* Herman Melville (1819–1891), whose most famous novel is *Moby Dick;* Mark Twain (1835–1910), who wrote the delightful *Adventures of Tom Sawyer* and *Adventures of Huckleberry Finn;* and, finally, Stephen Crane (1871–1900), whose *Red Badge of Courage* was perhaps the first novel to depict war in its true brutality and horror.

The American poet Henry Wadsworth Longfellow (1807–1882) told romantic stories in verse, the best known of which is probably his *Hiawatha*. John Greenleaf Whittier (1807–1892) was both a poet and a humanist, who used his verse as a vehicle largely to disseminate his views opposing slavery and other inequities. Walt Whitman (1819–1892) wrote poems, especially his collection called *Leaves of Grass,* which sang the praises of America, its peoples and their democratic way of life; Emily Dickinson (1830–1886) wrote powerful but uncomplicated poetry which charmed both children and adults and still does.

Many fine German writers graced the century of the 1800s. A select few are Ernst Theodor Amadeus Hoffmann (1776–1822), who wrote the imaginative short stories upon which the composer Offenbach's opera *Tales of Hoffmann* is based; the brothers Grimm, Jacob (1785–1863) and Wilhelm (1786–1859), who compiled fairy tales which are beloved to this day in virtually every nation of the earth; Gottfried Keller (1819–1890), a Swiss who was perhaps the outstanding writer of short stories in all German literature; and Thomas Mann (1875–1955), whose *Buddenbrooks* is considered to be one of the great novels of the period.

The nineteenth-century German poets Joseph Eichendorff (1788–1857), Heinrich Heine (1797–1856) and Eduard Morike (1804–1875), and the later Rainer Maria Rilke (1875–1926), all were important to German poetry and to Western literature. No dramatists writing in the German language approached the great playwrights of the eighteenth century such as Goethe, Lessing and Schiller, but the Austrian Franz Grillparzer (1791–1872) and the Germans Hermann Sudermann (1857–1928) and Gerhart Hauptmann (1862–1946) made important contributions to the literature of the theater.

The Italian novelist Alessandro Manzoni (1785–1873) was also a poet of note; his great prose romance *I Promessi Sposi* is popular in Italy to this day, and is ranked with the great literature of Europe. Giovanni Verga (1840–1922) is noted for bringing the realistic novel to Italy, and Gabriele D'Annunzio (1863–1938) achieved well-deserved fame in prose, poetry and drama. Giacomo Leopardi (1798–1837) was Italy's most highly regarded lyric poet of the 1800s.

The Danish writer Hans Christian Andersen (1805–1875) became world famous for his enchanting fairy tales, which were translated into the many languages of Europe, Africa and Asia, as were the plays of the Norwegian dramatist Henrik Ibsen (1828–1906), such as *A Doll's House, Ghosts* and *The Pillars of Society*. Ibsen's innovations, his forthright approach to subjects previously taboo in the theater, as well as his intense power and brilliant characterizations, all had a tremendous effect on later playwrights and novelists.

An attempt to select from the overwhelming number of fine novelists, poets and dramatists of France in the 1800s leaves the historian bewildered at best, and certainly open to the criticism of both experts and partisans. The poetic prose writer François-Marie de Chateaubriand (1768–1848), a precursor of the Romantic movement wrote descriptions of nature which are considered to be without equal elsewhere in literature. The novelist Marie-Henri Beyle (1783–1842), who used the pen name Stendhal, was an expert in portraying the personalities and motives underlying his characters; in *The Red and the Black* he portrays a young man trying to climb the rungs of the complex French society; in *The Charterhouse of Parma* he deals with the complexities of Italian society.

Honoré de Balzac (1799–1850) wrote many novels in the style of the then increasingly popular school of realism, in an attempt to paint a picture of the whole of French society, his most famous probably being *Le Père Goriot,* an intricate character study. Alexandre Dumas (1802–1870) wrote romantic historical novels which for generations have enthralled young and old alike; *The Three Musketeers* and *The Count of Monte Cristo* are perhaps the best known of his many works. Victor Hugo (1802–1885), poet, dramatist and novelist of the French Romantic school, is famous worldwide for his *Les Misérables,* a novel whose complex story arises out of the theft of a loaf of bread by a poverty-stricken father, and for his classic *Hunchback of Notre Dame.* Gustave Flaubert (1821–1880) wrote one of the most famous novels of the century in his carefully crafted *Madame Bovary.*

Guy de Maupassant (1850–1893) was the master of the short story of the 1800s, able with his concise prose to evoke any emotion, picture any scene and draw any character. Émile Zola (1840–1902) wrote of the real problems of real people. Among his best-known novels is *Nana,* the story of a harlot, a woman of the streets. Zola is honored for his courageous part in the rescue and rehabilitation of Captain Dreyfus in the political-military scandal that shook the French nation in the late nineteenth century. Anatole France (1844–1924) was a great satirist and the leader of the French literati of the last decades of the 1800s. Among his best works are *The Crime of Sylvestre Bonnard* and *L'Orme du Mail,* a satire on French rural life.

At least a dozen French poets of the nineteenth century, in addition to the previously mentioned Victor Hugo, must be represented here by Alfred de Musset (1810–1857), the great Romantic lyricist, and Paul Verlaine (1844–1896), who was a member of the group called Symbolists—poets who espoused freedom of expression and technique, coupled with individual choice of subject matter, and who used symbols to express abstract or intangible ideas.

English and Irish writers of prose and poetry produced memorably in every phase of literary endeavor. Charles Lamb (1775–1834), essayist and critic, is perhaps best known to young people for the highly readable *Tales from Shakespeare,* written with his sister, Mary Lamb. The essayist-historian Thomas Carlyle (1795–1881), noted for his attention to detail, his violent denunciation of hypocrisy and his conviction that great men, rather than economics or climate or location, determine the course of history, is best remembered for his *Sartor Resartus* (a quasi-autobiography), and for his brilliant word picture *The French Revolution.* Thomas Babington Macaulay (1800–1859) was a colorful but often inaccurate and biased reporter of events and people; his *History of England from the Accession of James II* was widely read, as were his essays on great historical and literary figures such as Clive of India and the poets Milton and Byron. H. G. Wells (1866–1946), historian and novelist, who would later try to educate people with his *Outline of History* and other works, entertained them in the 1890s with scientific romances such as *The Time Machine* and *The War of The Worlds.*

In Britain a remarkable number of literary artists won international renown for novels which, even today, are regarded as leading examples of the genre. Sir Walter Scott (1771–1832) the Scottish poet, novelist, historian and biographer, is best known among almost countless other literary accomplishments for having invented the historical novel, two of the best known being the novels *Waverley* and *Ivanhoe,* and for his *History of Scotland.* William Makepeace Thackeray (1811–1863) reached new literary heights in his use of descriptive detail and in his ability to expose vicious social customs. Two of his novels, *Vanity Fair* and *Henry Esmond,* embody some of the ablest social criticism in all literature. In addition, *Vanity Fair* presents, in Becky Sharpe, a skillfully drawn female character seldom, if ever, surpassed by any novelist. The novels of Charles Dickens (1812–1870) portrayed pathos and humor, and created characters who became, in the eyes of the world, the essence of certain human types. His novels *Oliver Twist* and *David Copperfield* are particularly famed for such character studies, and in *A Tale of Two Cities,* a novel of the French Revolution, Dickens reveals his complete mastery of plot complexity.

Charles Dickens became the world's most popular writer, selling thousands of copies of his novels about the poor, the dispossessed and the hopeless of society.

Charlotte Brontë (1816–1855) enjoyed great fame during her lifetime for *Jane Eyre,* most highly regarded among her several novels. Her sister Emily (1818–1848) has been accorded even greater critical acclaim with the passage of time for her single novel, *Wuthering Heights,* and there is growing admiration for her lyrical poetry. George Eliot (the pen name of Mary Ann Evans, 1819–1880) has earned a special place in the regard of generation after generation for her picturization of rural England in novels such as *The Mill on the Floss* and *Silas Marner.*

The beloved author of *Alice in Wonderland,* Lewis Carroll (1832–1898), whose real name was Charles Dodgson, was also, surprisingly, a mathematician of note. Thomas Hardy (1840–1928), whose emotionally down-to-earth writing reflected a reaction against the prevailing sentimental outlook of the Victorians, yet conveyed the feeling that fate determines human destiny, created a series of five novels, best known of which are *The Return of the Native* and *Tess of the d'Uber-*

villes. Robert Louis Stevenson (1850–1894) wrote romances which have thrilled and charmed generation after generation. Among his most famed are *Treasure Island* and *Kidnapped.* His *Dr. Jekyll and Mr. Hyde* was an early study of the split-personality theme. Rudyard Kipling (1865–1936) wrote against a background of British rule of India and became known the world over as a great teller of tales, a champion of the British Empire, and a firm believer in white supremacy and imperialism, popularized at the time as "the white man's burden," in which it was seen as the duty of white, Caucasian peoples to bring civilization to "backward" peoples of the world. Among his most widely read works are *Kim, The Light That Failed, Captains Courageous* and the much-loved *Jungle Books.*

Outstanding English poets of the 1800s were William Wordsworth (1770–1850) a lover of nature who became a leader of the Romantic movement, as did the master of the ballad, Samuel Taylor Coleridge (1772–1834); Lord Byron (1788–1824), whose narrative poems include the highly regarded *Childe Harold's Pilgrimage* and *The Bride of Albydos;* the great lyric poet Percy Bysshe Shelley (1792–1822), whose ability to create pure beauty has never been surpassed, and whose *Ode to the West Wind* and *The Clouds* are examples of the enchantment he brought to any subject; John Keats (1795–1821), a Romantic poet with fine descriptive power, whose poems have a unique melodious sound; Alfred, Lord Tennyson (1809–1892), perhaps best known for his *Idylls of the King,* based on the legends of King Arthur's court; Robert Browning (1812–1889) and his wife, Elizabeth Barrett Browning (1806–1861), both of whom earned an important place in the poetry of the nineteenth century. Other important names are Matthew Arnold (1822–1888), noted for his narrative verse; Dante Gabriel Rossetti (1828–1882), painter and romantic poet, and Algernon Charles Swinburne (1837–1909), a popular poet as well as a playwright.

Art in the nineteenth century became very much a French province. Although other nations produced first-rate artists and in at least one case a great one— Vincent van Gogh (1853–1890) of Holland, who painted brilliant and colorful "Impressionist" canvases —the majority of the front-ranking artists of the 1800s were French. They included Jean-Auguste Ingres (1780–1867), portraitist and leader of the surviving Classical school; Eugène Delacroix (1798–1864), one of the first Romantic painters, who reacted against the limitations on color and technique imposed by the Classicists, and became noted for his use of color in historical paintings and murals; Jean-Baptiste Corot (1796–1875), the landscape artist, whose use of soft colors and tones seemed to presage the revolution in painting known as Impressionism, a mode which attempted to achieve desired effects by the use of "divided color." The new technique employed dabs of different colors which, when viewed at a distance, blended into one, often as if shimmering in the sunlight. The Frenchman Camille Pissarro (1830–1903), was a leader of the Impressionist school. He was a master at painting the look of sunlight and, later, the glow and atmosphere of the Paris avenues at night. Édouard Manet (1832–1883) also emphasized the varied looks of sunlight. In addition, Manet revived the bold effects of the Spaniard Velásquez. To do this, he used brilliant colors and painted from real life. Claude Monet (1840–1926) was most noted for his landscapes, in which he attempted to catch the illusive changes of light and clouds. Edgar Degas (1834–1917) was a French Impressionist most noted for his studies of the electric grace of dancers, of race horses and of seaside bathers, all caught in rhythmic poses; Auguste Renoir (1841–1919) specialized in portraits of the female figure, both clothed and nude.

The group of French painters who next came upon the scene were known as Post-Impressionists because they attempted to avoid the ephemeral effect usual in true Impressionism. Paul Cézanne (1839–1906) used solid colors and intersecting sharp planes to obtain the feel of both volume and distance. Paul Gauguin (1848–1903) used brilliant color combined with a rhythmic line. He is most noted for his almost primitive portraits done in the later years of his life, when he lived in Tahiti. Henri de Toulouse-Lautrec (1864–1901) was famed for his portraits of people of the theater, the cafés, the bars and streets of Paris.

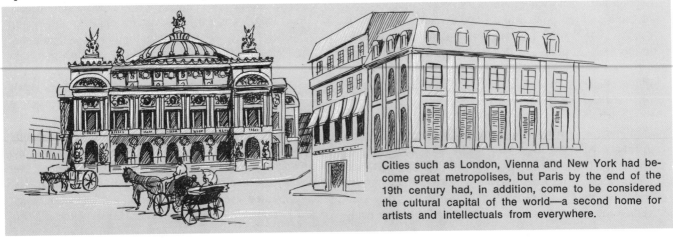

Cities such as London, Vienna and New York had become great metropolises, but Paris by the end of the 19th century had, in addition, come to be considered the cultural capital of the world—a second home for artists and intellectuals from everywhere.

Auguste Rodin (1840–1917), the French sculptor, lived and worked in Paris in the last half of the nineteenth century. Rodin was noted for being able to combine stark realism with extreme delicacy of modeling. His best-known works are probably *The Thinker* and *The Kiss*.

Two American painters who achieved fame in the nineteenth century were John Singer Sargent (1856–1925), portraitist to the great and near-great of Europe, and James Abbott McNeill Whistler (1834–1903), skilled landscape artist who became, ironically, most noted for his portrait of his mother and for the barbed edge of his witty tongue. Two noted English landscape painters of this century were John Constable (1776–1837) and Joseph Mallord William Turner (1775–1851). The Englishman Dante Gabriel Rossetti (1828–1882), previously mentioned as a poet, was also a painter, one of the founders of the Pre-Raphaelite movement, which aimed at recovering the spirit in art that prevailed prior to the Italian painter Raphael of the late 1400s.

Architecture during the 1800s produced little that was new, most buildings being designed "in the style of" past eras such as the Classical Greek, the Gothic, the Georgian or the Baroque. Toward the century's end, the Eiffel Tower, the work of the engineer Alexandre-Gustave Eiffel (1832–1923), was erected in Paris. At first its bold, functional, skeletonlike use of steel sweeping upward to great heights aroused bitter condemnation from art lovers, especially since the tower stood amidst the architectural glories of Paris. Yet it foretold the architecture of the future. The skyscrapers of concrete and steel which subsequently came into being in the world's great cities used many of the Eiffel Tower's engineering principles. The Woolworth Building in New York City, the world's tallest building at the time of its construction, is an example of the Eiffel Tower's influence on world architecture.

Music, from some points of view, had one of its most productive periods during the nineteenth century. During these years, the Romantic movement which had so strongly affected painting and the literary arts also invaded the world of musical composition. Outstanding work was done by German, Austrian, Italian, French, Polish, Belgian, Norwegian, Finnish and English writers of songs, operas and chamber music.

Ludwig van Beethoven (1770–1827), a German composer of Flemish descent, expressed by means of his music the heights and depths of emotion and the widest range of variations in the human spirit. Over the years, Beethoven has maintained a universal appeal comparable to that of Shakespeare in drama and poetry. His nine symphonies, his single opera, his choral masses and his piano concertos show his vast understanding of musical technique and great innovative skill, yet at no time does technique dominate his pure musical appeal. His work has affected every composer writing during and since his lifetime.

In the early years of the century the German Karl Maria von Weber (1786–1826) pioneered the Romantic movement in German music and played a key role in establishing the German national opera. Other German composers of the Romantic school were Giacomo Meyerbeer (1791–1864), who wrote operas in Italian and French; Felix Mendelssohn (1809–1847), who composed not for the opera but for the concert stage, for symphony orchestras and for the piano; Robert Schumann (1810–1856), who wrote symphonies, chamber music and a host of delightful songs; and Richard Wagner (1813–1883), who was a storm center around whom musical and social controversy raged. Wagner's operas, based on German legends and folk tales—operas such as *Tannhäuser, Lohengrin* and the four-part cycle *The Ring of the Nibelungs*—are performed as either operas or orchestral works all over the world to this day. Johannes Brahms (1833–1897), combining intellectual and emotional appeal, composed symphonies, piano concertos, chamber music and choral works which entitle him to a place among the all-time greats of musical composition.

The Austrian composer Franz Schubert (1797–1828) lived only thirty-one years, but left a vast amount of music, including ten symphonies, much enchanting chamber music and over six hundred delightful songs. Another Austrian, Hugo Wolf (1860–1903), is considered one of the great songwriters of musical history. The Austrian Johann Strauss the Elder (1804–1849) was the first to write dance music on an artistic level. He became known as the Father of the Waltz and wrote popular polkas, quadrilles and marches as well. His son Johann Strauss the Younger (1825–1899) became known as the Waltz King. Among his better-known compositions are "On the Beautiful Blue Danube" and "Tales from the Vienna Woods."

A group of Italian composers brought an entire new life to the musical theater, so that to this day the words "opera" and "Italy" seem almost synonymous. Gioacchino Rossini (1792–1868) wrote thirty-six delightful and very popular operas which sparkle with melody as well as with a very special humor. *The Barber of Seville* and *William Tell* are two of Rossini's most entertaining works. Giuseppi Verdi (1813–1901) added a high degree of intellect to the melodious operas with which he delighted nineteenth-century Europe. *Rigoletto* and *Il Trovatore* were among his early successes. *Aïda*, composed by Verdi at an age when most musicians have long since retired, reached a new pinnacle of achievement. Yet *Otello*, produced long past the commonly accepted retirement age, may be his greatest work, and *Falstaff* was presented to amazed opera lovers when the composer was eighty. Giacomo Puccini (1858–1924) combined the lovely melodiousness that the world had come to expect from Italian composers with an exciting sense of drama to produce such beautiful operas as *La*

Bohème and *Madame Butterfly.*

César Franck (1822–1890), Belgian composer and organist, wrote for the piano, the small orchestra and the full symphony orchestra. His work, with its use of counterpoint, at times reminds one of Bach.

In Russia a number of brilliant musicians earned a place among the great composers of all time: Peter Ilich Tchaikovsky (1840–1893), whose works include a number of outstanding symphonies and also ballets such as *Swan Lake* and *The Sleeping Beauty*—brilliantly orchestrated works with lovely melodies which keep the listener permanently captive; Aleksandr Borodin (1833–1887), composer of symphonies, string music, songs and the opera *Prince Igor,* which was finished by Nikolai Rimsky-Korsakov (1844–1908), a composer whose other contributions to music consist of several operas and symphonic poems, perhaps the best known being *Scheherazade,* as well as choral works and works for the piano; and Modest Moussorgsky (1835–1881), composer of songs and piano works whose opera *Boris Godunov* is also highly regarded.

Among the French composers who graced nineteenth-century music were Georges Bizet (1838–1875), whose *Carmen* is one of the half-dozen most popular operas ever written; Charles Gounod (1818–1893), whose operas *Faust* and *Romeo and Juliet* are still popular; and Claude Debussy (1862–1918), composer of *Afternoon of a Faun* and other orchestral works, who founded the Impressionist school of music.

The Polish composer Frédéric Chopin (1810–1849) belongs among the select few of all-time great musicians. His études, preludes, mazurkas, scherzos and ballades—almost all written for the piano—greatly enrich the musical world. The Hungarian composer and pianist Franz Liszt (1811–1886), the Finnish composer Jean Sibelius (1865–1957), and the great Norwegian composer Edvard Grieg (1843–1907) also made significant contributions to the music of the 1800s.

Chopin was honored by his contemporaries both for his compositions and for his piano concerts, which drew large and enthusiastic crowds.

ASIA, except for its Mediterranean Lands

The British rulers of India were troubled during this quarter century by the increasingly urgent drive for self-rule among native Indian peoples. The Indian nationalist movements were often anti-Christian and anti-British as well as pro-Indian. The situation was further complicated by the continuation of the age-old feuds between native Moslems and Hindus, by the threat of Russian expansion southward into Afghanistan (located on India's north), and by unrest in the neighboring country of Burma, on India's east.

In 1876, at the initiative of Prime Minister Disraeli, Queen Victoria was declared empress of India, the hope of Britain being that the Queen would become a rallying point for the diverse peoples of the subcontinent. The native princes, who still ruled their lands under the hegemony of the Crown, assembled in Delhi at a great ceremony, or durbar, to offer homage and loyalty to their Empress.

Between 1878 and 1881 the British became involved in the Second Afghan War, and, as a result, they gained control over Afghanistan's foreign policy, thereby limiting the Russian threat. Between 1885 and 1886 the Third Burmese War enabled Britain to annex the upper portions of Burma and to contain warlike Burmese fac-

tions. In effect, these lands became part of British India, greatly embittering the Burmese.

Terrible famines ravaged the Indian subcontinent in this twenty-five-year period, taking over seven million lives and crippling countless more. Toward the century's end, the nationalist movements of India became increasingly well organized. At the time, Mohandas K. Gandhi (1869–1948), a native of western India, was studying law at University College, Cambridge. In 1893, while in South Africa defending a lawsuit, he began a struggle to free Indian people who were indentured laborers there. Gandhi would one day become the political and spiritual leader of India and the symbol to oppressed peoples everywhere of nonviolent resistance.

The Chinese Empire was undermined and weakened by both the avaricious merchants of Europe and the pressure of Japanese imperialism during this last quarter of the nineteenth century. In 1894, Sun Yat-sen, a physician and the son of Chinese peasants, organized the first of several secret revolutionary societies, headquartered at Canton, which were dedicated to overthrowing the Manchu Dynasty. After the failure of the first of ten attempts to seize control of the Chinese government, Sun Yat-sen went overseas to solicit help from

Chinese residents of Honolulu and the United States. In 1896 he was kidnapped and held for ten days by the Chinese imperial representatives at their legation in London.

During 1894 and 1895, the Sino–Japanese War was fought over long-standing rivalries, especially in Korea. A victorious Japan forced humiliating terms upon China which included agreement to the independence of Korea (long considered to be within the Chinese sphere of influence), the payment of an indemnity of a large sum of money, the forced opening of four more ports to foreign commerce, and the ceding to Japan of the Chinese island of Formosa, or Taiwan. The Boxer Rebellion in China in 1900, designed to drive Westerners out of the land, is thought to have been secretly encouraged by the imperial court.

Unlike China, Japan was eager to copy Western methods. During the years 1879–1900, she completed a process of modernizing her industry.

By the end of the 1800s, France had acquired control of a major part of Indochina through a combination of military actions and advantageous treaties. The conquered area (to be called French Indochina) consisted of what is now known as North and South Vietnam plus Cambodia and Laos. Thailand, however, managed to resist being colonized by playing Britain and France against each other.

British and Dutch disputes over the Malay Peninsula and the islands of Indonesia were settled in treaties giving a clearer definition of the areas to be controlled by each.

OCEANIA

In 1898, the United States annexed the islands of Hawaii. The islands had been moving closer to union with the American republic for a number of years as American economic and military interests became increasingly predominant. In 1875, for example, Hawaiian sugar was admitted to the United States duty-free, and in 1877 the U.S. Navy had been given free use of Pearl Harbor as a coaling and naval station. Lydia Kamekeha Liliuokalani became queen in 1891. In 1893 the Queen promulgated a new constitution by means of a *coup d'état,* causing anxious American residents to organize a committee of safety. In 1893 the monarchy was abolished and American Marines landed "to protect life and property." The independent Republic of Hawaii was organized in 1894, and in 1897 a treaty of annexation was signed between the United States and the new republic. Formal transfer of the islands to the United States took place in 1898. In the same year, the Philippine Islands were annexed by the United States as a consequence of the Spanish–American War.

AFRICA, except for its Mediterranean Lands

Colonization of Africa below its Mediterranean lands was greatly accelerated during this quarter century. The explorations of the Welshman Henry M. Stanley—particularly his investigations into the Congo area, rich in rubber and ivory—had done much to open the continent to European colonization. The English were not at this time interested in moving into the Congo, but the Belgians under King Leopold II commissioned Stanley to lead a new expedition there, and by 1884 Belgium laid claim to the area.

A year later, in 1885, Germany took possession of the lands now called Cameroon (on the west coast of Africa) and Tanzania (on the east coast). In this same year, a congress of European powers met in Berlin to lay down diplomatic rules for the further partitioning of the immense African continent. This meeting in Berlin is often viewed as the beginning of modern African history.

Italy proclaimed a protectorate over Ethiopia in 1889, but seven years later a small African army defeated Italy and drove her armies from the area.

Between 1899 and 1902, a war was fought between Britain and the Dutch settlers in South Africa, known as Boers. After initial Boer successes, the British forces gradually forced the Boers to capitulate, and in a treaty signed at the city of Pretoria in 1902 the Dutch settlers swore allegiance to the British Crown.

Cecil Rhodes, an Englishman, merged the diamond mines of South Africa into the De Beers Mining Company and thus laid the foundation of modern industrial South Africa. The world-famous Rhodes Scholarships were established with funds provided by Rhodes's tremendous estates.

THE AMERICAS

In South America during the period from 1879 to 1883 Chile and Bolivia fought the War of the Pacific over the control of extensive nitrate fields. Chile was the eventual victor and retained control of the nitrates, valuable for manufacturing both fertilizer and explosives.

In Brazil, the great landowners forced the Emperor, Pedro II, to abdicate in 1888, and in 1889 the nation proclaimed itself a republic.

In North America, Mexico from 1876 to 1911 was under the dictatorship of Porfirio Díaz. Díaz promoted trade, built railroads and encouraged foreign investments, but he also did much to worsen the misery of the poverty-stricken common people of his country. In office continuously except for the period 1880–1884, he exploited the Mexican working and farm people, who were reduced to the status of peons. Education was neglected and personal freedom except among the elite was almost nonexistent in Mexico under Díaz.

The four-month-long Spanish–American War in 1898 deprived Spain of the last of her colonies in the New World, and made the United States a world power when the latter took over the Spanish colonies of Puerto Rico in the Caribbean, Guam in the Pacific, and the Philippines off the coast of Southeast Asia.

This twenty-five-year period saw the establishment in the United States of the Civil Service, a system of examinations used as a test of an individual's fitness for federal office; the first Pan-American Conference in 1889 to create closer relations among nations of the Western Hemisphere; the Sherman Anti-Trust Act in 1890 to limit and prevent monopoly in business and restraint of trade in any form; and the Spanish–American War in 1898.

There was much unrest and dissatisfaction among working people and constant agitation on the part of labor organizations in the United States during these last twenty-five years of the nineteenth century. There were strikes and riots. Troops were used against strikers "to protect property and prevent the obstruction of the mails." The Sherman Anti-Trust Act was used also as a device against organized labor when it could be pointed out that strikers were "in restraint of interstate commerce." Thus, business had a powerful weapon in the law to control organized labor.

In 1886, the American Federation of Labor was founded in the United States. Its purpose was to organize all workers by crafts and skills, and to obtain improved wages, hours and working conditions for them.

In Canada, the Canadian Pacific Railroad was completed in 1885, spanning the North American continent from the Atlantic Ocean in the East to the Pacific Ocean in the West.

In 1897, the discovery of gold in Canada's and Alaska's Klondike region, located along the great Yukon River and its tributaries, triggered the greatest gold rush in world history, as Americans, Europeans and Chinese endured unbelievably hard sea and land passages to reach this bleak land in search of the yellow metal and hoped-for great wealth.

THE CENTURIES OF EUROPEAN DOMINATION

A Look Back

The colonizing Europeans of these four centuries must have appeared united and indomitable to the dark-skinned natives of Asia, Africa and the Americas. The white faces of Italians, Portuguese, Spaniards, Frenchmen, Dutchmen and Englishmen must all have looked alike to the peoples of these lands. Similarly, the languages of the white man must have sounded alike in their unintelligibility. In addition, the white man's giant ships, his cannon and his hand guns must have appeared to give him power to be found only in the hands of gods, or perhaps of devils.

The truth of the matter was, of course, that the Europeans were far from united during these years. Upon occasion they wreaked upon one another worse punishments than they meted out to the natives of the lands they colonized; for these same centuries of European colonization of the New World, Asia and Africa were also centuries when religious wars were fought and nation after nation was attempting to dominate the rest of Europe. Strangely enough, they were also the years when Europeans wrote beautiful poetry and prose, painted many of mankind's loveliest pictures, and made greatly significant explorations into the physical and metaphysical nature of things.

Truly, the 1500s to the 1900s were the Centuries of European Domination; but they were also years when Europeans persecuted other Europeans and during which some of the greatest beauty ever created by man was accompanied by some of the most obscene ugliness.

VIII
THE TWENTIETH CENTURY
THE 74 YEARS FROM A.D. 1900 TO 1974

A Look Ahead

No man living during the 1800s could have predicted the changes which were going to take place in the next century. During the latter years of the 1800s, the continued domination of the earth by Europeans—and especially by Britons —seemed certain. The British Navy ruled the seas, and the European peoples regarded the peoples of Asia and Africa as the "white man's burden," inferior creatures whom the superior Europeans (and later also the superior Americans) must watch over and care for, while growing rich in the process.

In these opulent times, who could have foreseen the two world wars which would squander much of Europe's strength? Who could have foretold that the airplane would replace the seagoing vessel as the major means of transoceanic transportation, which would shorten travel time over the earth from weeks or months to hours?

Who could have foreseen that the world's center of economic and political power would move from Western Europe to the United States, and later that it would come to be divided among Europe, the United States, Russia, Japan and perhaps later China?

Who would have believed that man would walk on the moon? What man of the 1800s could have foretold that human beings would invent weapons capable of destroying civilization and perhaps all life on the earth?

Who could have foretold the total effect of technology upon the earth? Who would have dreamed that, what is commonly thought of as "progress" would poison the waters, lands and atmosphere and threaten to make the planet uninhabitable?

Ahead of the complacent Victorians lay the twentieth century. Changes and surprises awaited mankind as overwhelming as those that took place six thousand five hundred years or more before the birth of Christ, when men first banded together in fortified towns and thought of themselves as "civilized."

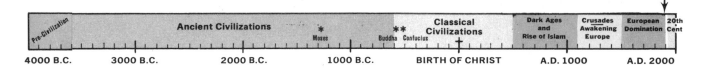

| Pre-Civilization | Ancient Civilizations | *Moses | **Buddha Confucius | Classical Civilizations | Dark Ages and Rise of Islam | Crusades Awakening Europe | European Domination | 20th Cent |

4000 B.C.   3000 B.C.   2000 B.C.   1000 B.C.   BIRTH OF CHRIST   A.D. 1000   A.D. 2000

1900 — 1918

Russian Domestic and Foreign Problems • The Russo–Japanese War • The Crumbling Ottoman Turkish Empire • The First World War • Communism in Russia • The Indian Nationalist Movement • The Chinese Republic • Automobiles, Radios, Airplanes

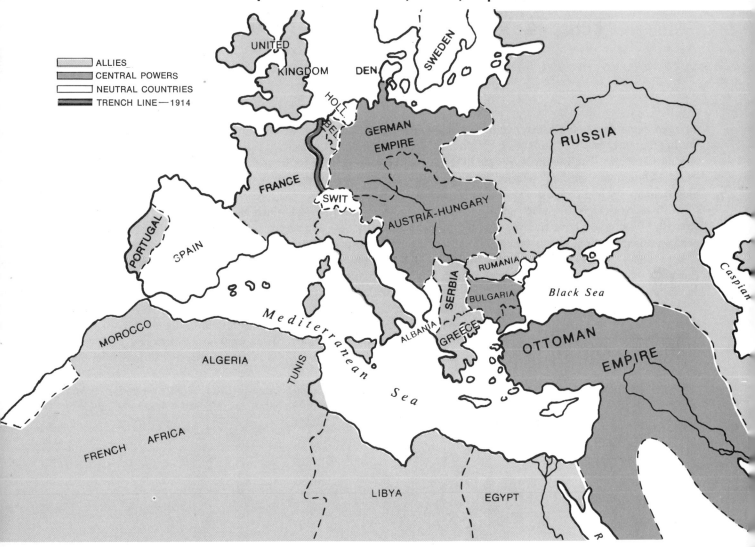

ALLIES
CENTRAL POWERS
NEUTRAL COUNTRIES
TRENCH LINE—1914

EUROPE and the Mediterranean World

The long-standing problems which would lead eventually to the First World War grew worse during the early years of the twentieth century. The deplorable condition of the Russian serfs, the declining Ottoman Empire and the ambitions of Germany and Austria to replace Ottoman rule in the lands left by the retreating Turks, countered by the determination of France, Britain and Russia to prevent German and Austrian expansion, made all Europe a powder keg.

To begin with, when Czar Nicholas II succeeded to the Russian throne in 1894, the wretched condition of the nation's people, the corruption among her government officials, and her heavy tax burden were reminiscent of pre-revolutionary France. In 1905, Czar Nicholas, frightened by a series of revolutions in Moscow and St. Petersburg, tried to relieve the hardships of his people by convening two representative assemblies called "dumas," but both times the liberal policies which the assemblies pursued frightened the Czar and he dismissed them. A third more conservative assembly rigidly repressed all revolutionary activities which were cropping up in Russia as a result of the condition of the serfs. A fourth duma, convened in 1912, was permitted to continue, but was given virtually no power except to act in an advisory capacity to the Czar in foreign affairs.

In the years 1904–5, Russia had been involved in war with her Pacific Ocean neighbor, Japan, and had been humiliatingly defeated by this island nation which had heretofore been regarded as a backward Asiatic land of little military power.

In 1907, Russia reached an agreement with Great Britain giving to each of them zones of influence in Persia. This Anglo-Russian treaty represented a diplomatic blow to the dreams of both Germany and Austria to dominate the Near East, and was the beginning of a long period of British-Russian cooperation. France and Britain reached a similar understanding. Beginning in 1904, this understanding gave the British a free hand in Egypt without competition from France, and the French were made free to rule Morocco without British interference. The agreement between them, which had its beginnings in the late 1800s, gave each of them separate areas to rule. It had come into being largely as a reaction to aggressive German colonization in the Near East, Africa, the Far East and Oceania. It later became the basis of British-French worldwide understanding after centuries of conflict and rivalry between them. Soon Britain would form a three-way alliance with Russia and France to be called the Triple Entente. Japan too, in the early 1900s, would become Britain's ally.

The second world peace conference was held at The Hague in Holland in 1907, and was characterized by much oratory but little action to ease the tensions growing in Europe.

Control of the crumbling Ottoman Empire was seized in 1908 by a group known as the "Young Turks" whose vigorous efforts to preserve the Turkish Empire proved largely unsuccessful. The Young Turks led the Ottoman armies against the rebellious European peoples of the Turkish Empire in the Balkan Wars of 1912 and 1913, but by the wars' end all of the European portions of the empire had broken free or been annexed by neighboring states. Prominent among the new independent nations were Bulgaria, Serbia (later to be part of Yugoslavia) and Rumania, with Serbia in a dominant position. There were many lesser Balkan peoples, however, trying to form separate nations. Italy in the meantime had seized the former Ottoman land of Libya in North Africa.

The dual monarchy of Austria-Hungary was pressing east into the Balkans, attempting to fill the vacuum of power left by the forced withdrawal of Turkey. Russia, Austria-Hungary's natural opponent for influence in this largely Slavic area, was too torn by domestic prob-

lems during this period to challenge her, so that much of the former Ottoman-ruled lands came under Austrian domination, but the area remained a powder keg of instability. Then, in 1914, Archduke Franz Ferdinand, heir to the throne of Austria, was assassinated in Serbia by a Bosnian, a member of one of the many Slavic peoples of the peninsula. Austria, backed by Germany, immediately seized upon this as an excuse to attack Serbia, hoping to increase her power there. Russia came to Serbia's aid; France, in turn, joined her ally Russia, and Britain followed quickly thereafter when the German armies invaded Belgium to get to France. Within weeks, most of Europe (excluding the Scandinavian countries and Switzerland) and eventually a large part of the rest of the world were plunged into the terrible period of World War I.

Much to the surprise of those who had anticipated a quick victory for the superbly trained and well-equipped German armies, a long war of attrition developed. In 1917, after three years of stalemate, the United States, angered by German submarine activities and fearful of the results of German victory, sent troops to join Britain, France and Russia. The American entry into the war proved the decisive factor in its outcome. On November 9, 1918, Kaiser Wilhelm II abdicated his throne and the German armies surrendered.

A list of the nations participating in the war with an indication of the casualties sustained by the main combatants, plus an estimate of the total materiel loss, will serve to give a statistical idea of the war's overwhelming size and destructiveness. Germany and her allies—the Central Powers—sustained the following approximate losses:

	DEAD	WOUNDED	MISSING
Germany	1,750,000	4,000,000	750,000
Austria-Hungary	1,000,000	2,750,000	750,000
Turkey and Bulgaria	500,000	1,000,000	100,000

The opposing armies—the Allies—were just as terribly hurt:

	DEAD	WOUNDED	MISSING
Russia	1,750,000	4,500,000	2,500,000
France	1,250,000	2,500,000	500,000
Great Britain	1,000,000	2,000,000	200,000
Italy	500,000	1,000,000	1,000,000
United States	81,000	220,000	4,000
Belgium	20,000	60,000	10,000

The other Allied nations in the war were Rumania, Greece, Portugal, Japan, Montenegro, Serbia, San Marino, Panama, Cuba, Siam, Liberia, China and Brazil.

The total monetary cost of the war to all the nations taking part has been carefully estimated to have exceeded $350 billion. Of course, no value can be placed on the misery, the suffering, the almost eight million dead soldiers and the countless dead civilians left in the war's wake.

British, French, and other Allied forces stopped the wave of advancing Germans at the Battle of the Marne. The two massive adversaries dug into the ground along a 400-mile front and for four terrible years lived, fought, and died in the trenches, always at least partially underground.

In 1917, in the midst of the war, two events of long-range significance occurred. The first was a revolution in Russia that forced the Czar to abdicate, followed by a second revolution, led by Nikolai Lenin and Leon Trotsky, that swept the nation into Communism. The second event of world import was the Balfour Declaration—a statement issued by Lord Balfour, the British Foreign Secretary, indicating that Britain favored the establishment of a Jewish National Homeland in Palestine.

European and American science, art and literature in the first eighteen years of the twentieth century remained as productive as in the explosive 1800s. In philosophy, the Englishmen Bertrand Russell (1872–1970) and Alfred North Whitehead (1861–1947), in their *Principia Mathematica,* set forth the principles of modern symbolic logic and also of what is known as the calculus of propositions. Oswald Spengler (1880–1936) demonstrated his theory that historical phenomena recur in a cyclical pattern and made the forecast that Western civilization, like its great predecessors, would inevitably decline.

Physicists Robert A. Milikan (1863–1953) and Ernest Rutherford (1871–1937) of England, Max von Laue (1879–1960) of Germany, and Niels Bohr (1885–1962) of Denmark all contributed substantially to the understanding of the structure of the atom. Great strides were made in astronomy by Ejnar Hertzsprung (born 1873) of Denmark and Henry Norris Russell (1877–1957) of England, who developed a graphic chart for classifying stars, known as the Hertzsprung-Russell Diagram, and also by Harlow Shapley (born

1885) of the United States, whose studies of star clusters and of stars of varying brightness gave a much more accurate picture of the size of our own Milky Way galaxy, and also a more realistic view of the location and importance of our solar system. Albert Einstein (1879–1955) published his special and general theories of relativity, which explained many discrepancies between experimental findings and Newtonian physics. In effect, Einstein detailed an entirely new explanation of gravitation, of light, and of the relationship between mass and energy. With the theories of Einstein, mankind stood on the threshold of a new universe of understanding.

In the early 1900s, important investigations were made of the part played in heredity by chromosomes, bodies revealed by the microscope to exist in the nucleus of all living cells.

Count Ferdinand von Zeppelin, in the year 1900, made the initial launching of one of the rigid-framed airships named for him. In 1903, the Americans Orville and Wilbur Wright flew the first airplane, a heavier-than-air ship, at Kitty Hawk, North Carolina. Shortly thereafter, in 1909, a Frenchman, Louis Blériot, flew an airplane across the English Channel. From 1914 to 1918 airplanes were used widely for reconnaissance and strafing in the First World War; and in 1919, two Englishmen, John Alcock and Arthur Whitten Brown, made the first nonstop transatlantic flight, taking off from Newfoundland and landing in Galway, Ireland.

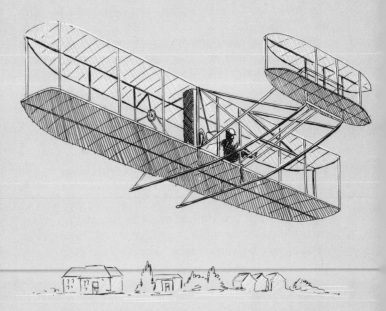

Orville and Wilbur Wright, building on the developments of aviation pioneers of several nations, made the first successful flight in a heavier-than-air machine in 1903. In 1908, a plane piloted by Orville Wright remained aloft for an unbelievable one hour and fifteen minutes. In the same year, the brothers demonstrated their machine throughout Europe, receiving plaudits everywhere.

The automobile came into widespread use during the early years of the twentieth century, thanks in good part to the inventions of an American, Charles F. Kettering, which included lighting and ignition systems and the self-starter. In 1913, the diesel-electric railway engine was developed in Sweden; it would later replace the steam engine as the power source of most railroads. Synthetic fibers such as rayon and cellophane were first marketed in the United States, and the polymer Bakelite, which was the first of the family of such plastics as nylon and Dacron, was discovered in America. In 1917 Clarence Birdseye of the United States began the development of the quick freezing of foods for packaging and sale.

Explorers reached the North and South Poles, and the Arctic and Antarctic areas around the poles were explored. Names such as Frederick A. Cook of England, Robert E. Peary of the United States, Roald Amundsen of Norway, and Robert F. Scott and Ernest H. Shackleton of Britain are the best known among the legion of courageous men from many nations who early explored the two polar regions.

The investigations into the human psyche by Sigmund Freud, Alfred Adler and others in the 1800s influenced the writing in the early twentieth century of many novels concerned with the fears, frustrations and anxieties of contemporary life. Among the most highly acclaimed of these novels were *The Magic Mountain* by the German Thomas Mann (1875–1955), which gives a view of the confusion of life prior to the First World War through the eyes of a young man in an Alpine tuberculosis sanatorium; *Ulysses,* an innovative presentation by the Irishman James Joyce (1882–1941) of the thoughts of one distraught human being in a period of less than twenty-four hours; and *Sons and Lovers,* by D. H. Lawrence (1885–1930), an Englishman, which is an account of the turmoil of a young man torn between his attachment for his mother and his awakening need for young women of his own age.

In the early 1900s, there was much restless experimentation among painters attempting to express ideas, moods and thoughts inexplicable through conventional methods of painting. Henri Matisse (1869–1954), of France, became the leader of one such group. Matisse utilized flat, decorative patterns with unusual color schemes built up in sections. A group of artists called Futurists tried to suggest movement by showing the same scene at successive moments. Another group, the Cubists, changed the natural shape of objects by representing them as interesting cubes, spheres, cylinders and pyramids. Other artists studied the art of African Negroes and South Sea Island natives, and transposed their primitive designs into modern sculpture and painting. Amedeo Modigliani (1884–1920), an Italian, painted strangely elongated figures derived in part from African primitive sources.

A movement known as Surrealism was exemplified by Salvador Dali (born 1904) of Spain, who painted with precise realism, but combined objects in groupings totally foreign to their actual existence. Out of this mode, he (and other Surrealists) attained an emotional unreality justified by the artists as a means of securing effects otherwise unobtainable. Another Spaniard, Pablo Picasso (born 1881), made his home in France, and epitomized in his work the experimentalism of modern art in a lavish and diverse outpouring of painting and sculpture. An amazingly original artist, Picasso, who died in 1973, continued to experiment and to change his style every few years. In the early 1900s, an important school of art grew up in Mexico. It abandoned the slavish copying of European art of previous Mexican artists and utilized bold colors and vigorous strokes to depict Mexican life and legends.

The development of new building materials and mass-production techniques brought significant changes to architecture in the first quarter of the twentieth century. The use of structural steel in the Eiffel Tower in the nineteenth century foretold the American skyscrapers, which became the prototype of urban structures the world over. One style—product of twentieth-century materials and methods—characterized housing developments, government buildings, industrial plants, hospitals, schools and even homes almost everywhere.

Music and drama were enriched in the twentieth century by contributors from many nations. No attempt is made here to limit the contributions to those produced during this eighteen-year period (1900–1918), but instead the following paragraphs attempt to give a scanning view of the key people in the first seventy-three years of the twentieth century.

In music, Maurice Ravel (1875–1937) of France is noted for the rhythm and melodic content of his work, of which the ballet *Daphnis and Chloe* and the fine instrumental piece *Bolero* are widely admired. Ralph Vaughan Williams (1872–1958) of England produced nine symphonies, a number of choral works, operas and some delightful chamber music. Béla Bartók (1881–1945) of Hungary is noted for his research into Hungarian folk music. Partly as a result of his research he wrote the opera *Bluebeard's Castle* and a quantity of choral music and violin and piano concertos, as well as other works of note. Manuel de Falla (1876–1946) of Spain demonstrated the rhythm and color of Spanish music as well as its depth of passion and its occasional harshness.

Sergei Rachmaninov (1873–1943), Russian composer and conductor, produced three piano concertos and a number of operas, symphonies, piano pieces and songs. His music is noted for its emotional appeal and rhythm. Igor Stravinsky (1882–1971), also of Russia, brought an exciting and controversial approach to music, as epitomized in *The Fire Bird* and in other ballets. The same excitement and ingenuity are evident in his two operas and in a number of his violin and piano concertos. Other important twentieth-century Russian composers include Sergei Prokofiev (1891–1953) and Dmitri Shostakovich (born 1906).

A number of English and American composers were indicating the beginnings of serious musicianship and composition in two nations that previously had been largely dependent upon foreign imports in the field of music. Such Englishmen as Arnold Bax (1883–1953) and William Walton (born 1902), and the Americans Aaron Copland (born 1900) and Leonard Bernstein (born 1918), were beginning to make an important impact on the musical world.

In addition to these more "classical" composers, two musical forms were growing up in America which would later be exported and enjoyed all over the world. The first was based upon American Negro rhythms and songs and would be known by a variety of names over the decades, such as the blues, Dixieland, jazz, boogie-woogie, swing and, most recently, rock 'n' roll. Just a few of the performer-composers who have enriched the jazz era are Edward K. "Duke" Ellington (born 1899), a prolific composer and arranger; Louis "Satchmo" Armstrong (1900–1971), an outstanding and beloved trumpet player; Leon B. "Bix" Beiderbecke (1903–1931), a clarinetist and composer who is thought to have introduced jazz forms years ahead of his time; and Benjamin D. "Benny" Goodman (born 1909), noted for his fine musicianship and for introducing what is called the "swing era." Many other jazz performers and composers should be mentioned, but space limits us to the most interesting musical group of the 1960s, a band of fine young musicians from England known as the Beatles, who have influenced, even revolutionized, every facet of popular music, particularly the modern form of jazz called rock 'n' roll.

The second American development was a kind of folk music known as "Country and Western." It had (and has) a rhythm, a tang and a distinctiveness which are widely appealing.

Twentieth-century drama in Ireland was alive, innovative and vigorously presented at Dublin's famous Abbey Theatre. Here the plays of many fine playwrights were first staged. Among them, the works of Sean O'-Casey (1880–1964) are outstanding. His *Juno and the Paycock* and *Within the Gates* are representative of O'Casey's poetic style and of the influence which the turmoil of the Irish revolutionary movement had upon it. Other Irish dramatists of the early 1900s who should be mentioned are William Butler Yeats (1865–1939), Lady Gregory (1859–1932), John Millington Synge (1871–1909), and St. John Ervine (1883–1971).

In England, George Bernard Shaw (1856–1950), although born in Ireland, came to dominate English theater. His *Saint Joan, Man and Superman, Candida* and *Pygmalion* are representative of his enormous contribution. A few of the other distinguished English dramatists of the 1900s are John Galsworthy (1867–1933), Noël Coward (1899–1973) and James M. Barrie (1860–1937).

In Russia, the Moscow Theater was graced by such great writers as Anton Chekhov and Maxim Gorki. The Russian theater itself was setting new standards and making innovations in acting and in directing (the "method" system) which the rest of the world would for decades attempt to emulate. In Germany, Gerhart Hauptmann was that nation's outstanding dramatist of the early 1900s. Other names of importance in the German theater of the period are Max Reinhardt (1873–1943) and Franz Werfel (1890–1945).

Italy's Luigi Pirandello (1867–1936) wrote realistic yet imaginative plays. Belgium's Maurice Maeterlinck (1862–1949) became best known for his play *The Blue Bird*. Important names in the French theater of the 1900s are Henry Bernstein (1876–1953), Jules Romains (born 1885) and Jean-Paul Sartre (born 1905).

In the United States, Eugene O'Neill (1888–1953) achieved a fame second only to Shaw's in writing plays in the English language. Among his outstanding contributions are *The Emperor Jones, Anna Christie, Strange Interlude* and *Mourning Becomes Electra*. Other important names in the American theater of the 1900s, again to name but a few, are Robert E. Sherwood (1896–1955), Marc Connelly (born 1890), George S. Kaufman (1889–1961), Moss Hart (1904–1961), Tennessee Williams (born 1912) and Arthur Miller (born 1915).

ASIA, except for its Mediterranean Lands

This was a period of great unrest for most of Asia. The Indian subcontinent, for example, was continually disturbed by anti-Moslem and anti-Hindu agitation and by the disruptive tactics of the Indian nationalist movements—the same divisive forces which had been disturbing the land for some time. Ironically, attempts by the British to improve the condition of the natives often angered the Indians. For example, the University Act of 1904, which was calculated to improve higher education in India by having British educators, methods and funds play a greater role, was construed by the people as interference in one of their few remaining semi-independent institutions. Again, when the British partitioned the Bengal area into two administrative units for the purpose of greater efficiency, they overlooked the language and religious groupings within the area. This oversight gave rise to intense opposition among the native peoples. An organization called the All-India Moslem League was formed in 1906 as a reaction to this opposition. The League affirmed its loyalty to the British government, but asked for separate representation for Moslems from the Hindus in future reforms—a continuation of the long-standing antipathy between India's two main religious groups.

The British tried to reorganize Indian agriculture, to establish rural banks, to pass laws punishing British soldiers for abuse of natives, to revive the study of Indian archaeology—but all did little to make the Indians content under British rule. When the Bengal poet Sir Rabindranath Tagore was awarded the Nobel Prize for literature in 1913, however, native pride and self-respect increased markedly.

Almost from the beginning of World War I, India cooperated with Britain and provided men and money for the Allied effort. The Moslem League in India, however, had by this time become anti-British and opposed participation in the war, taking the viewpoint that Britain would favor Hindus over Muslims in postwar acts. In 1914, Sikhs from British India were denied entrance into British Canada, and there were resultant riots throughout the Indian subcontinent. By the middle of the war nationalist movements were no longer controlled by native moderates, and by the war's end their members were often violent and revolutionary in their demands for home rule.

In 1900, Chinese reaction to foreign intervention and to government by imperial Manchu decree gave rise to the Boxer Rebellion, which drew its name from the secret "Society of the Clenched Fist," dedicated to driving foreigners and Christianity from China. The rebellion was suppressed by the twelve foreign powers involved in the China trade. Chinese officials were severely punished and the nation was burdened with heavy fines.

Five years later, in 1905, the exclusion from the United States of Chinese immigrants resulted in a boycott of American goods by the Chinese. Throughout China there was a growing spirit of nationalism. Sun Yat-sen continued his efforts, begun in the previous century, to oust the Manchu rulers, and in 1911 revolution swept through the west and the south of China. Sun Yat-sen, recently returned from Europe, was elected president of the United Provinces of China, and in 1912 the boy Emperor resigned. Later, Sun Yat-sen offered to step down to unify the nation, and a military man, Yuan Shih-K'ai, became president. Sun Yat-sen now became head of the nationalist party which opposed the new military regime because of its antidemocratic actions.

Japan, victorious in 1904–5 in the Russo–Japanese War, had continued to increase its military and naval strength. In 1910 she formally annexed Korea and began to spread her hegemony over other neighboring lands and waters. In 1916 she placed territorial demands on China and in 1917 was granted special rights in Manchuria and Inner Mongolia, as well as commercial rights in Shantung and in parts of the Yangtze Valley.

Japan entered World War I as an ally of Britain, and in 1914, after declaring war on the Central Powers, demanded withdrawal of the German fleet from the China Seas. Japanese naval forces then occupied a number of German-owned islands, among them the Marshalls and the Marianas, and bombarded and captured the German fortress at Tsingtao on the coast of the Chinese mainland.

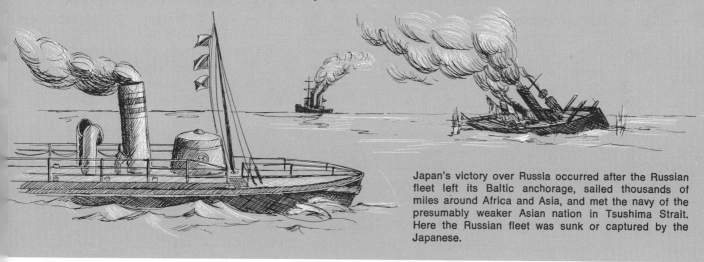

Japan's victory over Russia occurred after the Russian fleet left its Baltic anchorage, sailed thousands of miles around Africa and Asia, and met the navy of the presumably weaker Asian nation in Tsushima Strait. Here the Russian fleet was sunk or captured by the Japanese.

OCEANIA

In 1900, Hawaii was annexed as a territory of the United States. In the same year, the government of the Philippine Islands was organized under United States sovereignty.

The varied states of Australia were united in 1901 and given the semi-independent status of a commonwealth within the British Empire, and in the same year the first Australian Parliament convened. It was inclined

to pass high tariffs to protect Australian-produced goods, and was strongly opposed to the immigration of Orientals into the land. Australia entered World War I in 1914 on the side of the Allies. In the early years of the war, while Japan was overrunning German islands north of the equator, Australian and New Zealand troops aboard British vessels were conquering other German islands in the Southern Hemisphere. Before the war's end,

Australia had furnished more than 300,000 men to overseas service, mostly in the Dardanelles (Turkish) campaign.

New Zealand in the year 1907 was awarded the status of a dominion—a free, self-ruling political unit within the British Empire. The dominion of New Zealand supported Great Britain and the Allied cause in World War I and sent 117,000 men to service overseas, joining with Australian forces to form what became known as the Anzac Divisions.

AFRICA, except for its Mediterranean Lands

The victory of Britain in 1902 over the Dutch Boers established British control over South Africa. In 1910 the Union of South Africa was created by combining the Orange Free State, the Transvaal, Natal and the Cape of Good Hope.

In 1908 the "Congo Free State," which had previously been regarded as the personal property of the King of Belgium, was turned over to the Belgian government and renamed the Belgian Congo.

THE AMERICAS

During the late 1800s and the early years of the 1900s, the poor, the dispossessed, the ambitious and the adventurous of Central and Eastern Europe poured into the United States in search of a better life. Theodore Roosevelt became the nation's twenty-sixth president in 1901, a time of great change for the growing country and the Western Hemisphere as a whole. Roosevelt is best remembered, perhaps, for his actions to control and limit the expanding power of big business in the United States, and for his aggressiveness in foreign policy. He played an important role in making the United States a world power, modernizing the United States Army and Navy, and restating the Monroe Doctrine, which strongly affirmed the United States position in opposition to European military and political activities in the Western Hemisphere.

William Howard Taft became president in 1909, and Woodrow Wilson, inaugurated in 1913, was in office during the First World War. Wilson played an important part in the realignment of the nations of Europe under the Treaty of Versailles after the war, but his attempts to bring the United States into the world peace organization called the League of Nations ended in failure.

A listing of the key events occurring in the Western Hemisphere during these eighteen years will serve to give a broad view of this time of great changes. In 1903, for example, the Wright brothers made the first successful powered flight, and in the same year the first transatlantic radio communication was accomplished. In 1905 Alberta and Saskatchewan became provinces of Canada, and in 1906 construction was begun on the Panama Canal, linking the Atlantic and Pacific Oceans. The construction of the canal was to require almost nine years and to cost many lives before its completion in 1914. The first "Model T" Ford was manufactured in 1908.

Between the years 1910 and 1917, Mexico went through a period of revolution and instability under several weak, short-lived regimes. In 1917 a new constitution was adopted and Venustiano Carranza was elected president, beginning a period of greater stability for the Mexican people.

In the year 1912 the Northwest Territories were added to Canada. During the period 1912–1916, the use of United States Marines to establish orderly government and to supervise elections in Haiti, the Dominican Republic and Nicaragua led to widespread distrust of the United States motives throughout Latin America.

In 1917 the United States and Canada entered World War I, the same year that the United States purchased the Virgin Islands from Denmark.

Immigrants by the millions poured into the United States, often to find there poverty and bigotry instead of the Promised Land. Many returned home discouraged, but the majority stayed to overcome all obstacles and find a place in the New World.

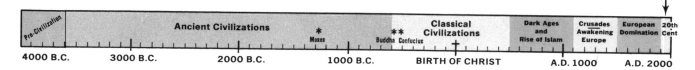

| Pre-Civilization | Ancient Civilizations | | Classical Civilizations | Dark Ages and Rise of Islam | Crusades Awakening Europe | European Domination | 20th Cent |

* Moses

** Buddha Confucius

4000 B.C.   3000 B.C.   2000 B.C.   1000 B.C.   BIRTH OF CHRIST   A.D. 1000   A.D. 2000

1918 — 1930

The Treaty of Versailles • **The League of Nations** • **Mussolini, the First of the Dictators** • **Byrd, Remarque, Hemingway** • **Mahatma Gandhi in India** • **Chiang Kai-shek in China** • **The Stock Market Crash of 1929**

EMPIRES AFTER WORLD WAR I

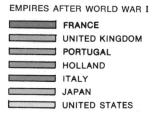
FRANCE
UNITED KINGDOM
PORTUGAL
HOLLAND
ITALY
JAPAN
UNITED STATES

EUROPE and the Mediterranean World

World War I left Europe shattered. The German Empire no longer existed; in its place at the war's end was a destitute new German state, the "Weimar Republic" (so known because it was founded in the city of Weimar), shorn of Germany's former possessions in Africa and the Pacific, and burdened with the obligation of paying $315 billion in reparations to the victorious Allies. France, although she was one of the victors, had experienced great devastation and impoverishment, and was left bitter and suspicious of every German move.

The Treaty of Versailles in 1919 at the war's end solved none of Europe's basic problems, and its punitive measures against Germany left that nation's people sullen and resentful. The various international enactments and agreements which followed the treaty were similarly ineffectual. These included the establishment in 1920 of the League of Nations; in 1924 of the Dawes Plan of aid to Germany; in 1925 of the Locarno Pact for mutual defense; in 1928 of the Kellogg-Briand Pact renouncing all aggressive war; and, also in 1928, of the Young Plan for further aid to Germany by placing a moratorium on her payment of war debts and reparations to the Allies. In 1922, in the midst of these peace-making efforts, Benito Mussolini (the first of a new group of dictators who were to seize power in European nations) led his private army called Fascists in a march on Rome and took control of the Italian government.

An Irish Free State, independent of Britain, was established in Dublin in 1922. The new Irish state included all but approximately the northern fifth of the island. A year later, France and Belgium occupied the Ruhr Valley in western Germany, in the hope of bolstering their economies by controlling this rich industrial area. They used as an excuse for the occupation the fact that Germany had defaulted in her payment of reparations.

The Austro-Hungarian Empire was also in a state of collapse by the end of World War I. Austria, the German-speaking portion of the empire, became a republic. Of the rest of the empire, part was divided into the separate states of Hungary and Czechoslovakia and part was joined with Serbia to form Yugoslavia. To prevent the resurgence of Teutonic power, the treaty forbade alliance or union of Austria with Germany at any future time. Poland reemerged as a completely independent nation, formed largely out of the divisions of the old kingdom that had been taken over in the past by Germany, Austria and Russia.

In 1919 the Ottoman Empire, reduced in size to only the area that is present-day Turkey, became a republic led by Kemal Ataturk, a powerful and progressive leader. Ataturk set out to modernize Turkey, ruthlessly eliminating those Moslem religious traditions which he felt inhibited his nation's progress. Thus, the fez and the veil (among similar things) were no longer to be seen in the streets of Istanbul and Ankara.

In Russia, now called the Union of Soviet Socialist Republics, Joseph Stalin became dictator upon the death of Lenin in 1924. In the Balkan Peninsula, Greece and Albania became republics. In 1926, Ibn Saud became ruler of the Arabian Peninsula, which he was later to rename Saudi Arabia.

Scientists and artists of Europe and America continued their great productivity in the years following the First World War. In astronomy during this period, Arthur S. Eddington (1882–1944), an Englishman, verified Einstein's prediction that a ray of light would have its direction deflected as it passed through the gravitational field of a large mass such as that of a planet or a star; Edwin Hubble (1889–1953), of the United States, did work that made possible measurement of the vast distances between stellar galaxies; and Georges Lemaître (born 1894), of Belgium, who had earlier introduced the concept of the "expanding universe"—which postulated that the galaxies were rushing away from one another at tremendous speeds—to explain many heretofore puzzling observations, now saw his theory being accepted. In physics, much important work was done to advance understanding of the structure of the atom. Among the more important contributors were Louis-Victor de Broglie (born 1892), of France; Wolfgang Pauli (1900–1958), of Austria; and Paul A. Dirac (born 1902), of Britain.

In 1930, the first modern digital computer was put into operation in the United States, at the Massachusetts Institute of Technology, by Vannevar Bush and his associates.

Kemal Ataturk, Turkey's first president, instituted sweeping reforms in an attempt to bring his nation into the mainstream of modern life. He wrote a democratic constitution, granted the right to vote to both men and women, expanded educational facilities, and did much to improve industry and agriculture.

In England, in 1929, Alexander Fleming (1881–1955) announced that the common mold Penicillium had the effect of inhibiting the growth of certain disease-causing bacteria. The introduction of sulfa drugs (also bacteria inhibiting) would not be made until a few years later—by Gerhard Domagk (1895–1964), of Germany—but sulfas would find practical use in medicine before penicillin.

Commercial radio broadcasting had its beginnings in 1920 under the leadership of Frank Conrad (1874–1941), of the United States. In 1926, John L. Baird (1888–1941), of England, made the first successful demonstration of television broadcasting, the result of the contributions of many men, important among them being that of Vladimir Zworykin, a Russian American. The first sound motion pictures were introduced in 1927, as was the process for producing colored cinemas invented by H. T. Kalmus.

In the years 1928 through 1930, Sir Hubert Wilkins (1888–1958), under the auspices of the American Geographical Society, flew over and mapped more than eighty thousand square miles of Antarctica. During the same period, Commander Richard E. Byrd (1888–1957) of the United States led an expedition to the South Pole, using ships and airplanes, and established a base on Ross Barrier which he called Little America and which became a center for scientific observations to be made by his expedition.

The postwar years from 1918 to 1936 saw a continuing production of the psychological novels which had arisen out of the work of the psychoanalysts. The American Thomas Wolfe (1900–1938) wrote *Look Homeward Angel,* a novel telling of the inner problems of a young man who felt himself a misfit in his native land; the Frenchman Marcel Proust (1871–1922) wrote, in *Remembrance of Things Past,* of the psychological problems of sensitive French people. The emotional impact of what was often a brutal world on the lives of sensitive people was the subject of many outstanding novels of the time, among which were *The Counterfeiters,* by André Gide of France (1869–1951); *The Sun Also Rises,* by the American writer Ernest Hemingway (1899–1961); and *All Quiet on the Western Front,* by Erich Maria Remarque (1898–1970) of Germany.

ASIA, except for its Mediterranean Lands

The Third Afghan War occurred in 1919, when Amir Amanullah of Afghanistan appealed to India's Moslems to rise against their British rulers. However, the Amir received little aid from his Indian coreligionists, and the war ended with no territorial changes.

Although the ancient enmity between Moslems and Hindus was in no way abated during this time, all India regardless of religion was aflame with anti-British feeling and was agitating for complete freedom from all foreign rule. In 1920, Mohandas K. Gandhi, soon to be called the Mahatma, the "great-souled one," was assuming leadership of the Indian nationalist movement. He called for nonviolence, for days of fasting, and for civil disobedience. Gandhi, who was educated in the West, was a devout Hindu who, however, believed in equality for all and rejected the Hindu concept of untouchability —the belief that some persons were of so low a caste by heredity that it would defile members of a higher caste to touch them. Often, because they were ignorant of his plans and aims, his people or their British rulers turned to violence. In 1919 in the city of Amritsar, located in north India, a British general, Reginald Dyer, ordered his Gurkha troops from Nepal to fire on an unarmed assembly (reportedly listening to anti-British speeches) until their ammunition was exhausted. Three hundred seventy-nine persons were killed and twelve hundred wounded. When only mild official censure of General Dyer resulted, anti-British feeling reached fever pitch.

During this period (about 1923) a Communist Party was established in India. Tensions mounted, and Gandhi, who was not himself a Communist, was im-

Mahatma Gandhi became an inspiration to millions of his countrymen and won the devotion and admiration of all nations and peoples of subsequent times who strove for freedom yet abjured violence.

prisoned in 1924 and again in 1930. There were repeated strikes and work stoppages throughout the land. Jawaharlal Nehru, second in command to Gandhi, and the man who would one day be India's first prime minister, introduced a proposal for public and governmental consideration which would give India dominion status within the British Empire, her own constitution and, of course, self-rule.

In 1919, Koreans rioted and openly rebelled against their Japanese rulers, and were mercilessly repressed. However, civil government was substituted for the existing military regime, and the Koreans were promised greater self-rule.

A great earthquake leveled Tokyo and other Japanese cities in 1923. Damage was tremendous, and the lives lost numbered in the hundreds of thousands. Many nations throughout the world came to the aid of Japan with money, medicines and food.

In China between 1920 and 1926, local military dictators called "warlords" assumed the actual leadership of the nation. Each made himself the real government in a specific area of China, while the national government had little actual power and was barely able to maintain a foreign service with functioning envoys to other governments.

Much of China's problem stemmed from this weakening of the central government by the warlords and from Western capitulation to the Japanese territorial demands made at Versailles. On May 4, 1919, a student demonstration and strike against Western betrayal and capitulation to Japanese demands (and Chinese government agreement to these demands) was joined by workers and even some merchants. From this time on, public demonstration became a widely used technique in China. A movement to educate the people to read and write in vernacular Chinese was begun. Western ideas and philosophy became available as a part of the common man's education, and thus China was brought into contact with the mainstream of world affairs.

In 1924 the first Kuomintang (Chinese Nationalist Party) congress, headed by Sun Yat-sen, admitted Communists to the party and welcomed Russian advisers. Sun Yat-sen was not himself a Communist, but China's need was great, and help from any source was welcome.

Sun Yat-sen, who had been the first president of the Chinese Republic, died in 1925 and was replaced as party leader by his chief of staff, Chiang Kai-shek. Rivalry between the government and the Communists prevented China from developing adequate defenses against Japan, whose military leaders, ever on the search for more land, threatened to seize additional portions of the nation. In 1927 Chiang Kai-shek mounted a drive for undisputed leadership of China, massacring many of the Chinese Communist Party leaders in Shanghai, and later launching an expedition into the north to eliminate Communists and local warlords there. In 1928, Chiang Kai-shek became the nation's president, and a year later China's capital was moved to Nanking.

In Southeast Asia, nationalist movements were arising in many nations. Often, revolt seemed the only possible means to arrive at some form of self-government, and the only help available was from Communist groups, which were usually Chinese. Between 1926 and 1927 a Communist rebellion in Indonesia was quelled and its leader, Sukarno, imprisoned. A year later, in 1928, a Communist Party was organized in Malaya.

AFRICA, except for its Mediterranean Lands

The German colonies of Africa were taken over by the victorious Allies at the end of World War I. Under the Treaty of Versailles, the French and the British divided the Cameroons and Togoland. The British also took most of German East Africa, renaming it Tanganyika; the western portions of the colony were absorbed into the Belgian Congo; and the Union of South Africa claimed German Southwest Africa. At the war's end, the only independent nations on the African continent were Ethiopia and Liberia.

THE AMERICAS

In 1918, a beaten Germany had sued for a peace which German leaders hoped would be based on the "Fourteen Points" of United States President Woodrow Wilson. Wilson, along with Prime Ministers Lloyd George of England, Georges Clemenceau of France and Vittorio Emanuele Orlando of Italy, played a major role in formulating the Treaty of Versailles which ended World War I, and also in establishing the League of Nations, which was designed to be a meeting ground of the nations of the world to prevent future wars. Despite the part played by President Wilson in the League's formation, the United States Senate failed to ratify the treaty, due, in part, to a return to isolationism by the American people and in part to Congressional rebellion against Wilson's strong wartime leadership. As a result, the United States did not join the League. In 1920, the Nineteenth Amendment to the United States Constitution guaranteed the right to vote to all women, the culmination of at least sixty years of continuous effort by dedicated women throughout the nation.

In 1922, the Washington Naval Disarmament Conference fixed and limited the ratio of naval tonnage between the three great naval powers, the United States, Great Britain and Japan. Japan was now one of the world's great powers, a force to be reckoned with on land as well as on sea.

The 1920s were the years of the "flaming youth" in the United States. The bob-haired, short-skirted, cigarette-smoking, flask-carrying young Americans of the "Roaring Twenties" symbolized to many people the utter degradation of this postwar world. This was also a time of great prosperity in the United States, as contrasted with Europe's general postwar poverty. The twenties in America were a time of widespread lawlessness too, emanating at least in part from the experiment in prohibition which had made illegal the sale of intoxicating liquors, but which at the same time made the sale of illegal liquor very profitable to criminals, who banded together in gangs and came to be called "gangsters."

In these post–World War I years the United States government and people were driven by an almost unreasoning fear of Communism, and they viewed events in Russia and China with consternation. Any sympathetic action of Americans toward these events was regarded with gravest suspicion. The nation reverted to some extent to its prewar isolationism and adopted strong tariffs to protect American products against competition from foreign-made goods.

Warren G. Harding became the twenty-first United States president in 1921 and died in office in 1923, to be succeeded by Vice-President Calvin Coolidge. Scandalous actions of Harding's Secretary of the Interior, Albert Fall, in leasing government oil reserves (notably the Teapot Dome Reserve) to private persons and Secretary Fall's sudden affluence badly blemished the Harding administration's record.

Charles A. Lindbergh made the first solo airplane flight across the Atlantic Ocean in 1927, flying 3,600 miles in thirty-three and a half hours from New York to Paris.

In 1928, in the midst of this period of prosperity, flamboyance and lawlessness, Herbert Hoover—a hero internationally for his work in bringing American food, clothing and other relief to millions of starving Europeans—was elected president. One year later, in 1929, the stock market crashed, and the United States's economy collapsed, followed shortly by the collapse of the already desperately shaky economies of much of the rest of the world. In the depths of business and economic depression, free "soup lines" for the poor became a common sight in American cities. Unemployment reached an all-time high, and industrial paralysis spread over the nation.

The carefree flapper and the man selling apples on street corner became contrasting symbols of the wasteful plenty and degrading poverty that existed simultaneously in the United States during the 1920s.

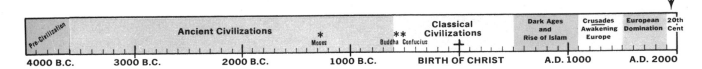

| Pre-Civilization | Ancient Civilizations | *Moses | **Buddha Confucius | Classical Civilizations | Dark Ages and Rise of Islam | Crusades Awakening Europe | European Domination | 20th Cent |

| 4000 B.C. | 3000 B.C. | 2000 B.C. | 1000 B.C. | BIRTH OF CHRIST | A.D. 1000 | A.D. 2000 |

1930 — 1942

Worldwide Economic Depression • The Dictators: Mussolini, Hitler, Franco and Stalin • The Second World War • The Rome-Berlin-Tokyo Axis • Toynbee, Keynes, Steinbeck, Fermi • Continued Striving for Self-Rule in Asia

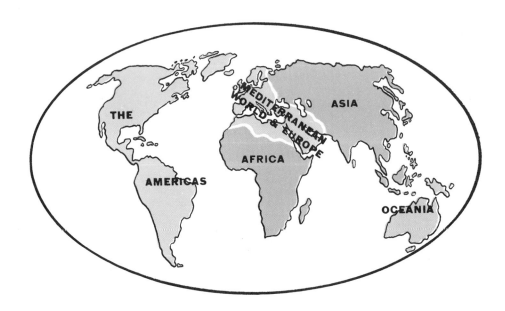

EUROPE and the Mediterranean World

By 1931, economic depression had almost totally engulfed the United States and had reached out to further depress the already shaky economies of Europe to a point where the actual survival of many in them in their pre-depression form seemed in doubt. Some European countries, such as England and France, adopted measures similar to those undertaken in the United States, where attempts were made to revive the economy by remedies within the democratic framework. In Germany, Italy and Spain, however, revolutions led by extreme conservatives rejected democratic institutions and adopted attitudes favoring, instead, "right-wing" regimented and controlled economies with strong one-man rule, in many ways not unlike the "left-wing" rigidly regimented and controlled economy of Soviet Russia, where much of the power was also in the hands of one man.

The first such right-wing revolution had taken place in Italy in 1922 under the leadership of Mussolini, but the most important was to occur in Germany, where Adolf Hitler in the 1920s organized and led a party called the National Socialists, or "Nazis," and in 1933 became chancellor of Germany. Under Nazism, Germany, once known as one of the most cultivated and religious countries in all Europe, now came to be known for acts of extreme political terrorism and cruelty. By 1934, Hitler had ruthlessly eliminated any opponents who would have resisted him, especially Catholics, Jews and liberals. Thousands of his opponents were killed outright. Other thousands were sentenced to a living death in prisons called concentration camps, where many were systematically eliminated by torture, starvation, disease, gassing and incineration. Two years later, in 1936, Hitler sent Nazi troops to reoccupy the strategic Rhineland, which had been demilitarized under the Locarno Pact of 1925.

Adolf Hitler rose to power in Germany by skillfully playing upon the contrasting emotions of fear and pride in the German people and by seizing absolute control of all sources of information—newspapers, books, radio—so that the nation's people could always be persuaded to believe what he wished them to believe.

Beginning the same year, civil war in Spain shattered that republic. When it ended, three years later, the right-wing leader General Francisco Franco, who had been aided by Hitler of Germany and Mussolini of Italy, was dictator of all Spain. In 1938, Austria was forcibly incorporated into the German Reich when German troops invaded and occupied Vienna, thus ending Austria's existence as a separate power. In 1938, Czechoslovakia too was brought by force under German control, with only its province of Slovakia remaining independent.

In 1939, Hitler, of rightist Germany, and Stalin, of leftist Russia, made a nonaggression pact in which they pledged not to go to war against each other and agreed to divide the border nation of Poland between them. With Germany's eastern front now secured against Russian attack, Hitler felt free to implement his agreement with Russia by bombing and invading Poland. Several months later, German troops invaded Holland, Belgium and France. Thus World War II began—although in the judgment of many historians it had actually begun in 1931 when the Japanese invaded China. France surrendered on June 22, 1940, and was in part occupied, in part controlled by the German military while maintaining the appearance of self-rule. Germany then began

Charles de Gaulle had tried in vain to persuade the leaders of France to prepare for a mechanized war with Germany and to fearlessly resist German aggression. With the fall of France, he made himself leader of the French government in exile and organized resistance from London. After the war, he was twice to become President of France and to wield great influence in world affairs.

a mass bombing of Britain of such ferocity that the capitulation of the island seemed inevitable. The capitulation, however, never occurred. In fact, Britain, led by Winston Churchill, was to withstand all that Hitler could hurl against her and rebound to become a key opponent and, in later years, the staging area for the Allied forces from the west that would aid in the defeat of Nazi Germany.

Winston Churchill had long warned his people first against the Communist dictator Josef Stalin of Soviet Russia and later against the Fascist dictators Benito Mussolini of Italy and Adolf Hitler of Germany. He became Britain's Prime Minister at the beginning of the Second World War, made his peace (for the time) with Stalin, and inspired Britain to survive the terrible bombings of London and other cities, and to rebound to play a key role in the eventual defeat of the Axis powers.

Hitler, having defeated France and thinking his western front secure, ignored his nonaggression pact with Russia and attacked her along his eastern front. This move, which German military strategists had long opposed, divided Hitler's forces between east and west, and thus he could at no time bring the full strength of German arms to bear on either front. It was to prove a fatal error.

Russia, from 1930 to the beginning of World War II, had become more and more a left-wing dictatorship, seemingly as completely regimented as the right-wing dictatorships in Germany, Italy and Spain. The Balkan nations of Greece, Yugoslavia and Rumania meanwhile survived precariously between the ambitious Germans, Italians and Russians located on or near their borders, but by 1942 most of the Balkans and other Eastern European nations were fighting a war of survival against Germany.

Outstanding contributions in the arts and sciences were made by Europeans and Americans despite the turbulence of these years of depression, dictatorship and war.

Josef Stalin of the Soviet Union became one of the powerful and ruthless dictators who seized power in European nations in the years between the First and Second World Wars. Stalin ruled Russia for 29 years. He led his people in the defeat of the Axis powers, yet sent countless numbers of his own countrymen to labor camps or to their deaths for opposition to his views. He helped make his nation one of the most feared and powerful on earth.

Beginning in 1934, for example, Arnold J. Toynbee (born 1889), of England, published his ten-volume *Study of History*. In 1936, John Maynard Keynes (1883–1946), also of England, published his *General Theory of Employment, Interest and Money* and thereby introduced what became known as "Keynesian economics." Toynbee and Keynes became the two most influential twentieth-century writers on political and economic matters.

Giants in the Earth, by Ole Rölvaag (1876–1931), an outstanding novel published in 1930, depicted the hardships endured by Norwegian settlers on the American frontier in Minnesota. Other important novels describing the economic trials and the bitterness of the depression years were *Tobacco Road,* by Erskine Caldwell (born 1903), and *The Grapes of Wrath,* by John Steinbeck (1902–1968). An Englishman, Aldous Huxley (1894–1963), grandson of the great biologist Thomas Huxley, wrote a prophetic novel *Brave New World,* which described the ultimate effect of industrial mechanization upon the human spirit and upon society as a whole.

Drama, music, painting and sculpture, like the novel, reflected the hardships of the worldwide depression during the turbulent 1930s. Most European nations as well as the United States instituted governmental programs in support of the arts and of artists. Out of these programs (most of which had been abandoned by the beginning of the Second World War) came a variety and quantity of plays, paintings, sculpture, operas and symphonies which (except for a diminution during the war years) rose to a peak which has continued to grow up to the present day. So vast is this output, so numerous the artists, so varied the techniques, that the recorder of history shies at making judgments and must wait until the test of time has been applied to this superabundance of creativity.

Work was done in physics which significantly broadened the understanding of atomic structure and which would within a few years lead to the development of atomic and hydrogen weapons. Among the important thinkers in atomic science were Ernest O. Lawrence (1901–1958) of the United States, who in 1931 invented the cyclotron; Otto Hahn (1879–1968) and Lise Meitner (1878–1968) of Germany, who did basic research and analysis in the study of the nucleus of the atom; and Enrico Fermi (1901–1954), born in Italy, who was one of the key students of nuclear theory and who later built the first nuclear reactor, at the University of Chicago in the United States.

The source of the sun's energy as well as that of other stars was explained by Hans A. Bethe (born 1906) in a paper published in 1939. Conquest of both the Arctic and the Antarctic regions was furthered in this twelve-year period by Russian, British, Canadian and American scientific expeditions.

ASIA, except for its Mediterranean Lands

In 1930 the Indian National Congress, led by Gandhi and Nehru, voted for complete independence from Britain. From this time on there would be no compromise in the firm but nonviolent drive of the Indian peoples toward political freedom, so that by 1940 Sir Stafford Cripps, a British emissary to India, recommended to his government that India be set free. The Moslem League of India declared that its goal was to have a separate country from the Hindus, which they intended to call Pakistan. In 1942 the Indian leaders Gandhi, Nehru and Abul Kalam Azad rejected an offer of autonomy because it was not to become effective until after the war.

During this period, the Chinese Republic under Chiang Kai-shek (Sun Yat-sen's successor) was torn by struggles with its dissident warlords, and was troubled also by the less open rebellion of the Chinese Communists. This turbulence created a situation which encouraged the ambitious Japanese to invade Manchuria in 1931. By 1936, Mao Tse-tung had gained control of the Communist Party in China, and in the same year the Japanese formed an alliance with Germany and Italy known as the Rome-Berlin-Tokyo Axis. By 1937, the Japanese had mounted a full-scale war against China. In 1940 the Japanese also invaded French Indochina, attacking Haiphong in Vietnam, where they installed a puppet government to replace the French-appointed rulers.

In 1941, Japan attacked simultaneously the United States's naval and air installations at Pearl Harbor in Hawaii, the American-held Pacific islands of Guam, Midway and the Philippines, and British-held Hongkong and Malaya. Japan thus became an active participant in World War II on the side of Germany and Italy, both of whom promptly declared war on the United States, and the latter became a combatant on the Allied side, against the three Axis powers.

OCEANIA

In 1934, under the United States's Tydings-McDuffie Act, the first plans for an independent Philippines were outlined. Australia and New Zealand joined Britain and her allies in World War II, as they had in World War I.

AFRICA

In 1935, Fascist Italy attacked the relatively helpless African nation of Ethiopia. This attack set a precedent for the European dictatorships, which, within the next few years, would each be guilty of several unprovoked attacks against smaller nations. The League of Nations proved totally ineffective and did little to stop the aggression against Ethiopia, thus sounding its own death knell as a world peace-keeping organization.

In 1936, Farouk became king of Egypt. Although nominally independent, Egypt was a base for British troops in North Africa during World War II. These troops would not be withdrawn until 1956. Major battles of the Second World War were fought in the deserts of North Africa by opposing forces led by the famous generals Erwin Rommel of Germany and Bernard Law Montgomery of Britain, with ultimate victory going to the British, who were strongly aided by United States forces.

THE AMERICAS

In 1931 the British Parliament passed the Statute of Westminster, which made all of the dominions of the British Empire (Canada among them) independent of British rule and partners of Britain rather than her subordinates in the affairs of the empire.

The depression which followed the stock-market crash of 1929 lay like a pall over American industry, agriculture and labor. By 1932, fifteen million Americans were out of work, and farmers and businessmen alike suffered ruin and despair. The American slump radiated out and aggravated the economic problems of the rest of the nations of the earth.

Franklin Delano Roosevelt was elected president of the United States in 1932. His administration inaugurated what was called the New Deal, which was a multifaceted attempt to stimulate the economy into renewed prosperity while, it was hoped, keeping the government's control of business and labor within the limits of a democratic framework. Under the New Deal, Congress enacted programs which, among other things, enabled the government to employ young men in road-building and reforestation and to build and operate dams which would furnish cheap electrical power and control soil erosion and floods. Many of these programs were popularly known by letters such as AAA (Agricultural Adjustment Act), CCC (Civilian Conservation Corps), and WPA (Works Progress Administration). Farmers were given subsidies; the work week was shortened; minimum wages were established; and Social Security (a form of old-age insurance) was made national and compulsory. There was, in addition, a mass expenditure of public funds to stimulate employment and business.

In Mexico, Lázaro Cárdenas was elected president in 1934. His government instituted land and labor reforms and gave the vote to women. The Cárdenas government in 1938 expropriated all foreign-owned oil properties, mostly of U.S. citizens—an act much criticized in the United States.

In the midst of this, the specter of war was growing in Europe, and millions of U.S. workers and billions of U.S. dollars were being channeled into the production of planes, guns, tanks and bullets.

In 1939 the Second World War began with Germany's invasion of Poland, and Canada almost immediately entered the war on the side of Britain and the other Allied nations. The United States declared its neutrality, but the succession of events and its own vital interests seemed to draw the nation inevitably closer to participation on the side of the Allies and opposed to the Axis powers of Nazi Germany, Fascist Italy, and Japan. In 1941, after Japan attacked Pearl Harbor in Hawaii, President Roosevelt asked the United States Senate to make formal declaration of war upon Japan and, a few days later, upon Italy and Germany.

Franklin Delano Roosevelt was elected President of the United States for an unprecedented four terms. Like other leaders of his time, he was confronted with the problems of the Depression. He attempted to solve them with such projects as the Tennessee Valley Authority, or TVA, as it was called. TVA built dams along the river which brought electricity to half a million homes, created tremendous power for industry, and provided thousands of square miles of outdoor recreational lands.

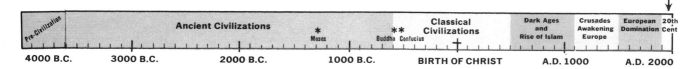

Pre-Civilization	Ancient Civilizations	*Moses	**Buddha Confucius	Classical Civilizations	Dark Ages and Rise of Islam	Crusades Awakening Europe	European Domination	20th Cent

4000 B.C. 3000 B.C. 2000 B.C. 1000 B.C. BIRTH OF CHRIST A.D. 1000 A.D. 2000

1942 — 1954

The Atom Bomb • **The End of the Second World War** • **The Nuremberg Trials** • **Camus, Wouk** •
Jet Engines, Computers • **The Cold War** • **India Gains Independence** • **The Korean War** •
The Berlin Blockade • **Communist Revolutions in Asia** • **The French and Indochina War**

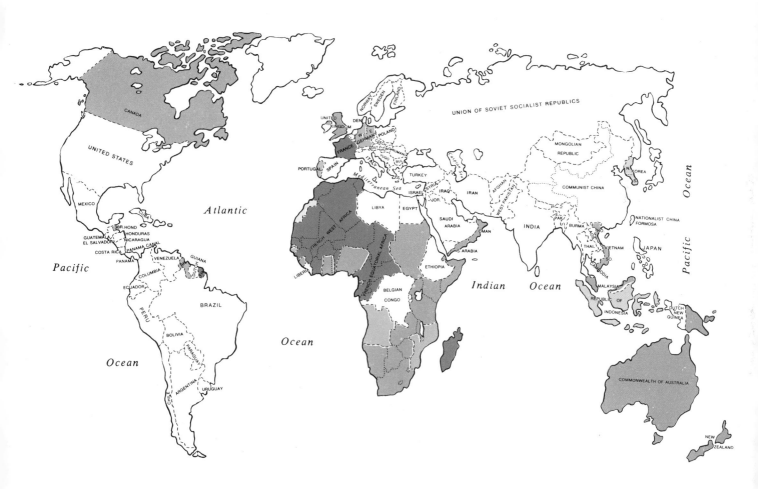

WORLD **EMPIRES AND COLONIES:**

FRANCE
PORTUGAL
UNITED KINGDOM

EUROPE and the Mediterranean World

The leaders of the Allied nations during the key years of the Second World War were Winston Churchill of England, Joseph Stalin of the Soviet Union, Charles de Gaulle of France (who organized French resistance from his sanctuary in the British Isles) and Franklin Delano Roosevelt of the United States. The leaders of the Axis powers were Adolf Hitler of Germany, Benito Mussolini of Italy, and Emperor Hirohito of Japan.

In 1942 the tide began to turn against the Axis. In the battle of El Alamein in North Africa, British troops outfought Italian and German armies, pushing them back as far as Tunisia. On the Russian front, after fighting bitterly and suffering almost unbearable losses for months during the harsh winter, Soviet troops regained possession of the city of Stalingrad and encircled the vast German armies there, inflicting terrible losses upon them. They then began to push the Nazi forces back toward Germany all along the long front.

From 1942 through 1945 the Germans were harassed by increasingly effective resistance movements in countries such as France and the Netherlands, which Nazi troops had captured and occupied early in the war. Not only did the citizenry in these nations grow ever more adept at undermining the efforts of the occupying German forces, but they were aided by their own soldiers who had escaped to England or North Africa and returned secretly to their homelands to engage in sabotage and espionage against the occupying forces.

On June 6, 1944, the designated day, or "D Day" as it is called in military parlance, powerful Allied armies commanded by the United States general Dwight D. Eisenhower crossed the English Channel and landed in the French province of Normandy. Germany now faced a two-front land war, with the Russian Army on its east and the American-British-French forces on its west. Despite occasional setbacks, the Allied drive into Europe proved too powerful for the Germans to repel. Early in 1945, the key Western leaders, Winston Churchill, Joseph Stalin and Franklin Roosevelt, met at the Russian city of Yalta on the Black Sea to lay plans for the final assault against the Axis. Included in their plans was an agreement that the Russians would attack Japan at the end of the European phase of the war. President Roosevelt's role at Yalta has been much criticized by those in the United States who felt that the Allies' decisions there gave rise to the postwar strength of Russia and China, which has been used subsequently against American interests.

Eleven months after D Day, on May 8, 1945, the German armies surrendered unconditionally to the Allied commander in chief, General Dwight D. Eisenhower, in a schoolhouse at Reims, France. The Italian Army and Navy had surrendered almost two years earlier, in September of 1943, so the German capitulation signaled the end of the European phase of the war. The Japanese, however, continued to fight for three months, until August of 1945.

The worldwide scope of the war and its terrible destructiveness can best be understood by listing the nations actively involved and the deaths resulting directly and indirectly from it. These included, among the nations of Europe and the Mediterranean world, Belgium, Egypt, Luxembourg, the Netherlands, Norway, Poland, Turkey, the United Kingdom and France on the side of the Allies; Bulgaria, Finland, Germany, Hungary and Rumania on the Axis side. The North and South American countries of Argentina, Bolivia, Brazil, Canada, Colombia, Costa Rica, Cuba, El Salvador, Guatemala, Haiti, Honduras, Mexico, Nicaragua, Panama and Uruguay and the United States joined the Allied powers, as did the African states of Ethiopia, Liberia and the Union of South Africa. In addition, the Asian and Pacific states of India, China, Australia and New Zealand fought with the Allies. Japan, of course, was one of the three key Axis powers.

A total of almost ten million military personnel (Axis and Allied combined) died in the war. Civilian deaths are estimated to have been between twelve and fifteen million. The wounded, the permanently disabled, the millions who were made homeless total almost astronomical figures.

Beginning in 1945, labor governments in Great Britain nationalized many industries and set up the National Health Service, the purpose of which was to give free medical and surgical care to every resident of Britain.

Yugoslavia, which had been occupied by the Nazis during much of the war, became a republic in 1945, and a Communist, Josip Broz, popularly called Tito, became the nation's premier.

The United Nations was established in 1945, first by representatives of fifty nations meeting in San Francisco from April 25 to June 26 to draft a charter, and later in the year by the ratification of the charter by twenty-

The Charter of the United Nations was signed at San Francisco on June 26, 1945, and later ratified by a majority of the fifty-one signatory nations. It was signed by the Secretary of State Stettinius with President Truman and Mrs. Eleanor Roosevelt looking on.

nine of these nations. The permanent seat of the U.N. was to be in the United States. The organization was created to help maintain world peace and, it was hoped, to promote political, economic and social conditions conducive to peace.

The Nuremberg trials, which began in 1945, made an unprecedented use of the legal process to punish government and military men for their activities in causing or carrying out war. Nazi leaders were accused and tried for crimes, foremost of which was intentionally causing the war. Many Nazi leaders were charged also with mass murder, enslavement, looting and various atrocities against Jews, Catholics and such ethnic groups as Poles and Czechs. Of twenty-two key officials of Germany who were tried, three were acquitted; the rest received sentences ranging from ten years to death.

By the end of 1945, France adopted a new constitution and, under it, inaugurated the Fourth French Republic, with Charles de Gaulle as its president. De Gaulle served for only a few months, resigning when he felt the nation did not solidly support him.

At the termination of the war, Germany was divided into four zones, each of which was occupied by one of the principal Allied nations—Russia, Britain, France and the United States. Problems and differences escalated into what was called the "Cold War," which was to drive a wedge between these nations formerly allied against the Axis forces. On the one side in this Cold War would be the non-Communist countries of the West; on the other side, Russia and the combination of Communist nations which the Soviets had put together at the end of the Second World War. These Communist nations included Poland, Czechoslovakia, Hungary, Rumania and Yugoslavia. The tensions between the Communist nations of Eastern Europe and the non-Communist nations of Western Europe were to become most intense in defeated Germany. In 1948 the zones of Germany which were occupied by England, France and the United States were combined to form a new nation popularly called "West Germany." Konrad Adenauer became West Germany's first chancellor in 1949. The zone occupied by Russia became Communist "East Germany," another satellite among Russia's Communist group of nations. These two divisions of Germany, the one backed by the Soviets, the other by the Western nations, faced each other across a barrier of misunderstanding, mistrust and fear.

The city of Berlin, two hundred miles deep within Communist East Germany, was also divided (as was all of Germany) at the war's end into sectors occupied by the four great powers. In 1949, after a series of disagreements, French, English and American access to their sectors of Berlin through Communist East Germany was cut off by Russian forces. This became known as the Berlin Blockade. More than two million West Berliners were then supplied with food and other necessities for eleven months by British and American airplanes. This herculean feat finally broke the Communist blockade so that the Soviets again permitted land vehicles to cross the Communist portion of Germany and bring supplies to the city. In another symptom of the Cold War, the nations of Western Europe joined with the United States and Canada to form the North Atlantic Treaty Organization (NATO), a mutual-defense group aimed at curtailing Russian expansion. In 1952, certain nations of Europe joined forces to form the European Coal and Steel Combine, designed to eliminate tariffs between member nations on the key products of coal and steel and thereby to improve their economic conditions.

The airlift of food and supplies to the people of blockaded Berlin was accomplished by vast armadas of British and American aircraft which flew into the city both day and night. As much as 4,100 tons of food and coal were brought into Berlin in a single twenty-four-hour period.

Joseph Stalin, dictator of Russia, died in 1953, and the world watched to see who would replace him and where the Soviet state would go under new leadership.

In 1948 the British mandate over Palestine (in existence since the end of World War I) came to an end. The United Nations General Assembly voted to partition Palestine into two states, one Jewish and one Arab. A provisional Israeli government declared the tiny nation of Israel to be independent of the rest of Palestine. In a resultant war, Israel defeated a coalition of Arab nations which attempted to crush it.

In 1949, the Republic of Ireland (Eire) was proclaimed as an independent nation. Shortly thereafter, the British House of Commons recognized its independence, but maintained that the six counties which made up Northern Ireland would continue to be a part of the United Kingdom. Thus, after eight hundred years of struggle, part of Ireland achieved freedom from England, but the fact that Northern Ireland remained a part of the United Kingdom was to cause continuing disruptions and bloodshed.

This twelve-year period also witnessed many accomplishments in science and the arts. To begin with, the development of the atomic bomb in the United States, with the aid of scientists from Great Britain, Italy, Hungary and Germany, had been, of necessity, preceded by a tremendous expansion of knowledge of nuclear structure among the world's physicists. However, once the bombs were developed, and used against Japan, these same scientists, driven by concern and guilt over the bomb's potential for devastation, devoted themselves to writing and lecturing all over the earth against the future employment of atomic weapons, and to seeking nonmilitary uses for the atomic processes which their research had made available. In the United States, civilian control of future atomic developments was assured (it was hoped) by the founding in 1946 of the Atomic Energy Commission, a nonmilitary organization. As an illustration of how the new knowledge could be put to nonwar use, prototype power-generating plants based on atomic energy were developed to run the machines of power-hungry world industry.

The highly sophisticated calculating machines called computers were being further developed and put into use in universities and other centers of research in Europe and America.

Radio-carbon dating, a method for ascertaining the age of certain kinds of fossils, was devised by Willard F. Libby (born 1908), of the United States.

Much important research was done in genetics, especially into the structure of DNA. This chemical, found in the nucleus of every living cell, is felt to be the storehouse of hereditary traits and the means by which all forms of life reproduce offspring with characteristics identical to those of themselves and of their ancestors.

Between 1940 and 1945, scientists in Britain, aided later by researchers in the United States, developed radar, a system for locating distant objects such as enemy aircraft by using electromagnetic waves. Radar later proved to have a wide variety of other military and many civilian uses.

Toward the end of the Second World War the jet engine was developed in Britain and Germany. It became apparent that future air travel would be based upon jet-powered planes rather than upon the previous source of power, the internal-combustion engine.

Many fine novels were written about World War II by men who had experienced it. Perhaps the most widely known works were produced by three Americans: Norman Mailer, who wrote *The Naked and The Dead;* Irwin Shaw, the author of *The Young Lions;* and Herman Wouk, who wrote *The Caine Mutiny*. Other literary and artistic works were produced in an unprecedented volume during this period, but are still too close to the present day for any objective evaluation to be made of them. The writings of novelist and playwright Albert Camus, of France (1913–1960), however, demand attention for the lucidity of their presentation and for their keen understanding of and penetration into the problems of the human conscience.

ASIA, except for its Mediterranean Lands

Japan was to continue fighting in World War II for only three months after the Germans capitulated—that is, until August 15, 1945. The entry of Russian troops into the Pacific theater of operations in 1945 played little more than a token part in the Japanese surrender, for the devastation wrought by the dropping of two atomic bombs by the Americans on two Japanese cities quickly brought the Pacific phase of the war to an end. The first such bomb, dropped on the city of Hiroshima, caused 150,000 casualties out of its 350,000 population. A second bomb dropped on the city of Nagasaki caused at least 80,000 casualties out of a population of 200,000.

In 1947, after the end of World War II, by agreement between the peoples of the Indian subcontinent and the government of Great Britain, India was partitioned into two nations—a Hindu state, to be called India, and a Moslem state, to be called Pakistan. Because there were two concentrations of Moslems in the subcontinent, one in the western area and the other in the northeast, Pakistan was divided into two separate parts, East Pakistan and West Pakistan, with India lying between them and separating them by distances averaging a thousand miles. A few small states in the Indian subcontinent such as Hyderabad and Kashmir remained, for the time, under the rule of their native princes and outside the new Hindu and Moslem nations. Kashmir was later absorbed into the Republic of India,

Before dropping the first atomic bomb, Allied planes distributed leaflets over Japan for 11 days, warning of imminent destruction if Japan did not surrender unconditionally at once. On August 6, 1945, the first atomic bomb was dropped upon Hiroshima. Seventy-five percent of the city was destroyed in a few minutes.

despite its large Moslem population, but the area has remained a source of contention between India and Pakistan to this day. Jawaharlal Nehru became India's first prime minister and Liaquat Ali Khan the first prime minister of Pakistan.

The turmoil resulting from the partition, and the fears and recriminations accompanying the new independence, led to two tragic events: the assassination of Mahatma Gandhi in 1948 and that of Ali Khan of Pakistan three years later.

In 1951, Ceylon became a self-governing dominion of the British Empire. In the same year, India began a five-year program designed to further her own economic development. India signed treaties concerning economic and defense matters with the Soviet Union, France and China.

China, during the postwar years, was torn by civil war between the Nationalist government forces led by President Chiang Kai-shek, supported by the United States, and the Chinese Communist forces led by Mao Tse-tung, supported by Soviet Russia. By the year 1949, the Communists won control of mainland China, and Chiang Kai-shek was forced to move with what remained of his Nationalist army to the island of Formosa, also called Taiwan.

Japanese rule of Korea ceased in 1945 at the end of World War II. The withdrawing Japanese troops were replaced in North Korea by Russian forces and in South Korea by United States forces. The thirty-eighth parallel acted as the dividing line between them. A Communist state was fostered in Korea's north by the Soviets, and a republic was nurtured in the south by the United States. After elections had established independent governments in the two areas of Korea, both the United States and Russia withdrew their troops in 1948 and 1949, but both left military advisers behind and furnished vast amounts of military aid to their client nations.

In 1950, hostilities broke out between North and South Korea which escalated into a full-fledged war. The United States (and certain other members of the United Nations) became deeply involved in supplying forces to fight on the side of South Korea. Eventually, Chinese Communist forces came to the aid of North Korea. The war ended in 1953, after more than three years of fighting and a million deaths, and after two and a half million persons had been made homeless, when it became apparent that neither side could achieve victory. There were no significant territorial changes and few, if any, problems solved in this war between the two parts of Korea.

Similar problems developed in parts of Southeast Asia. The several thousand islands of Dutch Indonesia, for example, had been occupied by the Japanese during the Second World War (between 1942 and 1945), and, as in Korea, the Japanese troops were expelled at the war's end. Here too the European colonial power, in this case Holland, was forced to grant independence to its colony, which then formed a republic under the leadership of Achmed Sukarno. Burma too was established as an independent republic in 1948, free from ties to Great Britain.

In Vietnam, Laos and Cambodia, the three states constituting French Indochina, independence was more

The civil war in China between government troops and the Communist forces laid waste millions of acres, destroyed whole towns, and left countless numbers of Chinese homeless and starving.

difficult to achieve. Here, after the Japanese were expelled at the end of World War II, nationalists seized North Vietnam in 1945 under the leadership of Communist-trained Ho Chi Minh. Returning French forces, unable to expel the insurgent forces under Ho Chi Minh, became embroiled in 1946 in a prolonged war with them. In 1949, France recognized the limited independence of Laos, Cambodia and Vietnam within a French Union of Nations, but this limited freedom failed to satisfy Ho Chi Minh or his followers, and the war continued. In 1950, despite United States economic and military aid, the French military position was becoming increasingly untenable. In 1954 a truce was signed, dividing Vietnam into two nations—North Vietnam, under the Communists, and South Vietnam, whose non-Communist leadership enjoyed limited popular support. The truce called for elections to be held no later than July 1956 to decide the political future of both North and South Vietnam. The cost of the war to France and the French Union of Nations at this point totaled at least a quarter of a million human casualties, of which ninety thousand were dead or missing. France had poured $4 billion into the conflict, the United States about $2 billion.

OCEANIA

Australia, New Zealand, and most of the other islands of the Pacific were involved in World War II on the Allied side.

In 1946, after the war had ended, the Philippine Islands were granted their independence by the United States. Manuel A. Roxas was elected to serve as the first Filipino president.

Australia and New Zealand joined the United States in 1949 in a mutual-defense pact that became known as ANZUS. From this time forth, these two British dominions of the Pacific would look often to the United States for guidance and help in matters of military aid and foreign policy.

AFRICA

The Axis forces had been completely expelled from Africa during World War II. There was a growing spirit of nationalism among the peoples of the remaining European colonies in Africa, and an increasing demand for self-rule. In 1951, the former Italian colony of Libya was made a free state by United Nations action.

THE AMERICAS

Franklin Delano Roosevelt died on April 12, 1945, in the last year of World War II, at the beginning of his fourth term as president of the United States. He was succeeded by Vice-President Harry S. Truman, who made the decision to use the atomic bomb against Japan, a decision which has since drastically affected the course of human affairs. World War II ended during Truman's administration, with the surrender of Germany on May 8, 1945, and of Japan on August 15, 1945.

In the year 1946, during President Truman's first term in office, the United Nations world organization held its first meeting, in the city of San Francisco in California. The North Atlantic Treaty Organization (NATO) was formed in 1949 during the Truman years, with the stated purpose of defending Western Europe against aggression and of promoting its general economic and political welfare. Truman's administration was responsible for the Truman Doctrine of "resistance to international aggression" (which was usually expected to be Communist); for the Marshall Plan of aid to the war-torn nations of Europe; and for the formation of the Organization of American States, which was dedicated to promoting the welfare and safety of all the countries of the Western Hemisphere.

Most United States international activities during this period seemed to evolve from the nation's intense and almost unreasoning fear of Communism. For example, the Cold War in Europe between the Communist and non-Communist nations continually plagued the Truman administration. During Truman's second term (to which he was elected in 1948) the nation became involved in the Korean War in Asia, also an expression of the antipathy between the Communist and non-Communist worlds. In Korea, in 1950, the United States came into violent conflict for the first time with growing Asian nationalism, and for the first time she committed troops to an Asian land war. The General Assembly of the United Nations endorsed this United States military intervention in the war on the side of South Korea against Communist North Korea. Several other United Nations members furnished troops as well as materiel to aid in what was at the time designated a "police action" rather than a war.

In 1952, General Dwight D. Eisenhower, who had been commander of all Allied forces in the European phase of World War II, was elected president of the United States. During his first year in office, the Korean War was settled, in some part as a result of his efforts. The boundary between North and South Korea, however, and the political, economic and ideological differences between the two divisions of the Korean Peninsula remained unchanged.

Russia tested its first atomic bomb in 1949 while Truman was president. By 1954, during the Eisenhower administration, both the United States and Russia had perfected the even more destructive hydrogen bomb. Throughout both the Truman and the Eisenhower administrations, there were confrontations between the two atomic giants—in Berlin, in the Near East, in Korea and in Hungary—confrontations which in pre-atomic times might well have led to war between them. That this did not happen is largely felt to be a result of the widespread dread of the universal and irreversible desolation which would result from an atomic war.

During the Eisenhower years, fear of Communism in the United States reached such great proportions that many otherwise reasonable persons were unable to think on this subject with any degree of reliability. This fear invaded the home, the shop, even the Congress of the United States. In the Senate, investigations to search out Communists or Communist sympathizers based on merest rumor and often slander were pursued under the leadership of Senator Joseph R. McCarthy. These investigations ruined the careers of many persons who were later found to be innocent. McCarthy and his team of "investigators" also diverted the nation's, and the government's, attention from important matters and exaggerated the crippling paranoia which already troubled so much of the nation. That is not to say that there were no Communist sympathizers or other persons willing to transmit official secrets to the Soviets for reasons of personal profit or political conviction. During these years, for example, two Americans, Julius and Ethel Rosenberg, were found guilty of such actions under the Espionage Act of 1917 and were executed. Leading lawyers have indicated, however, that imprisonment would have been a more likely sentence in less troubled times, and would have allowed the period of time required to resolve certain doubts and reservations in the Rosenberg case.

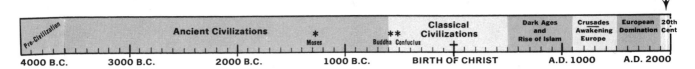

1954 — 1966

The European Common Market • Khrushchev in Russia and de Gaulle in France • Schism in World Communism • France and China Detonate Nuclear Weapons • New Nations of Africa • Escalation of the Vietnamese War • Space Exploration

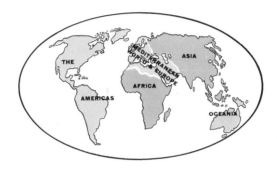

EUROPE and the Mediterranean World

During this period the nations of western Europe moved to restore economic stability to a continent ravaged by World War II. In 1957, for instance, West Germany, Italy, France, the Netherlands, Belgium and Luxembourg agreed to form a "Common Market" in which all tariffs on goods traded between them would gradually be abolished. Great Britain, which was not a member of this Common Market, made a slower economic recovery, due in some part to her exclusion from it. Perhaps nowhere was the contrast between levels of economic recovery so marked as between the great prosperity of West Germany, which enjoyed the rich trade benefits of being in the Common Market, and Communist East Germany, which was virtually isolated from trading with Western Europe.

In 1957, Harold Macmillan, a former war hero as well as a long-time Conservative member of the British government, became Britain's prime minister. He attempted to guide his nation through seven years of economic difficulty at home and declining influence abroad.

The Fourth Republic of France, which came into being at the end of World War II, had adopted a new constitution which contained many of the weaknesses of earlier French constitutions. In addition, the voice of the French people was divided among many competing political parties. This resulted in an unprecedented number of changes of government leadership between 1944 and 1954. During these years, French armies fought almost continually throughout the world to main-

tain France's empire, but with little success. In the end, France was forced to grant independence, first, to her Southeast Asian colony of Indochina (in 1954) and, later, to her North African colonies of Tunisia and Morocco.

In 1958, amidst considerable turmoil in both France and Algeria, General Charles de Gaulle, who had been the leader of French resistance forces in World War II, and the nation's first president after the war's end, again became head of the French state. A new constitution giving him great power was approved by a popular referendum. President de Gaulle entered upon the leadership of France harboring ill-feeling toward France's former allies, Great Britain and the United States, because of actions taken by them to bypass his authority during the Allied invasion of France in World War II and their attempts to exclude him afterward from the government of France. In addition, de Gaulle had long disapproved of the West's inability to make accommodations with Communist Russia and China. He felt also that United States leadership in Europe often did not serve Europe's best interests and was certainly often directed toward other than France's welfare.

During this period, de Gaulle took steps calculated to improve French relations with Russia and China, and (in 1960) France detonated her first atomic bomb, thus becoming third in the select group of nations (along with Russia and the United States) able to manufacture and use these fearful weapons. De Gaulle expelled NATO troops from their bases in France, so that France became in effect a buffer zone between East and West and thus, in de Gaulle's view, better suited to act as peacemaker between the Communist and non-Communist worlds.

In 1955, Nikita Khrushchev became prime minister of the Soviet Union, filling the vacancy left by the death of Joseph Stalin in 1953. An uprising in Hungary against Russian domination was repressed by the Soviets, but later, under Khrushchev's leadership, the world would see the Soviets take many steps to ease tensions within the Soviet Union and its satellites, and also to better relations with the West. Anti-Communist feeling was so strong among Western nations, however, that they were reluctant to believe that the changes were bona fide and to respond to them in kind.

Soviet Russia put a man into space orbit in 1961, as did the United States shortly thereafter. These two superpowers would continue to vie with each other in space exploration, as they would in military, economic and political matters, throughout the 1960s.

During these years, a deepening schism developed between Russia and China. The split between the two Communist giants disproved the theory of monolithic Communism and cast doubt on the wisdom of many in the Western nations who had insisted that all Communist nations would inevitably take the same political paths, regardless of their different national interests.

In 1955, oil-rich Iraq joined with Britain, Turkey, Iran and Pakistan in a mutual-defense agreement, called the Baghdad Pact, which was designed to control Russian expansion into the Mediterranean area.

The Suez Canal Zone was evacuated by British troops in 1956, and control of the canal was assumed by Egypt. Although Egypt reaffirmed her support of freedom of navigation of the canal by all nations, she refused to grant freedom of passage to Israeli ships. Israel, Britain and France then attacked Egypt in order to regain control of the canal, but, with easy victory in sight, they withdrew upon the insistence of the United States and other members of the Security Council of the United Nations.

In 1958, Egypt and Syria gave up their separate national sovereignties to form a new nation called the United Arab Republic. Gamal Abdel Nasser of Egypt became the UAR's first president, and Cairo its capital city. Syria, however, was later to withdraw from this union.

The Mediterranean island of Cyprus was repeatedly torn by conflict between its Greek and Turkish populations—a racial division within the island which had fomented a state of unrest since the conquest of Cyprus by the Ottoman Turks centuries before.

There was growing friction and hostility between the Arab countries and the state of Israel, and the ever present danger of renewed outbreak of war.

In 1962, after seven years of civil conflict, Algeria was finally granted independence by France. This was accomplished by the determination and statesmanship of French President Charles de Gaulle in the face of tremendous opposition from French landholders in Algeria and the French conservatives at home who felt that de Gaulle was their representative and would act to retain Algeria as a colony to the bitter end. De Gaulle, on the other hand, recognized that Algeria must eventually be freed. His courage in working out a solution saved much bloodshed and retained a relationship between France and Algeria, who have become commercially closer and have developed a mutual respect not thought possible during the years of rebellion.

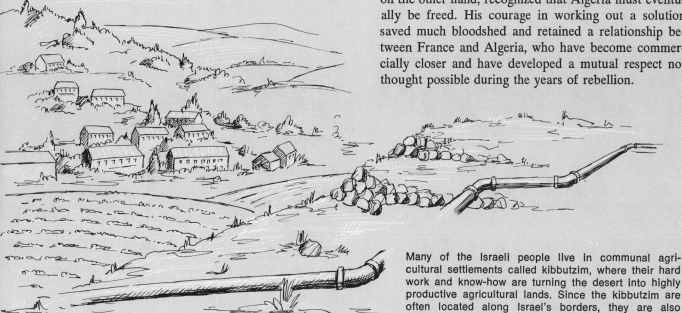

Many of the Israeli people live in communal agricultural settlements called kibbutzim, where their hard work and know-how are turning the desert into highly productive agricultural lands. Since the kibbutzim are often located along Israel's borders, they are also fortresses against Arab guerilla attacks.

ASIA, except for its Mediterranean Lands

The new Hindu nation of India was beset with problems rising from both internal and external causes. The French settlements which still existed in the subcontinent were transferred to the new government of India without incident, but Portugal held fast to her colonies of Goa and Damao. In 1955 India broke off diplomatic relations with Portugal, and in 1961 she invaded and conquered these remaining Portuguese-ruled areas.

There was trouble, too, between China and India, with border clashes in 1959 and large-scale fighting in 1962. In the year 1964, India's Prime Minister Nehru died and was succeeded by Lal Bahadur Shastri, who lived to govern just two years. Shastri was succeeded as prime minister in 1966 by Nehru's daughter, Mrs. Indira Gandhi. Pakistan and India had problems over the state of Kashmir which were alleviated in 1958 by an exchange of territory, arranged to place more of Kashmir's Moslems under Pakistani rule.

The people of Ceylon agreed in 1956 that Sinhalese should be the official language of their island dominion.

The Chinese Communists, meanwhile, were consolidating their hold on mainland China and threatening the Nationalist Chinese who, under Chiang Kai-shek, had fled to the island of Taiwan (Formosa). The small islands between Taiwan and the mainland were bombarded frequently by Communist gunfire.

Soviet Russia was showing increased antagonism toward the People's Republic of China. In 1959, Soviet reaction to Chinese–Indian border friction caused a near-breach between the two Communist giants. There were rumors of economic and political problems within China, and there were also contradictory stories of fantastic progress; but the ban on travel between China, the world's most populous nation, and the countries of the West made knowledge of China's internal affairs difficult to confirm. It seemed apparent, however, that a struggle for the control of the nation was developing in 1966 or earlier between the local Communist chiefs in certain cities and the national leaders such as Mao Tse-tung, aided by the Chinese Army. This struggle became known as the Cultural Revolution.

During this period, the People's Republic of China detonated a series of atomic devices and thereby became the fourth nation in the "nuclear club," along with France, Russia and the United States.

Japan was recovering from the effects of the Second World War at a rate which rivaled that of the nations of the European Common Market. In 1960, Japan and the United States signed a mutual-security pact; in 1965, Japan and Korea signed a treaty after almost fifty years of diplomatic and military differences. The Olympic Games were held in Tokyo in 1964, an indication of Japan's renewed acceptance as an honored member of the world community.

In Southeast Asia, the people of Malaya, who had come under British rule in the late 1800s and early 1900s, voted for self-rule. As a result, in August of 1957 the British protectorate over Malaya ended, and the nation became an independent member of the British Commonwealth. The crown colony of Singapore (located on the southern tip of the Malay Peninsula) also became a self-governing state in 1959 and was later incorporated into the new federation called Malaysia, which included Malaya, Sarawak, Brunei and British Borneo. Singapore was to withdraw from the federation shortly, however, to become an independent state in the British Commonwealth. In 1964 there was trouble along the border between Malaysia and Indonesia, and for a time it appeared that a full-scale war might result.

The Geneva Conference of 1954 had divided French Indochina into four small nations: Laos, Cambodia, Communist North Vietnam, and non-Communist South Vietnam. A general election was to have been held in 1956 to reunite the two Vietnams under a government of the people's choice, but fighting broke out in South Vietnam between government troops and a nationalist guerrilla group which called itself the Vietcong, or National Liberation Front. The United States began to pour ever greater amounts of military aid and advisers into the land to help the government of South Vietnam, and the scheduled elections to permit the people of North and South to choose a government for the entire land were never held.

In 1960 there was rebellion in Laos by the Pathet Lao, a nationalist group which was supported by Ho Chi Minh's Communist North Vietnamese. Civil war developed in which three factions—right-wing, left-wing and neutralist—contended for control of the nation. A conference at Geneva in 1962 established a coalition government in Laos under the neutralist leader Prince Souvanna Phouma.

The conflict in South Vietnam between the National Liberation Front and the South Vietnam government continued to grow worse. In 1964 there were 24,000 United States military advisers aiding the government of South Vietnam. An incident in the Bay of Tonkin in which the United States claimed that one of its destroyers was attacked by North Vietnamese forces evoked a violent United States retaliation. American planes began bombing North Vietnam, concentrating especially upon the supply roads from North Vietnam to the south, popularly called the Ho Chi Minh Trail. Those portions of this supply route which passed through neighboring Laos were also heavily bombed. By 1965, the North Vietnamese cities of Hanoi and Haiphong, hundreds of miles to the north, were under attack by United States planes, and by the summer of 1966 the United States announced that it had 250,000 troops (and later in the year 400,000) in South Vietnam. The extent of United States participation in the war in Indochina was causing worldwide consternation. Fear was growing that China might enter the war on the side of North Vietnam and that World War III would ensue.

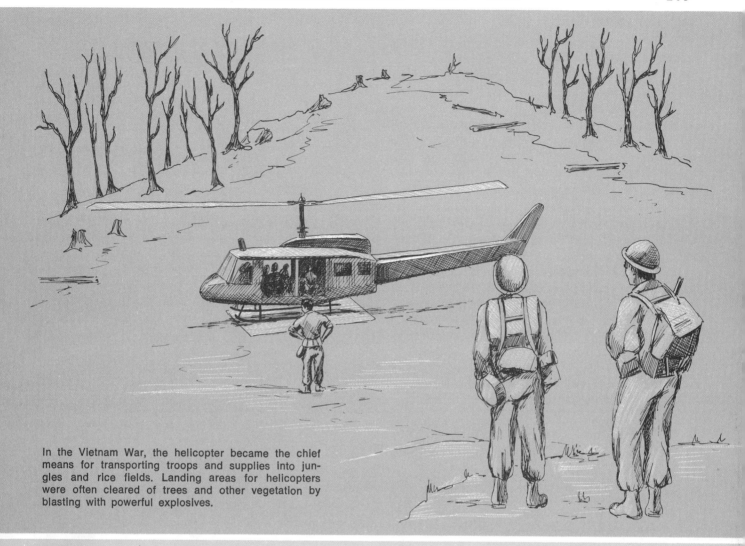

In the Vietnam War, the helicopter became the chief means for transporting troops and supplies into jungles and rice fields. Landing areas for helicopters were often cleared of trees and other vegetation by blasting with powerful explosives.

OCEANIA

Australia and New Zealand enjoyed a high measure of prosperity during these postwar years as wool prices soared and the market for their wool and various other products expanded. There was concern, however, that if their best customer, Great Britain, were admitted to the European Common Market, she would use less of their products, since her main sources of supply might become European.

Australia, New Zealand, Thailand, the Philippines and Pakistan joined the United States, Great Britain and France in the mutual-defense Southeast Asia Treaty Organization (SEATO), designed to contain expanding Asian nationalism, which was often Communist-led.

Hawaii became the fiftieth state of the United States of America in 1959.

AFRICA, except for its Mediterranean Lands

In the nine years between 1956 and 1965, thirty-three former European colonies in Africa achieved independence, so that by the middle sixties almost all of Africa was free of European rule. Most of the transitions from colony to independent statehood were accomplished in an orderly manner, but the Belgian Congo was a tragic exception. Its people were ill-prepared for the withdrawal of Belgian law and order, and underwent a chaotic period in which tribal warfare and political assassinations were widespread. As had happened elsewhere, both Communist and anti-Communist nations tried to take advantage of the turmoil to increase their

own influence. In 1960, United Nations troops were used in an attempt to help return orderly government to the Congo. In 1961, Dag Hammarskjold, secretary general of the United Nations, was killed on a peace mission to the Congo when his plane crashed in Northern Rhodesia. United Nations troops were not withdrawn from the Congo until 1964.

A very different situation, but one equally disheartening, existed in the Union of South Africa and in Rhodesia, where small white minorities maintained rigid control over the lands and denied participation in their own government to the black majorities.

THE AMERICAS

Many of the nations of South America and the Caribbean were governed by conservative dictatorships, often with a general or other military man as head of state. These dictatorships frequently enjoyed a close relationship with the United States government, which tended to support them as an alternative to what it feared might be left-wing or Communist revolution. Argentina under Juan Perón, Cuba under Fulgencio Batista, and Haiti under François Duvalier were outstanding examples of such Western Hemisphere dictatorships.

In the United States, during President Eisenhower's administration, Secretary of State John Foster Dulles was the key figure in world affairs. Dulles strongly advocated and implemented a policy of worldwide "containment" of Communism—an expansion of the policies of the Truman administration. American troops and installations, as a result of this policy, came to be spread around the earth. The Soviet Union was encircled with United States military establishments armed with atom-bomb carrying planes and rockets. In addition, the United States, during these years, took over the world-wide policing responsibilities which Great Britain had carried in the 1800s and early 1900s.

Two new states, Hawaii and Alaska, joined the Union during the Eisenhower years. During Eisenhower's term in office, Dr. Jonas E. Salk perfected the first polio vaccine; and the U.S. Supreme Court handed down the landmark decisions ending legal segregation of blacks and whites in the nation's public schools. Eisenhower's last months in office were blemished when Soviet Russia shot down a U.S. spy plane, called a U-2, over Soviet territory. This incident caused the Soviets to cancel a long-awaited summit conference between President Eisenhower and the Soviet leader, Nikita Khrushchev.

In 1960, John F. Kennedy became the thirty-fifth president of the United States. He brought to the office a spirit of youthfulness and an urgency to "get America moving again" after what Kennedy contended were the less active years of the Eisenhower administration. He and his brother Robert Kennedy (who was in his Cabinet as attorney general) played a major role in the effort to secure and maintain the civil rights of minority groups, which brought hope of first-class citizenship to millions of American Negroes.

President Kennedy made beginning attempts also to improve American relations with the Communist world, and with the United States's dissident former ally France. He continued and accelerated the space program begun under President Eisenhower.

During the Kennedy administration, thousands of black and white persons took part in several marches through Southern states, demonstrating for equal civil rights for United States Negroes. These marches were often led by such men as Dr. Martin Luther King, a black minister and civil-rights leader. Violence often erupted during these marches when the demonstrators passed through parts of highly segregated states such as Alabama and Mississippi.

The black American's drive for equality and against segregation was led by Nobel Prize winner Dr. Martin Luther King, Jr., who adopted the practices of nonviolence and civil disobedience that had been employed in India by Mahatma Gandhi.

In 1959, revolution in Cuba led by Fidel Castro swept away the island's rightist dictatorship under Batista, and installed in its place a dictatorship of the far left which established a close relationship with Communist China and Russia. When, in 1961, the Russians began to install atomic emplacements in Cuba just ninety miles from the state of Florida, one of the most explosive confrontations of the Cold War occurred. However, like similar confrontations between the atomic giants in Berlin, the Near East and Korea, it was settled without war.

President Kennedy was assassinated in Dallas, Texas, in November of 1963, and was succeeded by Vice-President Lyndon B. Johnson. Johnson continued the Kennedy space and civil-rights programs and at first enjoyed one of the most productive relationships with Congress in the history of the American presidency.

In 1964, Johnson was reelected president. Running against Republican Senator Barry Goldwater, Johnson won the largest majority vote ever until then given an American president. A part of the overwhelming vote given Johnson was due to the fact that he stated that he was unalterably opposed to sending "American boys to fight in Vietnam," whereas Goldwater strongly favored a strong enough United States commitment in men and materiel to win the war. Yet, after Johnson's election, his anxiety and preoccupation with the worsening situation in South Vietnam led him to commit ever more American men and materiel to that Asian war. By the end of 1966, the United States had over 400,000 men fighting in Vietnam. A growing antiwar movement among Americans was undermining President Johnson's political effectiveness and his control of his own political party.

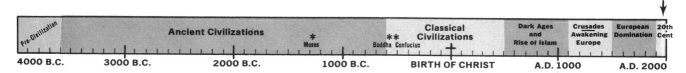

Pre-Civilization	Ancient Civilizations	* Moses	** Buddha Confucius	Classical Civilizations	Dark Ages and Rise of Islam	Crusades Awakening Europe	European Domination	20th Cent

4000 B.C.   3000 B.C.   2000 B.C.   1000 B.C.   BIRTH OF CHRIST   A.D. 1000   A.D. 2000

1966 — 1974

Arab–Israeli War and Oil Diplomacy • Religious and Economic Conflict in Northern Ireland • SALT Talks • Bangladesh Formed Out of East Pakistan • United States Withdraws From Vietnam • Civil War in Nigeria • Watergate Scandals • Environmental Pollution • Energy Crisis

THE WORLD TODAY

LOCATIONS OF WARS
1. NORTHERN IRELAND
2. CZECHOSLOVAKIA
3. MIDDLE EAST
4. BIAFRA
5. EAST AND WEST PAKISTAN
6. VIETNAM
— SOVIET BUFFER STATES

The period from 1966 to 1974 was, over all the earth, one of violence, dissatisfaction and pressure from individuals and groups for political, economic and moral change. Some of the events of these years will no doubt have a continuing impact on history. Others, which at the time monopolized world attention, will prove to have been important only in their own time, and only to the people directly involved.

The event which undoubtedly would have been the most significant one in these years did not take place: despite several dangerously provocative situations, the nuclear powers managed to avoid a head-on conflict. Furthermore, they entertained a number of proposals with the hope of making future confrontations between them less likely to occur, and less dangerous if they did.

More difficult to evaluate was the widespread disaffection of young people with the standards and the life styles of their parents. This disaffection was expressed in ways as varied as the length and style of their hair, their use of illegal drugs (as opposed to their parents' accepted use of alcohol and tobacco), their refusal in many cases to accept military service, their rebellion against accepted sexual mores, and, all too frequently, their resort to violence against life and property—the latter especially where the lives and the property symbolized establishment or government practices with which the young people strongly disagreed.

Equally difficult to assess were problems arising from the new ease of international air travel—problems such as the spread of communicable disease by travelers, the smuggling of drugs and other contraband, and, unique to our times, the hijacking of commercial airliners (often with one hundred or more passengers aboard) by lone individuals as well as by disciplined members of political organizations.

Less difficult to evaluate (although there was no absolute consensus here either) was the widespread pollution of the earth, its waters and its atmosphere by the very technology that had been confidently expected to elevate the quality of human life and to eliminate drudgery from it.

Problems of this period, however, were not confined to the new or the bizarre. There were, as in all previous times, revolution, religious war and civil war. For mankind, some things had changed little in five thousand years of civilization.

EUROPE and the Mediterranean World

During much of this period, relations between Russia and China were worsened by numerous clashes along their several-thousand-mile common border. The question arose as to whether or not the Soviets were being moved closer to *détente* with the West by this schism between themselves and the other great Communist power. Yet, by the end of 1972, relationships between China and Russia seemed to have enjoyed a reversal and apparently were improving.

On the other hand, war in the Middle East in 1967 between Israel (armed with French and, later, American weapons) and the Arab states (who had been largely armed and equipped by the Soviets) was definitely driving Russia further away from the United States and the other Western powers. In this war, Israel enjoyed a lightning victory over the far more numerous Arabs within a period of only six days. The victorious Israelis occupied strategically important portions of Egypt, Jordan and Syria. These occupied areas, which Israel felt were vital to her security, became a new source of Arab–Israeli friction. On October 6, 1973, Egypt and Syria attacked Israel in a resurgence of a war that quickly became a bloody testing ground for new Soviet and United States weaponry. The Arab states began withholding their oil—vital to the industrial nations—from the powers they considered friendly to Israel, and a peace conference between Egypt and Israel was quickly arranged. Negotiations in this first face-to-face meeting between Arabs and Israelis began in Geneva, Switzerland, in December of 1973.

In 1968, still another event worsened Russia's relationship with the West, when Soviet forces, along with those of the Communist nations of Poland, East Germany, Hungary and Bulgaria, invaded their fellow-Communist state of Czechoslovakia. The invasion presumably had been triggered by a growing liberalism in Czechoslovakia and by a movement in that country away from orthodox Communism as conceived by Russia; but a glance at a map of Europe suggests that the underlying

The people of Czechoslovakia awoke on the morning of August 21, 1968, to find 70,000 Russian, Polish, and East German troops, whose tanks were placed in strategic locations, in control of their country. Czechoslovakia's leaders were arrested and taken to Moscow for "consultations."

cause of the invasion might well have been purely geographical and military, for a Western-oriented Czechoslovakia might well have been the first crack in the wall of Communist buffer states that the Soviet Union had built between itself and Western Europe.

France, under de Gaulle, continued to move away from its former allies Britain and the United States, and toward a rapprochement with Russia. For example, France, like the Soviets, sided with the Arabs in the Arab–Israeli War, taking a position opposite to that of Britain and the United States. In addition, de Gaulle worked to keep Britain out of the European Common Market. He announced in 1969 that he would prefer his nation and the rest of Europe to totally abandon NATO, the West's mutual-defense group, and to be far less dependent on the United States. France was torn in 1968 by student riots and a nationwide labor strike, but by the year's end de Gaulle had won strong support in national elections, and a degree of calm returned.

In 1969, however, in a strange reversal of French public opinion, President de Gaulle resigned when a national referendum failed to give him the reforms and the powers he felt were necessary to the nation's well-being. The question immediately arose as to whether his resignation would open the door to British membership in the European Common Market.

The death of de Gaulle on November 9, 1970, brought home to the whole world, even those who had occasion to disagree with him most heatedly, that France and the world had lost a great and farsighted leader.

January 24, 1965, saw the passing of Britain's great statesman Sir Winston Churchill, who had served the empire in two world wars and who had wielded inestimable influence on the world during his ninety years.

Great Britain took several steps which she hoped would bring her closer to the burgeoning economies of the nations of Europe. She announced that British money, within a stated period, would be based upon the decimal system (as were the monies of Continental Europe), and her clocks would be set one hour ahead, also to coincide with those of most Continental nations. In late 1972, after more than two years of intense negotiations, Great Britain, the Republic of Ireland (Eire) and Denmark entered the European Common Market, making that organization an economic factor to rival Japan, Soviet Russia and even the United States.

In a hotly contested reversal of past British policy, Parliament sharply curtailed immigration to the United Kingdom of brown-skinned persons from Britain's former colonies in Asia and Africa.

In 1969, violence broke out between the Protestants and the Roman Catholics of Northern Ireland (the six counties which, unlike the Republic of Ireland to their south, are part of the United Kingdom), who had a several-hundred-year history of violence against each other. Their differences were over economic and political matters as well as over religious doctrines. By the end of 1972, it had become apparent that the problem would have to be settled by the entire Irish people through their government in Dublin, the capital of the Republic of Ireland, and the English government in London.

In Helsinki, Finland, in 1969, Soviet Russia and the United States began the often postponed strategic-arms limitation talks, commonly referred to as the SALT talks. These talks were widely welcomed as a hoped-for beginning of an end to the nightmare of nuclear-arms competition. The second round of SALT talks took place in April 1970 in Vienna, Austria.

By the end of 1972, it was readily apparent that the Soviet Union had achieved so much nuclear weaponry that neither she nor the United States could consider a nuclear decision to any political problem. In that year also, Russia demonstrated that she was one of the world's great sea powers by her ability to move her warships freely into the Mediterranean Sea and thence into the Indian Ocean, and the Atlantic and Pacific Oceans as well.

Encouraging among world events was a nonaggression pact concluded by West Germany and Soviet Russia, due in large measure to West German Chancellor Willy Brandt, who had worked long and hard to achieve a *détente* between his nation and the Soviets. In 1971, Brandt was awarded the Nobel Peace Prize for this achievement. In 1972, East and West Germany signed a treaty making travel between them by their nationals more normal. In signing this treaty, each in effect recognized the other, making such things as membership in the United Nations a possibility for both. Also encouraging in world happenings was the continuation of the SALT talks in 1971 between the United States and Soviet Russia, and the apparently broad scope of the treaties arrived at by the two superpowers. Later in 1972, President Richard M. Nixon of the United States made a much-publicized visit to Soviet Russia to sign these treaties.

Competition in space exploration between the two superpowers continued in this six-year period, with the United States putting greater emphasis on manned flights and Russia upon unmanned expeditions. The United States landed two manned flights on the moon in 1969; a third met near-disaster in 1970. The Soviets explored the moon with ingenious mechanical devices and sent several unmanned probes to other planets, as did the United States. During 1971, both nations explored the vicinity and the surface of the planet Mars, using unmanned space ships. Also during 1971, the Soviets suffered the loss by death of three astronauts, the crew of their earth-orbiting Soyez II. For the next two years, Russia confined herself to unmanned missions, but toward the end of 1973, successfully launched and returned to earth a manned flight, the first since the tragic Soyez II incident. In May of 1972, a joint American-Soviet space effort to be launched in July of 1975 was announced.

ASIA, except for its Mediterranean Lands

India celebrated its twentieth anniversary as an independent nation in 1967 amidst almost overwhelming political and economic problems. During this anniversary year, the nation was troubled by food riots, language disputes, and bitter conflicts between workers and management. In the meantime, the government seemed to be providing indecisive and uncertain leadership. There was little doubt that strong measures were required to control the nation's almost malignant rate of population increase. In 1968, sterilization clinics were established throughout the land, and classes were begun to teach birth-control methods. As always, there were bloody clashes between India's Hindus and Moslems.

In 1969, Prime Minister Indira Gandhi won reelection. The old Congress Party, of which she was the head, showed surprising strength and unity. Yet, after the elections the party split into warring factions. Violence, resulting frequently from the anger and frustration of the people, swept over much of the subcontinent time and again.

The twentieth anniversary of the founding of Pakistan occurred also in 1967. On the surface, Pakistan appeared to be enjoying an economic boom, but in actual fact only an insignificant percentage of her people shared in her much-vaunted prosperity, and only one in seven Pakistanis could read or write his name. In 1968, political unrest became so widespread that riots were common throughout the nation; there was at least one attempt on the life of General Ayub Khan, the nation's president. As a result, in 1969, Ayub Khan announced his retirement in favor of yet another general, Agha Mohammed Yahya Khan.

The problems of Pakistan were made worse by the fact that the eastern and western parts of the nation were separated by an almost one-thousand-mile expanse of Indian territory. The eastern section was subordinate to and mistreated by the western section where government headquarters were located. East Pakistan's fiery leaders demanded autonomy and even, in some cases, total severance from West Pakistan.

In 1970, in the midst of these problems, one of the worst disasters in recent history took place in East Pakistan, when tidal waves driven by hurricane winds swept over its coasts and offshore islands, leaving nearly 500,000 dead. Countless more were to die of the starvation and disease that followed in the storm's wake. Despite this tragedy, a local independence movement chose an East Pakistan assembly to frame a new constitution and select a new leader. It was hoped by these acts to correct some of the inequities between the eastern and western portions of the nation. The dominant West Pakistanis, however, were not to permit this to be. In 1971, they sent eighty thousand troops to "restore order" in East Pakistan and arrested its newly chosen leader. Thousands of the east's other leaders and intellectuals were executed. Ten million East Pakistanis now fled into neighboring India, where the already overtaxed economy could barely sustain the native Indian population. In late 1971, India declared war upon Pakistan, partly to solve this refugee problem and partly to deal her historic enemy, the Moslems, a crushing blow. Within two weeks, Pakistan was defeated and East Pakistan gained its freedom, forming a new nation, Bangladesh ("Bengal nation"), and the latest terrible chapter of the Indian subcontinent came to a close.

The twenty-five-foot-high-wall of water driven into East Pakistan by hurricane winds killed hundreds of thousands of people, destroyed whole towns, ruined crops, and left 3,500,000 people homeless. Early in 1971 the same area was racked by civil war and later in the year overrun by enemy troops in a war between Pakistan and her neighbor, India.

China in 1969 marked twenty years of Mao Tse-tung leadership, twenty years since the day in Peking in 1949 when Mao had proclaimed the birth of the People's Republic of China. The mood of the celebration, however, was pensive, for, although much had been accomplished, the nation had suffered dangerous and turbulent times (not the least of these being the three years immediately preceding this twentieth anniversary). The problems remained unresolved, and the leader, Mao Tse-tung, was very old.

Among the accomplishments which could be listed on this anniversary was the fact that China had been unified by a government that had proved strong and effective. The nation had recovered from the damage wrought by the Japanese invasion and the destruction of World War II. Much of the bitterness resulting from the civil war between the old government and the present Communist regime had been forgotten, too. By 1967, the crops of China had reached record proportions (although still not enough to totally sustain the nation), and the future, on the surface at least, looked secure.

In these twenty years, China had brought her Western-trained scientists back home, and they had made her a nuclear power.

On the debit side was the fear of war with the United States, and the even more obsessive fear of war with Russia. Mao Tse-tung felt that internally also the nation had become divided and that local Communist leaders were too much interested in self-aggrandizement and personal glory. In late 1965, therefore, Mao launched the "Great Proletarian Cultural Revolution" to bring China back to the ideals which he believed composed true Communism. To do this, Mao had to destroy in part the political establishment which he himself had played such a large part in building. In the process, the nation was sorely tried, the industrial and agricultural advances of the regime's first seventeen years were badly damaged, and many of the old leaders were eliminated. The "Red Guard" of young people under the aegis of Mao took to the streets, and bloody battles were fought, while the Army seemed to lend its support first to one side, then to the other. In mid-1968, with the nation almost in anarchy, the Cultural Revolution was brough to a halt and the young Red Guards were sent back to the farms, factories and schools.

These internal problems were paralleled by an extremely isolationist and ambiguous foreign policy, and there were clashes at China's embassy in London between embassy personnel and the local citizenry. Similar incidents occurred in other world capitals.

In 1969, quiet returned to China's cities, and strong efforts were made to rebuild her industry and agriculture. It became apparent at this time that the power of the military had been greatly enhanced, and that it now had a greater voice in the nation's affairs. The year 1970 saw a definite lessening of China's isolationism. Leaders of certain foreign powers were welcomed to visit the nation. Canada, the next-door neighbor of the United States, recognized the Peking regime. This was followed shortly by recognition by Italy, Austria, Belgium and Chile. Talks between the United States and Communist China were resumed in Warsaw, as China embarked on a new and bold foreign policy seemingly stemming from the nation's newly gained self-confidence and conviction that its way of life was the one right way for the future. In fact, so drastic was this turnabout that in 1971 some American athletes were welcomed as visitors to China. Later, arrangements were made for the American President, Richard M. Nixon, to visit China for conferences with Chinese leaders. In 1972 President Nixon made the visit to China which reversed more than twenty years of American anti-Communist-China policy. Later in 1972, China was admitted to the United Nations, after having been refused admission for two decades.

Another far-reaching revolution of the twentieth century occurred in Japan. At the turn of the century,

The Red Guards, Mao's teen-age legions and spokesmen, went on rampages, mouthing the party leader's words as if they were sacred and incontrovertible, spreading confusion and terror wherever they went.

Japan's defeat of czarist Russia had thrilled the subjugated peoples of Asia, who for the first time realized that an Asian nation could defeat a great European power. Perhaps the people of Europe who thought of themselves as invincible should have analyzed Japan's victory more deeply, for time may well reveal that it signaled the eventual return of the center of world power from Europe to the Asian land mass.

The chronology of events which brought about this Japanese elevation to world power is worth review. In the middle 1800s Japan was an isolated, largely agricultural nation of little industrial importance. By the time of the Second World War, she had developed a military-industrial complex that came close to conquering much of the rest of Asia and, for a short period, put the United States very much on the defensive. By the year 1972, Japan was seen to be the world's third most productive nation (after the United States and Soviet Russia), a superpower in her own right; her people enjoyed a standard of living which had been elevated from a bare subsistence level to approximately that of the industrial nations of Europe; and this standard of living was growing at a rate that indicated it might someday achieve for the Japanese a material well-being to rival that of the people of the United States.

Some statistics are in order: In 1970, Japan produced fully half of the world's ships, ranked second only to the United States in automobile manufacturing, was third in steel production, and actually dominated the entire world in such items as cameras and radios. Her fishing and canning industries had put Japanese products on the shelves of the food markets of the world, and the nation was second only to the United States in manufacturing fabrics and finished articles of clothing. Japan's rate of industrial growth, if maintained, would one day enable her to surpass Soviet Russia and eventually even the United States—this with far less population and a mere fraction of their natural resources.

In Southeast Asia, the drives of various peoples toward independent government—called "people's wars of national liberation"—were encouraged by Maoist example and even, in some cases, by actual Maoist Communist leadership. The British colony of Hongkong on China's southeastern coast was beset with repeated rebellion by Mao-inspired natives during these years, but British control remained intact. In 1968, however, Great Britain announced that her armed forces would be withdrawn from Singapore and Malaysia by the end of 1971, and the governments of these areas began to look to the United States for military support against rebellious nationalists (usually Communists), a support formerly obtained from Britain.

The United States in 1968 ceased its bombing attacks on North Vietnam by order of President Johnson, and later under President Nixon began to make large-scale withdrawals of its troops. However, an incursion in 1970 during the Nixon administration into neighboring Cambodia by combined United States and South Vietnamese forces, and an invasion in 1971 into Laos by South Vietnamese troops supported by United States aid, raised grave doubts.

The situation was made worse by United States' mining of Haiphong Harbor in 1972 and the most destructive bombing yet of North Vietnamese cities over Christmas of that year. Yet, in 1973, a peace arrangement was reached which saw the withdrawal of all American troops. War continued, however, between North and South Vietnam at a far lower but still considerable intensity.

During this period, young people protested in various nations of Asia (as they did in Europe, South America and the United States) against many circumstances which they considered to be unacceptable. In China the Red Guard tried to "purify" the revolution by violent application of Maoist precepts; in Burma and Pakistan students rioted against autocratic military governments; and in Japan there were widespread demonstrations against numerous social, economic, and political conditions.

A major breakthrough in agricultural techniques was accomplished in Luzon in the Philippines, where a new "miracle rice" was developed which yielded crops often as much as eight times the usual harvests. The potential of this new rice to improve the general welfare of the peoples of Asia and other impoverished areas of the earth was felt to be very great.

OCEANIA

Many islands of the Pacific were moving from quiescent isolationism into the stream of modern life. The jet airplane and the radio, which brought goods, tourists and news to these remote places on the earth, made such a metamorphosis possible, if not, indeed, inevitable. A strong drive toward self-determination among the various island peoples brought the roles of the colonial powers under repeated challenge. Among colonial nations, France attempted to maintain undiminished control over holdings in New Caledonia and the Society Islands; the United States returned the island of Okinawa, seized in World War II, to Japan, although American military establishments were maintained on several Pacific islands; and Britain acknowledged the independence of certain of its colonies in the Gilbert and Fiji groups.

AFRICA, except for its Mediterranean Lands

Most of the new nations of Africa, although inexperienced in self-government and in many cases only recently elevated from dependence on tribal controls operating within colonial governments, were relatively successful in holding elections and establishing democratic procedures of government. Successful military coups replaced elected leaders in Sierra Leone and Togo, but similar efforts to establish military dictatorships apparently failed in Ghana, Senegal and Uganda. For the most part, government procedures in the new states of Africa were more orderly than might have been anticipated.

There were two areas of tragic exception. The first was Nigeria, where civil war broke out in 1967 between the federal government and the nation's southeastern section, which, in 1967, had declared itself an independent state under the name of the Republic of Biafra. The Biafrans were traditionally better educated and technically far more competent than the other Nigerians. The war lasted until January of 1970, and by its end hundreds of thousands of Biafrans had died in battle or from disease and starvation. The war had resolved few of the disagreements between the Nigerian government and the people of Biafra.

The second area of exception to orderly government was in the African continent's southern portions, where white minorities in the state of Rhodesia and in the Union of South Africa enacted measures effectively depriving black citizens of many of their most basic political and social rights.

THE AMERICAS

Long-standing problems in Latin America intensified in the last years of the 1960s. Exploding populations, monopolization of land by the few, one-crop economies, and illiteracy all combined to increase the hunger and poverty that had traditionally characterized the Spanish- and Portuguese-speaking nations of South America. In 1968, conditions were made even more serious by a drought which drastically reduced crops in many Caribbean and South American countries.

By 1970, this accumulation of problems had given rise to widespread violence and terrorism, especially in South America. The struggle was joined between those who had traditionally wielded power and those political groups whose avowed aim was to establish new systems which would, presumably, be more responsive to the overpowering needs of the common people. Revolutionary acts included kidnappings and assassinations, from which not even major diplomats of foreign nations could be protected. In Argentina and Bolivia, elected presidents were forced out of office by the military, while in Chile a socialist, Salvador Allende Gossens, was elected president, thus becoming the first Marxist ever chosen by democratic procedure to head a Western Hemisphere nation. It is noteworthy that in a time when violence and revolution marked the resistance to social change in most South American nations, Allende's election was by orderly process and not by revolution or military coup. Yet by the end of 1972, Chile's economic problems were becoming more acute, and dissatisfaction with the Allende government more apparent. In September of 1973, the government of Chile was violently overthrown by the army. Hundreds of Chileans were executed, and President Allende himself was either murdered or committed suicide—a sad end to what had been a government elected in an orderly manner in South America's most law-abiding nation.

The United States was divided more in 1967 over the war in Vietnam and over the militant efforts of black Americans to improve their economic and social status than she had been by any problem at any time since the Civil War more than a century before. The issues raised by these two national problems stood at the very heart of the American way of life and raised for re-examination conclusions long unchallenged. In 1968, protest by opponents of the war and by blacks against social and economic injustices reached a peak and brought about a violent "backlash" of reaction among millions of people who disagreed with both the antiwar and the black protesters. As a result of these divisions within the nation, President Lyndon B. Johnson announced that he would not be a candidate for reelection to the presidency, and, at the same time, that he was ordering a cessation of United States bombing in North Vietnam.

Two civil-rights leaders were brutally assassinated during this period: Dr. Martin Luther King, Jr., a leading practitioner of nonviolence in the fight for Negro equality, and Robert F. Kennedy, a candidate for nomination for the presidency and a brother of the assassinated President John F. Kennedy.

Richard M. Nixon was elected in 1968 to succeed President Johnson, partly upon his promise to end United States involvement in Indochina, and partly because there was a general feeling of need for a change in national leadership.

Like other nations, the United States faced serious problems both new and old. The rapid increase in its population came to be seen by some as a danger to future well being as did the pollution of its land, air and water and the disproportionate amount of poverty in this the richest nation on earth. These domestic problems as well as the explosive situation in the eastern Mediterranean between the Arab states and Israel, and the continued strain of abrasive contacts between Communist and non-Communist nations elsewhere, confronted the new President, Richard M. Nixon, when he took office in January of 1969. The first year of President Nixon's term was relatively free of the violent protest which had marked Lyndon Johnson's last years in office. The American people were still divided, and they still strongly demonstrated their feelings on the grave issues dividing them, but the violence of the preceding year had subsided.

In the United States, protest marches and demonstrations, which had been employed by Civil Rights supporters, became a widely used vehicle for expressing dissent about many subjects. Great numbers of people, predominantly young, joined in protests against the war in Vietnam; against pollution of the nation's lands, air, and waters; against unfair treatment of minorities; against university policies; and against corporations and news media for such activities as manufacturing chemicals for warfare and, they felt, presenting biased news accounts.

Nonetheless, the year 1970 found many Americans disappointed in Richard Nixon's handling of the presidency, despite undeniable evidence of progress in a number of difficult and dangerous situations. In foreign affairs particularly there was justification for at least a cautious optimism. There was a marked decline in the level of fighting in Vietnam. In addition, the civil war in Nigeria came to an end after three years of fratricidal bloodletting, and the conflict between Arabs and Israelis in the Middle East, while no nearer a solution than ever, at least continued at a level which permitted the hope that a world crisis in that area might be avoided. Meanwhile, despite continued turmoil throughout the world, the strategic-arms limitation talks (SALT) between Soviet Russia and the United States were going forward. Most important, in a drastic reversal of a policy of limited contact with Communist China which he had long supported, President Nixon made arrangements in 1971 to visit China in the following year and to confer with her leaders.

The vague disquiet which, even so, troubled a significant portion of the American population seemed based on a feeling that little true progress was being made in solving the nation's deepest problems. When, in April of 1970, the United States launched an offensive into Cambodia against North Vietnamese forces operating there, a new wave of protest swept over the nation. These protests were especially violent in the nation's universities. The repressive actions undertaken by governmental and quasi-governmental agencies to suppress this student reaction in which several students were killed or wounded, were particularly disturbing to many observers.

By the end of 1970, evidence of government spying and record-keeping of the affairs of private citizens (even into the affairs of members of the United States Congress) added to public disillusionment.

In 1971, disclosures to the public by former United States employees of government papers marked "Secret" —the most important of them the so-called "Pentagon Papers," a history of events relative to the Vietnam War—caused a storm of debate and controversy. These papers revealed to the nation for the first time the step-by-step involvement of the United States in this Asian land war and undermined the public's trust in the honesty of its elected officials.

Even the successful accomplishment in 1969 of the space missions of Apollo 11 and 12 failed to lift national spirits more than temporarily. While American astronauts walked on the surface of the moon, many Americans asked themselves why it should be easier to accomplish such miracles of technology than to solve the social and economic ills that beset the nation. A subsequent mission designated as Apollo 13 suffered a near-disaster in 1970, causing the Apollo 14 mission to be postponed until 1971. The American aspiration to explore outer space seemed to diminish in intensity, as did the hold of the expeditions on the public imagination. Moon explorations in 1971 and 1972, while successful, were viewed with far less enthusiasm by the American people. During 1973, America launched earth-orbiting vehicles called Skylabs, whose crews performed and participated in many scientific experiments, not the least of which was the study of the effect of prolonged weightlessness upon themselves. Skylab 1, after being successfully returned, was followed by Skylab 2, which was in orbit 59 days. Skylab 3, launched in November of 1973, was scheduled to keep its astronauts in space a record 85 days. Meanwhile, the United States' unmanned vehicle Pioneer 10, which had been launched on March 2, 1972, made its closest approach to Jupiter (81,000 miles) on December 3, 1973. Unmanned vehicle Mariner 10, launched on November 3, 1973, was scheduled to come within 3,000 miles of the planet Venus on February 5, 1974, and within 621 miles of Mercury on March 29, 1974. Equally exciting was the approach toward the end of 1973 of the unusual comet Kohoutek—though it failed to justify predictions that it would be the brightest comet visible from the earth in the twentieth century.

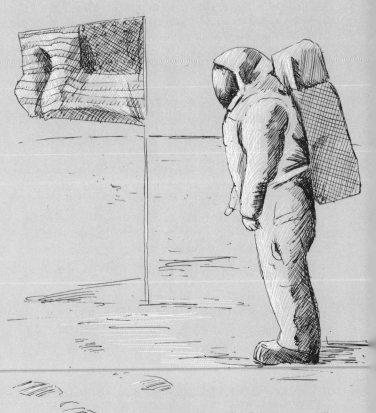

Neil Armstrong, the first man to walk on the moon, spoke the following words as he stepped onto the moon's surface: "That's one small step for a man, one giant leap for mankind." His words, as he spoke them, were carried by radio and television to viewers and listeners around the earth.

President Nixon in 1971 made a reversal of a long-standing position when he chose to remedy a worsening national economic situation by adopting economic measures long recommended by the opposing party. These included the freezing of prices and wages and, in late 1971, the devaluation of the American dollar. In 1972, President Nixon made still other reversals of long-standing United States policy and most particularly his own personal policy by making much-publicized visits of friendship to both Communist China and Communist Russia.

In November of 1972, Richard Nixon was reelected by a landslide majority to a second term as president. It was becoming apparent that some kind of negotiated end to the United States participation in the Vietnam War was in the making. When a cease-fire was signed in early 1973, many Americans insisted that this could and should have been accomplished four years earlier, avoiding the loss of thousands of lives and billions of dollars and the destruction of much of Indo-China.

Dissatisfaction with the Nixon presidency rose when evidence surfaced of a wide variety of illegal acts by highly placed White House staff people and by members of a special committee that had been formed to reelect Mr. Nixon. Many Americans suspected even the president himself of complicity in these matters. These acts were epitomized during the presidential campaign of 1972 by a break-in into the Democratic headquarters, located at the Watergate office building in Washington, D.C. By mid 1973, the "Watergate Affair" and other illegal acts by Nixon associates had severely damaged the president's governing ability.

Later in the year, the involvement of Vice-president Spiro Agnew in bribe-taking and other unlawful acts while he had been governor of Maryland, and even while he was vice-president, had further undermined confidence in the Nixon administration. Vice-president Agnew resigned his office in disgrace in the fall of 1973 after being fined and receiving a suspended sentence from the court. He was replaced by Congressman Gerald R. Ford, who was nominated by President Nixon and confirmed by the Congress. Vice-president Ford's selection was the first use of the Twenty-fifth Amendment, which had been enacted in 1965 and had taken effect in 1967, to fill vice-presidential vacancies. In the meantime, impeachment of President Nixon occupied much of the thought of the people of the nation as weil as its lawmakers in Washington.

In the United States and elsewhere, severe weather had so greatly damaged crops that food shortages were becoming almost worldwide. In addition, inflation seemed beyond control, due in some part to these food shortages and in some part to the unstable monies of many nations, but especially of the American dollar. The nagging worries over pollution, noise and nuclear war made it apparent that the employment of modern science had created unforeseen problems. The warnings of environmental specialists that the new technology posed dangers to the continuance of life on earth were becoming louder and more urgent. On top of this, the realization of a growing shortage of energy, particularly energy derived from petroleum, brought a crisis atmosphere to the United States and to the other industrial nations.

MAN'S JOURNEY THROUGH TIME

A Look Back

We have come a long way. In these few pages we have followed the story of man from the formation of his home, the earth, somewhat less than five billion years ago, to the threat, in the present era, of its destruction by atomic warfare or by other facets of man's technology.

In truth, man has been an inhabitant of this planet the merest fraction of its billion of years, and civilizations have flourished upon the earth during only a small fraction of that fraction.

We have seen how the first of these civilizations took form about five or six thousand years ago, near the eastern end of the Mediterranean Sea, followed shortly by civilizations in India and China. We made the amazing discovery that these first civilizations existed for almost half of the total of all civilized time (this total includes, of course, the twentieth century), and that the peoples of these ancient civilizations invented the wheel, several methods of writing and various systems of mathematics, architecture and government, as well as strong moral and ethical codes, and that they laid the foundations of most modern religions.

Yet, despite these accomplishments, we saw how these ancient civilizations gradually succumbed to a combination of internal decay and barbarian attacks, so that, one thousand years before the birth of Christ, only China of the original ancient cultures remained remotely recognizable. The inventions and the learning of the ancient peoples, however, did not disappear with them. Instead, they spread to nearby lands, and, later, in some cases even returned to their areas of origin, where they were put to use by new societies.

By 600 B.C., in what historians call the Classical Age, new civilizations were flourishing. China, India, Persia, Greece and Rome were the great names of this Classical period, and the contributions each of them made to science, art, philosophy, religion and government were very great. Yet, less than one thousand years later, by the end of the second century after the birth of Christ, Rome too, the last of the Classical civilizations, had begun to weaken before a combination of internal change and barbarian attacks. By A.D. 500 the European portion of the Roman Empire no longer existed, but its eastern portion, called at the time Byzantium and located in Mediterranean Asia, with its capital city at Constantinople, was to last almost one thousand years longer.

During this one thousand years, from A.D. 500 to 1500, the great contributions again were to come from Asian civilizations located in China, in India, in the Moslem lands and in Byzantium. Europe during this period was reduced to a patchwork of feudal states with power too widely scattered to permit more than sporadic attempts to rekindle the glories of the Classical past. The Christian Church in Europe and in Byzantium during this era preserved much of the scholarship and learning of the Greeks and the Romans, as did the Moslems in their great cities.

Beginning about A.D. 1500, Europe's renewed contacts with the East, first through the Crusades and later through trade and exploration, sparked a Renaissance in the arts and sciences which would enable the nations of Europe to dominate the rest of the world for the next four hundred years. Strangely enough, with this Renaissance in Europe, the nations of Asia and Africa sank into a torpor from which they have not fully recovered to this day. Japan is an exception to this lethargy of the Eastern nations, as is China under its present government.

The twentieth century burst upon the world as if to change everything in which mankind had previously believed. By 1967, many of the political, social and economic attitudes of the previous era had been rejected; two worldwide wars had been fought; and long-established governments and ways of life had been superseded by new governments with widely different cultural patterns.

Technological advances provided the people of this twentieth century with products and gadgets never before dreamed of, ranging from a host of man-made materials and fabrics to automobiles, airplanes and television.

The space age was part of this technological explosion. In 1957, Russia launched man's first artificial earth satellite, and the United States followed shortly with a similar feat. Thereafter, exploring space and putting a man on the moon seemed to become just another area in which the Communist and non-Communist nations could seek advantage over one another and hope to gain prestige in the eyes of the rest of the world.

Four series of events of the twentieth century stand out above all others in importance. The first was the development of weapons of such great destructive power that their use could conceivably mean the end of civilization and, indeed, of man himself. The second was the rebellion of subject peoples all over the earth against colonial masters. The third was the shifting of the center of world power so that it no longer resided solely in Great Britain, but had become divided among several locations—one in the combined nations of Great Britain and Western Europe, one in Soviet Russia, one in the United States, one in Japan, and one looming on the horizon in the Peoples' Republic of China. The fourth series of twentieth-century happenings which stand out above all others was the increasing pollution of the lands, seas and atmosphere by the effluvium of man's technological developments, the massive increase in the number of human beings upon the earth, and the chilling realization that the long-predicted shortage of fossil fuels had suddenly become not a matter to be considered in the vague future, but a current reality.

IX
MAN'S JOURNEY THROUGH TIME

A Look Ahead

And where does mankind go from here?

If we are to judge solely by the record, present-day society too will fall prey to conflicts over ideology and religion, to bitter wars for survival, and to the struggle for food, for land, for wealth and for power. The five years preceding this writing in 1973 have seen, after fifty centuries of civilization, a major part of the earth's people still going to bed hungry; have seen two religious wars in progress (in the Indian subcontinent, Hindus versus Moslems, and in Ireland, Christians versus Christians); have seen a war in the eastern Mediterranean between Arabs and Jews; have seen a war in Indochina over differing ideologies, and a conflict along the Russian-Chinese border between two nations of like ideology.

The record of civilization suggests that man will not hesitate to use any new weapon to fight his wars. As weaponry changed in the past from stone to bronze to steel, as the means of delivering weapons evolved from slings to bows to the horse to the tank to the airplane, all were adapted to man's struggles to gain ascendancy over other men. What, honesty makes us ask, has changed in the human condition to allow us to believe that hydrogen weapons delivered by intercontinental missiles will not also be used?

And yet, one demands, why must this be so? Why cannot the same minds that have solved some of mankind's seemingly insolvable problems and cured many of its seemingly incurable diseases, find the solutions and cures to the problems and diseases of human society? On the answer to this question would seem to depend mankind's survival.